ISBN 978-0-483-19215-7
PIBN 10793937

AN

# ADDRESS

DELIVERED BEFORE

## THE SOCIETY OF THE ALUMNI

OF

### DARTMOUTH COLLEGE,

AT THEIR FIRST TRIENNIAL MEETING,

JULY 25, 1855.

BY

SAMUEL GILMAN BROWN,

PROFESSOR IN THE COLLEGE.

WITH AN ACCOUNT OF THE PROCEEDINGS OF THE SOCIETY.

---

PUBLISHED BY REQUEST.

---

CONCORD, N. H.:
PRESS OF McFARLAND & JENKS.
1856.

Ō

**OREGO**
**RULI**
**CO.**

1

U.S./

2

3

4

5

AN

# ADDRESS,

DELIVERED BEFORE

## THE SOCIETY OF THE ALUMNI

OF

## DARTMOUTH COLLEGE,

AT THEIR FIRST TRIENNIAL MEETING,

JULY 25, 1855.

BY

SAMUEL GILMAN BROWN.

WITH AN ACCOUNT OF THE PROCEEDINGS OF THE SOCIETY.

PUBLISHED BY REQUEST.

———

CONCORD, N. H.:
PRESS OF McFARLAND & JENKS.
1856.

# ADDRESS.

---

GENTLEMEN OF THE ALUMNI:

You cannot feel too deeply, nor can I strongly enough express, the disappointment under which we all labor, that no one of the eminent men whom you earnestly solicited, fresh from fields of hard won fame, from toil and strife in that great world which, from our retreats, we look upon with curiosity and perhaps envy, should have inaugurated this your filial enterprise; should have stood here as the organ and minister of that ever benignant Mother, who waits in matronly dignity this day, to receive the congratulations of her children — her arms outstretched, as of old — a mother's welcome on her tongue — a mother's pride overflowing her heart. Next to a failure, I am afraid you will think it, that almost on the eve of our festival, the surely not ungrateful labor should have been thrown upon hands already overtasked with the duties of the season. And yet you will remember, I am sure, that this is a day of enjoyment and not of criticism — a day of indulgence and festivity, of retrospection and of hope.

It is singular that we come together as a body of Alumni, in a public and formal manner, now for the

first time. Lustrum after lustrum has passed unnoticed. The semi-centennial year of the College,
deserving to be marked by the whitest stone, signal-
ized by that great decision which gave its charter
new force and vitality, was marked by no general
gathering as to a jubilee. And now, reckoning *ab
incunabulis gentis*, a little more than a hundred years
have passed since was first cast into the soil of a
quiet town in Connecticut, the seed whose mature
and transplanted product here spreads its shade and
offers its fruit.

The occasion determines, in general, the subject
proper to occupy our attention. Our thoughts turn
first and instinctively to the College which early nur-
tured us, which opened for our inspection the science
and literature of the world, led us onward with encouragement, and gave us some discipline for the
sterner scenes of life. Our attention might naturally
be called altogether to its history; to what it promised and what it has performed. Yet to follow such
a plan to any good purpose, looking to the discerning
of principles, would require great care and exactness,
and a more protracted consideration than we are
allowed; while to neglect it entirely — to recall none
of the memories which are struggling for utterance —
none of the central elements in the life of the College
— would seem unnatural and unfilial.

One great difficulty lies in so selecting from ample,
but unordered materials, as not to go beyond the pro-
prieties of the day, and in so combining them as to
give a unity of interest. Perhaps we shall best meet
the wishes of the Association by looking at some of
the objects, methods and difficulties of the College,

while we refer, so far as may be necessary, to the noticeable epochs and incidents in its history; so shall we the better judge how far we have reason to congratulate ourselves to-day, and for what it becomes us still to hope and strive.

A college is to be distinguished from a university, on the one hand, and from an academy, or special school, on the other. An attempt to unite elements that are properly distinct, and perhaps incongruous, or to compel either institution to perform the functions of the others, would be for the injury of all. In the spiritless compound would be found neither the sharpness of the acid, nor the vigor of the alkali. To give a high sounding name and a profusion of nominal officers, with no scholars to be taught, and no funds to support the empty dignity, is a fault on the one side, just as calling the mind back from liberal excursions over the field of the largest knowledge, and binding it to a single special course of study, would be a fault on the other. Different schools may move with harmony and mutual profit side by side, or in concentric orbits, each silently affecting, but not disturbing the other, but those cannot be blended without mutual injury, whose objects and methods, whose discipline and culture, are radically diverse.

A university has been defined to be " a sort of corporate establishment, instituted for the intellectual elevation of the community by means of publicly recognized teachers." " It exists for the purpose of training the people intellectually at that highest stage where education, strictly so called, ends, and the business of life begins. It is not an establishment for drilling boys, but for stimulating, enlightening, directing and elevating young men."* A part of this definition will apply to our colleges. They are public institutions, whose object is to furnish the highest general education; an education which shall liberalize the mind and amply prepare it for professional study, or any sphere of active life. A college, then, in striving to realize its idea as an institution for a truly liberal education, aims primarily to impart a kind and degree of knowledge best suited to the nature of her pupil, and the ends she would subserve. She gives him some idea of the ever enlarging scope of the sciences; a knowledge of languages and of nations; a knowledge of civil economy, and of the laws of his own being. The inferior kinds of learning she subordinates to the superior; and by presenting knowledge in its vital organic connections, and not as if isolated, confers upon every part due honor. She unites discipline with attainment. She endeavors at once to inform and invigorate; so that what is highest in dignity may control the life, and the educated man, like a well trained army under a wise and energetic general, may move irresistibly over the fields of conquest.

So, too, within the scope of her abilities, would the college, as a disciplinary school, control and direct every moral faculty. She would fortify the student against the sorcery of pleasure. She would lay her hand upon every petulant temper, and soothe it to calmness; upon every ignoble purpose, and crush it out of existence. Every mind vacillating between the lower and the higher aims of life she would fix beyond possibility of change, that it might steadfastly

---

* North British Review, May, 1855.

hold on its way toward whatever is magnanimous and gentle, and pure and true.

Beside these influences, there are in every college others, beyond and without the prescribed curriculum, bearing with constant and effective pressure upon the mind, modifying and shaping its affections; influences none the less potent, because unseen and intangible; influences made up of all the traditions of the place, of all objects of art and culture, of prevailing opinions and customs, of the achievements and fame of its scholars; influences most effective with the finest minds, stimulating them to large endeavor, giving more seriousness to their meditations, more earnestness to their efforts; influences which gather strength with the rolling years, and become more potent with every name upon the enlarging catalogue.

This fact it is, among others, which gives a peculiar importance to the external condition of the college, the state of its buildings and grounds, its cabinets and apparatus. The observatory on the hill is an ever-present witness to the splendid achievements of the mind in one of the most mysterious fields of its labor. The library — how does it draw with ten thousand attractions toward scholarship and thought, and intellectual accomplishment. So too will the college edifices, if there be any architectural virtue in them, always be eloquent; for architecture is peculiarly public and universal in its influence. Its structures are built for the wear of centuries. Their beauty is not ripe till ages have rolled over them; till the footsteps of pilgrims have worn the pavements; till the record of saints is sculptured on their votive tablets; till the shrine of genius is erected within their enclosures; till the faith, and love, and endeavor of generations, have sunk into their walls. Thus does a noble structure become a living representative, a kind of incarnation of the institution, the state, the age. And as the life of Athens still lingers, still shines in her ruined Parthenon, so does the existence and authority of a college or university become visible and tangible through its venerable buildings. In them it lives, though its officers and students pass away year by year towards

> "The unfathomable gulf, where all is still."

It grows hoary and venerable amidst the fluctuations of society,— a rock which the swift-rushing currents of time chafe and wear, but cannot move,— touching with influences sombre and gentle every finer soul, and moulding it all the more effectively, because by a pressure so soft, yet so constant.

To an imaginative mind every object of picturesqueness or beauty becomes an object of love. The spire that leaps heavenward, the bell that swings in the turret, each

> ——— "jutty, frieze,
> Buttress or coigne of vantage,"

where the temple-haunting martlet

> "Hath made his pendent bed and procreant cradle,"

is seized by the fancy and clung to with ever-increasing tenacity.

Perhaps we do not give prominence enough to these intangible, evanescent influences — the education of the sympathies, tastes, affections, prejudices if you please — the moving springs of the life of man, which no future methods nor vicissitudes will essentially change. I have sometimes thought that in many a European university the least potent element of education is that of direct instruction. The *religio loci*, the recollections and traditions, the quiet walks, the lofty chapels, the spacious halls — these, during the most impressible years, are silently giving shape and direction to the life. Toward these centres come trooping the memories of the distinguished in science and letters, from Bacon to Whewell; from Spenser, a poor student, receiving in 1573 his first degree, to Tennyson, whose accumulated honors the plaudits of the theatre have scarcely ceased to echo. Lives there a soul so dull and earth-creeping as not to be touched by such influences? "In those apartments," says the university to her docile pupil, "in those apartments, over yonder gateway, Newton elaborated his Principia; in that lodge died Richard Bentley; yonder the musical voice of Heber pronounced his prize poem; in that senate house stands the statue of William Pitt; in that hall Bacon, and Barrow, and Usher, and Burke, and Berkeley, look down from the silent canvas; that desk was once eloquent with the voice of Chalmers, of Stewart, of Arnold; the wondrous arch which spans yonder chapel was thrown across by a builder whose genius has been the marvel of every succeeding architect, but whose modesty and humility thought it of no consequence to record his name. Go you, my son, and by assiduous labor, by fidelity, by noble purpose, by magnanimous effort, deserve what they attained. 'Remember, resemble, persevere.' Let your life, like theirs, be wrought into that of the age in which you live, for the welfare of man, for the glory of God." Are they few upon whom such influences are most powerful? In the fullest extent it may be so; yet the same may in part be said of the whole process of education; for it is a discouraging thought, that by the majority so little of instruction seems to be retained. Still we may underestimate the influences of education, both the direct and the indirect, even on the least promising. Much must be thrown into the common stock of impressions, sentiments, habits, which can be traced to no specific source, which cannot well be weighed or measured, but which is not to be disregarded in the final result on character. And there are always some minds sensitive to the noblest influences. If one such, of the highest order, comes in a quarter of a century, it is enough. The ponderous bells, "swinging slow with solemn roar," which caught the music-loving ear of Milton, and suggested the solemn lines in the Penseroso,— the "distant spires and antique towers," which prompted Gray's ode on the "Distant Prospect of Eton College,"— the "cloistered seclusion," and "grand halls, hung round with pictures by Verrio and Lely," which moved the imagination of Charles Lamb to writing the "Recollections of Christ's Hospital"— all these were doing a very evident work for the cultivation and refinement, the stability even, and the fame of England — for the cultivation and delight of all to whom Milton, and Gray, and Lamb are still compauions and friends.

It was to realize some such idea of instruction and discipline, and general influence, that our fathers — trained in the severe schools of the old world, remembering the learning of Cudworth, and Hooker, and Taylor, and Milton, and Baxter, and such as they, and fearing the perils of ignorance — devised that course of education, at once thorough and liberal, on which all the culture of an ample commonwealth might be grafted. They regarded the college, not in its relations to individuals alone, but as a power in the state, as the germ in which were held inclosed the organic forces which should at last blossom into the fullest, richest, most varied and complete forms of cultivated life. As the ideas at the basis of the public education were mean or liberal, contracted and distorted, or expansive and true, so, they thought, would in a large degree be the character of the commonwealth. Let us be grateful, thrice grateful, to them for their manly wisdom and their practical insight. The theories which would banish whatever learning cannot be turned to immediate account, which exalt an economical art at the expense of the more profound and far-reaching science ; which value the soul itself because it contrives so many ingenious machines, and not the machines as the mere ministers of the soul or evidences of its greatness, such theories they never heard of, or heard only to despise.

Hence they caught up those old languages which the subtle genius of the Greek and Roman had elaborated, in which are hidden all the civilization of antiquity ; hence they seized the high mathematics, among whose pure and severe demonstrations the serene spirits of Copernicus and Newton were wont to move ; and made them the immovable and ample foundation on which all other knowledge and discipline might rest. Upon and about this they gathered the theoretical and practical learning of the times.

They taught the mind to know and master itself; then thoroughly to master whatever science, whatever art came within the scope of its inquiries. They conceived the idea of " a complete and generous education," somewhat according to the suggestion of Milton, as "that which fits a man to perform justly, skillfully, and magnanimously, all the offices, both private and public, of peace and war"— a result none the less to be aimed at, and striven for, though impossible fully to realize. It matters little that they were unacquainted with many things familiar to us. They had a purpose and plan, and did not work at random. They laid a foundation in anticipation of a structure far costlier, more ample and more beautiful than they themselves were able to rear.

With the hope of intellectual discipline, they also associated the idea of a religious culture. They seemed equally anxious to avoid irreligious learning and ignorant religion. They would save learning from sciolism and infidelity, and religion from bigotry and superstition. They were imbued with the general spirit of that theology of the seventeenth century, which, whether right or wrong, was never contemptible. Religious and theological learning was felt to be important, not merely as furnishing a moral guide, but as invigorating and inspiring the intellect; as raising us to the highest objects of contemplation, and affording the most substantial and fruit-bearing knowledge. The motto for the seal of Harvard College, adopted as early as 1650, was, "*In Christi gloriam.*" Somewhat later another was used, similar in import, " *Christo et ecclesiæ.*" One of the laws, liberties and orders of Harvard College, established by President Dunster as early as 1642,* announces, that "every one should consider the main end of his life and studies, to know God and Jesus Christ, which is eternal life;" and the next statute is: "Seeing the Lord giveth wisdom, every one shall seriously, by prayer in secret, seek wisdom of him."†

The spirit in which Yale College was established was the same. Its corporation, composed entirely of clerical members, is a living and permanent evidence of its character. It was the religious element, and not a mere abstract love of learning, which stimulated the efforts of the fathers of the state, and drew forth funds from the liberal.

This spirit it was preëminently, which presided over the establishment of Dartmouth College. It is now a hundred years since Moor's school, founded by Eleazer Wheelock, took its name from the benevolent farmer in Lebanon, Connecticut, who gave it a house and two acres of land. It was instituted for the education of Indian youth, in order that they might afterward carry back to their own people the seeds, both of civilization and Christianity. The history of that preliminary effort, its motives, its natural growth out of the spirit of the times, is yet to be written. A few years witnessed an enlargement, to some extent, of the school, and a still greater expansion of the ideas and purposes of its founders. They were no longer satisfied with a simple Indian school, but wished for a college, with a sufficiently ample charter, and larger immunities and privileges. They sought for it a situation where they might neither interfere with others, nor be overshadowed and hindered by others.

* Quincy's Hist. of Harv. Univ., 1, 515.　† Ib., 1, 515.

One plan, not very seriously entertained, perhaps, was to remove it to lands on the Mississippi, given to officers engaged in the old French war; another, to establish it in Berkshire county, Massachusetts, where liberal subscriptions were raised; still another, to fix it at the city of Albany. Nor was it till after much travel, and the inspection of many places, that it was decided to rest upon these pine-clad plains, beneath the shadows of the granite mountains. Why this particular ground was selected; why in preference especially to the spot four miles south, the junction of streams, marking the courses of traffic, and offering the most favorable sites, I do not know; but this *region* was fixed upon through the liberal offers of Gov. Wentworth, both of land for its funds, and of his aid in securing a charter; and still further, in order that here, on the boundaries of two States, and far away under the northern skies, beyond any other college, it might be near the tribes whose welfare was a prominent design of its benefactors, and still be within reach of "English youth," as the charter terms them, to which it was freely open.

The charter of the college, dated in 1769, was drawn up with great care and skill. "Dartmouth College," said Mr. Webster, in 1818, "was established under a charter granted by the Provincial government; but a better constitution for a college, or one more adapted to the condition of things under the present, in all material respects, could not now be framed. Nothing in it was found to need alteration at the Revolution. * * * * A charter of more liberal sentiments, of wiser provisions, drawn with more care, or in a better spirit, could not be expected at any time, or from any source."* The year 1770 witnessed the first clearing in the woods; the building a few log huts, and the partial erection of a college edifice; and more than all, the actual commencement of instruction. The motto of the college seal, "*Vox clamantis in deserto*," was vividly indicative of the actual condition of things. The inhabitants of the region were very few, and there was no prospect of rapid increase: it was difficult to conjecture whence the students should come, or how they could get here. There has hardly been a college established of late years, in our new States, which has not at its opening given a fairer promise of immediate prosperity.

The first twelve or thirteen years were years of special trial. Funds were small, instruction necessarily limited, and students few. The Revolutionary war, though it did not interrupt the college exercises and disperse the students, as at Harvard and Yale, must have diminished their number, and materially affected their spirit. In 1781 and '82 the number of graduates was only four; no larger than the first class that left the college. But from that time for thirty years, during the generally prosperous administration of the second President Wheelock and his coadjutors, it were moderate and almost stinted praise to say that the college moved onward with ever-increasing strength, offering the most reliable proof of the value of its discipline in the general stability and excellence, and the occasional eminence of its sons.

The venerable Eleazer Wheelock closed his active and variously useful life April 24, 1779. His "last will and testament" concerning the college, as ex-

* Works of Daniel Webster, vol. v., p. 499.

pressed in one of his narratives, is worthy the companion of the Edwardses and Brainerds of the age. "It is my purpose, by the grace of God, to leave nothing undone within my power, which is suitable to be done, that this school of the prophets may be, and long continue to be, a pure fountain. And I do with my whole heart, *will* this my purpose to my *successors in the presidency of this seminary, to the latest posterity; and it is my last will, never to be revoked; and to God I commit it;* and my only hope and confidence for the execution of it are in Him alone, who has already done great things, and does still own it as his cause; and blessed be his name, that every present member of it, as well as great numbers abroad, I trust, do join their hearty amen with me."

The year 1798 is distinguished by the establishment of the Medical School — a school illustrated by the genius of Nathan Smith, its projector and founder; of whom it has not been thought invidious to say that he did "more for the improvement of physic and surgery in New-England than any other man"* of his time; by the taste and skill of Cyrus Perkins; by the exquisite facility and penetration of James Freeman Dana; by the elegant learning and refinement, and all-embracing scholarship of Daniel Oliver; by the still longer and more ample services of others, whom I need not and ought not to mention, for the worth of them is so fresh in your memories; and still more generally and widely honored by the skill and success of those who have gone from it to their various posts of duty in the world.

Of the studies and discipline of that earlier period,

---

* Kingsley's notice of Yale Coll., Quart. Reg., Feb., 1836, p. 207.

I have not been able to learn a great deal. The requisitions for admission were low, the means of fitting for college were very imperfect, and many of the studies inadequately pursued. I remember hearing one of the older graduates say that the first lesson of his class in mathematics was twenty pages in Euclid, the instructor remarking that he should require only the captions of the propositions, but if any doubted the truth of them he might read the demonstrations, though for *his* part his mind was perfectly satisfied. In stories like this, however, we must allow something to the genius of the narrator, and may fairly be of the mind of that earnest reader of the travels of Capt. Lemuel Gulliver, when he roundly and independently asserted that " there were *some* things in the book which he could *not* believe."

To some important events in the history of the college — the founding of the two prominent Literary Societies, whose libraries have acquired so much value — the writing and acting of plays — the Quarter days — the *Carmen Sœculare* — we can barely allude.

Other early customs must be passed over almost as lightly. Owing in part to the later period at which Dartmouth was founded, and in part to its position, some methods of restraint and control familiar to the universities of England, and the oldest colleges in New-England, were never adopted in ours.

"The punishment of boxing or cuffing," once in vogue at Yale and Harvard, was never introduced here. According to President Woolsey, "It was applied before the Faculty to the luckless offender, by the President, towards whom the culprit, in a standing position, inclined his head, while the blows fell in quick succession upon either ear. No one seems to have been served in this way except freshmen and commencing 'sophimores.'" At Harvard the energy of such modes of discipline was still more remarkable. On one occasion, according to the historian, a student, for speaking blasphemous words, was "sentenced to be publicly whipped before all the scholars. The exercise took place in the library, in presence of the Students, the Faculty, and such of the Overseers as chose to attend. The offender kneeled, the president prayed, the discipline was administered, and the solemnities closed by another prayer from the President." * Such ignoble punishments were dispensed with about the middle of the last century.

Another practice, quite as unusual now, continued to a later time, and gathered some strength here — that custom of the seniors exacting a certain amount of service from the freshmen. In the older colleges, long established custom had grown into an unwritten system of common law, against the violation of which public opinion, and sometimes the civil law itself, was brought to bear. It was early enacted at Harvard, among other things, that " No freshman shall wear his hat in the college yard, unless it rains, hails or snows, provided he be on foot, and have not both hands full." " No freshman shall speak to a senior, with his hat on; or have it on in a senior's chamber, or in his own, if a senior be there. All freshmen shall be obliged to go on any errand * * * for any of his seniors, graduates or undergraduates, at any time, except in study hours."†

* Quincy, I., 189.   † Ib., II., 539.

Similar customs prevailed with us, though they never consolidated into a system. Perhaps they never worked over-smoothly; and at last, whether through the increasing ignorance and ineptitude of the freshmen, I will not say, the mistakes they made (if current reports be relied on) were so frequent — the almost miraculous changes which liquids and solids underwent in the passage from the shop where they were purchased, to the room where they were used, were so common — the oil sputtered so in the lamp, and the ink became so pale or so unctuous — that about the year 1795 the custom was entirely abandoned, and passed quietly away, among those few other usages which we remember with a smile.

Both these practices — the corporal punishment, and the subordination of one class to another — arose, and were sustained from the general feeling of society. The punishment was regarded much, I suppose, as the same is looked upon in the English schools of our day; and that one class should render a moderate service to another was a practical demonstration of the principle of reverence for orders and ranks, which was generally accepted as healthful.

The first quarter of the century covers the most critical period in the history of the College — a period of difficulties, of struggle and contest. I would rather pass it over, would not the omission seem more censurable than a reference to it. After the lapse of more than a generation, we view the agitating events of those days in the calm light of history, giving credit for sincerity and earnest endeavor to both sides, and preserving our interest mainly in the issues that were determined. How the contest came to be complicated with politics; how personal feeling, of necessity, inflamed the controversy, as the discussion became protracted and was found to involve such results, it is quite unnecessary to say. Let all that was temporary and accidental, all that was personal and private, sink into oblivion, and there yet rises before us a principle indestructible, and that cannot be forgotten — the faith and defence of which has added to the fame of many — the establishing of which has given security to every eleemosynary institution, to every charity in the land, if not, indeed, a stronger tenure to every most private trust. The guardians of the College were moved by a profound conviction of the justice, equity and vital consequence of the question. Otherwise, it might not then, at least, have received the thorough defence of Smith and Mason, Hopkinson and Webster, nor the luminous and ample decision of Marshall and Story — a decision which, not over-estimated, I suppose, in the judgment pronounced upon it by Chancellor Kent, has gone far beyond the immediate issue, and, by removing our colleges from the fluctuating influence of party and faction, has helped to make them what they should be — high neutral powers in the state; devoted to the establishing and inculcating of principles; where may shine the *lumen siccum* — the dry light of wisdom and learning, untinged by the vapors of the cave or the breath of the forum.

How earnest was the College for a thorough argument; what efforts she made to secure it, though, in her poverty, she was literally begging bread from door to door; how learned and subtle were the discussions; how long and anxiously the decision was waited for,

you, many of you well remember; and when at last
the tidings came — one week from Washington — and
the first sentence of the letter from Mr. Webster —
"All is safe and certain," — announced the result, the
hearts of many sprung up with unwonted elasticity.
The news was received by all friends of the College
with profound joy; by some with exultation, by others
with a more sober satisfaction, as at the demonstration
and establishing of a vital principle. Some, perhaps,
had already received monitions that the sands of their
glass were running with strange swiftness, and nearly
all were unusually divested of the feelings of personal
litigants.

The College was probably never in better spirit for
study, and every effort which becomes scholars, than
at the period when so much existed to divert the
attention. Revolutions are said to be fruitful of great
men, and thus, perhaps, we may in part account for it,
(*parvis componere magna*,) that so many of our distinguished alumni bear date from about that time. The
future was indeed uncertain, instructors few and overtasked, funds scanty, but there remained a spirit which
supplied every deficiency. The subjects familiarly
discussed — the solicitudes which the students in some
measure shared — the uncertainties under which they
labored — the sympathies which were excited — all
furnished the best stimulus for intellectual improvement, and the best assurance of thoughtfulness and
self-restraint.

The general course and spirit of every institution
largely depends on its ruling minds. May I, without
violation of propriety, advert to some of the men of
that, and a later day, whose names are indissolubly

associated with the progress of ours. Of the permanent instructors, one still remains to receive our congratulations,* one to whom the young may look up with reverence, and whom the old may greet as a friend; changed a little in appearance, like the old familiar house he has so long lived in, but within, the same generous heart and sagacious mind. Another † — it seems but as yesterday that his familiar and venerable form moved amongst us — was gathered to his fathers, full of years and of honor. How can we help remembering with gratitude his serene and pure life, his simplicity of character, his scrupulous and conspicuous integrity, his untiring fidelity. Of yet another who had some share in the general responsibilities of the day, some part in the multifarious works of instruction and government, it does not become me to speak. *Admiratione te potius quam temporalibus laudibus, et si natura suppeditet, æmulatione decoremus.*

If from the officers of the College we turn our attention to its board of Trustees for the first quarter of the century, we shall find quite an uncommon collection of persons of eminent intellectual ability. Some united thorough learning in the law with the far-reaching views of statesmen. Some were profound metaphysicians and theologians. There were men well versed in affairs, men of immovable firmness, of unsullied probity, of deep religious convictions.

There rises first before the memory the somewhat attenuated and angular form of Nathaniel Niles — a schoolmate of the elder Adams, whom he loved his life long, and mainly, it would seem, because at school John Adams was the terror of the big bad

---

* Rev. Dr. SHURTLEFF.    † Prof. ADAMS.

boys, who, in his absence, would oppress the little ones,—a graduate of Nassau Hall,—a follower of Jefferson in politics, yet practically rather conservative, and of Calvin in theology, yet apparently sometimes verging toward his opponents,—an acute metaphysician, a little inclined to the opposite side,—half author, in conjunction with Dr. Burton, of the "*Taste-scheme,*" so called, yet walking independently, and not precisely agreeing with his sharp-minded friend,—a great reader, keeping up remarkably with the progress of science, and renewing in his old age his knowledge of Latin,—a shrewd judge and an indefatigable opponent. Beside him stood Elijah Paine, with a physical frame "put together with sinews of brass,—his voice clear and audible at the distance of three quarters of a mile,"—remarkable for high-toned integrity,—clear-minded, honest-hearted and upright,—of whom it was said by a most competent judge,* "that the supposition of any thing like injustice or oppression where Elijah Paine was present, was a palpable absurdity, not to be believed for a moment,"—appearing sometimes to be severe when he really meant to be only just and true,—a little obstinate, perhaps, especially if any good or right thing was opposed, and perfectly inflexible if it was opposed by unfair and improper means.†

Side by side was seen Charles Marsh, a lawyer more thoroughly read than either—on whose "solid, immovable, quieting strength" one might lean and rest,—if erring, erring with a right purpose,—simple and with-

---

* The late Mr. WEST, of Charlestown.

† For the characters of Judge NILES and Judge PAINE, and in a degree for that of Mr. MARSH, the writer is much indebted to the recollection of Rev. JOSEPH TRACY, of Boston, and Rev. Dr. WHEELER, of Burlington.

out pretension, like his relative, Mr. Mason, but when once engaged in any cause, unflagging and unyielding, bringing to bear upon every subject the strength of a penetrating and tenacious understanding, and resting with perfect confidence and fearlessness upon his own convictions of both right and duty.

Of the same general character, of transparent purpose, of remarkable equanimity, undisturbed by difficulties, and serene in uprightness, was Timothy Farrar, whose eye was not dim, nor his natural force abated, though he was drawing toward the farthest verge of the ordinary limit of human life, and who finally, in 1847, was gathered to his grave in peace, at the extreme age of one hundred years. In contrast, yet in harmony, was seen Thomas W. Thompson — like Judge Paine, a graduate and a tutor of Harvard, — of courtly ways, refined and cultivated in manners, with deep religious convictions, and a supporter of every thing good in circumstances where a loose holding to principle would have subjected him to less inconvenience.

Contemporary with these were Rev. Drs. Payson and McFarland, whose praise was in all the churches, and whose names added dignity and strength to whatever society or institution they were connected with. And if we follow down the list, how soon do we come upon the ever-honored name of Ezekiel Webster, then in the fullness of uncommon manly beauty and undisputed intellectual preëminence.

> "His own fair countenance, his kingly forehead,
> \* \* \* \* \* \* \*
> The sense, and spirit, and the light divine,
> At the same moment in his steadfast eye,
> Were virtue's native crest, the immortal soul's
> Unconscious meek self-heraldry."

There was yet another, taken from us but as yesterday, whose name need not be uttered here beside that ever hospitable abode within the glance of our eye, alive still with his presence, its very walls exhaling the breath of courtesy and magnanimity, sagacity and wisdom.* But I pause. Am I not introducing you to a congregation of senators? Would that from the marble or the canvas every one of them looked down upon us in our halls or libraries, so that our vanity might be rebuked by their presence, and we insensibly lifted to higher regions of thought, of purpose, of life.

I do not propose to apply any very rigid text to the history of the College, yet it may be expected that we should at least refer to some of the characteristics which have marked her course. I think it may be said that she has endeavored to establish herself upon *principles*, both in literature and in morals. Some have thought her not supple and flexible enough. Her faults have not been on the side of vacillation and indecision.

She has generally been distinguished, farther, by a wise conservatism. She has not been hasty to accept new theories in education; she has not been impatient of the old methods, where they have been tested and their fruit demonstrated to be good. With all the cry and din that has sometimes been raised in favor of the immediately practical, she has never forgotten the need of studies speculative and recondite. She has given their proper place to facts, but has given a higher place to ideas. That which has been proved, that which is true, that which is good, she has clung

---

* To none but to those unfamiliar with Hanover is it necessary to mention the name of Mills Olcott.

to, biding her time, if some of her friends even have been doubtful.

Her course has at the same time been marked by a tempered and sure progress — a progress sure, because not spasmodic, but natural and healthful; because moderate, ascertained, and at every step, secured. She has had few impulses, either from a large accession of students, or from remarkable accumulation of funds, but has increased by gradual increments, to be tested at somewhat distant intervals. Her measures, even if not always approved, have not averted the affections of her friends; neither has she in general lagged behind their sympathies. She has endeavored so to adjust the harness, as to enable her to bend forward with all the weight of her accumulated strength, as well as to hold back when the vehicle would, by natural impulse, rush down the declivity with too much violence.

And that every energy may be rightly controlled, she has endeavored to pervade her discipline and her studies by religious ideas; ideas the most profound, most subtle, most lofty, and of widest scope. She would teach her students to contemplate affairs from a position high enough to embrace the amplest horizon, that in public life they may be statesmen of generous sympathies, of vigorous effort, of unsullied integrity; and that in every profession they may rise to the full dignity of their calling — in medicine, reverently searching into the mysteries of the wonderful microcosm, — in law, comprehending its grounds and principles, administering it with incorruptible fidelity, and obeying it as the voice of God, — and in theology, at once humble and daring, yielding to faith the things that belong to faith, yet soaring immeasurably beyond the farthest scope of philosophy under the guidance of revelation.

What then are some of the difficulties of realizing the aims of the College? One is found in the very extent of the ground to be gone over, compared with the time allowed for the work. Within the last thirty, and much more, the last fifty years, many new sciences have been created, and the boundaries of all have been greatly enlarged. Some modern languages, which then were hardly known amongst us, now form an essential part of the furniture of an educated man; without which he cannot enter upon the thorough and scientific study of any liberal profession; without which he can master neither history, nor criticism, nor art. The pursuit of philology, under the severe methods of later scholars, has given to the ancient languages a new life, and a modern interest. We cannot study our own language without knowing them. Old text-books are abandoned. Methods more thorough and more generous are rendered necessary. And yet the time of the curriculum has not increased, and therefore, relatively, is diminished. The danger then is, notwithstanding improved means, of superficial and not thorough learning, of minds inflated with conceit and not full with knowledge, nor humble under a conviction of ignorance. There is not a department which is not clamorous for more time for justice to itself, for profit to its pupils.

The only remedies are to make the standard of admission higher, or that some specific studies of the present college course should be relegated to the academies or special schools, or reserved for the few whose taste for them is strong, or trusted to that general and cultivated love of learning which urges its possessor into every attractive field; thus leaving ampler space to those studies reckoned fundamental, and more strictly disciplinary; — or still again, to add a year or two to the college course, so as to afford room for a more extensive pursuit of some studies, or the introduction of others of great importance. Whether changes like these be practicable, it is not my purpose to inquire. Either of the propositions would be determined in the affirmative, "were it not," as our venerable professor used sometimes to say, in deciding perplexing questions, "were it not for countervailing objections in the negative."

But against the last there lies a difficulty which also bears with much force against our present arrangement, viz., the general impatience and haste which urges the student, no less than society in general, toward the future. We forget the necessary chronology of intellectual progress. The expansion of the country, and the immense demand for educated, or partially educated labor, tempts the student to the course which is the shortest and swiftest. Long before he graduates he is enticed by lucrative and honorable offers, and is it strange that he should not always judge wisely? He begins his profession a year or two before he is graduated, that he may so much the sooner leap over the intervening space between himself and active life.

A still more important and essential difficulty in realizing the full idea of the College is found in the lack of means. No considerable literary or scientific community can be created without books, and instruments, and cabinets; and no constant, strong and pervading literary or scientific interest can be excited without such a community.

It might be unwise, it certainly would be ungrateful, to indicate the destitution under which we have labored: yet who that remembers the College Library as it existed a few years since, can be insensible to the plentiful lack of all the apparatus needed for modern scholarship? We cannot be too grateful to those benefactors among the living, as well as of the dead, whose generosity has supplied the most glaring deficiences, and given a direction to the gifts of the liberal, which we hope may be abundantly followed. The College has never received from a single source the ample donations with which some favored institutions have been endowed. Yet, not to mention those yet with us, let us remember with honor the names of Dartmouth, of Thornton, of Wentworth, of Phillips, of Evans, of Hall, of Reed, of Appleton, of Shattuck, of Chandler — familiar, many of them, in the annals of charity and public spirit. Nor let us forget the many on whose liberality the College has ever relied, and not in vain. It is difficult to compare the commercial value of the broad streams bearing fleets of traffickers upon their bosom, with the silver rills which fertilize a thousand hill-sides and meadows.

How far the College has attained all the objects for which it was founded; how far it has been a force in the State; how wisely it has mingled instruction with discipline; how promptly her course of study has followed the ever-flying boundaries of knowledge; how thorough, severe and generous has been her train-

ing ; with what wisdom and skill she has guided her
children ; whether her sons have done honor to themselves and to her, we shall leave others to determine.
Yet if in this northern region there is spread a wider
refinement, a gentler spirit, a deeper love and honor
of literature, of art, of liberty, of law ; if there be
diffused a more adequate idea of the nobler purposes
of life ; if in other States throughout the Confederacy,
if in other lands towards the rising and the setting
sun, there be found the eloquent orator ; the faithful
minister ; the missionary, learned, zealous and self-denying ; the physician, cunning to discern the secrets
of life ; the statesman, looking through the darkness
of coming years, conquering difficulties afar off, de-
vising safe remedies for most threatening evils ; if,
gratefully receiving among her officers the sons of
other colleges, older and younger than herself, she has
paid the debt to learning by contributing of her alumni to meet the similar wants of ancient universities at
home, and new schools abroad ; if the torches kind-
led at yonder altars have been borne " even and high"
towards all regions, signals everywhere of encouragement and joy ; — if names of the illustrious, memora-
ble from achievements in letters, in arts, in life, already chronicled in history, part and parcel hence-
forth forever of the fame of the land,—if such names
are found on her rolls, early or late,—if these evidences are patent to the world, may we not believe that
its founders and guardians, who nourished it by their
prayers and staked so much upon its defence, would
still (were such things permitted,) look down upon it
with satisfaction, and may we not be pardoned if we
cling to it with love and devotion ? Mistakes there

may have been, too little encouragement to the diligent, too little stimulus to the sluggish, now too much haste and then too little, yet in soundness of principle and sureness of result, could we reasonably have expected more ?

I have referred to differences in studies at different periods. Yet there is an advancement not covered by a knowledge of books, — not in attainment merely, but in the spirit of a scholar, — the inward life, the indescribable fervor, the inimitable beauty, the holy zeal, the expanse of mind, the magnanimity of soul ;— of those elements of a perfect education we cannot so well speak, nor compare the successive generations of students. Yet if the past is a fair prophet of the future, — if the next half century shall produce another Appleton, another Marsh, another Woodbury, another Wilde, another Webster, may we not be satisfied ?

These, Gentlemen of the Alumni, are some of the considerations, lying but too evidently on the surface, ordered with too little care, which have suggested themselves as not entirely unfit to the occasion, while we stand with a sober and tempered spirit to gather up the lessons of the past, to gird ourselves anew for the future. Through the favor of heaven, the College enjoys at least a fair degree of prosperity. You find her not in the heat and uncertainties of conflict, but in the beauty and affluence of peace ; not folding her robes about her to fall, but resting with serene confidence on the affection and generosity of her sons ; not, indeed, "winning her easy way" from one scene of enjoyment to another, yet her path beset by no unusual and insuperable obstacles. What she shall be must depend largely upon those whose early culture she has directed, and in whose fame and prosperity she may claim some little share.

May she yet have resources sufficient for every reasonable want; instruments wrought with cunning art for the most subtle or far-reaching operation of science; libraries ample for the student of widest research, ever enlarging with wise foresight, sheltered in apartments whose very air shall inspire the philosopher, the historian, the poet, and so protected that the first fire which our audacity is tempting shall not lay in ashes all our wealth. May she have some building, at least one, be it Chapel, or Hall, or Library, or all combined, of noble architecture, that we may look on with love and pride, whose image may rise first in the memory when her name is pronounced by her distant sons, and which may bind still closer together the increasing generation of her children, by offering a common subject of thought, a common bond of association. May every liberal art find increasing protection under the shadow of her wings. Above all, may she abound in that wisdom which ennobleth institutions no less than individual men, and more perfectly fulfil her first design of increasing sound learning, and diffusing pure religion. In the language of Thomas Fuller, "May her lamp never lack light for the oil, or oil for the light thereof. May the foot of sacrilege, if once offering to enter the gates thereof, stumble and rise no more. The Lord bless the labors of all students therein, that they may tend and end at his glory, their own salvation, the profit and honor of the church and commonwealth." With such a spirit, respectful of the counsels of age and ardent with the resolution of youth; sustained by filial hands that will never forget nor forsake, and planting her footsteps upon eternal truth, will she go on to fulfil her mission.

> Dum juga montis aper, fluvios dum piscis amabit,
> Dumque thymo pascentur apes, dum rore cicadæ;
> Semper honor, nomenque tuum, landesque manebunt.

# SUPPLEMENTARY.

IN accordance with the provisions of the Constitution, the Association of the Alumni of Dartmouth College met in the Chapel, on Wednesday, the 25th of July, 1855, and elected the officers of the Association for the current year, as follows :

JOEL PARKER, LL. D., *President.*

DANIEL BLAISDELL, ESQ.,
REV. SILAS AIKEN, D. D.,
RUFUS CHOATE, LL. D.,
REUBEN D. MUSSEY, LL. D.,
} *Vice-Presidents.*

PROF. E. D. SANBORN, *Secretary.*

PROF. JOHN S. WOODMAN, *Treasurer.*

PROF. IRA YOUNG,
IRA PERLEY, LL. D.,
ALBERT SMITH, M. D,
DANIEL CLARK, ESQ.,
JOHN P. HEALEY, ESQ.,
PROF. EDWARD A. LAWRENCE,
REV. NEWTON E. MARBLE,
} *Curators.*

PETER T. WASHBURN, JR., ESQ., *Chief Marshal.*

The *Secretary* proceeded to read the names of those of the Alumni who had deceased within the past year, and brief remarks upon their lives and characters were made by classmates and friends, until the hour appointed for the Oration.

After the Oration a Poem was delivered by *Park Benjamin*, Esq., of New-York, and an Oration by *Wendell Phillips*, Esq., of Boston, before the Literary Societies of the College.

The Association then proceeded to the further celebration of its Anniversary. No arrangements were made in contemplation of a publication, but it has been supposed that the subsequent transactions may prove, to those interested in the welfare of the College, an acceptable Appendix to the Oration ; and an attempt has been made to collect the *disjecta membra* with such success as warrants the belief that those who were present will recognize the general truthfulness, if not the precise accuracy, of the following Report of what transpired,

SUPER CŒNAM.

*The President of the Association :*

· Gentlemen,—The duty which falls upon my shoulders upon the present occasion seems just now to be of rather an onerous character. It is quite an easy matter, as you have perceived to-day, to make an excellent oration, or to deliver a racy poem; but to preside at the supplement to a dinner-table, after such an intellectual treat, is another affair altogether. I feel somewhat like the good deacon who maintained that the minister's salary of some two hundred and fifty dollars was quite enough, because it was so easy to preach ; and who thereupon was invited by the clergyman to occupy the pulpit. You may recollect that when he came to the sermonizing, after three or four ineffectual attempts to get hold of the thread of a discourse, he leaned over the desk in despair, and said to the audience : "My friends, if any of you think preaching is such a very easy matter, I wish you would just come up here and try it for yourselves."

If any one of you, my friends, thinks that presiding over the after dinner part of the performances at this Celebration is such an easy affair, I shall be pleased to have him come up here and try his hand at it.—As no one speaks, I suppose I must proceed to supply the pulpit as well as I may.

You are aware that this is the first public celebration of the Alumni of Dartmouth College. Something more than a quarter of a century since I had some agency in the formation of an association, which, after vainly endeavoring for three or four years to have a celebration in connection with a Commencement, expired without accomplishing the object for which it was instituted.

It has not been I think from any want of fraternal feeling on the part of the Graduates of this College, nor from any lack of interest in their Alma Mater, that the Institution has been somewhat behind others of a like character in the efficient organization of an association like the present ; but one prominent cause has been the wide dispersion of the Alumni of this College, which in all classes follows immediately upon graduation, and to the lack of facilities until recently for a reünion in the classic halls of their earlier days. There is probably no collegiate institution which has done more than Dartmouth to send the schoolmaster abroad. It is substantially, if not literally, the fact, that wherever there has been a patch of the country of sufficient ability to support a district school, there, or in the vicinity of that place, has been found a graduate of Dartmouth. Some of them have attained to the dignity of schoolmasters in other similar institutions. Commerce, manufactures, and agriculture throughout the Union have had the benefit of their labor. Some have acquired renown in the halls of legislation. As members of the learned professions, they have been scattered broad cast over the land. Some fill professional chairs in Medical Colleges. Others are dispensing justice from the bench. And of those who, with a self-sacrificing spirit, have taken their lives in their hands in order to carry the Gospel to the uttermost parts of the earth, Dartmouth has contributed her full share. It is no vain boasting in behalf of our Alma Mater, to say that wherever her sons have gone, the boundaries of science have been enlarged, truth and justice have been enforced, and the world has been made better because they have lived in it.

The difficulties which have interposed themselves in the way of a family gathering under the maternal roof-tree, have been partially overcome. The railways which intersect the country, whatever mischiefs they may have occasioned, have among their merits that of furnishing facilities for such an assemblage; and through their aid we have come up here at this time, under a constitution which declares that the object of the Association "shall be to unite in such meetings, exercises, and other measures as shall be appropriate to the Alumni of a literary institution, and as shall tend to strengthen the bonds which bind us to each other and to our common Alma Mater."

The question how the first part of this constitutional obligation is to be performed, has been readily answered. We have adopted the approved mode. We have had our joyous greetings and pleasant reminiscences. We have listened to a Discourse of marked ability and eloquence, pronounced at our request and for our edification; which is undoubtedly a proper measure for the Alumni of a literary institution. And we have just united in an exercise which is universally admitted to be one of the true modes of promoting good-fellowship. You all know the old proverb respecting the most direct way to a man's heart. A good dinner makes us wondrous kind. Judging from what I have observed around me, you are all just at this time most affectionately disposed towards each other. So far, very well.

But the mode in which the other part of our constitutional obligation is to be complied with ; the means which shall be taken, now and here, to strengthen the bonds which bind us to our common Alma Mater, do not appear quite so clearly. The questions, what does our good Mother desire of us? what can we do for her? and how increase our affection for her? are not as readily answered. In order to solve the first of these questions, we should consult her. How shall we get from the honored Lady some expression of her wishes? I have in my eye a gentleman who is her Chief Steward, and who doubtless could give us the information, if a way could be devised of extracting it from him. But how is this to be done? If we were assembled under old fashioned usages, with wine upon the board, I should have no difficulty. It would only be to call upon you to fill your glasses, and with a bumper to Alma Mater, we should have him on his feet forthwith. He would, by all the laws in such cases heretofore made and provided, be bound to respond to it. But our wise Mother furnishes no such means of acquiring information. She only points to "the old oaken bucket that hangs in the well."

In this "pursuit of knowledge under difficulties," it occurs to me that we are at this time very like children, and may act in that character. The little folks march and counter-march, hold meetings, have their parties, with toast and tea, and all kinds of imitations of their seniors, but when appealed to respecting the reality of the thing, they admit that it is only "make believe." Suppose we proceed upon that basis, try the virtue of "make believe," and see what will come of it.

Please fill your glasses with the pure element. Let us have a bumper to,—*Our Alma-Mater, and her worthy President.*

I beg leave, Gentlemen, to introduce the Reverend Dr. LORD.

*President Lord :* Mr. President,—You call upon me to represent the wishes of Dartmouth, at this festive gathering of her sons. Sir, she thinks of nothing, just now, but to please them. She has but one wish to-day ;—that they may have a merry meeting, and go in together, one and all, for a good time.

Sir, I have but a doubtful right to say a word on this occasion, beyond what is merely *ex officio ;* for I am not a son of the venerable Mother whose children have come up to do her honor. But I may claim the privilege of adoption, and of a child kept at home, in expressing to this goodly company the feelings of a brother's heart. In truth, I know no difference between your mother and my own, or her children and my own brethren ; and I love them, not as in duty bound, but as I cannot help, with all the affection of a natural kinsman. It is spontaneous, and I give it free utterance in an honest and hearty welcome.

I may also claim a yet higher right to speak, for many greet me here, the more generously because, on my part, the relationship has been so poorly earned, as children. I have a double joy in these festivities, and in giving a double welcome to this glowing brotherhood. I welcome all and several to this old homestead, to these old halls and haunts, and I go in with them for a warm meeting, and a good time. Sir, we shall have it. I see it in your eye. I saw it when, with your usual forecast and benevolence, you went out, just now, to shore all up safe below.

But you do not mean that this good time shall pass away and be forgotten. You mean to live hereafter. You are looking out for better times to come. You ask me to show cause why Dartmouth should continue to have the favor of her sons? My answer is a short one,—because Dartmouth is in her sons. There is no Dartmouth without her sons. They have made her what she is, and they constitute good and sufficient reasons why she should be sustained, and become a yet more prolific and propitious mother. You could not expect me to discuss these reasons. Why, Sir, there are three thousand of them—*numerus integer*—and of that entire number two thousand *supersunt adhuc*. A tithe of that surviving number represent here, this day, the strong heads and warm hearts of the whole living fraternity. Could I discuss even them? It would be out of taste. They would not thank me. They will speak for themselves.

But I will just take it upon me to say what Dartmouth is : that is, what her sons have made her, and what I trust she will be as long as she has sons to be called by her name. What have they made her?

Sir, God makes all things. But the ideas, the principles, that he, in his good providence, causes to pervade a learned institution, and by which it has a character, belong to the men whom it educates. It takes its impress from them. And, in my judgment, the sons of Dartmouth have made her, and she accordingly stands out this day :

1. A College which knows no party in the State; but is of and for the State, and for the whole of it :

2. A College which knows no denomination of the Church; but is of and for the whole of it :

3. A College which knows no order in ethics, no father in theology, no hierophant in philosophy, and acknowledges but one Master, who is in heaven :

4. A College which stands between Church and State as a mediator, not to unite them, not to constitute an ambitious and destructive Church-and-State-power; but to compose and harmonize these respective bodies in their distinct and independent but coördinate spheres, for the ends of righteousness and peace, and, by consequence, for the common good.

Mr. President, let Dartmouth and her sons be true to these principles, and she will have, if not the present favor of the State, or

Church, yet, what is of more account, and what will make her, in the long run, more subservient to the common good, the favor of Him who ruleth over all.

*The President :*—It is now quite a number of years,—(as my wife is not present to object, perhaps I may as well be frank, and say that it is more than forty years) since my name was enrolled among—of course among—the diligent students of the College. At that time the father of the Orator of the Association was one of the Tutors. As an instructor at that time, as an occupant of the sacred desk afterwards, and subsequently as the presiding officer of the College, he was unsurpassed. But it is not for me, upon this occasion, to pronounce his eulogy. It was my good fortune to be for one term under his instruction; and if my lessons in the recitation room did not tell as well as those of some others, (to use the language which at a former meeting to-day has, with much less reason, been applied to a most distinguished son of Dartmouth,) I will not hold him responsible. In fact, I must admit that I was somewhat stupid at that time, for it certainly did not then occur to me that nearly half a century afterwards I should come up here to listen to instruction from a son of my most respected Tutor. And yet there is perhaps some excuse for me ; for whatever you may now think, after the very interesting discourse to which you have listened to-day, I can assure you, Gentlemen, that the Orator was not thought much of fifty years since. And I don't propose to say much of him now, because, as you are aware, he is so well able to speak for himself. I merely give you, *The Orator of the Day.*

*Prof. Brown,* after thanking the President and Alumni for their generous reception of an address too hastily prepared, excused himself in a few words from intruding farther upon the attention of the Association, and proposed as a sentiment—

*Our Alma-Mater : Salve, magna parens frugum,  * * * Magna virûm.*

*The President :*—You are aware, Gentlemen, that there is in almost every community a venerable personage who is regarded as a kind of oracle in all matters relating to the weather and the crops, and respecting every singular and astonishing event. He is regularly appealed to upon every extraordinary occasion, but it is always expected of him that his memory shall not be able to recall any thing so marvellous in that line as the incident which has just happened. I regret that it is not in my power to make you acquainted with that renowned personage, "the oldest inhabitant;" but I can do much better than that; I can introduce to your notice one with whom you are already well acquainted, and one who is and has always been an oracle in relation to matters of much more importance than these ordinary marvels; one who has probably done more for the collegiate education of the elder half of us than any other man now living. I see you are at no loss to perceive where the index points, and you will heartily respond to,—*Long life and health to our venerable friend and instructor, Rev. Dr. Shurtleff.*

*Dr. Shurtleff:* Mr. President,—The unexpectedness of your call conspires with this delightful occasion to awaken emotions which I have no words to express. I discover so many cheerful faces here, which were once familiar in the halls of recitation, that I almost feel the need of a check, lest I should inadvertently call for an abstract of the last lesson.

I am doubtless acquainted with more of the Alumni of Dartmouth than any other man living, and to me they are all peculiar people; and I hesitate not to express the gratifying opinion, that no College in our land has produced a greater proportion, to say the least, of eminent and useful men than my own venerable Alma Mater. And while riding at anchor in the wane of life, during the last seventeen years, I have seemed repeatedly to live over again the thirty-eight years I spent in her service. In imagination I have seen her beloved sons in classes before me, and have followed them in their various ways from State to State, from continent to continent, and from kingdom to kingdom—accounting myself successful in all their prosperity, and happy in their happiness.

But, out of regard to your time and my own weakness, I will add only an expression of my fervent desire and prayer, that we and all the surviving Alumni of this cherished Institution may, through divine grace, be prepared to meet in a brighter world, where friends will part no more.

*The President:*—It will be recollected that the reading of the list of deceased members was suspended this morning, by a call for the formation of the procession. Although this is not the most appropriate time for such reminiscences, it seems expedient that this duty should not be left unfinished. Classmates and friends of the deceased will please favor us with memorials.

*The Secretary* proceeded with the roll.

*The President:*—I understand that letters have been written within a few days to divers gentlemen, especially requesting them to give us the benefit of their presence at these festivities, and that answers have been received from several who are unable to be here. We will remember—" *Our absent Friends.*"

Mr. Duncan, who has the letters in his possession, will please an-swer in their behalf.

It is suggested to me that just at this time Mr. Duncan himself is among "our absent friends." I am not aware of any process by which I can enforce his attendance.

Speaking of process reminds me,—*Salmon P. Chase!* Hearken to an indictment found against you by the grand inquest for the body of this Association. The jurors for the Association of the Alumni of Dartmouth College on their honor present, that you, Salmon P. Chase, were, on the —— day of ——, 1854, duly elected and commis-sioned to deliver an oration before the Association upon the pres-ent Anniversary—and the jurors aforesaid do further present, that you have failed and neglected so to do; in evil example to others in like case to offend, contrary to the form of the statutes in such case made and provided, and against the peace and dignity of the Association. What say you, Are you guilty of the offence with which you here stand charged, or not guilty?

*Hon. S. P. Chase:* Mr. President,—I do not know exactly by what authority this indictment is preferred against me; and perhaps I ought to plead to the jurisdiction of the Court in which I am ar-raigned. But I will not do that. I might stand mute, and refuse to plead at all; but then I too well know to what *peine fort et dur* I should expose myself, to be willing to risk its infliction.

As I have a complete defence upon the merits, however, I will nei-ther except to the jurisdiction, nor, by silence, incur the charge of contumacy.

It was with no little regret that I surrendered the expectation of addressing this ancient and honorable Society to-day. I fully in-tended to do so. I had appropriated to the duty of preparation a time altogether sufficient. I had indeed entered upon the perform-ance of that duty, but just then I was summoned to the discharge of a professional obligation which could not be postponed, and which occupied the whole time set apart for the preparation of an address for this occasion. It seemed to me, therefore, that I was only doing what became a loyal son of Dartmouth, and a faithful member of our fraternity, to announce at once to the proper authorities that it would be impossible for me to fulfil my engagement, in order that some other gentleman might be called upon in time for the performance of the duty which I could not discharge.

But, sir, I do not rest content with this vindication of myself. I not only claim a verdict of acquittal, but a vote of thanks. My com-pelled failure to address you really assumes the character of positive merit. It has been the means of procuring for us all the pleasure of listening to the extremely interesting and eloquent address, which we have heard from my able and accomplished friend, who sits near me (Professor BROWN). If I had been, in fact, a delinquent, you could easily pardon a delinquency which has been the occasion of such a gratification.

And now perhaps I ought to take my seat, but as the impulse is upon me I will say a few words, suggested by what has fallen from you about the wide dispersion of the sons of Dartmouth.

As you spoke I could not help thinking of the various circumstances under which I have met her children in the course of my own life.

It was under the charge of my own elder brother, a son of Dartmouth, that I, a mere boy, first sought the distant West — now no longer the West, but the centre of the Republic. There, with the venerable Bishop of Ohio, another son of Dartmouth, I found my first western home.

There, too, I remember to have met another of the children of our Alma Mater. He was a young man, of fine intellect and rich attainments, who had for a brief period resided in the commercial metropolis of Ohio, with a view to the practice of an honorable profession, in which he afterwards rose to deserved renown. He had become discontented or discouraged, I don't know which, and was on his return to New-England. Never before in his life, I believe — never since, certainly, was he known to retreat. But then he was certainly upon the back track. What the West lost, however, New-England gained. I need not give you his history. Thou, Mr. President, art the man.

Years afterward, when, myself a youthful graduate, I sought, by teaching, the means of a professional education, another son of Dartmouth, occupying a post in the Senate of the United States, cheered me by sympathy and aided me by counsel.

A little later, when returning to the West, I was obliged to undergo a brief probation in a lawyer's office, before I could enter upon the practice of the law. I found a kind welcome to office and library, from a gentleman whose useful and honorable life reflects distinction upon this venerable Institution whose alumnus he is. I am glad to see him among us to-day. He is not quite royal, for he may do wrong. But in name and nature he is always *Wright*.

While engaged in the practice of my profession, I could not be indifferent to the fortunes of those who had with me received the benediction of our Alma Mater, when from her peaceful shades we went forth into the world. The universal and inevitable law of dispersion was upon us. Almost every where in the Union were members of our class. One was a lawyer in New-Orleans; one a physician in Massachusetts; another was a minister of the gospel on the Ohio. Some had gone beyond the limits of the Union. One was Secretary of the State of Texas at the period of annexation; another, in the far distant islands of the Pacific, was engaged in the great work of making known to the heathen the unsearchable riches of Christ.

At a still later period it was my fortune to be chosen to represent the Empire State of the West in the Senate of the Union. There, again, I met the sons of Dartmouth. The regretted death of one of them (Mr. Norris) has been announced to-day. Of the other how shall I speak? How shall I describe the lofty grandeur of his intellect, the simple dignity of his manners, the kindness of his spirit? I will not attempt to do at all, what I must needs do so inadequately and unworthily. Dartmouth—New-Hampshire—the Union, has had but one WEBSTER, and can have no other.

Thus, Mr. President, every where are our brethren found. They do their part in the world, and truly the world is the better for their doing it. Every heart here will, I am sure, echo the aspiration of my own, God bless them, wherever they may be!

*The President :*—Hearken to the verdict of the jury; as it is duly recorded. The jury find the said Salmon P. Chase is guilty in manner and form, but in consideration of the extenuating circumstances to which he has referred, recommend him to mercy. And thereupon, having the advice of counsel, a full and free pardon is extended to him.

The remarks of the gentleman who has just received his pardon suggests a call upon—*The Class of* 1811. *The biggest class, of its size,—in its own opinion,—which had then graduated.** *It has still some claim to regard, inasmuch as it numbers among its members one " always Wright."* Judge Wright, of Ohio, Gentlemen.

*Judge Wright :*—It seems hardly justice to the absent and the departed, to call on *me, now,* to represent the class of 1811 — not only unused to this service, but *now,* travel-soiled, and very tired. For let me say, Sir, the class of 1811 is not to be trifled with—not at all to be spoken of slightly. It has made its mark in the annals of Dartmouth; aye, sir, and in other places of the earth.

Were there time it would be grateful to me, and perhaps useful to us all, to recall some of its names, and the course of their lives; to go back almost half a century to our joyous days here, and from that stand look forward into the future, — now become the past.

There was *Daniel Poor,* the Christian Missionary, so amiable and so earnest; unsurpassed in skill as a teacher of the heathen; unlimited in devotion to his Saviour; his bones reposing now among the spicy groves of Ceylon.

*Nathaniel H. Carter,* distinguished *here* for his exquisite classical taste, and afterwards, far and wide, as an elegant leader in the periodical literature of the time; especially by his graphic sketches of for-

---

* The Class of 1811 numbered *seventy-five.* Owing to various untoward circumstances, but *fifty-three* received their degrees in course. One graduated at Middlebury the same year. Two received their degrees with the Class of 1812. The honorary degree of A. M. was conferred upon another in 1822.

eign travel. "He touched nothing which he did not adorn." He has long since gone to his rest, in a foreign land.

There was *Lemuel H. Arnold*, who held, with good success, the helm of Government in that sister State, which once seemed so much to need a hand of extra firmness and power.

*William Cogswell*, also, has gone; so useful and so faithful as a Christian Teacher, and who did so much to strengthen the ties of men to their kindred.

*Ether Shepley*, distinguished as a statesman in the Senate of the Union, and still more as a jurist at the head of the Judiciary of Maine; a lawyer who blends the highest legal talent and learning, with the conscientiousness of a devoted Christian, still remains among us.

There was *Amos Kendall*, since Post-Master General; an office the most complex and harassing of all the departments of public service. To the deep disgrace of our country be it said, all our public men, worthy and unworthy, without distinction, are grossly abused, vilified, vituperated; and he shared the common lot. But now, when the frenzy of the moment has passed away, who doubts that Amos Kendall filled that office with distinguished ability and integrity.

Then there was another, not to be named in this presence, and yet not by any means to be omitted; a stripling in the class, not in mind but in body — for he was very young — long Chief Justice of this our State, where not only his own people, but the whole legal profession throughout the land, will ever remember him with deference and gratitude; now a distinguished Professor in the celebrated Law School at Cambridge; a man who can give honor to any station, and receive honor from none.

But I must stop — I might speak of others; of the whole class. But I am trespassing. I do no justice even to these. May I ask, Sir, to hear from yourself in relation to this class of 1811?

*The President:*—I always do every thing which I may by deputy. Brother Andrews is commissioned to respond to this call.

*A. Andrews, Esq.* : Mr. President,— Little did I think when I entered this hall that so humble an individual as myself would be called upon as your deputy to speak for the class of 1811. I feel myself unable to do justice to the merits of a class which contained so many members who have distinguished themselves in the various learned professions and other employments of life. They need no praise from me, and I shall not attempt to bestow it. But were I competent to the task I might, for a moment, recall to your mind other individuals of our class, who have passed away from earth, whose names are dear to our hearts.

I would name the elder *Goodwin*, who, having just opened an office in South Berwick, Me., his native town, for the practice of law, was suddenly called from his earthly toils and from friends who must have entertained high hopes of his usefulness and success. He was a young man of promising talents, winning address, and unblemished character.

The next name I would bring to your notice is that of *Woodbury.* He had read law, and commenced practice in Portsmouth, N. H. But afterwards he studied divinity, and settled in the gospel ministry in North Yarmouth, Me., in 1817. He died at Groton, Mass., in 1819. Mr. Woodbury was a gentleman of high moral worth, a good scholar, and an amiable man.

Other names crowd upon my memory, but I forbear. A word respecting some of those who have already been mentioned.

*Carter* was decidedly, in my humble opinion, the best classical scholar in the class. He devoted most of his life to literary pursuits, and his writings, both in poetry and prose, were highly creditable to himself and an honor to the class. He was courteous in his manners, upright in his morals, and social in his feelings.

Of *Poor* I have already spoken to-day, when his decease was announced at the meeting in the Chapel. In early college life he came to the determination to devote his whole life as a missionary in India. He has accomplished the task he so ardently desired. Mr. Poor was a persevering scholar, a philanthropist, and a Christian, and in his manners kind and obliging to all.

*Cogswell* knew more of the Class than any other man. He was an industrious man, performing *well* whatever he attempted, in less time than ordinary men. He was the author of several works :—I mention but one—a little pamphlet which we esteem very highly, because it contains a Sketch of the Life of each member of our Class.

And now, Mr. President, as I am about to resign my delegated trust to your hands, allow me to advise you, the next time you attempt to speak by deputy to so respectable an audience as the one over which you now preside, to be more discreet in your choice.

*The President :*—You perceive, gentlemen, that I was not mistaken respecting the opinion which the class of 1811 entertained of itself. I give you next—*Benjamin's Mess. Unlike his namesake of ancient times, the Poet has given, instead of receiving, a double portion of good cheer. We have had from him to-day Poetry and Truth.*

I understand that the Rev. Dr. Henry, of New-York, is responsible for Mr. Benjamin, who it appears is not present.

*Rev. Dr. Henry :* Mr. President,—You have taken me by surprise. I did not expect to be called up at all, still less to be called on to answer for our missing Poet. For I am not a poet, neither am I our poet's *keeper.* I declare to you I have not put him out of the way, as Cain did Abel ; and I resent the imputation your call on me implies. I have not the least doubt but that he is safe and well somewhere.

Though as to the rest, I am unable to conceive what claim you can have on him, or on me, if I were answerable for him; since you yourself admit that he has given us his whole "Benjamin's mess," and gone dinnerless away himself. Be this as it may, I shall decline answering for him.

[*The President :*—"You will please, then, to speak on your own behalf."]

Well, Sir, since I am unrighteously called up, though unprepared with any thing to say, and utterly incapable of continuing the strain of sparkling wit and humor, which you—witty yourself, like Falstaff, and the cause of wit in others—have elicited for the mirth and joyousness of this festive hour; yet I will try to speak an earnest word or two out of the deep feeling which this occasion has awakened.

I have not been here since, fifteen years ago, I had the honor to deliver the Phi Beta Kappa oration: and I have never seen so many of the sons of Dartmouth assembled together before. Sons of Dartmouth!—brethren all,—children of the same benignant Mother! Glorious old Mother of our minds! In eighty-four years she has brought forth nearly three thousand sons! That is the number, I believe, which the venerable President has just told us stands upon the catalogue as the *"numerus integer,"* the whole number of the Alumni ; of which I forget exactly how many he said (in academic catalogical phrase) *"qui supersunt adhuc,"* and I will thank him to mention it again.

[*President Lord,* in reply :—"Nearly two thousand *qui supersunt adhuc.*"]

. Three thousand sons ! of whom nearly two thousand are yet alive ! Wonderful old Mother! And she is as fruitfully vigorous as ever ; as capable of bringing forth children, and more so ; and she means, I don't doubt, to go on bringing forth thousands more of children, every eighty-four years to come, to the end of time.

. We have heard to-day, Sir, how the sons of Dartmouth are to be found every where in the world, doing honor to their Alma Mater and to themselves in the service of God, of their country, and of mankind. Our brother from Ohio, [Senator Chase] of whom his Alma Mater and his brethren may well be proud, and who has made his adopted State and all FREE States proud of him, has given us an amusing account, in his exquisite way, of his experiences in encountering the *ubiquitarian* sons of Dartmouth. I listened with pleasure and with pride; and I may be pardoned, on classic ground, for reciting the classic verse his account called to my mind—words which our Alma Mater has a better right to utter than *pius Æneas* had:

> " Quæ regio in terris nostri non plena laboris ?"

> Wherever you go, by sea or by land,
> Are the sons of Dartmouth, a glorious band.

Not exactly a literal rendering, perhaps, but I am sure you will think it a strictly true one.

Little, Sir, as I feel myself to have done to make my Alma Mater proud of me, I am proud to be reckoned among her sons. I am proud of my brethren. I am proud, and we all have reason to be proud, of our Mother. And she has, in my judgment, a special title to be held in honor by all lovers of sound culture throughout the land. Amidst all the fluctuations of public opinion, and the demands of the spirit of the age for practical studies, so called, she has faithfully adhered to the good old fashioned curriculum. She has understood that the special function of a college is *to train and discipline* the mind, rather than to impart pragmatically the greatest possible amount of mere knowledge. She has understood that it is just simply impossible to find any course of studies so admirably, so perfectly adapted to the true nurture, the harmonious development, and the thorough discipline of the human faculties, and so to the preparation of a youth for all the subsequent acquisitions and subsequent achievements of a man, in whatever sphere, as precisely the good old fashioned, thorough training in classical, mathematical, and logical studies. She has indeed admitted new studies; she has kept pace with the progress of science; but she has not diminished aught of the old, rigid, wholesome discipline. For this, as one devoted to the cause of good learning and public instruction in the University where the best years of my life have been spent, I hold our Alma Mater entitled to a tribute of homage which I am glad to have this opportunity to pay.

Before I sit down, Sir, there is one thing I would like to add. It is suggested by what our orator said of the College buildings here, and of the desirableness of something better, more suitable, more cultivating in architectual character. I heartily agree with what he so finely said. And, though it may not be quite proper for me to make the suggestion at this time, yet I cannot help observing that there is here a large and exceedingly valuable collection of books that ought to be better protected than they are in the edifice in which they are now sheltered; and a fire-proof library building—beautiful enough in form, proportion and expression to satisfy the fine taste of our accomplished orator—would be a fine testimonial of the filial love of the sons of Dartmouth for their benignant Mother. I trust you will pardon me for uttering the suggestion here.

Pardon me for having talked so long. When I complied with your kind request to speak on my own behalf, I only intended to try to express—what no words, however, can express—the boundless delight with which I find myself in the presence of so many of my brethren, Alumni of Dartmouth. I hope our next meeting will be a still more numerous assemblage. I wish we could see all the "*supersunt adhuc*," the near two thousand live sons of Dartmouth, assembled together at once! You say, Sir, that we should have to find some other place than this crowded, extra-propped-up hall. Let us fill the College Green, then, and stretch a canvas covering over it all. It would be a glorious reünion! for there is no finer, purer, more spiritual bond—and, outside the tender relations of the domestic circle, there is no stronger bond—than that which unites the lovers of good letters, and especially those who have received the nurture of their minds at a common source. Let us, Sir, ever cherish this bond; and wherever in the wide world the sons of Dartmouth meet, let it be with the heart-glad hand-grasp of true-hearted brothers.

*The President:—The Judiciary. We claim a present primary interest in that of New-Hampshire, Maine, and Vermont; and have had some good investments in that of the United States, and that of Massachusetts and other States too numerous to mention.*

Chief Justice Redfield, of Vt., is bound to answer for the Judiciary.

*Chief Justice Redfield:* Mr. President,—I shall not attempt to make a speech at this late hour, upon so dry and uninteresting a subject as the Judiciary. Nobody, as a general thing, cares much about the Judiciary, any way. It is always, to most men, a dull topic of discourse; and I have sometimes thought the least said or done upon that subject, the better. It is no doubt true, the world is governed too much, and as Chancellor Oxenstiern said to his son, "with very little wisdom often." Still, there are a good many who seem to fancy that all the ills of life are curable mainly by legislative and judicial reforms. These are, for the most part, men who have more confidence in themselves than in others, or than others have in them; men who don't like right well to trust Providence even.

It has thus happened that in this country, for the last ten years, almost all the States have been making more or less experiments upon their judicial systems, the tenure of judicial office, and the mode of appointment, till everything is brought into a state of painful uncertainty upon this subject. It has seemed to me that we were, in regard to the Judiciary, in this country, getting very much into the condition of the physician's patient. He said the truth was, it had been *doctored* too much : it was, in reality, dying of the medicine, rather than the disease.

I do not expect these judicial reformers to be equally frank in their confessions, but the condition of the public mind has been quite too much agitated, for the last few years, to be likely to cure the evils which no doubt exist, to some extent, in our judicial systems; and there seems more disposition among the politicians for reforms there, than among the people. Some of our States have quite recently declined to make the Judiciary elective, by a popular vote, even for a term of years—preferring that the judges should hold office by executive appointment, during good behavior; but in some States there is manifested a disposition to have the Judiciary more essentially popularized, as they call it. If by that they mean, to have the Judiciary a power in the State whose direction shall be shaped by the outward pressure—a mere stake, for demagogues and politicians to gamble over—let them beware. When that thing is once done it will be too late to retrace their steps! *Nulla vestigia retrorsum!*

And if any body, natural or artificial, has just cause to glory in the wisdom and independence of the Judiciary, it is Dartmouth College—our venerable, vigorous, and glorious Alma Mater. But for the Judiciary, and a Judiciary above the changing and hireling influences of the day or the age, even the name of Dartmouth College would have been among the things that were. *Illa fuit, et ingens gloria*, should already have concluded her brief history. She was not only the occasion, but the cause—the efficient cause—of establishing, through the independence of the National Judiciary, a most conservative and indispensable principle in the law and the life of corporations; and if in her turn she has contributed any thing to the credit of the judicial incumbents in the States named, we shall all rejoice. I could not, perhaps, be expected to say more upon this particular topic.

*The President:—The Orator of the United Literary Societies. Although we have not the honor of his name on the roll of our Alumni, we recognize it with pleasure as that of one of our most munificent benefactors.*

*Mr. Phillips* declined making a speech, but said he had heard of some tall specimens of the Graduates of Dartmouth College, and expressed a wish to hear from—

" *The tallest Graduate—the tallest Member of Congress, and the tallest Man present.*"

This led to a general call for *Mr. Wentworth*, of Illinois, who graduated in 1836.

*Mr. W. responded:*—I consider myself fortunate in being present at a meeting of so many of the Alumni, and hope to be equally fortunate on many similar occasions. My relatives are all in New-Hampshire. Whenever I visit them at this season, I always attend the Anniversary Exercises of my Alma Mater. But I am called out in consequence of my height. And what had Dartmouth College to do with that? From the days of Eleazer Wheelock to the present time, when did she add an inch to any one's stature? Perhaps gentlemen think all the Graduates stand upon their diplomas, and that my parchment was a little thicker than that of any other of the Graduates. Now, diplomas are very good things, but they will not do to stand upon in all cases. Yet I took one degree, and succeeded so well with it that I came back and got a second, and I succeeded a great deal better, and so all say who have tried the second degree.

The Faculty of Dartmouth College never claimed any credit for my height, and did their whole duty to make me think it was of no importance. It seems but yesterday that President Lord recited certain stanzas from Dr. Watts, which referred to me so plainly, that, had it been in Congress, and had Congress been an orderly body, I should have called him to order, for a personal allusion. I am not certain that I quote them correctly, but if I do not, President Lord will correct me :

> " Were I so tall 's to reach the Pole,
> " Or grasp the ocean with my span,
> " I must be measured by my soul :
> " The mind 's the standard of the man."

Now, by this standard, the eloquent orator of this afternoon, Mr. PHILLIPS, is a taller man than I am ; and hereafter, when he and I are together, and the tallest man is complimented, I shall insist that he come forward and do the blushing.

By this standard, as I look around these tables, I recognize a great many taller men than I am, and I wish to hear from them all. They need be under no embarrassment. They are at home now. If they make any mistakes, the Faculty are responsible. They came here like clay in the hands of the potter, and it is the fault of the Faculty if they have not been moulded into great men. If any were spoiled in making—and I have heard of such instances—here, among our own brethren, is the place to charge it upon the Faculty, and to give them such proof of it that they will confess, and perhaps try to remedy it. Here we are, brethren, back in the old ship-yard from which we were originally launched ; and if we have any defects, let us go into the old dock and lay ourselves up for repairs. Let us all speak with freedom, and if we speak amiss let us call upon President LORD to show cause for the Faculty's not being held responsible therefor.

We have been hearing of the influential, the potential men ; the officers of the National Cabinet, the Supreme Judges, the Senators, the Foreign Ambassadors, the Presidents and Professors of Colleges, the Missionaries, &c. &c., that have been graduates of Dartmouth College. All these references afford but additional cases where " distance lends enchantment to the view." Here, at these tables, I insist, are the jewels of Dartmouth College. Don't look at me so earnestly, gentlemen! You are the jewels! Look at yourselves! What have you done to add lustre to Dartmouth College ?

Preceding speakers have alluded to the distinction acquired by members of their respective classes. My class has not been out in the world long enough yet to do justice to itself without crowding its predecessors. We are not one and twenty yet. But we have the Governor of one of the most thriving States of the Confederacy —Hon. JAMES WILSON GRIMES, of Iowa. And I notice that another of that class has just been nominated as a candidate for Lt. Governor of Vermont—Hon. STODDARD B. COLBY. When we graduated, this would have been called extending our influence from one extremity of the Union to the other. But now, under our system of annexations and conquests, we can only say, from the centre to one extremity.

One instance of the influence of Dartmouth College upon the

youth of the West, and I must be excused. We have but little time here, and that should be divided among the largest number possible.

It is said that a western man never speaks any where without an allusion to his town, and that his hearers may always think themselves fortunate if he does not take out his map and ask them to purchase a lot. I believe Chicago has the best system of free schools in the world, with her school-houses extended to the remotest boundaries of the city, and open to all, without distinction of birth-place, color, or religion. Poor foreigners can step from the cars just bringing to them to our city, to any of our schools, and leave their children whilst they look up a house for a home. And all those schools, with their thousands of scholars, are under the immediate superintendance of J. C. DORE, Esq. And who will even undertake to calculate the immense advantages of his free instruction to the children of the poor foreigners and day laborers. Many of these children must receive from him such a stimulus for the paths of literature and science, as will induce them to come to his Alma Mater, and travel the paths which he has traveled before them so much to their profit.

Mr. President and Gentlemen: I hope to meet you all again, and as many more as can possibly be prevailed upon to be present at our future Anniversaries; and, whenever I do meet you, if I promptly respond to calls upon me to say a few words, it will be more from a desire to set a good example, than from a disposition to speak. For I really consider all the pleasure to be derived from these reünions to consist in the freedom and frankness with which we converse with each other; making the scene like that in the parents' house, when the numerous and long absent children return to greet each other upon life, health and prosperity; all forgetful of the past but its pleasures and instructions; all buoyant in the hopes of the future; all with a little something to tell for the delight of the household.

*The President:—The Reverend Clergy. In their orisons be all our sins remembered.*

Rev. Dr. PETERS, of New-York, is requested to speak of the Clergy.

*Dr. A. Peters* remarked that the scene to which he was here introduced was new and exciting, and yet it was old as his memory of College days. Since coming on to this ground, he said, I hardly know whether to consider myself old or young. I feel a kind of " Conflict of Ages" in my own person. It seems but a day since I was among the " *Hi Juvenes*" of the graduating class. On my arrival this morning I ran like a boy to find the old school-house, where I taught the village school during my " Senior vacation," and the way I governed sixty-one boys and girls was a caution. I looked, as I said, where the house was, and it was not there ! It has been moved away bodily, and another of larger dimensions and more durable materials erected in its place.

Changes have come over the town, the people, the College. The bridge across the river is burnt down, and Le Compt, who, we used to say, was like a Jew, because he kept the *Passover*, is gone from the toll-gatherer's hut; and I am reminded that it is forty years, save one, since I left these grounds, new fledged for life and labor. A whole generation has passed away,—except the remnants of it who mingle their scattered ranks with grey heads, and often with trembling steps, among their youthful successors,—and, young as I feel, and vigorous for new enterprise, I find myself among the old men who have left their grand children at home, to come here and renew their interest and sympathies in the scenes of College life.

I look for my teachers and only two remain [the venerable Professors Shurtleff and Muzzey, who were present] to cheer *us*, of those other days, with their familiar faces ; and only one of my classmates is present, though full one half of the class of 1816 are still living to honor their Alma Mater in the walks of respectability and usefulness which they adorn.

But, Mr. President, you have called on me to respond to a sentiment of honor to the Clergy, which you have been pleased to announce. I would not be diverted from this topic by the clustering memories to which I have alluded, and which the present gathering is so fitted to awaken.

Old Dartmouth has ever been famous among the Colleges for the number of its graduates who have entered the clerical profession ; and I am ever thankful for having been myself accounted worthy. of a place in the Christian ministry. But this ministry, as a profession, needs no advocacy from me. It stands high and prominent among the callings of the educated men of our country, and is certainly second to no other in the sphere of its usefulness. And more than this, I do but justly magnify a holy calling, by saying that it surpasses all other professions, in its adaptedness to promote the highest interests of man, in all the conditions and prospects of his being. It has to do both with things seen and things not seen; but the crown of its joy will be received, and the consummation of its benefits will be sung, in everlasting songs in the life eternal.

We honor the Clergy in the faithful discharge of their duties. We honor the Institutions whose training contributes to fill the ranks of a profession so indispensable to human well being, both here and hereafter. The Clergy are a blessing to the land, as preachers of righteousness and examples of self-denying piety and beneficence. More than the members of any other profession, they are at the head of our educational institutions. They are among the most prominent of the leaders of the great benevolent enterprises of the age, and of the conductors of the religious press. And last, not least, they are the Missionaries of the Church to bear the cross of Christ to foreign lands.

Our Alma Mater, Mr. President, has contributed its full share to provide for all these departments of usefulness and of high endeavor. I may be permitted to say that while I was Corresponding Secretary of the American Home Missionary Society, and had much to do with young men just entering the ministry, I had frequent occasion to admire the self-sacrificing enterprise of the sons of Dartmouth. If we wanted a man to occupy a position in advance of all others on our western borders—" to go to the jumping-off-place," as was sometimes said—we looked for him among the graduates of this Institution, and were sure to find him here, or among the sons of one of the northern Colleges.

Sir, I have said, very imperfectly, what perhaps I might have said better and more at large, had I been aware of your intention to call me up on this topic. If the Clergy of the sons of Dartmouth shall continue to honor their profession, as they have done in most cases, I doubt not that you, and all good men and true, who trace their early instruction to the same halls of learning and discipline, will not cease to honor them and to honor this home of our youthful and undying affections, on account of the large number it is raising up to preach glad tidings to the nations, and say unto Zion, "Thy God reigneth."

*The President:—Railroads.   We well remember that among their merits is that of giving facilities for this joyous reünion.*

Mr. Edwards, of Keene, who has had as much as most men to do with their construction, will please answer for the railroads.

*T. M. Edwards, Esq.:* Mr. President,—I am not unmindful of the honor of being called out on this occasion, but I am, nevertheless, admonished, by various indications, that it would not be prudent for me at this time, if ever, to enter upon a measured speech.

The lateness of the hour, the vacated seats around me, the sense of satiety, if not of weariness, resting upon the faces, " *eorum qui supersunt adhuc,*" to use a phrase quite familiar in these anniversary proceedings, all impress me with the truth and frequent applicability of that sage though somewhat trite maxim, that the better part of valor is discretion.

Beyond this I am not quite sure, you will permit me to say, that the subject which you have assigned to me is entirely in harmony with the topics which have engrossed attention through the day. We have been guests at a banquet exclusively literary and social. We have been engaged in communing in relation to the abstract; in relation to principles, truths and sentiments presented and illustrated in rich and glowing language, and interspersed with flashes of wit and humor. Now, every thing connected with the great feature in our system of internal improvements, to which your sentiment relates, is of a gross, material and merely practical character; and however much, even in its present imperfect state of development, it may have ministered, or may now be ministering, to the convenience and to the interest of individuals, and to the growth and prosperity of the country, it certainly presents no very fit theme for the poet or the orator, and could hardly prefer any other claim to admission into this presence, than the one to which you have referred in your opening remarks, viz., the facilities which it has furnished for bringing together, from distant parts of the country, so many of the scattered sons of this ancient College, and reüniting them at this friendly festival on the scene of their early and most cherished associations. So far as the Railroad has contributed to this result, it is entitled, here and now, to our favorable estimation and to our gratitude.

In this connection I must ask to be indulged in a passing notice of your very civil reference to myself, as having had some experience in railroad matters. It is true that to the neglect and abandonment of a profession, the study and practice of which is a very usual sequence to college life, I have devoted some years to the charge of the construction and management of a railroad; and there was a time when I should have regarded an allusion to this fact, as being, as it is now intended, complimentary, having idly supposed that in aiding in achieving a public risk of this character, I was contributing something to an important public benefaction. But so disastrous has been the result of many of the railroad enterprises in our own and the neighboring States, to those with whom they have originated, and by whom they have been sustained and carried on to completion, as you, Sir, I think, have some reason to know; that so far from claiming any credit here for the part which I have enacted, I am rather disposed to ignore the whole subject, and to be quite content if my connection with them shall not subject me to a visitation similar to that which you felt it your duty to inflict, for a very different offence, upon the honorable gentleman from Ohio, to wit, an arraignment on indictment found against me by the body of this Association. If I were compelled to plead, I should be obliged to confess, and could offer nothing in extenuation but the fact, of having aided somewhat in the work before alluded to, of promoting and facilitating this pleasant gathering, and, perchance, of much larger assemblages to be had at our future triennial meetings. This I should expect would at least be received in mitigation of punishment.

Having said all that I desire to say, Mr. President, in relation to this special assignment, I should very willingly, if time permitted, briefly refer to a more prominent topic of the occasion, viz., the present condition of the Institution towards which we sustain a common relation, and in the welfare and prosperity of which we feel a common interest.

Having passed the last week here, in a service connected with the College, I have had a more favorable opportunity of becoming acquainted with its existing arrangements, and of renewing and brightening my recollection of its earlier condition, than I could hope to have enjoyed under other circumstances.

The comparison of the past and the present, to which this renewed acquaintance has necessarily led, shews obviously much change and much improvement.

Without derogating from the great credit which is justly due to its founders, and early and later managers, but tendering all honor and gratitude to them for their timely, earnest, faithful and almost unrewarded labors, it is not too much, I believe, to say that there has been no period in its history when this great Educational Agency has possessed so large a power for usefulness, or has been so worthy of the regard, respect, and veneration of its Alumni, and of the confidence and patronage of the community, as at the present time. A largely increased number of students; enlarged accommodations; a more numerous corps of able and efficient instructors; more extensive libraries; other appliances for facilitating the acquisition of knowledge, newly added; a more comprehensive course of study; careful attention to moral as well as mental training; all furnish unerring indications that this Institution at least keeps pace with other kindred institutions, in the march of improvement, and prepares herself in advance to respond to a growing demand for a more varied, thorough, and profound collegiate education.

I will only add, Sir, that it must be the earnest wish of all her sons, as it is mine, that " Old Dartmouth " may long continue to occupy the honorable position which she has so long enjoyed among the literary institutions of the country.

*The President:*—We have heard from two of the learned professions. My friend, Mr. Ordronaux, furnishes a sentiment calling for a response from the other.

*The Medical Profession. Bonus Medicus custos populi.*

Dr. Mussey will please take us under his care.

*Mr. President,*—I had no expectation of being called upon for remarks upon this occasion. Had I been requested to give you a lecture on Surgical Anatomy, or to describe an amputation, or the method of dressing a broken leg, or of gouging an eye *secundum artem,* I would not hesitate to make the attempt, if the materials suitable for the demonstration were before me; but, vegetable eater as I have long been, and wholly untrained to making speeches over a table covered with the scattered and half devoured remains of animal carcasses, I must be permitted to decline the honor so kindly offered.

It is with no slight gratification that I have witnessed in this assembly the outpourings of wit under the inspiration of no other liquor than the pure beverage of Paradise. Why, Sir, this attic salt streams out at every pore, and fills our saloon with its sparkling atmosphere.

May every son of Dartmouth show his regard for the wine of Eden, by coming up to the altar of humanity and taking the solemn vow, *never to drink any other.*

*The President:*—As Dr. Mussey declines to make a demonstration, we turn to one of his successors, well known as a " *Great Medicine,*" and ask Dr. Peaslee to favor us with a prescription or a lecture.

*Dr. E. R. Peaslee:* Mr. President,—As the venerable Professor who has just spoken could better deliver a lecture on Surgery, I suppose that from me you would rather expect something on Anatomy and Physiology.

The *dispersive* tendencies of the Alumni of Dartmouth have been alluded to on this occasion, and I will venture to suggest an explanation of the fact. The students of this College are, most of them, fully developed men, physically, even when they enter College, the average age being three or four years more than in Yale and Harvard. Many of them have in fact previously acquired, by their own exertions, the means to defray the expenses of their education. Such men have of course acquired a habit of self-reliance; and when they have at length graduated and completed their professional studies, they go out determined and fully expecting to succeed; and they *keep going*, till they find a good place. As a body they seem to be thoroughly imbued with the sentiment expressed by Pope:

> " The mouse that ever sticks to *one poor hole*,
> Can never be a mouse of any soul."

So that you have to look the whole world over to find them, but when you *do* find them, it is generally in the right place.

Perhaps, Sir, you may be inclined to demand an apology from me for comparing the men of Dartmouth—*men* in the noblest sense of the word—with the diminutive animal just mentioned. But I have good authority, poetical and otherwise, for so doing. In the first place, the men of Dartmouth are, every where I believe, the "muscle" of the community of which they form a part: and this word is from the Latin *mus–culus*, as I have had occasion to say to young men. Burns has said—

> " The best laid plans of *mice and men*
> Oft gang awry."

And not much more elevated is Grainger's invocation:

> " Now, Muse, let's sing of rats!"

But it is not fit that I should occupy the time at this late hour. I propose, Sir, one of the Alumni of Dartmouth; who emigrated from this to another State, and who also *kept going* (upward) till he found himself in a very good place. I will not name him, lest I disturb that modesty which is as marked a characteristic as his rare merits. I propose—

*The Royall Professor of Law in Harvard University: Our President on this occasion.* In whatever *state* we find him, in whatever condition, in whatever *position*, he does honor alike to all. "*Omnis Aristippum decuit color, et* STATUS, *et res.*"

———

The Association here adjourned, to meet at the close of the public dinner on Commencement day: at which time the President, on taking the chair, said the members of the Association might now expect to hear from their absent friends, Mr. Duncan being no longer among the number.

Wm. H. Duncan, Esq., one of the Committee of Arrangements, read the following letters.

[FROM REV. BENNET TYLER, D. D.]

EAST WINDSOR HILL, July 23, 1855.

Rev. S. G. BROWN,

*Dear Sir :* Yours of the 20th inst. is just received. It would give me great pleasure to attend your Commencement if the state of my health and other engagements would permit. But I must deny myself the satisfaction. I regret it the more, on account of the meeting of the Alumni, which I should rejoice to attend, with the hope of meeting many of my former pupils, some of whom I have not seen since "*Pro auctoritate mihi commissa,*" *eos admittebam* "*ad gradum primum in artibus.*" I need not say how cordially I should greet them, as well as many others of the earlier and later graduates. Dartmouth may well be proud of her sons. I trust they will not be wanting in affection for their mother.

The few years of my life which were devoted to the interest of the College have awakened in my breast a regard for its welfare which I shall not cease to cherish while life lasts. That it may ever be the seat of sound learning and the centre of a healthful moral influence, is the prayer of

Yours most affectionately,

B. TYLER.

---

[FROM HON. RICHARD FLETCHER.]

BOSTON, July 25, 1855.

*Dear Sir :* When your favor, dated the 21st, and mailed the 23d instant, reached me, it was too late for me to return an answer, or go in person to Hanover in season for your dinner to-day. If your kind letter had been received at an earlier period, it would have given me much pleasure to have been present at the meeting of the Alumni.

With thanks for your obliging communication,

I am, very respectfully and truly yours,

RICHARD FLETCHER.

WM. H. DUNCAN, Esq.

---

[FROM HON. DANIEL M. CHRISTIE.]

DOVER, July 23, 1855.

*Dear Sir :* I have yours of the 20th, in which you, in behalf of the Committee of Arrangements, extend to me a polite and particular invitation to be present at the approaching Anniversary of the Alumni of Dartmouth College.

It would be highly gratifying to me to be with you on the occasion, but indispensable engagements will deprive me of that pleasure.

With assurances of much respect for the Committee, and the kindest regard for yourself,

I am your much obliged friend and servant,

DANIEL M. CHRISTIE.

WM. H. DUNCAN, Esq., Hanover.

---

[FROM REV. JOHN WHEELER, D. D.]

BURLINGTON, July 23, 1855.

To W. H. DUNCAN, Esq.,

*Dear Sir:* I regret that it will not be in my power to comply with the request of the Committee to be present at the gathering of the Alumni, at Dartmouth, this week. But, though absent in body, I would be present in spirit, and, by these presents, beg you to greet the multitude of brothers with the warmest expressions of fellowship.

I would add a word respecting my personal historical recollections of the period of my connection with College, (from 1812 to 1816) but it will be so much better done by the accomplished orator of the day, who I learn intends to speak of historical matters, that I will only say it was a *transition period* of the Institution ; one in which, rising from her couch of quiet growth, she cast off the bonds of childhood, and stepped forth with the vigorous development of a youthful Titan. And then "shaking her invincible locks," she seized her spear and went forth to battle for the rights of all the institutions of civilization and culture, that pertain to the being and growth of our beloved country. I now look upon her, irrespective of times, of parties, of persons, political or ecclesiastical, as then resisting a particular statute, in a lawful way, only that she might repose in the bosom of that law, which makes possible the freedom of social life, and which constitutes the harmony of cultivated humanity. The men who resolved for her; the men who counselled for her; the men who pleaded for her; and the men, who, in the Temple of National justice, determined and decided for her, are gone; — all gone, down to the dead. But she lives. She lives, the symbolic keystone in the arch of religious, literary and commercial institutions which are free; and from her high eminence now shines, radiant and effulgent, like a morning star, in her literary beauty. Thus she will live while her Alumni study her lessons and practice her virtues.

Your gathering is an occasion, when literary men, and great men, and benefactors, as such, are remembered ; but a day in which the men of physical labor and toil are usually forgotten. But it is by the sweat of their brow that the ease and the leisure, by which culture becomes possible to social life, is obtained. Talk as we may, think as we may, they substitute the $\pi o v \ \sigma \tau \tilde{\omega}$ on which society erects her structures, and by which she maintains her physical life. I call to mind one of these men, who learned his letters and his catechism by " light-wood candles;" who was but six weeks in any school, until by his own labor he paid for six months' tuition and board at an Academy, under the care of " Master Hubbard," afterward Professor of Mathematics in our College; Professor Hubbard, a man who should not be forgotten ; whose whole being, instead of working toward right lines and rectangles, was ever imparting a life of the affections, in graceful elipses and curvilinear lines, and now and then parabolic curves of perhaps indefinite extension.   Under this affectionate teacher, the young man made such progress that he soon taught school; but finally, with axe in hand, entered the woods of a mountain town, felled the trees for a farm, cast in the seed, and waited for his harvest.   Exchanges were made, and he was soon a country merchant, and was present at the commencement of Dartmouth College in 1816.   After the exercises of the day, as he was sitting in his chair, and bidding adieu to a Professor of the College, he said, " If the Trustees intend to test their rights by a suit at law, and should want means, I have a *thousand* dollars at their command."

The late Professor Adams has said if it had not been for this unsolicited, unsuspected, unthought of aid, the great case of Dartmouth College would not have been commenced.

And the late Charles Marsh has spoken of the offer, which was at once transmitted to the Board of Trustees, then in session, as a light breaking upon blank darkness.   It was a prophecy of hope, which at once fixed the resolution and determined the course of the Trustees.

What would the College now be without the aid of the " Industrial class;" without Chandler, and Appleton, and Evans, and Phillips —what would our students be without the numerous off-shoots from their class, and especially without their material aid in the progress of their studies ?

I beg to give you, as a sentiment for the occasion, and for every Commencement of Dartmouth College—

*The Industrial Classes of Society : — The strength of its physical life, the* που σιω *of its structures — the roots which have nourished us all.*

Yours with highest regard,

JOHN WHEELER.

At the close of the reading of this letter the name of the munificent donor being called for, the President said he understood it was John B. Wheeler, Esq., late of Orford, the father of President Wheeler.

----

[From Rt. Rev. Carlton Chase, D. D.]

Claremont, July 24, 1855.

*My dear Sir :* It is with difficulty I yield to the circumstances which deprive me of the pleasure of joining, in happy reünion, with the Alumni of an Institution whose son I am proud in claiming to be.

Such an assemblage of cultivated minds, drawn together by the noble sympathies of kindred scholarship; coming in, too, as well from the outposts of social progress, laden with the fresh observations of learned adventure, as from the various positions of honor and usefulness in the old fields of knowledge, enriched with stores of experience and wisdom, cannot fail to present an occasion for refined and exalted interchanges, such as does not often turn up in the course of our pursuits.

In contemplation of such an assemblage I feel impressed with the thought of the momentous issues which may depend on the character of the individuals who compose it, and on the use they make of the elevation to which knowledge has raised them. There is, indeed, intrinsic beauty in truth, which is of itself a reward to the scholar,— but if there be not also power and use, the moral world is a chimera.

I trust I shall be pardoned for thus briefly and hastily giving expression to the feelings which the habits of my sacred profession incline me to indulge in view of your meeting to-morrow. Let it be remembered, that the true scholar is one who receives light to yield it again.

I pray you, my dear Sir, in my behalf, to present to the brotherhood the assurance of the high consideration and respect with which

I am their, as also your most obliged servant,

CARLTON CHASE, *Class of* 1817.

WM. H. DUNCAN, Esq., *Chairman of Com., &c.*

---

[FROM HON. JOHN AIKEN.]

ANDOVER, July 21, 1855.

WM. H. DUNCAN, Esq.,

*My dear Sir:* I have just received your note, written in behalf of the Committee of Arrangements of the Society of Alumni of Dartmonth College, inviting me to be present at the approaching Anniversary; or, if that cannot be, to furnish some memorial for the dinner hour.

Let me assure you and your brethren of the Committee, and my brethren of the Society, that it would afford me very great pleasure to be present. It so happens, however, that the Trustees of Phillips Academy, of which body I have the honor to be a member, will hold their Annual Meeting on Tuesday next, and will occupy, in their necessary business, the whole of that day. I deem it my duty to attend this meeting, so that I could, at the very earliest, reach Hanover on the afternoon of Wednesday, after your dinner hour.

Though thus held back from your festivities, I shall be with you in spirit, and vie with the very best of you in crowning with honors our Alma Mater.

The occasion will be consecrated by many tender and precious recollections. My own College life, from 1815 to 1819, was filled with incidents of great moment, and to those immediately concerned, of thrilling interest.

Of the Hon. and Reverend Trustees of that day not one remains, and of my instructors in the College, Dr. SHURTLEFF, and Dr. BOND, of Philadelphia, are the only survivors. To the memory of the honored dead your orator has, no doubt paid the deserved and appropriate tribute. In passing let me thank Prof. BROWN for coming to the rescue in your hour of extremity. Though I thank him, let me tell him there is one topic appropriate to this occasion, to which he cannot do justice. He cannot speak in fitting terms of the character and doings of my loved and honored President, FRANCIS BROWN. This lack of service, made almost necessary by the relations which you orator sustains to the subject, I would, if I might, supply.

Pres. Brown entered on the duties of his office in the autumn of 1815, and closed his active duties as a teacher at the Commencement of 1819. His inaugural discourse, some portions of which I can still repeat, was in Latin, written, as was said, in part at least, at the taverns on his way to Hanover. He was in the prime of early manhood, being but 31 years old, and yet he had the dignity, the maturity and the wisdom of riper years.

In person Pres. Brown was singularly dignified and commanding : one of the very noblest specimens of manhood that my eyes ever beheld. And yet his dignity sat upon him so gracefully, that the beholder discovered at once that it was but one of the native properties of the outer man, and no exaggerated exponent of the dignity of the inner. His large, full blue eye, and genial, beaming face, invited confidence, yet his whole expression was so sagacious and so penetrating, that no student ever dreamed of deceiving him, or presumed on unbecoming familiarity with him. When the occasion required he could be *severe, terribly severe*. This severity, however, had nothing of personal anger in it, but savored rather of grief, or wounded love. To govern young men was his natural and easy work. The language of command he never, or seldom used. A *wish*, or *request*, expressed in the mildest and kindest form, was fully equivalent to a command, and we all took delight in pleasing him, for we both loved and honored him.

His talent for teaching was not inferior to his talent for governing, and this talent found occasion for abundant exercise. During his whole administration, the entire instruction of the senior class devolved on him, and from the end of his first year till his health began to fail, he heard the junior or sophomore class one recitation each day. For all these recitations he carefully prepared himself, so that no slipshod preparation on the part of a student could escape unexposed. If a topic should be started, or a book be referred to, with which the President was not familiar, he would, by sagacious questioning, draw out what the student knew of that topic or book, and then, by his sharper analysis, his keener and more penetrating insight, or his power of broader generalization, he was prepared to discuss the subject in a way that satisfied the student who furnished all the material, that the President understood the matter much better than he did himself. The mind of Pres. Brown was eminently sagacious and comprehensive, as well as discriminating.

Pres. Brown could not in truth be called a greatly learned man. Occupied as he had been, and at his period of life, this could not be. Yet he was a man of vigorous and cultivated mind, and a scholar. And he was capable of appreciating good learning, and all his influences tended toward a sound, thorough, and comprehensive scholarship. Accordingly in his day, though the Faculty of instruction was very inadequate, and greatly over taxed, consisting as it did of the President, two Professors and one or two Tutors, and the facilities in the way of libraries and apparatus exceedingly small, there was much earnest and effective study in the College. The Catalogue will show *small classes*, but a large proportion of *good scholars.*

The official life of the President was one of ceaseless toil. Vacations brought no rest to him. This was his season for begging money to meet the urgent wants of the College, and for taking counsel for its welfare. During the vacation of my Junior year, President Brown visited my native town, in the south part of the State, and collected of the farmers, in little sums, about $100, to help the College along in its deep distress and poverty.

The eminent legal counsel of the College had a very high opinion of President Brown. No man could measure him more accurately than the late JEREMIAH MASON. *He* regarded Mr. Brown as a very remarkable man; remarkable especially for the sagacity, clearness and strength of his judgment. More than once I have heard Mr. Mason say, "Mr. Brown understood the College Case thoroughly, and could have argued it with eminent ability."

In early manhood Mr. Brown was called to preside over a Board composed of men of great ability, dignity and wisdom; and yet, in all these elements of character, young as he was, he was not a whit behind the very chiefest of them.

I close with this sentiment:

" *The Memory of* PRESIDENT BROWN. *It is embalmed in the hearts of all his pupils.*"

Wishing for my brethren a most happy meeting, I subscribe myself,              Your and their friend and brother,

JOHN AIKEN.

---

[FROM HON. RUFUS CHOATE.]

BOSTON, July 25, 1855.

*My dear Sir:* Your letter inviting me to attend the meeting of the Alumni of Dartmouth College reached me at so late an hour that I could not accept the invitation, nor suitably express my regret that I was unable to do so.

I have heard with great pleasure of the proposal to form an Association of our Alumni, which should mark their memory and their love of our Alma Mater by a meeting at every Commencement, and had formed a general intention to be present at the first. I cannot doubt that the idea will be carried out, and that it will realize all the expectations of those who conceived it. Certainly my own affection for the now almost ancient school, and my sense of obligation to its teachings and its care, lose no strength as the happy days of my life there recede from me, nor does any thing which I have learned of other Colleges depress my estimation of its rank and claims. These I am sure are the sentiments of all the children of Dartmouth. To express and publish them, as well as to renew and strengthen the ties which unite all fellow students, will give a practical object and a real interest to these annual festivals. I hope some time to take my share in them.        I am very cordially,

Your friend and servant,
RUFUS CHOATE.

Daniel Blaisdell *and others, Committee of Alumni.*

---

[FROM HON. GEORGE W. NESMITH.]

Franklin, July 23, 1855.

Wm. H. Duncan, Esq.:

I thank you, my dear Sir, for your kind invitation to be present at the ensuing Anniversary of the Alumni of Dartmouth College. My business engagements must compel me to decline your invitation, as I shall be called to Malone, N. Y., on that day.

I appreciate highly your new Association. I can imagine nothing but pleasure and utility to flow from it. . I hope on some future occasion to be able to participate in your enjoyments.

Allow me to suggest to the wise managers of your organization the importance of establishing, for the use of all the sons of Dartmouth, a very broad and perfect platform upon which we can safely stand without jostling any off. We can see around us many beautiful erections of modern philanthropists, and more modern politicians, and we can copy therefrom all that is useful, and still leave much uncopied. But let me suggest to the wisdom that shall this year be assembled, if this annual feast is to be continued on our side of the Connecticut, the manifest propriety of extending forthwith a very perfect *wooden* platform from the house formerly inhabited by a renowned man by the name of Le Compt, thence westerly to the premises of the celebrated Dr. Lewis, in the ancient town of Norwich. As we would save the bodies of all our learned and unlearned fellow citizens from the peril of death by drowning, you are permitted to draw upon me for my plank to finish up this model and much needed platform.

Yours forever,
GEORGE W. NESMITH.

---

[FROM RICHARD B. KIMBALL, ESQ.]

West Lebanon, July 23, 1855.

*My dear Duncan:* Will you present my thanks to the Committee of Arrangements for the invitation you were kind enough to communicate, to be present at the exercises of the Society of the Alumni on Wednesday next. I am sorry I cannot be with you; and I request you distinctly to understand that it is because I must be on my way to New-York, and not because you have no wine at dinner; which you distinctly insinuate may be to me a trifling inconvenience! I am sure I should not notice this innuendo, except that your note, being semi-official in its character, it seems to me I am bound to repel it. There are many grave reasons why wine should not be furnished at a public dinner. Tell me, is it not expected that every guest shall be in a situation to get on his feet when called up? But what saith the ancient Roman?

> " Magnum hoc vitium vino est,
> *Pedes* captat primum."

Therefore away with the seductive article! Let us not offend our weaker brethren—weaker in legs, I mean, of course.

Seriously, it is an aggravation that I must leave here just as the children of " Old Dartmouth "—God bless her—are assembling for an interchange of happy thoughts and pleasing memories. Perhaps you will allow me to propose the following, that I may seem, to myself at least, to take some trifling part in your arrangements:

*Liberality of Sentiment: One of the softening graces of our humanity. May the Alumni of Dartmouth retain and cherish this offspring of an enlightened education.*

Yours truly,<br>RICHARD B. KIMBALL.

WM. H. DUNCAN, Esq., Hanover, N. H.

---

[FROM HON. HARRY HIBBARD.]

BATH, July 25, 1855.

*My dear Sir:* Through accident, your letter in behalf of the Committee of Arrangements, inviting me to be present at the meeting of the Alumni of Dartmouth to-day, has but just been received. It comes at an hour too late for me to say more than express the regret I feel at my inability, by reason of other engagements, to be with you upon an occasion which must draw around it so many incentives to enjoyment, not only from the intellectual and physical festivities of the present, but from the renewed associations and recalled memories of the cherished past.

Have the kindness to tender my acknowledgements to the other members of the Committee, and be assured that I am,

Most truly yours,<br>HARRY HIBBARD.

WILLIAM H. DUNCAN, Esq.

*The President:*—You are aware, gentlemen, that a short time since Alma Mater opened a little school — not by any means an infant school — which at the present rate of progress bids fair to rival not only Moor's Indian Charity School, but even the Classical Department itself. I give you, *" The Chandler School of Science and the Arts,"* and call upon the Visitors of that Foundation for a response.

*F. B. Hayes, Esq.,* one of the Board of Visitors of the Chandler School, replied :

*Mr. President:*—In obedience to your call, and at the request of my associate, I rise to respond to the sentiment with which you have honored the Scientific Department of this College. At this festival, when your Alma Mater is surrounded by her own distinguished children, her adopted sons might well be silent; and I had hoped, Sir, to have been permitted undisturbedly to listen to the words of wisdom or pleasant mirth falling from the lips of those about me, till now your order requires me to say something for the Chandler School.

It perhaps may not be known to your guests, Mr. President, that the founder of this School owed to the sons of Dartmouth the first earnest desire, which afterwards grew into a determination, to obtain a liberal education. As Mr. Chandler informed me shortly before his death, he was a laborer on a farm at Fryeburgh, Maine, at about the time he was twenty-one years of age. One evening he was sent on an errand to an inn in Fryeburgh, where he found two young men conversing upon an interesting topic in a manner which attracted his attention. He listened with deep interest to their discussion, and, upon leaving the house, inquired who these young men were, and was informed that they were students of Dartmouth College, returning to their homes after the close of a term. As Mr. Chandler related, in his walk to his home he reflected upon the subject of the conversation he had listened to, and felt keenly his inability to think and converse as those young men did, which deficiency he very properly attributed to the defects of his education. He said that it flashed across his mind that he must obtain a collegiate education, so as to have the pleasure and power these young men possessed in their intellectual attainments. After this determination, there were many difficulties in the way of accomplishing his wishes, but these difficulties vanished before his energetic character. He continued his agricultural labors, and interested his friends upon the subject dearest to his heart, until he procured the means and privilege of entering Phillips Exeter Academy, on the foundation provided for indigent students. His zeal in literary pursuits commended him to his friends, and with their assistance he obtained by loans what was necessary to defray his expenses while a student at Harvard College. After his graduation he was for many years a successful teacher, and entering at middle life into mercantile pursuits as a partner with one of his old pupils, he acquired an ample property, with which he determined to benefit his native State. The disposition of his wealth was made by him when he had given the subject many years of reflection, and was the result of his best judgment, formed after consultation with his friends, and earnest and frequent prayer that the Source of wisdom would guide him to a right decision. By his will, having suitably provided for numerous members of his family, and kindly remembered some of his friends, and contributed to objects of charity, he made the munificent bequest of fifty thousand dollars to this College, and the residue of his estate, amounting to more than thirty thousand dollars, he gave to the New-Hampshire Asylum for the Insane. Thus did this excellent man, having no children of his own, leave with Christian benevolence a rich inheritance to the youth, and the helpless and afflicted of his native State.

It gives me pleasure, Mr. President, to say for myself and associate, that we find, from our own observation as well as by the report of others, the Chandler School is doing its work well. It has not been the object, as you know, Sir, of its officers and managers to hold this department before the public with flattering promises of what it can do, and ostentatious display of what it has done. It has been supposed wiser that the progress of the School should be actually sure and steady, rather than apparently brilliant in the outset, lest it should have a fitful existence, and disappoint in the end the hopes of its friends and public expectation. By pursuing the more careful policy in its management, we trust we shall lay a deep and firm foundation for it, on which we can build a superstructure as enduring and beautiful as truth and virtue. The practical usefulness of this department will, it is hoped, be soon apparent to all. Its progress will be hand in hand with the Academical Department of the College, and all the Alumni and friends of the College will continue to feel a worthy pride in the undiminished honor and extending usefulness of this venerable Seat of Learning.

Having thus unworthily spoken to the subject of your sentiment, Mr. President, I should resume my seat, if the remembrance of the words of the orator of yesterday, the interesting letters that have just been read, and this Anniversary, did not excite in me emotions which compel me to ask your indulgence for a few moments longer.

This day completes the fiftieth Anniversary since there were graduated at this College two young men who were room-mates through their entire collegiate life, and were particularly noted by their fellow students for the friendship they manifested toward each other. Never did an unkind word pass from the lips, nor an unworthy thought rest for a moment in the breast of either of them injurious to the other. In scholarship they stood together, sharing equally in the highest honors of the College, the one delivering the Salutatory and the other the Valedictory oration before those who were gathered in these halls half a century ago to-day. Afterwards one was appointed to a tutorship, and the other to the preceptorship of Moor's School at this

College. In after life their paths were separated, but their hearts were undivided, and no one rejoiced more at the distinction of another, than did the one when his former chum was promoted to the elevated seat of President of the College. The friend rejoiced not only that his classmate had attained this dignity, but that the newly elected President was competent to fill, with honor to the College and the country, that high position during the most troublous and exciting times Dartmouth has experienced. I allude, as it has already occurred to you, Sir, to the season of the presidency of that distinguished man whose name the orator of yesterday could not utter, from sentiments of filial delicacy, but whose name on this Anniversary should receive full honor. At this fraternal meeting, when it is permissible to speak of matters of a personal nature, I hope I may be allowed, honored as I am in bearing the name of both these friends and classmates, to speak reverent words of the friend of the parent who would have, (how gladly!) if living, discharged the duty of friendship.

From my earliest youth, Sir, I have heard of the moral purity of the late President BROWN, and how well he performed his part when he was fighting in the front rank with great men in the cause of Dartmouth College. Not only from a parent's lips, but from others well qualified to form correct opinions upon the subject, the same story has been told me, all in honor of the energy, the prudence, the unflagging and self-sacrificing devotion of the late President. In an interview with Dartmouth's most distinguished son, I had a very interesting account of her great case, and of the distinguished service President Brown rendered the College. It is proper that we should preserve in fresh remembrance the services of the great and good men, who, doing what they could in their time, have passed to their reward ; and let us never forget, certainly we will not on this occasion, those who have been the founders and distinguished benefactors of this Institution.

In conclusion, Mr. President, I desire to offer as a sentiment,—
*Ever increasing and enduring prosperity to Dartmouth College, founded* ( to use the words of Mr. Webster) *by Eleazer Wheelock, re-founded by Francis Brown.*

*The President :*—Is there any further business before the Association, which now stands upon its adjournment.

*Professor Alpheus Crosby* made some remarks upon the great interest and enjoyment of the occasion,—classmates meeting classmates, and friends friends, in many cases after a long lapse of years, the departed brought to remembrance and their memory honored, and the strange, romantic history of the College reviewed,— *Vox clamatis in deserto.* He then remarked upon our obligation to impart, so far as we could, of what we had ourselves enjoyed, to those of our brethren who had been unable to come up to our festival, and made the following motions to that end :
1. " That the best thanks of the Association be presented to Pro-

fessor Brown for his valuable and eloquent Address, and that a copy of it be requested for the press."

2. "That a collection be now taken up for the purpose of defraying the expense of printing the Address, with an accompanying Sketch of the Proceedings of the Meeting, and sending a copy of the same to each Alumnus whose address can be ascertained."

These motions were seconded and adopted unanimously.

*The President:*—The present Association of the Alumni had its origin in a movement of the Class of 1827. It is highly proper that the motion for an enduring memorial of its proceedings should come from a member of that Class.

I give you as the closing sentiment, " *Our Alma Mater. We have diligently endeavored to strengthen the bonds which bind us to her, by faithfully complying with her wishes, expressed through her President, that we should have a good time.*"

Lightning Source UK Ltd.
Milton Keynes UK
UKHW011144051118
331792UK00005B/423/P

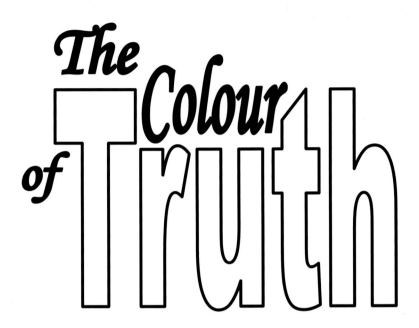

# The Colour of Truth

## Vol I: Patterns in Light

*(now with full-colour midsection)*

# The Colour of Truth

## Patterns in Light, Parallels in Life,

## & Principles to Live By

## Volume I: Patterns in Light

### Amazing Coincidence? ..or Intelligent Design?

Stephen T. Manning Ph.D.

**Perspectives on the Meaning of Life**

OTHER BOOKS BY THIS AUTHOR

The Colour of Truth Volume II: Parallels in Life

The Colour of Truth Volume III: Principles to Live By

Psychology, Symbolism, and the Sacred:
Confronting Religious Dysfunction in a Changing World

The Colour of Truth Volume I: Patterns in Light (3$^{rd}$ Ed. colour 2011)
ISBN: 978-1-906628-37-6
Published by CheckPoint Press, Ireland

EMAIL: EDITOR@CHECKPOINTPRESS.COM

WEBSITES: WWW.CHECKPOINTPRESS.COM & WWW.COLOR-OF-TRUTH.COM

COVER IMAGE "KALEIDOSCOPE" BY TODD SALAT, TAKEN ON LOCATION IN ALASKA
WWW.SALATSHOTS.COM

# TABLE OF CONTENTS

**PART ONE: OBSERVATIONS**

# TABLE OF CONTENTS

# TABLE OF CONTENTS

♣ **Diagrams and Illustrations: (pp 118-125)**

Fig. 1 The Allies and the Central Powers during WWI
Fig. 2 The United States and Eight Allies join the War in 1917
Fig. 3 Targets of Japanese Aggression During the War Years
Fig. 4 Various 'Opposition' Forces in the Twentieth Century
Fig. 5 The Remarkable Display of Red-White-Blue Symbolism
Fig. 6 Political Symbolism of the Middle East
Fig. 7 Nations of the Arab League c. 1960
Fig. 8 Properties of the Electromagnetic Spectrum
Fig. 9 Properties of the Color Spectrum
Fig. 10 Cosmic Symbolism
Fig. 11 Individual Triadic Archetypes and Chakras
Fig. 12 Symbolic Elements of the Greek Soul & Biblical Symbolism
Fig. 13 Atomic Structure
Fig. 14 DNA
Fig. 15 The Hindu Trimurti and A.U.M.
Fig. 16 Thematic Subdivisions of the Color Red
Fig. 17 Cosmic Circle; Nazi & Fascist Symbolism; the Holy Trinity
Fig. 18 Sexual Symbolism of the Tabernacle and the Temple
Fig. 19 Triadic Patterns of the Kabalistic Tree of Life
Fig. 20 Pre-Reformation Flags of Christianity
Fig. 21 Some Post-Reformation Christian Flags
Fig. 22 Flags Associated with Other Religions
Fig. 23 Cosmic Symbolism and Monotheistic Traditions
Fig. 24 Stages of Human Consciousness and the Triadic Archetype
Fig. 25 Animus & Anima / Jesus & Mary as Archetypes / Yin Yang
Fig. 26 Jungian Theory of Personality & Religious Theory
Fig. 27 Some Traditional Hero, Heroine, & Anti-Hero Figures

**Selected Features of the Triadic Archetype: Examples 1-8, pp 126-131**

    Example 1: Science / Quantum Physics
    Example 2: Ontological / Thematic
    Example 3: Psychological / Psychospiritual
    Example 4: Human / Relational / Social
    Example 5: Biblical / Judeo-Christian / Theological
    Example 6: Other Religious / Mystical / Mythological
    Example 7: Historical / Political / Sociological
    Example 8: Other Possible Representations

# TABLE OF CONTENTS

**TABLES**

# INTRODUCTION

W hen it comes to the great questions of life; *"Why are we here? What's life all about? Is there a God.. an afterlife?"* we invariably turn to our education and belief systems for answers. Unfortunately, academic disciplines and religious traditions are so often at variance when it comes to these particular questions; not only with each other, but also within their respective fields. Indeed, the incongruity of differing philosophies and ideologies throughout history, and the resultant discord between cultures and religions suggests a fundamental lack of universality within many, if not most of those systems. As a result dissension, disharmony, superstition and ignorance continue to afflict humanity in its most pernicious forms, and the quest for a universal taxonomy; a self-evident 'theory of everything' whose unifying principles stand upon their own merit continues to preoccupy the minds and hearts of true seekers and peacemakers everywhere.

This book is born of that quest: The search for a unified and self-evident 'theory of everything'. It is the result of a long, laborious, and deeply personal journey of investigation and discovery. Compiled painstakingly from research spanning many years; *The Color of Truth* is a new and pioneering exposé of previously undocumented facts and formulas that indicate the existence of synchronistic patterns, parallels, and principles that arguably affect—if not actually direct—the course of human history.

Originally intended for just one volume entitled *The Color of Truth: Patterns in Light, Parallels in Life, and Principles to Live By;* the extensive research has led ever-deeper into the alcoves of history, science, nature, religion, and the mechanics of the human psyche. As a result the source material has expanded to the point where, for practical reasons, three consecutive volumes are needed to accommodate the data. These three volumes will be presented under the following headings:

**The Color of Truth Volume I: PATTERNS IN LIGHT**
Amazing Coincidence.. or Intelligent Design?

**The Color of Truth Volume II: PARALLELS IN LIFE**
Historical Synchronicity and the Meaning of Life

**The Color of Truth Volume III: PRINCIPLES TO LIVE BY**
Applying the Triadic Archetype in Your Life

# INTRODUCTION

This series of books and planned books focuses upon a new phenomenon—or at least a newly-recorded phenomenon—that of the *substantial archetype* defined here by the author as:

> The substantial manifestation in natural and human history of preexistent cosmic themes, patterns, and principles that govern science, underwrite history, and directly (albeit usually subliminally) influence human consciousness.

In other words, a study of visible and tangible signs in nature, history, and society that who knows may, perhaps one-day, help resolve the perennial human quest for the elusive 'meaning of life'.

As we progress through the evidence of the following pages, my sincere and earnest request is merely this: That we place our preconceived notions and judgments temporarily aside and simply allow truth to be her own witness.

STM 2007


Update October 2011

The first and second editions of this book were produced using 'modern' print-on-demand technology, which at the time could only produce black-and-white results for competitive markets. Thankfully, with recent advances in colour-printing technology, we have now realized our original intention to produce this book in colour.

We hope this will add considerably to your enjoyment of this book, as well as a fuller appreciation of the phenomenon of the triadic archetype.

STM 2011

# ABSTRACT: VOLUME I – PATTERNS IN LIGHT

One universal constant underwrites all forms of matter and energy on the planet. That universal constant is light – the central feature in the known electromagnetic spectrum. Studied scientifically, the properties of light may be categorized in both empirical and philosophical terms inasmuch as color —the visible aspect of light—can be measured;

(a) *Mathematically* in terms of its wavelengths.
(b) *Evidentially* in terms of its physiological and psychological effects upon us.
(c) *Philosophically*; in terms of its traditional symbolic values, especially where present in national, political, religious, or pseudo-religious symbolism and practices.

This book approaches some of the standard scientific and religious theories of our day from a perspective that re-evaluates them against the fundamental properties of light itself. Because, as *the* fundamental feature of life on Earth, light contains intrinsic formulae that must, by virtue of natural transference, be present in all other life forms. Where there is transference of intrinsic formulae, then most assuredly there will be a parallel transfer of related principles…

Testing this 'chromo-numeric' theory against historical facts and the more recent findings of psychology and subatomic physics, we uncover an amazingly consistent visible-yet-subliminal 'universal language' not only present in the natural world, but also apparently underwriting all aspects of human development and history.

After presenting truly dramatic evidence that establishes thematic connections between science, religion, sociology, history, politics, psychology, medicine, art, and human relations, we explore possible applications of this archetypal 'credibility-test' against contemporary paradigms and belief systems, and in the process offer what may be termed a self-evident 'truth-formula' from where we may begin to reassess and re-evaluate our personal, cultural, and traditional value-systems and beliefs.

# TECHNICAL FOREWORD

Thank you for purchasing this book. To facilitate better understanding, a variety of charts, tables, and illustrations are interspersed throughout the text as listed in the Table of Contents. For practical reasons, the diagrams are at the center of the book, arranged in general order of discussion. References to such will be noted in the main text in parenthesis with the following symbol (♣) and with a figure (♣ 1) or (see fig.2 ♣) for example. Flag illustrations have been adjusted to fit the diagram boxes and therefore may not be to scale. If those diagrams are not in colour, please go to the *Color of Truth* website for full-colour views at the following web address: http://color-of-truth.com/

When dealing with certain subjects, it is unavoidable that we must at times use specialized terms. Accordingly, the first entry of any such term is marked in the text *in italics*, accompanied with an explanatory footnote, or with a brief explanation (in parenthesis) in the text itself. In each case, any such entry will also be listed in the Glossary at the rear of the book.

Arabic numerals (1, 2, 3…) are used to identify endnotes; also to be found at the rear of the book.

Not wishing to offend any particular group of readers, 'inverted commas' are generally used to highlight any particular word or phrase (such as 'God' or 'Allah' or 'truth' for example) whose meaning may be indefinite, indistinct, or ambiguous to readers of different cultures or beliefs. Italics too may be used in certain cases where special emphasis is required.

Unless otherwise indicated all unmarked dates are to be read as "of the current era" whether or not they are accompanied by the suffix 'CE'. The abbreviation 'BCE' ("before the common era") is used in place of the more traditional 'B.C.' ("before Christ").

Gratitude is respectfully extended to all those whose writings or opinions are referenced in this work. Under the international 'fair rules' copyright doctrine, reference is duly made in the text as well as in the Bibliography at the rear of the book. In their first mention, or when accompanying direct quotes, the titles of any such referenced works or websites will be written *in italics*. Apologies are offered if any references have been omitted either in error or due to absent sources.

Regarding the historical facts and scientific data recorded in this work; care has been taken to present only that which is both accurate, and easily verifiable. Whenever any such information departs from traditional views, references have been made duly available. If in any doubt, the reader is respectfully encouraged to check those sources for themselves.

Wanting to achieve the broadest circulation possible, these books have been printed in both European and American formats, which regrettably do not always match either with each other, or with other forms of English. I therefore ask the reader's indulgence if as a result, some of the formatting and spellings seem unfamiliar (particularly 'color' vs 'colour').

Finally; because we are dealing with so many interconnected topics throughout this series of books, and because material from successive volumes depends upon an incorporated understanding of previous books; certain material must be repeated in succeeding volumes from time to time. This may require only a brief synopsis here and there, or a specially-tailored introduction for example, but at times (such as in the book *Psychology Symbolism and the Scared*) this may require the repetition of a complete chapter or two. In the case of any such necessary duplication, and with the exception of tables and diagrams, the repeated material will not constitute more than 10% of the finished work.

Any further technical questions or enquiries should be directed to CheckPoint Press at the address at the front of the book.

Thank you, and happy reading.

STM 2011

"Meaningful coincidences are unthinkable as pure chance – the more they multiply and the greater and more exact the correspondence is...they can no longer be regarded as pure chance, but, for the lack of a causal explanation, have to be thought of as meaningful arrangements."

Dr. Carl Gustav Jung
(1875-1961)

# ARCHETYPES – WHAT ARE THEY?

Archetypes may be described as timeless themes and patterns common to all humanity regardless of nationality, culture, creed, or the era in which we live

Representing the collective psychological blueprint of humanity, archetypes inhabit our dreams, our mythologies and our folklore

Believed to originate in the depths of the collective subconscious; archetypes not only reflect who we are; they hint at what we could be

But archetypes are themes, not things. Shadows, not substance – or at least that's what we thought..

This book documents a unique and pioneering breakthrough in understanding these vital archetypes, and by association; the very meaning of life itself

# PART ONE

# OBSERVATIONS

*Patterns and parallels recorded in nature and human history that suggest the existence of primordial principles and themes underwriting all aspects of life on Earth*

# CHAPTER ONE

# EVIDENCE OF A PATTERN

*We open with a dramatic and colorful display of interconnected events of the twentieth century, of organizations, nations, and individuals, linked together by patterns, forces, and super-coincidences that all but defy rational explanation.*

Nineteen seventeen was a very busy year in Europe. The First World War had already raged for three horrifying years, filling the mucky, rat infested trenches of the Somme with the blood of a whole generation. As the tears of a million mothers fell amongst the stark and treeless battlefields of Verdun, Ypres, and the Marne; and French, British, and Russian forces combated the seemingly overwhelming might of the German Army, fevered murmurings of bloody revolt simmered throughout Imperial Russia.

In the United States, President Woodrow Wilson's optimistic declaration for a "Peace Without Victory" echoed the profound reluctance of the American people to be drawn into the carnage of war in a very distant and troubled Europe. Unfortunately for the Americans however, the hasty departure of the Russian military to deal with the unrest at home depleted the allied ranks significantly, thus bolstering German confidence and prompting further advances into allied territory. Subsequent military provocations and political intransigence would eventually force a reluctant America to stir from her diplomatic neutrality until finally, like a gentle giant roused to wrath the USA declared war upon Germany in April of 1917. Seven months later the 42$^{nd}$ Rainbow Division of the U.S. Third Army was dispatched to France. Thus the United States took her place in the 'war to end all wars' and the tide of battle soon began to turn. In the same month of November 1917 Russia, having already lost more than a million men in the war finally succumbed to the Marxist urgings of Trotsky and Lenin. The Bolsheviks would soon transform Imperial Russia into the fledgling Soviet Union, thus creating the socio-political environment that would foster seventy years of communist-sponsored global development and expansion.[*]

At the same time in the Middle East, an intrepid 'Lawrence of Arabia' stirred armed revolt amongst the pro-British Arabs with dramatic and legendary successes. The audacious taking of Aqaba, and the subsequent Turkish surrender of Jerusalem would end four hundred years of Ottoman rule in Palestine leading to the fall of Baghdad the same year. This provided the backdrop for the introduction of the highly contentious *Balfour Declaration*, a British-sponsored initiative that formally recognized the Jewish peoples' right to a homeland; whilst in a closely associated development the opposing *Arab Liberation Organization* simultaneously registered their new flag and constitution.

Parallel with both the rise of Bolshevism in Russia and the fall of the Ottoman Empire, 1917 also marked the four-hundredth anniversary of another kind of revolution when on October 31$^{st}$ 1517 a fiery Catholic Monk named Martin Luther nailed his *Ninety-Five Theses* to the Cathedral doors at Wittenberg in Germany, thus setting the Protestant Reformation into motion. The same year that saw the introduction of the Catholic Church's *First Code of Canon Law*, 1917 was also (a) the three-hundredth anniversary of the *Great Schism* when three separately-elected popes contested the Roman Catholic papacy for forty years; (b) the two-hundredth anniversary of the birth of Holy Roman Empress Maria Theresa of Austria who also reigned for a history-changing forty years (1840-1880); and (c) the one-hundredth anniversary of the births of influential American philosopher Henry David Thoreau and the Baha'i prophet Baha'u'llah, the latter suffering exile and imprisonment in Iraq; also for an intriguing forty years.

The year 1917 also saw 3 million Russian lives claimed by an epidemic of typhus, whilst in troubled Ireland beleaguered patriots immersed themselves in the struggle for political and religious freedom from a British Monarchy who, in a deft political move changed their traditional family name from the original Germanic 'Saxe-Coburg-Gotha' to the more politically-palatable 'House of Windsor'.[†] Imprisoned for her part in the 1916 Easter Rising, Countess Constance Markiewicz, aged forty when she joined the Irish Republican Sinn Fein party, would go on to become the first female parliamentarian in Europe in 1918.

---

[*] First known as the RSFSR: The Russian Soviet Federated Socialist Republic, est. July 1918
[†] Until the end of Victoria's reign the British Royal family was named 'House of Hanover'

Back in America meanwhile, the same year that saw the birth of future president John Fitzgerald Kennedy also witnessed the rise of the Women's Suffragette Movement and the election of the first woman member, pacifist Jeannette Rankin to the U.S. House of Representatives. This coincided interestingly with a purge on prostitution in both New Orleans and San Francisco – the two leading outposts of the industry. 1917 would also witness the introduction of the highly unpopular law of prohibition in the same year that an important literary monthly named *The Dial* arose in New York as the essential publication for new (and now mostly sober) writers. Forty years after the invention of the phonograph and the microphone, 1917 would also witness the production of the very first Technicolor film and the first Pulitzer Prize awarded in New York, whilst the Nobel Prize for Physics went to forty-year old Englishman Charles Glover for his work on x-rays. Other groundbreaking discoveries were being made that year too: In the field of subatomic science this was the year that Ernest Rutherford determined that nuclear fission was possible whilst simultaneously discovering the existence of the proton; whilst mathematician Johan Radon developed the three-dimensional theory for CT scans; a process that unfortunately would not see practical appliance for another forty years. The publication of psychologist Carl Gustav Jung's pioneering work *Psychology of the Unconscious* also arrived in 1917, the same year that his mentor, father of psychoanalysis Sigmund Freud published his controversial *Introduction to Psychoanalysis*, which in turn coincided with fellow German author Hermann Fernau's landmark work *The Coming Democracy,* an insightful critique of German attitudes and politics that would suffer proscription in his own homeland.

Meanwhile back in Central Asia, in profound contrast to the warmongers of Europe and once again, an intriguing forty years after Queen Victoria of England was crowned Empress of India, the indomitable Mahatma Gandhi tread the dusty roads in peaceful protest against British occupation – later to become one of the world's most respected spiritual leaders. 1917 would also see the birth of India's first female prime minister, the unrelated Mrs. Indira Gandhi who in 1999 was voted 'The Woman of the Millennium', outscoring such notables as Mother Theresa, Queen Elizabeth I, and Marie Cure... * and whilst all these world-shaping socio-political dramas were being played out; in a quiet, forgotten corner of Portugal 'Our Lady of Fatima' made her first mystical appearances to three little children, explicitly warning of "imminent danger" from Soviet Russia.

---

* Voters were international users of the BBC News Online service

Now you could justifiably ask why—other than due to the obvious connection with the year 1917—all these events are listed together in the same category; political, historical, scientific, technological, academic, mystical, religious… and what about all those number forties and four-hundreds …what's the big connection? And why the specific onus on notable women in history? Well, if you have read the introduction you will no doubt have concluded that these events are somehow linked to the theory of universal *archetypes*.[*] (If you haven't done so yet, please now take a moment to review the definition of 'archetypes' on pages x and xv at the front of the book.) Implausible though it might seem at present, we are about to discover that all of these apparently discrete occurrences are in fact connected at root by profound *subliminal* [†] themes and formulas, and although we will cover many more such examples as we advance through the book, we have chosen to open this work at this particular point in history for three specific reasons: Firstly, because this era is relatively recent history; the details of which are already familiar to most, and if not, can easily be checked by any wavering skeptics. Secondly, we begin here because of the crucial importance of this time period in respect to 20th century socio-political development and current world affairs. And thirdly and most importantly because of the simple fact that this confluence of interconnected events bears specific, undeniable witness to the existence of the aforementioned universal archetype in a unique way. Although we will be dealing continuously with the various aforementioned interconnections throughout the book; (scientific, numeric, religious etc.), amongst the most convincing evidence perhaps, are the dramatic parallels to be seen amongst the political colors and themes of the day. To understand exactly what we're talking about, let's now take a closer look…

**The 'Great War'**
We begin with a glance at the political circumstances that led to the start of the First World War in 1914—a horrendous global conflict unprecedented in scope and scale—a war that would last nearly four years and would eventually involve thirty-two nations in a complex parade of alliances and rivalries, in various stages of aggression and/or defense. Some nations would even change allegiances during the course of the war, thus compounding the already complicated and highly volatile political situation. But before we can get into specific details, let's first look at the major

---

[*] Archetype; an original model, or prototype. Please see full definitions on pages x and xv
[†] Subliminal; subconscious; below the threshold of conscious perception, yet affective

players and how they lined up in opposition to each other at the beginning of the war in 1914.

At the outbreak of the Great War there were two major military alliances standing in opposition to each other. These were known as the 'Triple Alliance' consisting of Germany, Austria-Hungary and Italy; and the 'Triple Entente' comprising Great Britain, France and Russia. These alliances had formed due to a combination of factors brought about chiefly by the intense nationalism of the day, compounded by political, ethnic, and economic rivalries, and then further driven by a collective urge towards military expansionism. Treaties with smaller or less powerful nations were constantly being drafted and signed as these two military triads muscled up with increasingly hostile intentions... and then, in the midst of all this political tension the Austrian heir apparent, Archduke Francis Ferdinand, went and got himself assassinated!

Apparently it was a Serb national, a member of the 'Black Hand' underground society and a student of the Russian revolutionaries who, driven by the nationalistic epidemic prevalent at the time decided that the Austrian Archduke should be relieved of his royal duties. This, in the eyes of the incensed Austria-Hungarians, gave them the license to declare war on Serbia who in turn called upon her allies for protection. In this case Serbia's allies included France, England, and Montenegro. Thus within a matter of days, five members of the two opposing triads (the Entente and the Alliance) would each declare war on their opponents. Italy was the sole exception, choosing to sit out the first year of the war before eventually switching allegiances and aligning herself with the group of nations that would later become known as 'The Allies' or 'The Associated Powers'. Their opponents, later to be known as the 'Central Powers' would consist of Germany, Austria-Hungary, The Ottoman Empire (Turkey), and Bulgaria. So, in the opening stages of the Great War in Europe, Germany and Austria-Hungary faced the combined nations of Serbia, Great Britain, France, Russia, and Montenegro (see fig.1 ♣).

The discerning reader will immediately notice that amongst these major players in the conflict we see a very clear unifying pattern in their choice of national colors. Could it simply be 'pure coincidence' that the entire active Allied nations at the outbreak of the war flew under red, white and blue flags? Is it also only 'pure coincidence' that we find no blue whatsoever in any of the Central Power's Flags? [*] Is there some other, simple explanation perhaps? Well, before we go any further let us first deal with this particular historical episode and, in considering the broad range available in the color spectrum ask ourselves what indeed is the statistical likelihood of these five nations flying under the same three colors at this specific point in history? Indeed, can any existing mathematical formula even accurately calculate such a unique conformation?

In fact, accurately calculating the statistical likelihood of such an arrangement is probably impossible. For in order to even begin to compute the odds we would first need a mutually-compatible 'common-denominator' through which to appraise the respective values of color, culture, politics and history. Provided we were successful in this endeavor, we would then need to use the same value-dynamics to evaluate the dispositions of all those who influenced the choosing of the colors for the flags at various points in history (including their personal psychological states) and all other related environmental factors. Then, we would have to somehow incorporate time and space into the formula, and all manner of assorted variables both tangible and abstract. All in all a difficult, if not impossible task I think you'll agree. There are so many variables when dealing with such a multifaceted topic as historical-political color choices over such a broad period of time, with so many interrelated factors far too diverse and impossible to measure through just one theoretical formula. However, despite the challenges presented by the absence of any such common denominator, theory, or quantifiable formula, we still have an important point to make and an issue to prove. So, in the spirit of true science and in order to put the notion of 'pure coincidence' to rest, let's try to come up with the simplest possible formula and see what figure we arrive at.

**Calculating the Odds**

First of all, we obviously need some idea of the varieties of colors available to flag makers at various times in history, to which end we review the *Flags of the World* website whereupon we discover that colored flags have been around for a long, long time. There are records for instance of dynastic banners being flown in China centuries ago, and many other examples since of empires, kingdoms, and dynasties in various parts of the world using pennants, standards, and other colors for identification both on and off the

---

[*] Although Italy's flag contained the blue trim of the Savoy arms until after WW II, Italy 'swapped sides' several times during each conflict and as such is not considered a 'core' player in these political formulas.

battlefield. Some modern national flags have clear connections to these centuries-old origins, whilst others appear to be the product of relatively recent political developments. The British 'Union Jack' for instance, first officially hoisted in 1801 CE was born out of the colors of three nations of the United Kingdom; England, Ireland, and Scotland, and was therefore 'adopted' from these previously independent countries each with their own national histories stretching back many centuries; whilst in contrast, the modern Palestinian flag or the flag of the United Nations have only been around for a few short years. As we shall soon see however, both classes of flags—both ancient and modern—follow the invisible rules of universal archetypes.

In Europe, our main area of interest for the moment, we note that national flags were first officially recognized with the formal registration of the Danish flag in 1218.[1] So, we know that flags and their colors have been a significant feature of European culture since at least the 13th century. In addition, we also know that the techniques for applying heraldic colors to banners, shields, and coats of arms have been available at least from the time of stained glass painting which, although known in Egypt as early as the 3rd century BCE, did not become established as an art form in Europe until the 8th century. Known then as 'painting with light' stained glass painting reached its zenith in France around the year 1200. The *Encarta Encyclopedia* informs us:

> The predominant colors used at this time were blue [especially for the background], red, yellow, and green. Violet, brown, and white with a green or blue cast were secondary, and pinkish shades served as flesh tones.

In addition, during the Gothic period; "A wider range of purples, dark green, and yellow hues were added to the French and English repertoire of colors." We are further informed that silver, tawny brown, olive green, and mosaics of reds, blues, and grays were increasingly incorporated into medieval art forms and heraldry before the 14th century. So, we may safely conclude that a wide range of colors was indeed available to various artisans in the Middle Ages. Furthermore, in 1533 a manual "for the production of paints and inks" was published in Augsburg, Germany. This further affirms that the technical ability to reproduce a variety of colors upon assorted surfaces was clearly possible at least from that time forwards. Obviously, the selection of recognized colors in medieval times was far fewer than the scores of different shades available to us today. Even so, it is clear that when craftsmen in the Middle Ages were directed to create banners, flags, shields, stained glass, or manuscripts, they usually had at least a dozen or so basic practical colors at their disposal. This fact then, will serve as the baseline for our calculations. For the purpose of our investigation therefore, and in order to ensure that our calculations remain very much on the conservative side, let's reduce these twelve basic colors to only seven central shades. This gives us; black and white, red, green, blue, yellow and purple, which, considering the variety of colors available to our ancestors and in use in *vexillology*[*] today (the study of flags) is a very modest selection indeed.[†]

In relating this selection of colors to the opening stages of the First World War, specifically to the five Allied nations of Russia, Great Britain, France, Serbia and Montenegro, we can quickly calculate that even with only seven colors to choose from, any one of these nations could have chosen a tricolor from thirty-five possible choices. Therefore, thirty-four of the possible tricolor combinations from these seven colors are *not* red, white and blue. If we now multiply 34 (the flag options) times itself five times (the 5 nations), we get 1,544,804,416 different possible line-ups containing five tricolor flags that are *not* all red white and blue across the board. In modern *short scale* [‡] mathematics (and all being equal) that is odds of; one billion, five hundred and forty four million, eight hundred and four thousand, four hundred and sixteen… to one! To reiterate: 1,544,804,416 different flag line-ups that are *not* red, white, and blue! Rather high odds don't you think? Would anyone like to explain this *phenomenon*? [§] Or, for that matter, would those who believe in 'pure coincidence' care to place a bet against the likelihood of this happening again? ..a possibility we will explore shortly. There doesn't appear to be any obvious explanation for this dramatic and stunning run of coincidences, yet we can clearly see that for some reason the Allies all chose red, white and blue over any other selections, whilst their active opponents have no blue whatsoever in their flags.

So why indeed did they choose red, white and blue at this specific time in history for obviously, it wasn't a previously agreed international political decision? Please remember that vexillologists have no uniformed explanation of why nations choose certain colors. In fact as already implied, these uncanny coincidences cannot be accounted for thematically or historically, with each nation listing different and often quite unrelated reasons for their particular color choices; blue is for the ocean, or for the

---

[*] Vexillology: The study of flags and their origins
[†] Technically, white is the presence of all colors, and black is the absence of color
[‡] Some EU countries use the 'long scale' which defines 'a billion' as a million millions
[§] Phenomenon; a thing, event, or occurrence perceivable by the mind; unusual or remarkable

sky, or for the morning… red for the blood spilt on the battleground, or for the proletariat, or for the sunset etc. Or in some cases it is simply a matter of family tradition as can be confirmed on the FOTW website. Therefore, if we were to factor in all the other personal and aforementioned environmental variables such as time, culture etc; then the odds of this five-nation, red-white-blue phenomenon occurring 'purely coincidentally' would probably rise by several billions. As psychoanalyst Carl Jung remarked:

> Meaningful coincidences are unthinkable as pure chance – the more they multiply and the greater and more exact the correspondence is…they can no longer be regarded as pure chance, but, for the lack of a causal explanation, have to be thought of as meaningful arrangements.

So, hoping we are all agreed that we do seem to have something of a mystery to solve, let's take another look at those events in Europe in 1917 that would so much affect the shape of the world we know today and see if there are any more clues as to this intriguing phenomenon.

**The Odds Go Up**
As battles continued to rage on European soil, and the first lumbering tanks clattered ominously through the cobbled streets of Belgium and France, many other nations declared their support for the Allies in various ways. Countries from as far afield as China, Japan, and South America declared war on the Central Powers at various times between 1914 and 1918, but as previously mentioned it was the full entry of the United States in April of 1917 that would eventually decide the outcome, and this is where we will now focus our attention. Before going further however, it should first be clarified that although more than thirty different nations became politically involved in one way or another in World War I, some of those nations (such as Italy and Romania for example) changed allegiances during the course of the conflict, and others, such as Belgium and Portugal, only had war declared *against* them without any significant response in return. Still others came in or out of the conflict at various stages, only cautiously "severing diplomatic relations" with the Central Powers, or engaging in other diplomatic maneuverings for various political or nationalistic motives. Accordingly, any such irresolute, tentative, unpredictable, or vacillating nations (relatively speaking) will not be considered 'core' players in these World War I political formulas. As we progress, the determining factors of 'core' vs. 'secondary' nations will become increasingly evident to the

11

reader, but the attentive reader will already have observed some of the intriguing thematic connections between particular historical events, color symbolism, and the cultural or political characteristics of specific nations.

To continue: As previously mentioned, unrest in Russia had prompted the withdrawal of the Russian military at about the same time as American Forces were arriving on the Western Front. The Russian Tsar, Emperor Nicholas II was forced to abdicate, making way for the formation of the Union of Soviet Socialist Republics by year's end (USSR) thus ensuring that the imperial red, white and blue would no longer fly at the head of the Russian military. Under the red flag of Communism, the Soviet Union would soon become the bitter enemy of her previous democratically inclined allies. So, as Russia transformed from an Imperial 'Christian' Empire into a God-denying ideological State, the 'righteous and God-fearing' Americans planted their own red, white and blue *Stars and Stripes* on European soil. Then, in direct response to the U.S. declaration of war in April of 1917 the following nations also formally declared war on Germany: Brazil, China, Costa Rica, Cuba, Greece, Liberia, Siam, and Panama. Yes, you've guessed it. Once again, we see a remarkable consistency in these nations' choices of colors. All of them contain white and blue, and six of the eight flags are red, white and blue, thereby bringing the 'coincidence' ratio up even more dramatically (see fig. 2 ♣).

What is possibly even more remarkable is that despite a completely different set of cultural and political conditions, the same color-related dynamic that was being played out between aggressive instigators and defenders in Europe was also evident in the conflicts of the Far East during this time. The targets of Japanese aggression before, during, and after the war years for example, namely Russia, China, and Korea, all had red, white and blue in their flags (♣ 3). As another fascist-type political regime imperial Japan was unique in the World War I scenario inasmuch as she used the Allies' declaration of war against Germany purely to advance her own territorial interests in Asia; siding with the Allies in order to justify seizing German-held territories in the Far East. Taking such actions including occupying Chinese, Russian, and Korean land during this period without contributing materially to the war effort in Europe, effectively put Japan in an 'aggressive dictatorship' class by itself, a situation that would continue through World War II.

So in review; we now have a total of fourteen different nations that declared war on Germany either (a); at the outset of war in 1914, or (b); in conjunction with the Americans in 1917. First, the five original members of the Allied camp; Serbia, Great Britain, France, Russia and Montenegro.

Then, with the Russian withdrawal and the arrival of U.S. Forces in April 1917, eight more nations joined the Allied ranks. Remarkably, all of these nations' flags contained blue and white colors, and twelve of them contained red, white and blue. In direct contrast, we see no blue at all in the colors of their 'core' opponents; and obviously therefore no red, white, and blue combinations (♣ 1 & 2). Would anyone now like to compute the odds of this being 'mere coincidence?'

By now the reader should be at least a little intrigued by the possible implications of these symbolic repetitions in recent history. But just in case any skepticism lingers, let us now drive home the point with the following remarkable list of replications of red-white-blue symbolism in subsequent 20$^{th}$ century political events (see 5 ♣):

- Three allied signatories signed the 1919 Treaty of Versailles that officially ended WWI: England, France, and the U.S.A.
- Three Nations were originally involved in founding the League of Nations in 1920: Norway, England, and France.
- Three nations came under persistent attack from Japan in the first half of the 20$^{th}$ century: Russia, Korea, and China.[*]
- Three nations froze Japanese assets in the Pacific prior to WW II: England, Holland, and the U.S.A.
- Only two nations substantially opposed Hitler and Stalin's move on Poland in 1939: England and France.
- On the same day that Pearl Harbor was attacked in 1941 Japan also launched attacks on; the Philippines, Guam, Wake Island, Midway Island, Hong Kong, British Malaya, and Thailand; all flying red-white-blue flags.[†]
- Resistance to Japanese aggression in the Pacific during WW II came chiefly from Australia, New Zealand, Britain and USA.
- Sixteen nations collaborated in the Korean War against the Soviet Union, China, and North Korea. Some supplied medicines and other logistics, but the active forces comprised twelve nations: United States, England, Australia, Thailand, New Zealand, Netherlands, France, Luxembourg, Canada, Philippines, South Africa, and Norway. Once again, all flying flags containing red, white, and blue.

---

[*] Several flags changed during this period – nevertheless maintaining archetypal integrity
[†] Some flags came into existence at a later date, such as Wake and Midway Islands

Again, in contrast to the afore-listed nations carrying the colors red, white, and blue, we witness the remarkable fact that their opponents in each case, whether it be the Axis or Central Powers, the Germans, the Soviets, or the Chinese, sharing that one aforementioned color-specific feature in common; no blue (4 ♣).* It is especially interesting to note that nations such as Russia, China, and Canada for example, whenever politically *aligned* with the central allied nations such as the United States, France, and England during times of significant historical importance, also had red, white, and blue in their flags; later to lose the blue when internal politics necessitated their withdrawal from allied coalitions. And in the forty-day opening battle in Iraq that commenced in March of 2003, is it any great surprise to note that the three main contributing nations were the United States, Britain, and Australia; three red-white-blue nations in opposition to a regime sporting no blue in its colors?

Furthermore, and in addition to the aforementioned *chromatic* † sequences, another dramatic 20th century color-dynamic is observable in the symbolic signatures of those longstanding adversaries, the Arabs and the Jews. We will later deal with this topic in more depth, but for now is it not intriguing to note that in the various 20th century wars between Israel and her Arab neighbors there is an absolute consistency in their respective choices of colors. Israel, with her blue and white flag has intermittently been supported by England, France, the United States, the League of Nations, and the United Nations, all flying under red, white, and blue or variations thereof. In opposition, the combined nations of Egypt, Syria, Lebanon, the PLO, the Soviet Union, and the Arab League sport not a shade of blue between them (♣ 6 & 7)‡ Likewise, the great majority of fascist and neo-Nazi colors of the 20th century display deep reds and blacks and are conspicuously devoid of blues (♣ 17), and whilst there may indeed be occasional exceptions to any given rule, it is in the consistent color-choices of such 'core' nations, groups, and organizations wherein we observe the highest level of consistency. Obviously *something* is causing this to happen. Even in the latest political animosities born of militant religious extremism that in turn has spawned the horrors of global terrorism, we see a remarkable consistency in the color symbolism separating the core combatants:

---

* North Korea is a special exception, as technically it doesn't exist as a discrete nation, and the forced division of the country in 1953 remains unrecognized by South Korea
† Chromatic; of, or relating to colors
‡ This rule applies specifically to pre-1960 Arab League nations directly engaged in the struggle against Israeli sovereignty. In recent years, a smattering of blues has surfaced in the colors of 'new' albeit not-politically-prominent, nor militarily active, afro-Muslim nations

England, the United States, and Israel, with intermittent support from Australia and New Zealand, and a now red, white, blue Russia on the one side, vs. Iraq, Iran, Syria, Hezbollah, Hamas, the PLO, the Taliban, Al Quaida, Chechnyan Rebels, and various other groups and nations who (we are told) harbor and support anti-American and anti-democratic agencies on the other. In each case the colors reflect the same patterns; blues, whites, and reds on the one side, and an absence of blue on the other. The facts are plain to see. For some yet-unexplained reason, during these world-changing events or crucial periods of history, the colors, as much as the politics and ideologies appear to separate and identify the warring factions. However, it should equally be emphasized that when nations chose the path of ambiguity or political indecision (such as Italy during the war years), they should no longer be considered 'core' players in these historical formulas during these specific times, at least not as long as they vacillate between priorities. 'Core' players are thus defined by their solid and committed defense of—or attack upon—key issues or agencies of historical importance, one way or the other.

**In Summary**

After observing the evidence so far, it seems fair to say that we either have an amazingly unusual series of coincidences bordering in fact on the incredible, or that 'something else' is influencing this extraordinary phenomenon. Nations, organizations, and 'core' individuals certainly *appear* to be following some unconscious color-based pattern that places them in predetermined positions or situations at certain times in history, identifiable in the first instance by their choice of national colors – as if indeed there was some sort of secret or clandestine 'color code' underlying international relations. And we haven't even begun to account for those other 'coincidences' yet—historical, scientific, technological, academic, numeric, mystical, religious—linked to this topic of political symbolism.

But what are the causes of these apparently-synchronistic events? *Something* is obviously causing these formulas and patterns to surface in conjunction with socio-political values. But what is that something? Could it really be mere chance; at odds of billions to one? Common sense suggests not. But again; exactly what type of subliminal influence or energy, or effect, force, or authority could possibly be engineering this enigma? How indeed could such a phenomenon occur consistently and systematically in the first place in a world populated with freethinking, intelligent human beings *without* our conscious awareness; or at least without being formally acknowledged or recorded as a historical occurrence? Clearly the evidence is there, but for some reason we haven't noticed it before. In a world full of scientific theories and religious speculations – how could we have possibly missed it?

The implications are disquieting to say the least. For isn't the concept of subliminal orchestration—cosmic or otherwise—a fundamental challenge to the common conviction that we, and *only* we, are the ultimate shapers of our own destinies – at least at the personal level? After all, we are autonomous beings aren't we? Even religious fundamentalists promote the belief that man is a being of consciousness and relative independence, capable of making informed personal choices and is thus fully responsible for those choices. Environmental conditions aside, we each choose our paths in life consciously whether good or bad, right? So surely there is some simple explanation for why recent political history revolves around certain color-themes, or for why our forefathers chose these particular color patterns in the first place. But if so, then what is it ...and why isn't it already part of the historical record? Indeed, why have so many vexillologists already concluded that political color-choices are only connected (if at all) through arbitrary tradition and culture, as opposed to the suggestion here; that there is a profound universal or archetypal link to be observed in these patterns?

Well of course it is far too premature to be forming any firm conclusions. But one possible explanation implied above that would fit with the evidence so far is that there is some yet-unidentified *subconscious* or *supra-conscious* cause behind this phenomenon. Something discernible but as-yet-undocumented in other words. A subliminal, yet very 'real' phenomenon whose influence in history is marked by these undeniable patterns—otherwise inexplicable—except by a radical belief in incredible coincidences. But this then reinforces the question; is it really feasible that collectively we are somehow being unconsciously influenced? That our lives and histories are somehow interwoven into a yet-unknown cosmic tapestry? Could something as pervasive and elementary as our political-historical color-choices reveal evidence of a collective (albeit subconscious) thematic unity? Or proof of subliminal cultural identities perhaps? Or even, speculatively, of a historical synchronicity; of predetermined historical paths or courses; that we are in some way unconsciously involved in fulfilling a greater plan? A 'providential plan' in history perhaps, that can apparently affect nations, ideologies, and individual destinies like so many pieces on a cosmic chessboard at least to *some* extent?

Or, (please bear with me here), could these subliminal color-choices be evidence of a hidden collective psychology; proof of the existence of a place or state of mind, or state of *being* perhaps where universal themes and principles overrule human consciousness; an uncharted cosmic phenomenon that apparently leaves corresponding color-signatures marking those times in history where it was either most salient, or most at threat? Finally, is there in fact any further evidence to suggest that there is really anything more than 'mere coincidence' to observe here?

My firm and resounding answer to this is an emphatic YES. For, in the following chapters we will explore proof after undeniable proof of the substantial-yet-subliminal existence of archetypal patterns in natural science and human history. Most specifically we will focus on what I term *Universal Substantial Archetypes;* in particular the *Triadic Archetype* centering upon the colors white, blue, red and associated data as the most dramatic and pervasive example of universal symbolism and activity. But we will also look at other archetypal models and themes in social theory, in religion, in mythology and art, in science, numerology, psychology, history, and in politics – already hinted at in this opening chapter. In doing so we will uncover a wealth of untapped parallels, patterns, and principles— exciting connections that most assuredly have something of significance to teach us. For if we are to accept eminent social scientist Carl Jung's expert opinion: "Meaningful coincidences are unthinkable as pure chance."

This then is the primary purpose of this book: To introduce the reader to just such evidence, and presuming that the facts will indeed confirm the theory, to then invite the reader—both experts and laypersons alike—to apply these new archetypal theories to their own specific disciplines and/or lives as the case may be. Subsequent volumes will expound upon the facts, data, and theories suggested here; but before we get too far ahead of ourselves risking possible charges of presumption or exaggeration, let us remind ourselves that these color-patterns, and specifically the political colors of the 20th century, are only one small part of the visible proofs for the archetypal formulas uncovered and explored in this book. So in the interests of scientific *objectivity* [*] and before we explore any other aspects of these universal archetypes in depth, we must first research the elementary dynamics of light and color for any clues as to the reasons for the aforementioned political color-choices.

To do this, we must now take a closer look at the phenomenon of light itself; the visible aspect of cosmic energy, the foundation of color, and the primary source of life on Earth.

---

[*] Objective; lack of personal bias; detached observation; impartial.

# CHAPTER TWO

# LIGHT, COLOR, & US

*Here we look at the basic properties of light and color, including an overview and summary of historical theories on the subject with a view to better understanding any physical factors that may lie behind the color-coincidence phenomenon of Chapter One.*

W
e begin with this discussion on light and color simply because we, like all the elements that constitute life in our universe, are constructed of light-energy in one form or another. As such, light underwrites most, if not all of the natural laws. For that reason a basic understanding of the place of light and color—as well as any associated phenomena such as the color-coincidences of Chapter One—is obviously key to this work. The reader is therefore encouraged to stick with some of the more technical stuff as we create a solid foundation for understanding many of the topics discussed in this work as a whole.

The first point to be clearly made is that light is visible energy and colors are different components of that light-energy which, when blended, form natural or 'white' light. Science measures light and color as well as other energy-forms such as heat and sound-waves using the electromagnetic spectrum; the recognized range of cosmic magnetism and electricity. Visible light rests near the center of this spectrum, and although the electromagnetic spectrum is in theory 'infinite', light itself comprises only about $1/60^{th}$ of the currently known range. For those of us whose physics or natural science may need an update, other properties of the electromagnetic spectrum include gamma rays, x-rays, ultraviolet and infrared light, microwaves, and radio-waves (see fig.8 ♣).

For most of us of course color is consciously perceived through our eyes, but what many may not have considered is whether colors have any *other* effect upon us other than visual stimulation? After all, each of the other aforementioned components of the electromagnetic spectrum from radio waves to microwaves have measurable, other-than-visual effects upon us. The implication is therefore, that based upon the evidence that radio waves, lasers and microwaves have affective substance in relation to the human body (think music, sunburn, or TV dinners) then perhaps color, which after all is just another aspect of the electromagnetic spectrum, may also have previously unrecognized *substantial* effects on human beings. Makes sense doesn't it? In fact, it not only makes sense but was confirmed over a century ago by French psychologist Charles Féré who demonstrated the unseen effects of colored lights on his clients. Charles Darwin too reported similar effects when using colored lights to affect plant growth. The evidence for this will be discussed as we progress, but suffice for now to accept the possibility that light and color operate in several substantial dimensions other than the purely visible.

## A Little History – A Little Science

The scientific study of color is known today as chromatics, a field of knowledge whose origins date at least as far back as the ancient Greeks, but it wasn't until the late 1600s CE that science really began to understand the intrinsic properties of light and color. This began with the English philosopher and scientist Sir Isaac Newton who is perhaps best known for getting hit on the head with apples, and then discovering the formula for gravity. However, he was also an avid chromatist. Newton was the first to split natural sunlight into the color spectrum using a prism in 1672 CE. Recognizing that 'white' light actually contained all the colors of the rainbow in its pure form eventually led other scientists to the understanding that our perception of any given color depended upon the various degrees of absorption or reflection of light by the surfaces of objects around us. In other words, it was found that 'white' light (natural sunlight) bathed the surface of the earth, and various surfaces either reflected or absorbed the differing light waves thus producing the different colors that we see. For example; plants appear green in daylight because they reflect the green light-waves whilst absorbing the other colors. In the same manner rose petals appear red because they reflect red light-waves whilst absorbing green and all the other light waves. Our eyes, which contain light-sensitive cones that can distinguish between red, green, and deep blue (the full range of the color spectrum) then notice this reflected light and this is how we 'see' color. If we reduce the surrounding light substantially, the color properties change; remove all light, and color disappears altogether. Surfaces that appear white in daylight are actually reflecting all the colors, whilst those that appear black are reflecting none, a fact that can be proven by painting all of the colors of the rainbow on a disc and then spinning the disc quickly. One might expect that as the colors are thus perceived in chorus one would see the same effect as if mixing all the pigments together in a bowl; a dirty, dark, mucky brown? But no: Instead, as the disc speeds up and the colors appear to merge into one due to the speed, the disc appears white. This confirms that from a visual perspective 'white' is actually a combination of all the colors (as Newton discovered) whereas black on the other hand is actually not a true color in the scientific sense, but actually the *absence* of color, or the absence of light. This point carries considerable symbolic meaning and is worth remembering for future reference.

In modern chromatics scientists measure light waves (color) in nanometers (nm)[*] by special apparatus that identifies their numeric properties; "The longest wavelength that we can see is deep red at 700nm. The shortest wavelength visible to humans is deep blue, or violet at 400nm."[2] So, tentatively at least, we can attribute the number 400 to deep-blues, and the number 700 to deep-reds (see 9 ♣). Although many still argue the *subjective*[†] nature of color perception, Newton's seven original colors of the spectrum are still generally recognized as the truest natural model, as confirmed in the colors of the rainbow. Thus we can establish that deep-red and blue-violet respectively define the outer limits of the visible spectrum, with green, the color traditionally regarded as the color of nature resting at the center. Here it is worth noting that plants that reflect green light must by default be absorbing the red and blue ends of the spectrum in order to stimulate growth. Later we will see how this bears witness to a fundamental masculine-feminine-union process at the heart of creation. This point too is a fundamental worth remembering.

At the very high end of the electromagnetic spectrum, energy-waves are known as 'cosmic rays' and they travel throughout the universe by stimulating atomic particles to reflect or generate energy or light. Light then converts into other forms of energy on earth chiefly through photosynthesis whereby plants absorb sunlight, and then, through a series of chemical reactions convert that light-energy into matter (such as leaves and fruit) for consumption as fuel for other species. In an interesting development recent

---

[*] One billionth ($10^{-9}$) of a meter
[†] Subjective; particular to a given individual; personal; limited; introspective; not objective

studies have found that the innate chemicals that determine the color of natural foods such as fruits and vegetables contain disease-fighting properties. This is a new discovery for which we have few scientific facts at present, although promoters of vegetarianism such as the health-and-fitness lecturer Paul Volk in his *New Start Plus* series of presentations produces convincing data to support the claim that if one "chooses all the colors of the rainbow in one's choice of natural foods, then one receives all of the essential proteins, starches, carbohydrates, and minerals necessary for a healthy life."[3] Volk adds that nature appears to have thus 'color-coded' our food so that a meal that is naturally attractive and balanced to our eye is also good for our health, a concept also echoed in *The Color Code; A Revolutionary Eating Plan for Optimum Health (2002).*[4] This adds considerable weight to the notion that color itself, when present in food sources has inherent biophysical values.

Further supporting the possibility of color's substantial effects on humans is the arrival in the Western sphere of many 'mystical' sciences that claim associations between color, sound, and parts of the human body. For example, the ancient Tantric spiritual system familiar to Hindus and Buddhists as well as the Chinese Art of Feng Shui are centered upon the belief that in surrounding ourselves with appropriate visual and audible stimuli we can affect our physiological, psychological, and spiritual well-being. Despite the early skepticism of conventional medicine to such claims, an abundance of evidence continues to mount in support of these precepts, details of which will be discussed later. Moreover, once it became apparent that light-wave frequencies could indeed be measured in waves per second or 'Hertz' (Hz) * the *empirical*,[†] and therefore 'physical' and effectual aspect to color was confirmed as a scientific fact. This in turn opened up a new avenue of chromo-sensory research. For instance, we hear sounds that operate between 16 Hz to 20,000 Hz at wavelength speeds of only around 33 meters per second, whilst light waves operate at 300,000,000 meters per second on a much higher frequency between approximately 400 billion Hz for deep red, to about 700 billion Hz for deep blue.[‡] Color light-waves in other words, were found to operate in time and space as part of the electromagnetic spectrum in a manner that paralleled sound waves. This naturally led to speculation about what other parallels may exist linking sound and light. According to the British-based *Colour Energy* website there

---

* 'Hz' is the abbreviated form of 'hertz' a unit of frequency measurement
† Empirical; derived from observation or experiment; provable; testable; scientific
‡ Sound waves' speeds increases with temperature, and are more effectively conducted in solids than gases

are some "forty octaves between the spectrums of light and sound..."[5] (here's our familiar number forty once again). In principle this suggests that if we can respond emotionally to the sound of Mozart for instance (or Metallica if you prefer) just because our ears are physically receptive to the frequencies of music, then why indeed shouldn't light-wave frequencies be having a similar, albeit largely unnoticed effect on us through our visual or psychobiological senses? The apparent absence of other-than-visual stimuli surely doesn't rule out a resultant effect? Indeed, when watching the effects of a 'silent' dog-whistle on our canine companions, who would be so foolish as to argue that there is no sound just because we can't hear it? Our limited physical senses (sight, smell, hearing, taste, and touch) are obviously insufficient to register the full dimensions of the electromagnetic spectrum; elements that undoubtedly continue their cosmic activities regardless of our conscious recognition or lack thereof.

Consider also the fact that sightless aspects of nature such as vegetables and minerals, or even sightless animals that dwell underground or in the depths of the ocean are not themselves conscious of the presence of light and color, yet they nevertheless remain part of an interdependent world that is wholly dependent upon sunlight. They are thus directly affected by an energy-source of which they are completely unconscious. In other words, because elements of the electromagnetic spectrum are known to be active in time and space beyond the range of normal human sensory perceptions, we may reasonably assume the existence of supra-sensory, cause-and-effect forces or 'agents' (but not necessarily 'agents' in a personalized sense) that subconsciously or supra-consciously affect us. This concept ties in neatly with the notion of subliminal influences affecting political color-choices as seen in Chapter One.

With this awareness however come immediate and challenging questions including; (i) how far beyond human cognition do these forces / agents operate; (ii) how exactly, and to what extent do they interact with, or affect us; (iii) how can we access them; and (iv) what cosmic secrets are contained within their energy-fields or modes of operation? When we further recognize that human beings are not just physical beings but also comprise psychological (mental, intellectual, emotional) and 'spiritual' aspects (the latter term soon to be clarified), isn't it reasonable to assume that psycho-spiritual and psycho-biological aspects of the human make-up are in turn subject to substantial effects from subliminal sources, including chromatic influences?

**Expert Opinions**

Now things get very interesting because although they have sometimes used different terminologies and approaches, several eminent scientists, authors, and scholars in history including Paracelsus, Immanuel Kant, Johann Wolfgang von Goethe, Novalis, Rudolf Steiner, James Clerk Maxwell, Charles Darwin, Ludwig Wittgenstein, Albert Einstein, Carl Gustav Jung, Faber Birren, Edgar Cayce, Max Lüscher, and many more, have each hinted at some of the conclusions presented in this work. [*]

Respected modern psychologists too, as well as many 'alternative healing' practitioners have developed treatment programs utilizing color properties or color-theory in some form or another, and there is growing public interest in these ideas.[6] From 'healing your inner child' to improving your golf swing, or to simply growing bigger tomatoes, the concepts are basically the same. Each of the respective experts has recognized that color in various forms contains intrinsic properties that affect us in different ways, often without our conscious awareness. Even as far back as Newton's time *synesthetic* [†] (or interconnected) theories linking sound and color were in vogue, and many other color-related theories since (some more or les fantastic) have tried to link differing *taxonomies*[‡] including the various human senses; sight with sound, or sight with touch, taste, or smell. We have already heard the claim that there are forty parallel octaves between light and sound, which theoretically at least, links seeing and hearing, and mirrors that odd coincidence noted in Chapter One where we read that the invention of the phonograph and the arrival of the first Technicolor film were also an interesting forty years apart. The numerical aspects of this phenomenon will be discussed in due course.

Meanwhile, research scientists continue experimenting with the psychological effects of light and color, whilst other specialists expound on the *chromodynamic*[§] properties of quantum physics. [**] Art historians too continue to theorize about intriguing cross-cultural parallels amongst the shades and hues of the classic masters, and search for meaningful color-patterns in contemporary works. Much has also been written about the properties of color in mystical religious traditions, as well as the role of color in mythology, folklore, and popular symbolism, and as seen in Chapter One, we now also have tentative evidence of a systematic socio-political

---

[*] Please refer to Bibliography for a comprehensive listing of color-related works
[†] Synesthetic; meaning interconnected--when one sensation evokes stimulation of another
[‡] Taxonomy; classification system; ordered groups and classes; a systematic listing
[§] Chromodynamic; activity associated with colors (specific to this work)
[**] This field of study is known as quantum chromodynamics: chromosomes, chromomeres

dimension to the phenomenon of color.

However, although many of the aforementioned pioneers and scholars may indeed have made ground-breaking discoveries in the field; to the best of my knowledge no one has yet formulated a comprehensive and workable, unified theory of light and color that encompasses both the natural-scientific *and* the socio-political-religious realms.

Of course this is not so surprising, given the fact that any such theory required the abovementioned socio-political dimension, and therefore was unlikely to be presented until the dramatic unfolding of 20th century political events complete with their striking color-patterns as listed in Chapter One. And whilst painfully aware—in relation to the various experts and specialists—of the limits of my own scientific knowledge; it seems to me that in the discovery of these symbolic socio-political parallels we might indeed be holding a significant clue to the proverbial 'missing piece' of the chromatic puzzle that has thus far baffled many an eminent scholar in the quest for a unified theory.

In recognizing the authenticity of these historical 'super-coincidences' as described in Chapter One, we may also consider the possibility that history has overlooked and underestimated the importance of color; this seemingly innocuous aspect of everyday life.

Naturally, with this new information at hand the question now arises; can we at last expect to see the development of a comprehensive, universal theory of color that in turn will shed more light (excuse the pun) not only on the archetypal phenomena presented in this work but also perhaps on other important aspects of life on this planet?

**Color Codes and Categories**

In the introduction to his intriguing work *Color and Meaning (1999)* the respected art historian and scholar John Gage comments on "the history of art as a unifying subject" where he states his personal belief that any debate about color "can only rest on the detailed examination of case histories."[7] This is in support of an earlier statement where he declares,

> There is no 'scientific' art history... It is a pursuit which can be followed only by introducing a consideration of the literature, religion, science and technology of the age in question...

In short, although speaking specifically in context of his own field of expertise Gage is recognizing the fact that most scholarly attempts to codify the attributes and mechanisms of light and color so far have been 'subjectively' influenced, that is, undermined by the prevailing social environment and by individual scholars' preconceptions. This of course applies to both the period under scrutiny *and* the environment from which the scholar launches the investigation. Gage notes for example that from Renaissance times onwards there was a prevailing perception, still evident in conservative aspects of our cultures today, that black was a mark of refinement and distinction and that bright colors should be disdained. This view undoubtedly had considerable influence on the color-theorists of the day. Gage also draws attention to the confusing use of similar terms in various languages for very different colors, thus rendering an accurate tracing of color-theory that corresponds with modern themes, concepts, and color-terms almost impossible. In other words, despite there being many different (and often progressive) theories on the subject, there is at present no strictly axiomatic; that is, no self-evident, absolute, or truly 'objective' theoretical understanding of the intrinsic qualities of light and color. This is obviously a bit of a problem for us as we attempt to discern the meaning (if any) behind the color-coincidences of our opening chapter. Nevertheless, as we shall soon see, this lack of consensus amongst chromatists need not be an insurmountable obstacle to our quest.

In a somewhat divergent view to Gage, in the introduction to his scholarly and encyclopedic work *Color Codes (1995)* professor Charles Riley II also notes the tremendous difficulties of formulating a comprehensive color-theory when he writes:

> The topic of color has become a watershed for thinking about models and about art that is created by systems simply because it is such a devourer of models and systems. It has attracted and ultimately confounded systematic innovators in philosophy and psychology, as well as writers, painters, and composers who attempt to use precompositional systems.[8]

Riley goes on to suggest that because each individual perceives color differently, any attempt to systematically codify color behavior(s) or value(s) is relative, and therefore rather "senseless." But of course, we could say the same of practically all classification systems that involve individual perceptions that attempt to comprehend mysterious topics. For short of the purely mathematical formulas of arithmetic and calculus, most philosophical or psychological systems are at very best *somewhat* subjective and therefore at least *partially* relative. With respect to the specific term

25

'precompositional' as used here, it appears that we may have overlooked the fact that discrete colors can now be defined numerically, and thus not *only* through the subjective view of the observer. This presents a purely pragmatic and systematic base for evaluating color in scientific terms that is devoid of cultural or philosophical opinions, and is thus unaffected by the confabulations of human history and any dissenting scholarship on the topic so far.

But Gage and Riley's points are very well taken, because they both draw specific attention to one crucial attribute of color that bears direct relevance to this work; its apparent inexplicability; its mysteriousness; its capacity to evade being categorically defined by scholars – at least so far. But interestingly, this fact doesn't really concern us other than to note the lack of full human understanding of the field. Here we need to emphasize that we are not explicitly concerned in this work with discerning how well humanity has or has not understood and interpreted light and color through the ages; but rather with identifying the actual effects and attributes of light and color as a cosmic entity that *acts out upon man* regardless of our personal perceptions, academic understandings, cultural interpretations, or theoretical assumptions or presumptions – or lack thereof. Fascinating though it would be to trace the history of mankind's struggle to rationally encapsulate this phenomenon—(something already well covered in Gage and Riley's books)—we are more concerned today with the overt and covert *effects* of light and color, and the probable causes and effects of such. Therefore, when reading Gage and Riley's insightful commentaries on the profusion of theories, codes, and color-systems developed throughout the ages, we can see that they refer mainly to the record of various subjective human viewpoints. In short, everyone has had their personal opinion, and no doubt will continue to do so.

But what if we are more concerned today with documenting actual cosmic truths; rather than mere subjective opinions? Where should we go for that rare experience? In answering this question, and in an attempt to highlight the difference between subjective and objective reality let us consider one famous work of art as an example; the enigmatic *Mona Lisa*.

Subjective appraisals of Leonardo Da Vinci's famous 16th century painting have varied from time to time and from place to place. Who is that woman they ask? Was she a local Florentine merchant's daughter, or Da Vinci's mistress perhaps? Maybe she was just an invention of Leonardo's sprightly imagination, or perhaps as some suggest, this is a self-portrait of Leonardo only in feminine form? Who indeed can say for sure? Sometimes the painting itself is even known by different names: *La Jioconda* in Italy for example, or *Mona Lisa* in Britain, or *La Jocunde* in France. But whatever the title, or indeed whoever she was, the debate continues as to what exactly she was smiling about? The mind boggles with the possibilities. Five hundred years and counting, and secondary, subjective opinions continue to differ.. and we're only talking about one painting here, not the awesome phenomenon of light itself. No wonder there are so many differing opinions and theories when it comes to the topic of color.

This brief example of the *Mona Lisa* debate shows us that subjective, secondary opinions on any subject can ultimately only be qualified by checking directly with the source. We need to go back to the origins in other words. Obviously, only Leonardo himself can answer some of these questions. But unless we discover some way of resurrecting him we are clearly stuck with the debate. Opinions will continue to differ simply because each has originated in a place distant from the original artist, devoid of his thoughts and perceptions. And whilst it might justly be argued that a work of art belongs equally to the observer as to the creator (albeit in differing ways), surely, if one were chiefly interested in the truth of the matter, one would expect greater insights about the purpose and meaning of the *Mona Lisa* from Leonardo himself?

Secondary appraisals might be very interesting and insightful, but removed as they are from the mind of the artist may, as we have seen, suffer the inclusion or exclusion of factors necessary for an accurate grasp of the piece. Subjective opinions after-the-fact are thus often out of concert with the creator's original ideas. But this does not necessarily disqualify them. Just like the various color theories reported upon by Riley and Gage, such opinions can still have important historical significance without actually speaking to the meaning and purpose of the original at all. There is considerable academic validity and benefits to be had from many speculative sciences. The fields of philosophy and theology for example are comprised in great part of subjective material that may or may not eventually prove to be 'true' in a literal sense, but they remain fascinating fields of study nevertheless and remain an important part of humanity's quest for understanding. But with due respect to previous research on the topic of color, our interest here today is in objective observations rather than subjective opinions – no matter how 'colorful' those opinions may be. For as any philosopher will tell you, there is a vast difference between a subjective truth, and Truth (with a capital 'T') as an objective reality.

When dealing with a single work of art the issue of subjective bias may not be all that important, but when dealing with a phenomenon that breathes life into all that we are—namely light and energy—perhaps we need to be more prudent in our opinions, and more broad-minded and universal in our approach. Certainly, when considering the fact that light and color comprise the center of the known electromagnetic spectrum, and remain the primary evidence of far-flung galaxies, surely only the most all-inclusive and objective theories should be applied in its understanding? After all, from microbes to megastars we are all children of light, right?

Hence the color-theories so eminently reported upon by Gage and Riley in their scholarly works by-and-large reflect these subjective-historical limitations as should be expected, and therefore clash, overlap, merge, and even contradict each other in many ways. Hence the logical conclusion proffered that a comprehensive theory of color is out of reach.

But herein lies the secret. Because even as the various incompatible color-models highlight the difficulties of using philosophical or metaphysical classification systems to try to encompass a medium as enigmatic as light or color, they also hint at the unbounded scope of any such 'subject' that so persistently escapes the intellectual categorization processes. No less so perhaps, than the transcendent concepts of 'God' or 'Truth' (with a capital 'T') or even of the Universe itself continue, in similar manner, to defy comprehensive academic boundaries or definitions.

This fact in itself might be our biggest clue to solving the enigma of color. Perhaps we lose something essential to the very character of such multidimensional concepts by trying to drag them into the purely intellectual realm, where we vainly attempt to digest them by first carving them into manageable, rational bytes? However, being intrinsically 'more' than we can grasp intellectually (at least for now) such ubiquitous 'subjects' continue to evade academic encapsulation, or at very best suffer greatly in the categorization process. The subject under scrutiny; God, Ultimate Reality, Truth, or in this case light and color must either be reduced to a mere shadow of itself in order to fit into established and often pedantic categories or, we must humbly admit to our dismal lack of comprehension, a far-too-rare occurrence amongst all but the most courageous of thinkers. In other words perhaps the topic of light and color is simply too ubiquitous to be compartmentalized. Too universal to be boxed. Too 'big' to be bound, as it were?

It seems we are left with a conundrum. For if esteemed professors of the art world cannot assemble a comprehensive theory of color, then how indeed are we generalists supposed to do so?

The answer to this question is actually simpler than one might expect. In fact, I believe simplicity is the key.

**Simple Secrets**

In my opinion we first need to assess light and color from the aforementioned 'purely scientific' perspective, broken down first of all into its most fundamental particles and energies and then build up our theory from there. Not through culturally-tainted human speculations and conjecture, but by using science and mathematics. Once we have established a solid scientific base we can then add the cultural, philosophical, and historical components, but only in a secondary mode: First the known facts, and then the theory and opinions – but *only* if they match with the facts.

Could it be possible in other words that in trying to understand the mind-boggling range of applications and effects of color in history, that we have become embroiled in far too many subjective theoretical nuances that may detract from a clear and objective grasp of the essential material? Indeed, perhaps the very reason we continue to have such difficulty defining the nature of light and color is because we have failed to understand that light and color are intrinsically and *hypostatically* * bound by the same archetypal principles that bind cosmic law; the same characteristics incidentally, that not only bind the sciences and nature, but which are also symbolically evident in the world's major religions and mythologies?

In other words, perhaps light and color are so much a part of the essential fabric of life, are so elemental and so omnipresent, that any limited intellectual attempts at *comprehensive* evaluation are currently relatively futile. Rather like trying to define the world of art using only a sketchpad and pencil: Sketching indeed may be 'art' but art is not simply sketching. Or trying to understand all scientific thought through the relatively limited vocabulary of the biologist, or the chemist. Chemistry may be science, but science is not merely chemistry. Or for that matter, trying to understand universal truths through a relatively limited cultural or religious perspective. We simply cannot hope to evaluate a universal theme with any degree of objectivity or completeness whilst bound by personal and environmental limitations whether scientific, philosophical, cultural *or* religious. This rather obvious fact however has not prevented human institutions—in particular religious institutions—from declaring their own patently limited understandings and interpretations of life (in many cases) as 'absolute truths.'[9] In contrast, not having the luxury of faith-based creeds to define or at least accommodate transcendent mysteries, science quite rightly declares any such 'mysterious truths' open to skeptical analysis and experimentation, and boldly rejects any absolutisms that lack empirical proofs.

---

* Hypostatic; the intrinsic essence; the substance; the underlying reality

29

Sadly, the resultant tension between the credulous and the skeptical mindset has often led to hostile polarizations, but I believe they need not necessarily be viewed as insoluble opposites. In fact, there is already a well-established forum for this discussion. No less a figure than the esteemed William James (1842-1910 CE) considered an icon in the study of religion and psychology was himself a pioneering advocate of "radical empiricism" that is; the acceptance and exploration of all human experiences both physical and metaphysical. Carl Gustav Jung, eminent psychoanalyst, also held this view. Templeton Prize winner Ian Barbour in turn puts forth convincing arguments for supporting dialogue and integration between the fields of science and religion in his 2000 book *When Science Meets Religion*. However, this is not to suggest that mere beliefs or unqualified opinions should have equal footing with the proofs of empirical science, but rather that we allow for the possibility of other truth forms that contribute to, or arise out of, the mystical and religious experiences of humanity. Perhaps with a little patience (and maybe even a prayer or two) we can thus devise a comprehensive 'middle' way to uncover the secrets of the universe. In studying the enigmatic topics of light and color for instance, if we allow for a possible 'sacred' or metaphysical dimension *without* losing the scientific mindset, we open up a second avenue of approach not only to this specific topic, but also to many longstanding religious and scientific mysteries as well. If, as has been suggested, we can successfully read the enigma of light and color primarily in scientific terms, including its manifestations in mythology and symbolism for instance, then perhaps we can later apply a similar approach in evaluating and understanding other paranormal, mystical, and religious phenomena? Keep our eyes and ears firmly on the facts in other words, whilst keeping an open mind and heart to *the possibility* of associated mystical, or supra-sensory influences. Maybe it is time for science to rediscover its soul, and for religion to recover its reason? The combined results might prove very interesting indeed.

Thus we arrive at a point where we place the study of light and color in the same *ontological* [*] realm as the concepts of 'God' 'Truth' and 'Ultimate Reality' and continue to ask questions. Armed with a sort of empirical spirituality if-you-like, we can now begin to acknowledge that the struggle for ontological understanding has as much to do with (i) recognizing and controlling our own subjectivity, (ii) taking into consideration the limits of precompositional taxonomies, and (iii) to do with curbing our persistent impulses to mythical-religious speculations; as it has to do with tenaciously

---

[*] Ontology; the study of the nature of being; of existence itself

rooting out the data that ultimately confirms all revelation, both scientific *and* religious.

For at the end of the day all of the evidence points to a universe that functions as an interdependent coalescence of *symbiotic* * elements, 'each' (as identified by us) ultimately inseparable from each other, and from the greater whole. Despite the marvelous advances in understanding in recent years, we would perhaps be advised to acknowledge that in context to the universe-at-large, all classification systems within the current realm of human knowledge are indeed relatively limited, and therefore somewhat synthetic in relation to truly universal laws, principles, and realities.

And what indeed could be more universal than that cosmic pulse of energy that brings light and color to our world; that nourishes and sustains us, visible in the sun, reflected in the moonlight, and illuminating the night sky with the timeless twinkle of a trillion distant stars?

---

* Symbiotic: A relationship of mutual dependence or benefit

# CHAPTER THREE

# BODY, MIND, & SPIRIT

*Having just discussed the difficulties of using limited and often subjective human classification systems to attempt to categorize entities that are fundamentally unitive in character, we must of necessity now attempt to do just that--to define the indefinable--to classify the experience of being human into three recognizably-discrete parts that are in reality inseparable; namely body, mind, and spirit. We will then use this information to better identify the sociological and psychobiological effects of light and color in relation both to the documented flag phenomenon of Chapter One, as well as to our theory of a universal triadic archetype.*

Imperfect though they may be, our various academic and philosophical taxonomies are all that we have at present. Clearly defining between seemingly-discrete aspects of the experience of being human is especially challenging inasmuch as between each of these three facets; the physical, psychological, and spiritual (or body, mind and soul), there is as previously stated, a necessary symbiotic interdependence that makes categorizing very difficult. For example, how does one differentiate between the *physical* sensations that accompany excitement or fear, and the associated *emotions* thereof? Or who will define the difference between *emotional* stimulus or *intellectual* discernment or; the *feelings* arising out of a *spiritual* experience such as joy or happiness, or the *physical* and *psychological* aspects of bodily pain... or for that matter, the *thought processes* and *feelings* involved in prayer and meditation, encompassing both *spiritual* and *mental* faculties? And what about romantic 'chemistry' – that quixotic mix of sexuality and scintillating conversation? Where exactly is the dividing line between the psychological and the biological? How indeed do we draw those categorizing lines? What exactly is 'psychological'? What is 'biological'? What indeed is 'spiritual'? Here, we see the necessity for, and yet the limitations of *epistemological** categories and the complex challenges that arise from their use.

Nevertheless, for understanding certain color values in relation to human experience it is important to make reasonably clear distinctions between these three aspects of human nature so that we may more accurately identify and understand the dynamics of those interdependent relationships and how color may affect us through them. In order then to better understand the terms 'physical' 'emotional' and 'spiritual' in context of this work, let us now add a few clarifying adjectives which should help us avoid unnecessary confusion. Please understand that we are not attempting to re-define these words for the reader other than as a reference for this work. No doubt we could have a wonderfully stimulating (and probably endless) debate about the terminology here, but I hope we can move beyond the individual words themselves and grasp the essential meanings and themes at the roots of each term:

- **Physical:** To do with the body. Physiological. Biological. Tangible. Substantial. Matter. Corporeal. Material. Physically quantifiable. The five physical senses; sight, hearing, touch, taste and smell. Action.

- **Mental:** To do with the mind, emotions, or intellect. Perception. Cognition. Thinking. Affecting one emotionally. Desires and moods. Psychological. Rational. Planning. Conceptual. Reasoning. *(Note: It is generally recognized that the human mind is subdivided into emotional and rational aspects).*

- **Spiritual:** To do with inner spirit, or soul. Associated with the spiritual or noumenal realm. Ethereal. Mystical-contemplative. Our connecting point with God. The immortal or immaterial aspect. The search for higher purpose, or The Divine. The transcendent or 'Unknown Realm.' Pure religion (a very rare thing).

One immediately notices that we are attempting to categorize the whole human experience into three distinct albeit generalized groupings, with no nebulous 'mystery' concepts hanging around backstage in case we discover something non-categorical and have nowhere left to put it. This is purposefully done. Whilst recognizing that certain religious or philosophical belief systems expound additional categories differentiating between 'spirit'

---

* Epistemology; the branch of philosophy that deals with the nature of knowledge

and 'soul' for example, or between 'mind' 'intellect' and 'emotions,' or even between 'the flesh' and 'the body'; for our purposes here today it is best to keep these categories to a bare, and understandable minimum. This is chiefly because the purpose and intention of this work is to clarify rather than to create more mystery and confusion. There is quite enough already.

Therefore, although we risk a little non-specificity by reducing these concepts to an elementary triad of 'physical, mental, and spiritual' the value and importance of this will become clear as we progress. Before we move on however, and in order to help frame our general understandings from this point forwards, a few clarifying words about the spirit-mind-body paradigm are required.

**Soul Searching**

The noted philosopher and psychologist William James whose writings in matters of religion and psychology remain pertinent over a century after first printing, defined the essential human being as comprising three identifiable yet interdependent parts; (i) the material self, (ii) the social self, and (iii) the spiritual self. These definitions correspond to our body, mind, and spirit triad inasmuch as the first definition (material) relates to the physical and active elements of our lives. The second (social) relates to the interpretive and intercommunicating elements, which are very much associated with the functions of the mind and the intellect; whilst the third aspect obviously corresponds to the realm of spirit or soul.

In turn this triad is reflected in other *psychospiritual* [*] mottos in common use such as *'Eternal, Internal, External'* or *'Concept, Plan, and Action'* or even Kundalini Yoga's *'Healthy, Happy, Holy'* (when sequentially adjusted of course). But of particular import to us today is recognizing the fact that amongst these three categories of human experience (physical, mental, spiritual) the physical, active, and external world is the most familiar to us. In other words, we know and understand far more about the material world and our own physical bodies than we do about the mind, or the spirit-soul, with even the most miniscule aspects of physiology such as quarks, atoms, molecules, *chromosomes*, [†] and DNA already extensively cataloged and documented by science; not to mention the rest of our physical environment; minerals, plants, animals, and the geography of our solar system.

---

[*] Psychospiritual; relating to the mind and the spirit – in context of this work, specifically to the Psychospiritual Theory

[†] Chromosomes; threadlike strands within DNA

After this comes the intellectual-emotional category, the study of the mind and its functions; a field that includes psychology and psychiatry, and arguably overlaps into philosophy, sociology, education and anthropology as well as other areas, but a field that in comparison to our knowledge of the physical world is still very far from complete. Then, trailing a very long way behind (in terms of the completeness of our scientific knowledge and understanding) comes the spiritual dimension, the noumenal realm—the haunt of spirit or soul—which raises a very interesting observation: For is it not well documented in various religious texts that 'God' or 'Jehovah' or 'Allah' supposedly exists primarily on the spiritual plane? One would expect therefore, that if God truly exists primarily in the spiritual sphere, then knowledge of this spiritual realm, the 'home' of the Creator—or of Ultimate Reality—should be foremost in our source of understanding of the meaning of life? It seems logical to me that we should first understand the spiritual environment from which creation supposedly sprang before we can properly understand the resultant psychological and physical realms. But we don't, do we? This in turn prompts a second, and more disturbing realization. For if the source of all knowledge and truth indeed dwells in the spiritual realm, and we have yet to properly document it; then this apparently 'unnatural' and inverted state of affairs (whereby humanity's physical and intellectual knowledge greatly outweighs our current knowledge of the so-called 'spiritual' realm) implies a profound, and very disturbing state of human ignorance of the true fundamentals of life. Apparently, we are working in reverse. We don't yet know the essential meaning of life but nonetheless spend our lives busily engaged in the process of living. Like a map without a key, or a jigsaw-puzzle without a picture, we can but guess at the original, complete, or foundational meanings of much that we uncover in our physical, psychological, and religious pursuits. In the words of William James;

> The further limits of our being plunge, it seems to me, into an altogether other dimension of existence from the sensible and merely "understandable" world. Name it the mystical region, or the supernatural region, whichever you choose. So far as our ideal impulses originate in this region (and most of them do originate in it, for we find them possessing us in a way for which we cannot articulately account), we belong to it in a more intimate sense than that in which we belong to the visible world, for we belong in the most intimate sense wherever our ideals belong.[10]

Or, in more poetic terms from Melville's *Moby Dick (1851)*: "Our souls are like those orphans whose unwedded mothers die in bearing them: the secret of our paternity lies in their grave, and we must there to learn it."[11]

Remembering that this is a systematic and methodical work, but nevertheless an investigative work that allows for the possibility of other-than-empirical truth forms, then any hypothetical 'ifs' concerning the possible existence of God, or Allah, or Nirvana etc., need to be given particular, and respectful space. Consequently, if we are to accord our respective religious philosophies any credibility whatsoever, or for that matter the findings of eminent scholars such as William James, then 'the key' to universal truth (or the meaning of life) must lie somewhere in the so-called 'spiritual' realm. Paradoxically however, we cannot possibly hope to grasp it substantially until it is somehow made manifest in the conscious, and/or physical realms. In other words, for man to progress to a fuller understanding of the meaning of life the truths of the spiritual realm must in the long run be revealed (or discovered) in forms that can be understood by the earth-bound conscious mind, and perhaps more importantly, by the *collective* human consciousness. Spiritual truths in other words, must take on material or sensible forms. At the very least, they must be translatable into rational, self-evident hypotheses. Whether this requires a great outpouring of scientific revelation and understanding or a greatly-enhanced state of human spirituality is inconsequential to the outcome: A conscious and substantial union between humanity and universal truth(s) whereby we become fully and truly the masters of our earthly domain. One might even describe such a union as the fulfillment of our original Biblical destinies to be made "in the image and likeness of God."[12]

But not being able to identify or exactly define 'God' or 'spirit' puts us in a very awkward spot. For if God is indeed 'spirit' then obviously, how can we legitimately claim to be made in His or Her image if we know little or nothing about things spiritual? Without such knowledge, how do we dare to make any such claims or judgments? Please note that the term used here is "know" and not "believe" for indeed anyone is at liberty to believe anything they wish. Problems always arise however when we substitute beliefs for knowledge, and then claim to know them as truth. The sincere statements; "But I honestly *thought*.." or "I really *believed*.." usually precede an admission of error.

At best, beliefs should be reasonable extensions of existing knowledge and not replacements for it. A temporary stepping-stone on the way to knowledge, but never ever a destination in themselves. No more and no less than a bridge from the known to the unknown.

Sadly however, religious beliefs in particular have become for many, a convenient escape from the responsibilities of the *true* religious quest, or for that matter, the sincere quest for scientific truth. Approaching the religious quest with admirable sincerity, initiates regularly find themselves being directed to simply 'develop their (denominational) faith' and are thus surreptitiously invited to surrender the individual truth-quest in exchange for a life of direction, indoctrination, and the security of the group. And herein lies the great personal dilemma; the disturbing choice between faith or knowledge; between emotional security and the yet-unknown; between spoon-fed religiosity and the true spiritual quest.

**Faith or Knowledge?**
We will discuss the subject of 'faith-over-reason' in more depth later on, but for the sake of clarity we first need to establish a couple of important principles before speaking on color as a spiritual-religious phenomenon. This issue is particularly germane inasmuch as many who read this book will be directly challenged to change their current views and beliefs. With over 70% of the world's population claiming affiliation with one of the major religions, and a further 20% reportedly having at least *some* religious beliefs, it is extremely important that those who do glance over these pages are confronted kindly but firmly with the subtle yet fateful effects of superstition and credulity.

Metaphorically speaking, living purely 'in faith' is like taking up residence on a bridge whose destination is shrouded in fog – and then making no attempt to cross it. Hoping that no-one is sawing through the supporting ropes as we sit suspended over the foggy abyss, we shut our minds to the disquieting possibility that we may not be on secure ground, and focus instead on erecting walls—creating an illusion—making ourselves feel safe and comfortable in our chosen location.

But wise explorers have never set up camps on bridges, let alone tried to build fortresses there. For a start, bridges weren't designed for that purpose; there is nowhere to lay a solid foundation, and one's tactical options are extremely limited. Secondly, any such actions only generate a false sense of destination and block the route for other seekers, as well as placing the bridge itself at risk. You simply cannot build an establishment on a bridge and expect to populate it without somehow misleading the potential inhabitants about the depth and quality of the foundations. By the same rule, you cannot build rock-solid religious institutions 'purely upon faith' without employing misleading dogmatics somewhere along the line, and then finding credulous souls to believe in them.

Surely, we have wallowed in spiritual ignorance for long enough. In a world populated with intelligent beings the very fact that a mystery exists in the first place should be a stimulus for tenacious searching, and *not* a justification for turning blind faith into a sovereign virtue. Faith is ratified in truth, and therefore has nothing to fear from it. It is only when faith is detached from reality—when it becomes a superstitious fantasy—that it need fear scrutiny and exposure. This is when religious faith manifests itself as a defensive neurosis. But then, any such 'faith' is not really faith at all. Such faith is merely a substitute; a replacement for reality. But faith should never ever become a substitute for reality. Ironically, it is just such 'faith'— when beliefs become more important than reality—that lies behind the staunchest resistance to (God's?) newly revealed scientific truths. Hence the tragic *dichotomy* * whereby religious *beliefs* actually become more absolute in the minds of believers than the 'absolute truths' they purport to allude to. And as long as we promote this reversal of the knowledge-over-beliefs principle, we are going to have problems: Misdirection of the innocent; exploitation of the unlearned; and the promotion of false authorities that block true education whilst promoting elitism, exclusivity, and religious prejudice are but a few examples. Sadly, this is the precise model employed by many popular religions, who by-and-large tend to discourage their members from 'outside' soul-searching, often arguing of course that such is a 'danger to the faith'.

But I propose that faith should be an encouragement towards—and not a barrier to—universal knowledge: A pointer on the way; a signpost if you like, but not the destination itself. Obviously, we have to find some better way of accessing the spiritual realm and/or the realm of Universal Truth(s) if we are to solve this perennial problem. Perhaps we need fewer believers and more courageous questers? Fewer credulous creeds, and more skeptical critiques? Less acceptance and more searching?

However we label it, we certainly need to find another approach besides blind faith; that is of course unless we are at peace with the prospect of a future riddled with semantic confusions and the excesses of religious fundamentalism. This again prompts the question; if not through pure science or pure religion, then where do we go for answers? Could this goal of accessing the *noumenal* † realm finally be realized through the agency of universal archetypes manifested in sensory and/or substantial forms? In other words, might there be clues as to the very meaning of life hidden

---

* Dichotomy; division into two usually-contradictory parts
† Noumenal; not of the physical senses; metaphysical or psychological term for spirit or soul

within the color-patterns of nature and human history? Hidden in that intangible place that both envelops *and* bridges nature and science, and myth and mystery? Could the universe—itself a child of light—be modeled along archetypal chromatic lines one wonders? Modeled along lines that we reflect and recognize—albeit subconsciously—at such a profound level that despite the fact that the evidence of our subliminal responses are all around us we haven't been fully aware of them? As we read through the following reports the reader is invited to consider the very real possibility that this is precisely what has been happening.

So, having established the crucial-yet-problematic place of faith as a tool in the learning process, let us now briefly review some of the work done by the aforementioned experts and scholars under the three interconnected and interdependent categories of 'physical' 'mental' and 'spiritual.' Based upon this foundation we may then approach in more depth the colors specific to the triadic archetype. Namely red, white, and blue.

## Color as a Physical Influence

Since ancient times, there has been no shortage of experimentation and investigation into the other-than-visible properties of light. In her book entitled *The Healing Power of Color (1998)* Betty Wood does us a great service by providing a veritable who's-who of those persons involved in the quest for a fuller understanding of color in our lives. She also presents a very convincing case relating specifically to the healing properties of color. Interestingly, the subtitle on the cover of her book is *Using Color to Improve Your Mental, Physical, and Spiritual Well-Being.* Wood opens with an account of research experiments that prove that under controlled circumstances light has identical physiological effects upon both sighted *and* blind children. She later quotes Faber Birren, a world authority on color and light as saying; "..color affects muscular tension, cortical activity (brain waves), heart rate, respiration, and other functions of the autonomic nervous system."[13] She also names Nobel Prize winner Neils Finsen of Denmark as one of the pioneers of light research who founded a Light Institute for the cure of tuberculosis in the early 1900s, and who reported many 'amazing cures' amongst his patients, simply by exposing them to sunlight and ultraviolet light. Today of course, it is commonly known that vitamin D is produced in the human body through such exposure, and it has been found that many skin disorders such as psoriasis or herpes sores can be cured through either exposure to natural sunlight or to ultraviolet or infrared rays. Indeed, baths of light have even replaced blood transfusions as a more effective treatment for premature jaundiced babies and much experimentation with dyes, drugs, and light combinations continue by those who believe there is great potential in the use of light-treatments particularly for healing. In recent years, practices as diverse as acupuncture, homeopathy, chiropractic, biofeedback, feng-shui, and naturopathy have become increasingly popular, and today there are several emerging schools of thought that promote even more diverse, and less intrusive healing techniques: That is, that instead of employing invasive surgeries or commercial drugs, alternative health practitioners promote unusual techniques such as using chants or music, or employing natural elements such as minerals and sunlight, or the aforementioned color-immersion baths as health treatments.

Inger Naess, the originator of the *Color Energy Corporation* in Canada also covers this topic in some depth in her booklet entitled *An Introduction To Color Energy (1998)* which is also interestingly subtitled; *Color Energy for Body and Soul.* Inside, a variety of advice is offered on the effective use of color baths under the headings 'physically' and 'mentally,' and her findings—like all the various authors researched—further corroborate the discoveries of this work. In dental work too it is now standard practice to use lasers and ultraviolet light in specialized treatments.

So even from the evidence so far we may reasonably conclude that apart from those other components of the electromagnetic spectrum which we already *know* have physically quantifiable effects upon us (lasers, microwaves etc), we can now absolutely confirm that natural light as well as individual colors have direct physiological effects, and are therefore not *only* visual phenomena. How exactly to measure or quantify those physiological effects of course is quite another matter. However, as research and experiments in this field continue to amass evidence, proving that people do respond physically (both consciously *and* unconsciously) to color in their environment, it seems increasingly likely that we will witness the development of progressive fields of color-therapy for physical ailments. For now though in context of this work a simple factual recognition of the biophysical and effectual properties of color and light upon human beings is sufficient to our needs.

## Color as a Mental / Emotional Influence

In like manner, much experimentation has been undertaken regarding the possible influences of light and color on the human mind. Some of these experiments were prompted by the S.A.D. phenomenon (seasonal affective disorder) where persons deprived of sunlight for extended periods were known to suffer various forms of stress and depression, the most effective cure being simple exposure to sunlight. Wood informs us that the director of clinical services in a Californian County Probation Department claimed consistent success with the use of a 'pink room' for calming down aggressive offenders. Violent youngsters were simply placed inside this small room, and contrary to the usual reaction when placed in confinement, an almost immediate calming effect was reported that apparently lasted for some time afterwards. Studies were also conducted in both hospitals and mental institutions where it was noted that the color of the internal surroundings had a very definite effect upon the patients. In some cases, those effects were physical, such as elevated heart rates and blood pressure. In other cases, patients displayed distinct unease when placed in certain colored rooms, or showed reluctance to travel down specifically-colored corridors. Evidence also suggests that different types of lighting affect the study atmosphere in schools, and that exposing groups of people to colored lights can produce a predetermined effect, such as the reported case in 1932 when a violent crowd was apparently calmed by using blue light.

In the field of modern psychology the famous Lüscher Color Test in existence since the early 1970s has also proven a credible method of evaluating personality types and behaviors solely upon the client's choice of color-paired cards, whilst psychologist Dr. Taylor Hartman's 1998 book *The Color Code* applies color-values to varieties of human behavior that directly correspond to the central premises of this work. For example, the simple fact that the fashion world follows design parameters based upon the general public's instinctive likes or dislikes confirms the direct link between color and emotion. This further corroborates the idea that our thoughts and actions are indeed being substantially influenced, albeit subconsciously, by colors in the environment.

## Color as a Spiritual Influence

For the average layman the terms 'spiritual' and 'religious' are synonymous and often even inseparable, although scholars quite rightly continue to explore the considerable differences between the two; differentiating between *orthodox* * religious practice vs. various forms of mysticism for example, and associated religious states of being. This religious-spiritual debate will be visited in more depth later on. For now however, in order to temporarily facilitate clarity and understanding we will simply acknowledge the fact that for most religious adherents, the rites, rituals, and symbolism of their chosen faith traditions play a very important part in creating,

---

* Orthodox; adhering to the accepted viewpoint; usually conservative; mainstream religious

stimulating, or facilitating the personal 'spiritual' experience as each person understands it to be. Certainly from the perspective of this work, it is enough for now to recognize two basic facts. Firstly, the strong traditional connection between religion and spirituality, and secondly, the mysterious and intangible nature of all things currently labeled 'spiritual.' Despite much proselytizing that appears to suggest otherwise, the plain fact is that whenever we deal with matters 'spiritual' we enter a relatively unknown and unfamiliar realm. For as already mentioned, when compared to the physical or mental spheres the spiritual or supernatural realm remains an area of great mystery for most of us, and therefore should (if we are wise) be approached with considerable humility and respect. Certainly, none of us should be engaged in absolute or unqualified declarations about such an indefinable aspect of existence…

On January 3rd 1945 Edgar Cayce, the renowned mystic and healer, passed away. He had baffled the medical world with his ability to pinpoint injuries and diagnose illnesses in patients whilst in an unconscious trance, apparently having no recollection of the events that transpired afterwards. A humble man who was reluctant to take personal credit for his gifts, he had a special interest in 'auras'; that is, the light that supposedly emanates from all of us but which can only be observed by certain gifted individuals. (This is one explanation given for the presence of 'haloes' around holy people and angels in religious art). Edgar Cayce claims to have had this gift and it is difficult to doubt his sincerity based upon his devout life of faith, his success in discerning patients' problems, and his life of service to others. The last booklet he wrote was a fifteen-page essay simply entitled *Auras (1973)[14]* and the very last paragraph opens with the statement; "Colors reflect the soul and the spirit, the mind and the body,.." (spiritual, mental, physical?) In his essay, he not only gives a concise exposition of his understanding of the physical, emotional and spiritual effects of color on humans, but his findings (I am pleased to say) exactly corroborate the concepts and formulas uncovered in this book.

Betty Wood also touches on the association between color and the human spirit when she describes color-healing practices which encourage the subject to visualize certain colors with a view to either encouraging or repelling influential spirits, and as we will later discover, the Christian Bible too contains specific references to particular colors which are intriguingly consistent across a broad swathe of different religions and assorted sacred texts. In addition, many modern Churches have apparently (and at least somewhat unwittingly) color-coordinated the vestments of their clergy according to the theme of the service or liturgical calendar; patterns also evident in certain mystical movements such as modern Kabalism, the Hindu chakras, and ancient Greek, Egyptian, and Roman religions. The patterns are strikingly consistent throughout. From the Aztecs of Central America to the Norse gods and heroes of Scandinavia, and from Ancient Persia to the Native North American tribes. Without apparent awareness of the archetypal nature of these symbol-forms or of the religious practices of distant cultures, various faith traditions through the ages have consistently incorporated certain color-specific rituals or paraphernalia when calling upon particular deities. Or, have chosen the same colors and symbols for specific theme-related tasks such as ritual sacrifice, marriage, victory in war, a good harvest, or to bless a newborn child; examples of which will be presented in due course. Once again, just as in the color-patterns of Chapter One, there are remarkable consistencies in the chromatic characteristics and core themes that transcend the usual anthropological explanations or any theory of random probability.

Although we have yet to review the evidence in detail we should by now be in fair agreement that color, as a vital component of original 'white' sunlight plays a critical, fundamentally-necessary, and highly influential part in our daily lives; simultaneously both (i) actually-and-philosophically, and (ii) consciously-and-subliminally.

We should be equally agreed that within the three categories of physical, emotional, and spiritual (as previously defined) color is definitely playing an active part in human relationships as well as affecting our interactions with the environment at large, but for the most part without our full conscious awareness or understanding.

We have also witnessed the amazingly consistent patterns of 20$^{th}$ century political history centering upon the red, white, and blue formula, an intriguing phenomenon yet to be fully explained, and we have hinted at the unfolding of a great and enlightening chromo-dynamic theory based upon a 'universal triadic archetype'.

So, in order to progress to a better understanding of the possible causes or meanings of the political color-sequences of Chapter One and any possible connections with our spirit, mind, and body theory, we now need to take a closer look at what science, history, and our various color-experts have to say specifically about the colors white, blue, and red, and see if there may be any sort of sequence or pattern that will help us explain this intriguing phenomenon.

# CHAPTER FOUR

# COLOR IN SCIENCE & HISTORY

*On the foundation of proofs that show that light and color substantially affect the three dimensions of the human experience; body, mind, and spirit, we will now explore the colors white, blue, and red, with a view to establishing their specific effects and values according to the scientific-historical perspective. Mythological and religious associations with these particular colors will be examined separately and in more depth in upcoming chapters. Regarding the four remaining colors mentioned in Chapter One (green, purple, yellow-gold, and black) since they feature in our central theme for the most part in a secondary or supporting role we will simply summarize their value-properties here, only addressing them as-and-when further clarifications or explanations are necessary.*

There are many sources for information gathering available to us today, perhaps none quite so captivating and popular as the Internet. But although a rich source for color-related information, the Internet is also a forum for posting all sorts of subjective, unqualified, irregular, and possibly erroneous opinions, so naturally we have to be discerning about where we glean our supporting information. Interestingly, in using the Internet as a source of color-data, it is relatively easy to prove the point made in Chapter Two about the problems caused in education by subjective theorizing, for as yet no built-in filters have been established against the posting of unqualified opinions. In the same vein however it is equally interesting to note that as far as color-related information goes, the more 'qualified' websites are relatively consistent in their findings. In particular those hosted by traditionally-certified professionals in their respective fields; art historians, anthropologists, social scientists, and psychologists for example. Therefore, when dealing with 'non-traditional' sources such as mystics and mediums, or with specific religious theory, I have tended to ratify or dismiss any particular theory against the evidence presented in this book, and in accordance with the qualified reports of the aforementioned professional sources. This same rule applies to enthusiastic amateurs or pseudo-scientists in various color-related fields. Accordingly, the reader may expect to find reference only to collaborative, and mostly 'professional' websites. But this should not be misunderstood as an act of elitist bias on my part, especially as I expect my own research to come under similar scrutiny. I suppose differentiating between 'professional' and 'other sources' could technically be termed 'discrimination' inasmuch as we must discriminate between that which is more or less credible, but this does not automatically exclude any specific source or commentary. For example, the aforementioned spiritual healer Edgar Cayce, although much respected in New Age circles still struggles to be labeled anything other than 'a pseudo-scientist' by strict empiricists. Carl Jung too, suffers criticism for the same reasons. Nevertheless, you will find the opinions of both Cayce and Jung on the subjects of color and archetypal symbolism much quoted by me, chiefly because they are in agreement with my own independent findings in almost every parallel. And whilst such selectiveness will naturally open me to charges of seeking specifically-collaborative sources to support my own theories, I can but follow the evidence where it leads. In short, considering the this work is based upon the logical and systematic arrangement of scientific facts, historical data, and rational theory, I return once again to the original argument that we need only stick to the facts, and simply allow truth to be her own witness. So with respect to any differing opinions on the topic, let us now review the following summaries of our aforementioned 'qualified' sources, remembering that we are chiefly concerned with establishing the central tenets or themes that the respective experts agree correspond to any given color.

## The 'Color' White

Science informs us that when all colors are combined in light we get the impression of white. Conceptually speaking, in relation to our human ability to see colors white therefore represents 'everything'. In relation to the source of color, white represents 'the origin', and in relation to the individuality of colors, white represents 'unity' or 'wholeness'. As the source of energy for our planet, white light (from the sun) also holds the position of life-source. Supporting this, scientific experiments reported by Faber Birren in his book *Light, Color and Environment (1969)*[15] include research data that confirms white light's effect on animal breeding habits and its ability to influence the quality of produce from captive animals (such as eggs, milk, fur etc.). In another work entitled *The Symbolism of Color (1988)* Birren reports that tomato seedlings, as well as other commercial crops responded most favorably to stimulation from "warm white lamps" (although red lamps also had the effect of accelerated growth).

In Western culture, white is generally seen as a symbol of purity or goodness such as in the colors of the 'white knight' or the 'lone ranger' in their heroic adventures and escapades. Baptisms and weddings use white to convey purity, but in apparent contrast Eastern cultures regularly use white as the color of mourning. It should be noted though that this association with death is not necessarily contradictory or 'negative' per se, but can be read as Eastern culture's more wholesome understanding of the nature of death as a spiritual advancement, rather than as a mere cessation of life. Furthermore, in those societies where black was the usual order of the day for practical or cultural reasons (such as nomadic Muslim tribes) then the use of white for special occasions marked a symbolic departure from the norm. Also reinforcing the general understanding that the color white represents goodness and purity, even in the vocal arts a pure vowel tone in singing is known as 'a white tone'.

Placing moral or political judgments aside, one of the more notable uses of the term 'whites' in political history was the description of the counter-revolutionary forces fighting against Communism in the Russian Civil War (1918–1921). Their Bolshevik opponents of course were 'the Reds'. In Asia too the Korean people reportedly earned the title "The People in White" from their invading neighbors due to a consistent national spirituality and because of the unusual fact that they never forcefully invaded another country. However, another report suggests that the label "The People in White" came from an imperial decree that the peasantry wear white when members of the royal family died – which apparently, was a very regular occurrence in a nobility consisting of hundreds of members. Nevertheless, as in many countries worldwide white is generally understood to symbolize purity, innocence, spirituality, and morality. Interestingly enough though, the red-white-blue South Korean flag remains a leading example of religio-political symbolism as identified in this book, with its red and blue yin-yang symbol on a white background.

White is present in a great many national flags of course but what is worth noting from a symbolic perspective is the ambiguous nature of white. Present in both totalitarian as well as democratic colors (such as Nazi Germany, or Great Britain for example), the 'color' white may justifiably be interpreted in either positive or negative fashion: In some cases for instance we may be looking at the actual presence of white whilst in other cases, we may simply be observing the absence of color. An informed discernment is essential, and will become clearer as we progress.

In contemporary understandings of the color white Edgar Cayce the spiritual healer returns to natural dynamics in saying that white is the perfect aura. "If our souls were in perfect balance, then all our color vibrations would blend and we would have an aura of pure white". In her book *The Healing Power of Color,* color-healer Betty Wood describes white as a most sacred color associated with "wholeness, purity, innocence, and spiritual authority," whilst Indian Vedic scholar Vijaya Kumar's *Colour Therapy* booklet associates white with purity, self-illumination, and the Divine. Psychologist and author Taylor Hartman lists white as the 'peacemaker' characteristic, whilst the Sherwin-Williams Co., who specialize in painting and decorating give this description of the influence of white on moods: "White purifies, energizes, unifies; in combination, enlivens all other colors." Finally, in his fascinating book *The Secret Language of Symbols* psychologist Dr. David Fontana notes: "White represents purity, virginity and the transcendent... For Tibetans, white is the color of Meru, the mountain 'at the center of the world' embodying ascent to enlightenment.[16] All-in-all I think, a pretty convincing argument of white's archetypal value as that of a pure, uncorrupted place of relationship with the Universe and 'the Divine'.

**The Color Blue**
Although the Encarta Encyclopedia lists deep blue and violet as the same color, we make a necessary differentiation between blue, and the colors violet, indigo, and purple for reasons that will soon become clear. In this presentation therefore, 'blue' represents all shades between sky blue and royal blue, such as the blue of the United Nations flag and the blue in the French flag.

Beginning with the observation that blue shades rest at one extreme of the color spectrum—in opposition to reds—we should draw attention to the evidence of Chapter One where none of the axis or communist nations central to 20th century conflicts contained blue in their flags at the time of conflict. However without exception, they all contained red. As we will see in a moment, there are possible subliminal connections between the values attributed to the colors blue and red, and their respective political counterparts. In *The Secret Language of Symbols* for instance, Fontana focuses upon the feminine attributes summarizing the color blue as;

..the hue of the intellect, peace and contemplation. It represents water and coolness, and symbolizes the sky, infinity, the emptiness from which existence arises... the color of the Virgin as Queen of Heaven... denotes faith, compassion and the waters of baptism. ...the goddess of love.[17]

Also reflected in the British-based website *Color Affects*, and in her book *The Beginner's Guide to Colour Psychology (1998)* author Angela Wright describes blue as:

..the colour of the mind.. (that) affects us mentally, rather than the physical reaction we have to red. Strong blues will stimulate clear thought and lighter, soft blues will calm the mind and aid concentration. Consequently it is serene and mentally calming. It is the colour of clear communication.[18]

Vijaya Kumar supports this blue-as-thinking concept when he notes that blue is "the center of communication, self-expression, knowledge and wisdom... where we find our higher potential and absorb our dreams."[19] This too suggests a contrast between physical reds and more contemplative blues. In addition, in scientific experiments conducted under blue-colored glass by John Ott,[20] the results were almost exactly opposite to those carried out under red-tinted glass. Captive animals were pacified, the pregnancy rate increased significantly, and the ratio of females born increased 50% whilst that of newborn males decreased 50%. This suggests a direct correlation between the color blue and the female gender: Blue effected positive female results, whilst red light did the same for the males. Interestingly enough, in the war years, there existed an unspoken tradition of prostitutes wearing blue as a badge of their profession, another interesting albeit obscure connection with female sexuality.

Our three respected authors on the subject of color-healing and auras; Edgar Cayce, Ingaer Naess, and Betty Wood, collectively agree that "blue...moves us towards the more spiritual aspects of life and away from the physical level." Ingaer Naess continues, describing blue as "a peaceful and relaxing color" ...having "a pacifying effect." It is also "spiritually stimulating, being the color of the soul, and of purity." Although this appears to merge blue values with those of white, we should remember that this is not an exact science, and in many cases 'expert' opinions are still tinged with a liberal dose of subjectivity. In any case, the progression away from red and towards white is at least a limited confirmation of our central theory so far. Cayce reiterates these higher concepts stating that "blue has always been the color of the spirit, the symbol of contemplation, prayer and heaven". In his concluding color chart he too attributes "spiritual, artistic, and selflessness" to the color blue. Betty Wood also goes into considerable depth in describing the values connected to blue including its cultural association with "truth, revelation, wisdom, loyalty, fertility, constancy, and chastity" – concepts that are also reflected in traditional heraldry which attributed the values of truth and loyalty to the color blue. Not surprisingly, Wood also connects blue with "the feminine principle, the Great Mother… (and) comfort, peace, compassion, healing." In an interesting note on a chapter about healing, Wood adds that blue "is only superceded by its higher counterpart.. indigo, the ray of spirituality" (sometimes known as purple). The reader is invited to remember this fact for later reference. Our painter-decorators define the properties of the color blue on mood as; "relaxing, refreshing, cooling, producing tranquil feelings and peaceful moods".

Finally on the subject of moods, if we look at common language 'mood' is a regular partner to the term 'blue'. For example; "a fit of the blues, feeling blue, singing the blues, being in a blue mood, etc.." all of which may be associated with the mind and the emotions, and the traditional feminine position.

## The Color Red

In the visible spectrum, red has the longest wavelengths and is therefore the strongest color, the easiest one to see. For the purposes of this text, under the designation 'red' are included the other reds such as scarlet and crimson, whose numeric value is also in the 700 nm range, and who ascribe to the same symbolic properties as deep red.

In ancient writings and manuscripts red was the first recognized color recorded. Even Aristotle only recorded three colors of the rainbow; red, yellow and green, all of which are in the red half of the color spectrum, suggesting that color awareness amongst humans began with recognizing red and has developed along the spectrum towards the blue hues as time progressed. As we will soon see, this fact corresponds to our previous acknowledgement of humanity's historical fixation with things physical and material.

Angela Wright's website list the positive properties of red as follows: "Physical, physical courage, strength, warmth, energy, basic survival, 'fight or flight', stimulation, masculinity, excitement." The author also notes what she sees as the more 'negative' aspects of the color red such as defiance and aggression, an interesting aspect of red that is evident in some of the following examples – which we will address shortly.

In recent political history the most notable use of the term 'Reds' is in reference to Communists or communist sympathizers, and as previously mentioned in the Russian Civil War of 1918-21 the red Bolshevik forces directly opposed the 'white' Tsarist forces. The Soviet Red Army and the Chinese Red Army also derived their names from a communist military ideology that could arguably be defined as 'a collective political affiliation with a noticeably 'non-spiritual' and generally-patriarchal social order. Red also factored integrally in the colors of Fascism and Nazism, and perhaps somewhat surprisingly was one of the two central colors of pre-Reformation Christianity, as well as modern Islam (more on this later). As already mentioned, scientific experiments using red-tinted glass have also reported some amazing results: John Ott reports that captive animals became more aggressive under red light, their appetites and weight increased, and pregnancy rates decreased although the *ratio* of male births actually increased. Ott also discovered that the human male is more stimulated by red radiation than his female counterpart. In addition to all these associations with the physical and the masculine, modern color healers associate red with "will, power, life, vitality and energy," but insist that red "is never used for any type of mental healing" [21] which is another point worthy of special note for later reference. Also symbolic of "blood, battles and wars, heroism and courage, and pioneering, leadership-type people" in medieval heraldry red was the color of the warrior, the martyr, and representative of courage and strength.[22] Sexual energy and procreation, as well as all things corporeal are connected to the color red. Thus red is reflective of the strongest and basest emotions, such as rage, lust and anger, as well as the more noble heroic masculine virtues. Kumar too notes that red is associated "with our most primal instincts, procreation and aggression," and Fontana summarizes the properties of red as follows:

> Symbolizing the life-force as expressed through the animal world, red is the energy coursing through the body, the color that flushes the face and swims before the eyes in violent arousal. Red is the color of war and its god, Mars, and of the greatest of the Roman gods, Jupiter. It is the color of masculinity and activity.[23]

The text of the Lüscher Color Test further notes; "the outgoing actions of attack and conquest are represented by the color red," (which also has) "...a decidedly stimulating effect upon the nervous system."[24] This recognition of the hostile aspects of masculinity brings a little more complexity to the possible symbolic interpretation of the color red, and the reader should be made aware that there are indeed mitigating factors that we will address in due course. For now though, the recognition of the primary *masculine and active* aspects associated with the color red are sufficient to our task.

As previously mentioned, mixing red with black is considered "the worst possible combination... but red can be either positive or negative". Cayce tells us that in ancient symbolism red represented the body (as opposed to the spirit), and in his color chart Cayce gives us the three words; "force, vigor, energy".. to define red, whilst our contemporary decorators list the effects of red on mood as "empowering, stimulating, dramatizing, competing, and stimulating passion". Finally, there is the use of the word 'red' in common language, such as 'seeing red' (anger), 'red-blooded' (strong and high-spirited), and getting the 'red carpet treatment' (being treated with respect, or as a hero).

**Conceptual Values of White, Blue, and Red**

So, to summarize our findings so far: With a very few perspicuous exceptions that migrate across the categories, we see a consistent, historical symbolic association between (i) the color red, masculinity, and physical activity (both constructive and destructive); (ii) between the color blue, femininity, emotions, and mental procedures; and (iii) between the color white and wholeness, light, and high spirituality. Even allowing for the occasional differences in cultural interpretations, this brief overview of the values traditionally attributed by science and society to these three specific colors brings us to the inescapable conclusion that we are indeed adopting certain colors according to universal themes, which in turn correspond to the physical properties of the visible spectrum. As University of Illinois professor Olivia Guide states in her 1999 article *Color Coding,* regarding the natural responses of students to certain colors:

> Typically, blue may be described as soothing, sad, or moody; yellow as cheerful and upbeat. Black is associated with somberness, evil, or death; white with transcendence and purity. The language used by students, and often by the teacher, implies that such associations are not based in symbolic conventions, but are natural, unmediated human responses.[25]

So, blue is perceived as an 'emotional' color, and white as 'spiritual'. Please take particular note of her summarizing statement: "..that such associations are NOT based in symbolic conventions, but are natural, unmediated human responses." In other words, these automatic reactions to colors are *not* due solely to our respective cultural programming as has often been claimed, but rather emerge from somewhere in the deep subconscious. Or, perhaps we might say from the archetypal realm; the 'high super-consciousness'?

Leaping straight into the conceptual fray, the astute reader will already have noticed the direct and substantial correlation between the three dimensions of the human being previously discussed; body, mind, and spirit – and the colors red, blue, and white respectively. If we now reproduce the two sets of definitions already summarized and place them together; our body-mind-spirit summary with our red-blue-white color values; we arrive at a very interesting parallel-triad centered on both these themes. This triadic formula where the colors white, blue, and red generally correspond with the spirit, mind, and body theme respectively will now form the basis of our enquiries into the theory of a universal, chromatic-based, triadic archetype:

> **White**: Spiritual. Origin. Soul. Inspiration. Creative. Containing all colors. Wholeness: To do with inner spirit, or soul. Associated with the spiritual or noumenal realm. Our connecting point with God. The immortal aspect. The search for higher purpose, or the Divine. Ethereal. Pure religion; a very rare phenomenon

> **Blue**: Emotional. Feminine. Sympathetic. Wisdom. Mental: To do with the mind, emotions, or intellect. Psychological. Rational. Affecting one emotionally: Desires and moods. Perception. Thinking. Cognition. Planning. Conceptual.

> **Red:** Physical. Masculine. Body. Action. Corporeal: To do with the body. Physiological. Tangible. Substantial. Matter. Energy. Activity. The five physical senses; sight, hearing, touch, taste and smell. Physically quantifiable.

Thus we establish the existence of a conceptual, multidimensional, archetypal triad that (initially) incorporates at least five dimensions of existence in harmonious, although admittedly rather general terms. Corresponding neatly not only with the physical structure of the color spectrum—whose opposite ends are represented by deep red and deep blue respectively—but also with the 'masculine-feminine-origin', and the 'inspiration-plan-action' triads as already discovered in our findings and summarized below as.

(1) The spirit, mind, and body triad
(2) The origin, female, and male triad
(3) The inspiration, contemplation, and action triad
(4) The white, blue, and red triad of the color spectrum
(5) The white, blue, and red flag phenomena of 20th century political history

Add to this the interesting fact that crocodile eggs will hatch as either female or male depending upon the temperature of the nest: a warm (red) nest produces male offspring, whilst a cool (blue) nest produces females; and we have yet another intriguing connection to support our findings that can be dated back 200 million years or so. Specifically, that the warm high-energy wavelengths at the red end of the spectrum somehow relate to masculinity whilst the cooler blues relate to femininity. Accordingly, and based upon the recognized consensual color values of white, blue, and red, we observe a formulaic progression that hints at a profound connection between this chromatic archetype and a natural order that in ideal circumstances would originate in 'inspirational' white (contains all colors), through to wise, thinking-and-planning blue (the feminine, nurturing color), and finally to active, reproductive, physical red – (the masculine energy-color).

Temporarily putting aside any debates about exceptions to this general rule, let us now simply evaluate these color-values in context with the few token examples illustrated in Table A and see whether we may actually be "on to something?" …as Sherlock Holmes would say.

## Table A: Five Comparative Parallels

| Electromagnetic | White | Blue | Red |
| --- | --- | --- | --- |
| Human | Spirit | Mind | Body |
| Logical | Inspiration | Contemplation | Action |
| Gender | Origin | Female | Male |
| Political | White | Blue | Red |

Although we have yet to explore social and religious theory, it is patently clear that there is a profound series of subconscious (or supra-conscious) associations here. The real question of course is what exactly do these examples this tell us other than recording the fact that masculinity and femininity somehow correspond to the electromagnetic spectrum; to physical and mental values; to political themes; and to the colors red and blue in some subliminal dimension? What else have we got here other than a quaint, perhaps even intriguing theory that links colors, flags, gender, and general concepts?

The answer to this question is dramatic indeed. Because this token display of archetypal properties in relation to man and his world is only the proverbial 'tip of the iceberg', with the greater part of the interconnected meanings of universal semiotics yet to be exposed. Indeed, the proofs to come suggest—if not indeed confirm—that our very development as a species is being paralleled subliminally-yet-substantially by this symbolic, archetypal language: A symbolic record that not only tracks and records our progress, but may arguably yet even prove to anticipate it. After all, until all the facts are in who indeed is to say what the limits and dimensions of this discovery might be?

When we add the intriguing fact that astrologists measuring the values of the cosmic spectrum have recently concluded that the overall general color of the universe is white, but that; " The universe started out young and blue, and grew gradually redder as the population of evolved 'red' giant stars built up…" [26] we are left in no doubt as to the cosmic propriety of these three colors in a specific and naturally-balanced sequence.

As we progress through this book and subsequent volumes presenting proof after proof of the triadic archetype in areas as diverse as quantum physics, holy scripture, art, mysticism, history, politics, and psychology, the reader will surely come to understand that whatever it is the experts decide we have uncovered here, it is certainly no mere run of remarkable coincidences.

Lastly, in reference to the other four colors discussed in Chapter One, and in order to give a balanced assessment of the findings of our afore-quoted experts, we offer the following provisional summary of color values as respectfully compiled by this author from their published conclusions. As previously explained, with all category and classification systems there will be some merging of concepts from color to color, as well as some cultural variations in their interpretation. But as we observed earlier there is a subtle, but oh-so-important difference between culturally-programmed responses to color and the "unmediated" archetypal responses as reported upon by professor Olivia Guide. The color green for example will have a specific, and quite different cultural identity for Irish or Arab peoples, as will the color orange have differing 'values' for South African Boers or Buddhist monks. But ultimately, and beyond these cultural variations, lies a deeper symbolism common to us all.

> **White:** Spiritual, Origin, Soul, Inspiration, Creative, Containing All Colors,
> **Blue:** Emotional, Feminine, Mind, Contemplation, Sympathetic, Wisdom
> **Red:** Physical, Masculine, Body, Action, Pragmatic,
> **Purple:** Sovereignty, Royalty, Sacred, Spiritual
> **Green:** Creation, Natural Balance, Reproduction, Center, Union, Harmony, Healing
> **Gold:** Of Ultimate Value, Presence of Value, Symbol of Sovereignty & Prosperity
> **Black:** Absence of Light, Primordial Darkness, Death, Chaos, Evil

To reiterate, this is what we are concerned with in this book; divining the primal, universal archetypal identity of key colors and their associated values and meanings, over and beyond any local views. This in turn brings us to a most important and sensitive point.

**The Color Black**
The reader will have noted the negative connotations associated with the color black in the list above. But it should be emphasized that we are concerned with the archetypal, and *not* merely cultural interpretations of the color black. Dark-skinned people should not take any slight from these findings, no more so than Caucasians should read white symbolism with an elitist ethnic slant. The primal symbolism associated with black has simply to do with its being the 'anti-color', because technically speaking black is not a color at all, but is in fact the absence of color and light.

In a philosophy that places light and color at the productive center of the equation, black must naturally represent non-light, non-color, and non-life; hence the terms "Darkness, Death, and Evil" rise as implicit metaphors. But as we will see, these are not necessarily truly accurate metaphors – at least not in combination. 'Evil' for example is in an altogether different category from darkness and death inasmuch as the latter two are essential to life itself. Evil, as we shall see, is not an essential component of life. This too will be discussed in due course.

Sadly, whilst it is highly likely that there are subliminal links between our cultural prejudices and universal color archetypes, it should be reiterated that the racial issue of skin color is, in my opinion, no more than a highly emotive distraction from the scientific study of color. Regardless of skin pigmentation we are all, literally, children of light. So please let's not be distracted by cultural bias here, nor make any ad-hoc associations that do not belong in what I hope will be regarded as a unifying, rather than divisive theory.

For just as each color has individual characteristics that give it its own specific identity, in reality, they all merge in the electromagnetic spectrum to form true light – which leads us to an interesting philosophical metaphor: For curiously enough it is impossible to accurately discern the 'trueness' of any particular color without the illuminating perspective of light. Hence, the first important moral principle that can be deduced from the dynamics of the color spectrum is that only those who stand in the universally-objective position (of light) are truly qualified to determine value.

# CHAPTER FIVE

# SYMBOLS, NUMBERS, & ANCIENT TRUTHS

*We now take a brief journey back in time, exploring the historical beginnings and subliminal origins of some of society's more familiar symbols. We do this in order to establish a clear lineal connection between; (i) preexistent natural elements; (ii) man's historical symbol-choices, and (iii) the color-dynamics of the electromagnetic spectrum, particularly the colors red, white, and blue. This exploration is undertaken to confirm the subliminal integrity of what might otherwise be perceived as 'merely arbitrary' choices in humanity's selection of religious and tribal symbols. Based upon these findings we will then move on to explore connections with other natural and social phenomena in subsequent chapters before summarizing the essential properties of the triadic archetype, and evaluating its possible meanings and applications for us today.*

Although not yet fully understood, the fact that archaeologists, explorers, anthropologists, and historians regularly unearth artifacts that contain culturally-diverse, yet globally-consistent symbols during their research and discoveries, further confirms that we are indeed connected through time and space, beyond cultural and ethnic borders by certain universal concepts. For along with colors and numbers, visible symbols are another aspect of universal language whose meanings transcend the limited world of words. In their consistent appearances and reappearances throughout history in diverse cultural, religious, and historical settings we are offered a profoundly valuable insight into human psychological and anthropological development. Coupled with the meanings and values of colors as outlined previously and supported both by Jungian theory and empirical data (which we will review shortly), apparently arbitrary historical decisions such as choosing tribal colors or selecting political symbols such as flags or insignia of office, now takes on an altogether new meaning. As we are about to see, many such symbols reflect cosmic truths that reside deep in the collective *psyche* [*] (or collective spirituality), yet despite their sensory and substantial forms have uncannily, somehow escaped formal conscious understanding or recognition.

Pervasive enough to affect the very patterns of history, the forces behind these phenomenon undoubtedly have archetypal (or noumenal) origins. But these particular symbols differ from traditional theoretical archetypes in that they are *sensory* and *substantial* and, being visible records of historical symbol-choices, thus escape to a great degree being obscured, obstructed, or camouflaged by individual (or collective) subjectivity.

In other words, the symbol forms discussed in this work; from political flags to religious icons are not 'mere' abstract theoretical concepts. They are actual, visible, and substantial entities written into the historical record. As such, these symbols represent astounding empirical insights for comprehending the development of the human psyche – and by implication, the very meaning of life itself. The challenge of course is to bring the profound meanings of these symbols out of their subconscious places of origin, and into the collective awareness where such knowledge can benefit us all. This is our task today.

However, considerable caution must be exercised in the interpretation process. For if inappropriate values are ascribed, then many symbols that do indeed contain profound insights risk loosing their full impact and credibility – an occurrence sadly prevalent in many pseudo-religious, pseudo-scientific, and pseudo-political settings. Therefore, in this brief study of universal symbol-systems connected specifically to the colors white, blue, and red, we will list only those examples whose meanings are stoutly confirmed by substantiations in other cultures or religions; examples such as the Sun and the Moon or the rainbow for instance; or the fire, air, water, and earth symbols of the ancient Greek fathers.

As a final point of clarification, please be aware that the following definitions are not offered as culturally-specific 'absolutes' but rather as amalgamations of core, consistent meanings, gathered painstakingly from a wide range of expert sociological and historical sources.

---

[*] Psyche; the spirit, soul, and/or mind – usually a psychological term

## Symbol Shapes and Forms

Physical symbols have three essential properties: (i) their shape or form, (ii) their color(s), and (iii) their value-meanings. Their colors (ii) and their general value-meanings (iii) will be dealt with continuously throughout the book, but their shapes and forms (i) now deserve a little extra clarification before we engage specific examples.

As far as the shapes and forms of symbols are concerned, we are primarily interested in anything that has parallels in the dynamics of the electromagnetic spectrum or/and, those forms that repeat regularly and consistently amongst human *iconography*: * The common triangle and the number three for example, or the number four and squares, or perhaps the number seven and the many mystical connections in religious symbolism.

This gives us cause to review fig.9 ♣, where we note in the first instance that the numbers 400 and 700 have been ascribed to the colors blue-violet and deep red respectively. The number 300 is also (possibly) prominent as the nanometer span separating (or bridging) these two colors. Hence the numbers 300, 400, and 700 can be associated—at least provisionally and theoretically—with the red, white, blue tricolor phenomenon of Chapter One. Following this line of logic, in according the numbers 400 and 700 to the colors blue and red, we might also reasonably apply the number 300 either to a full-spectrum rainbow, or to full-spectrum white. However, considering the fact that white is in fact the integrated blend of all colors, and therefore the theoretical origin of color, we might arguably be better off attributing either (a) the number 'one' for origin and cosmic unity; (b) no number at all; or (c) simply assign to white the number of infinity (whatever that may be).

But one other number that fits with our tentative findings so far that could possibly be assigned to white is the number of the speed of light. Interestingly, science informs us that the speed of light is 300,000,000 meters per second, which means that in one second alone light can circumnavigate the earth seven times: the numbers three and seven once again. These facts will come into play with considerable significance later on when we consider the probable cosmic links not only between archetypal numbers in ancient mythologies, but also in regards to modern mathematics and atomic physics.

To offer one intriguing example; if we accord the numbers one, four, and seven to the colors white, blue, and red respectively, we arrive at the mystical number twelve; incidentally, the number of the red, white, blue

---

* Iconography; the study of images or symbols

coalitions of countries that triumphed in the two World Wars, as reported in Chapter One. Perhaps this is truly 'only coincidence' once again, but in light of the numerous repetitions of the number twelve and its multiples in history and mythology, not to mention dozens of entries in the Bible and other scriptures; it is nonetheless very interesting (see Table B).

For now however, the main point is to draw the reader's attention to the possible secondary meanings of any symbols or patterns that employ the mystical numbers three, four, or seven—or multiples thereof—as there yet may be unrecognized connections. After all, it is hardly mere coincidence that these particular numbers are central to the major world religions and many ancient mythologies, as well as featuring prominently in the lives of many of history's greats.[*]

There remains the argument however, that the historical duplication of mystical numbers is simply arbitrary. For example, that mystical numbers are logically derived from ancient cultures' recognition of the twelve lunar cycles of the year divided into four segments of three months apiece. Or, that the mystical number seven is simply derived from the seven recognizable colors of the equally mystical rainbow as reflected in the Buddhist Vedic chakras for instance.

In any event, whether primevally associated with lunar cycles; with the *chromonumerics*[†] of light; or, with the long list of interrelated happenings of Chapter One; there is a notable lack of solid scientific explanation for this perennial surfacing of certain numbers in socio-religious history and iconography. But there they are, and there they remain all the same. Similarly, any triadic, quadratic, linear, or circular formulas could—in theory at least—be associated with chromonumeric properties; 300, 400, 700, and circular infinity, representing white, blue and red respectively. However, considering the vast array of numerological theories (many of which are at variance) and not wishing to embroil the reader in possibly distracting speculations at this point, let us simply acknowledge the interesting fact that the numbers three, four, and seven in particular are integral both to the color spectrum and to many commonly-used symbols and icons, as well as surfacing repeatedly in human history, especially in religion and mythology. Drawing attention to possible numeric associations at this time merely serves to prime us for future 'coincidental' connections along numeric lines, and adds a little more weight to a systematic theory of universal archetypes.

---

[*] This subject will be dealt with in more detail in *Volume II: Parallels in Life*
[†] Chromonumeric; relating to colors and numbers

## Table B: Selected Examples of Appearances of the Number Twelve

| | Mythology / Astrology / Religion | | Biblical / Political |
|---|---|---|---|
| 12 | Greek Olympian gods | 12 | Fountains at Elim (Exodus 15:27) |
| 12 | Egyptian deities (ennead & triad) | 12 | Stones on the Ephod breastplate |
| 12 | Roman gods and goddesses | 12 | Tribes of Israel (via Jacob) |
| 12 | Labours of Heracles (Greek) | 12 | Hebrew Judges & Prophets |
| 12 | Signs of the Western Zodiac | 12 | Months of Gehinnom (Judaism) |
| 12 | Realms of Norse mythology | 12 | Age of Jesus in the Temple |
| 12 | Gods of Norse mythology | 12 | Disciples of John the Baptist |
| 12 | Animals of the Chinese Zodiac | 12 | Apostles of Jesus |
| 12 | Cycles of Rta; Aryan mythology | 12 | Baskets of leftovers miracle |
| 12 | Divas (Hindu / Buddhist) | 12 | Girl raised from dead miracle |
| 12 | Yaksa Guardians (Japan) | 12 | Years of diseased woman miracle |
| 12 | Upper worlds; Polynesian myth | 12 | Angels; Book of Revelation |
| 12 | Avatars; Hindu Vishnu (messiah) | 12 | Gates of Heaven; Book of Rev. |
| 12 | Adityas; sun gods of Hinduism | 12 | Stars in woman's crown; Rev. |
| 12 | Idols of Crom Cruach (Celtic) | 12 | Fruits of the Tree of Life; Rev. |
| 12 | Members of a modern jury | 12 | Days of Christmas (to Epiphany) |
| 12 | Months of the year | 12 | Disciples of St. Columba |
| 12 | Carbon; and triple-alpha process | 12 | Carolingian French Kings (Vol II) |
| 12 | Colours; standard colour wheel | 12 | R-W-B coalition in WW I |
| 12 | Arabic tribes (of Ishmael) | 12 | R-W-B coalition in WW II |
| 12 | Yrs; Muhammad's visions to Hijra | 12 | R-W-B coalition in Korean War |
| 12 | Imams in Shi'ia Islam | 12 | Stars in European Flag |

## Symbolism and the Ancients

Let us continue by taking a brief look at some striking connections between our central chromonumerics and the combined sources of astrology, Judeo-Christian scriptures, and the metaphysical teachings of the Ancient Greeks who, as we shall soon see, had uncannily accurate understandings of principles that would not be ratified for centuries.

To begin with there is the aforementioned three-by-four numeric principle, abundant in its occurrences in mythology and religious symbolism, most probably inherited from the Ancient Egyptian Zodiac and later reflected in the twelve Greek Olympian gods and goddesses. These Greek Olympians later transmigrated into Roman mythology; Zeus became Jupiter, Ares became Mars, and Aphrodite became Venus for example. Worthy of note is the fact that the ancient Zodiac was itself logically divided into four seasonal groups of three. The twelve biblical sons of Jacob and the twelve tribes of Israel further correspond to this three-four pattern in ancient mythology and astrology, similarly represented on Aaron's (Moses brother's) golden priestly breastplate by twelve precious stones, likewise arranged in four groups of three. In the Islamic tradition too, Ishmael, the elder son of Abraham by Hagar the Egyptian maid, sired twelve sons of his own with his Egyptian wife, who in turn grew into twelve Arabic tribes. Several 120-year sequences also present themselves in biblical dynasties, including the Saul / David / Solomon series of forty-year consecutive rules, and Moses' three forty-year courses in the wilderness.[27] The twelve apostles of Jesus were also numerically connected to this theme, and there are some intriguing associations between the symbolic icons of the individual tribes of Israel such as animals, buildings, plants and the like that also coincide with the signs of the Zodiac, but regrettably (for us pattern-seekers) only in a handful of cases. As previously mentioned however, the signs of the Zodiac are themselves dynamically grouped into four central themes, each comprising three astrological signs that represent fire, water, air, and earth respectively. Each of these four primary elements have their own identity within symbolism but it is particularly worth noting that in combination these elements, when represented by the colors red, blue, white, and green not only represent all of creation but also encompass the full range of the color spectrum: Red and blue at opposing ends, green in the creative center, and white encompassing them all (10 ♣). Recalling our previous mention of the color green representing the central point of union of feminine-blue and masculine-red in the life generating process of photosynthesis itself, we see in these Zodiac themes a clear and direct parallel with natural dynamics. When we then compare this to the viewpoint of the Ancient Greeks who believed that life was made up of these abovementioned four factors; air (white), fire (red), earth (green), and water (blue), long, long before they had any understandings of the color spectrum or its apparent gender-related properties, we uncover an intriguing and very balanced match between those ancient metaphysical theories and the (then unknown) laws of natural science. The symbolism is uncannily accurate, and could even be represented figuratively in the form of squares or triangles (fours and threes), with each of the colors equilaterally distant at the apexes. In turn, this resonates with the molecular structures of certain gases, liquids, and solids that can theoretically be compared not only to the colors white, blue, and red; 'white' air and oxygen; blue oceans and rivers; red-brown earth etc., which in turn resonates with the temperature scale; white = cold, blue = cool, red = hot; but also to the spiritual, psychological, and physical triad respectively. (More on this later.) The fact that the Greeks also considered the human soul to be dualistically composed of fire and water (red and blue) stirs even more intrigue (12 ♣). Not because of the questionable physics of course, but because of the psychological or metaphysical notion of a masculine-and-feminine, active-contemplative, red-and-blue center to the human psyche; further confirmed by the 20th century findings of C.G. Jung concerning the subconscious existence of the *animus* and the *anima* which we will discuss in more detail in Part Two.[28] The question we should be asking of course is how ancient philosophers could hypothesize so accurately about scientific matters that were then well beyond their demonstrable reach? Where exactly did the inspiration come from to produce such enlightened theories if not from empirical observation? Could the answer lie in the perennial workings of psychospiritual archetypes one wonders?

**The Triangle:** Speaking of triads and archetypes, perhaps it is time to note the importance of the triangle both as a figurative and an abstract symbol that is key to this work. Clearly the triangle represents the number three, which in turn relates to the theology of the Christian Trinity, the Hindu Trimurti, and dozens of other religious and mythological triads such as in ancient Babylonian, Egyptian, Greek, and Roman religions. Historical associations with the number three-principle are innumerable, and are found in fields as far apart as human politics and atomic physics. Likewise, the design of the triangle corresponds in several ways to other conceptual trinities. For instance, David Fontana's book defines upward or downward-pointing triangles as representative of either male or female.[29] Considering the foundational place of triangles and sexuality in our gender-sensitive triadic formulas this affirmation of sexual properties is very interesting, and although it could be argued that the triangular design of the uterus, and the phallic symbolism of the pyramid represent female and male triangles respectively, for rather obvious reasons associated with whole human physiology (see fig.11 ♣), it is this writer's opinion that the symbolic positions are at least mutually reversible. Adding a little physical evidence to my theory is the fact that a water molecule ($H_2O$), symbolic of the feminine, is constructed along the lines of an isosceles triangle.

**The Sun:** This, probably the most primal icon is recognized as the preeminent male symbol often representing God the Father, as well as stimulating sun-worship via the various gods of myth; from the Sumerian god Shamash to Greece's Helios, or from the Egyptian Ra, to Lugh of the Celtic Isles. The association with fire and the color red (as opposed to cool blues) should not go unnoticed. After all, although it may appear white, yellow, or even orange from Earth, we all know that the Sun is basically a big ball of fire. As the source of all light and energy it is natural that ancient traditions would gravitate religiously towards this symbol of life. Often associated with gold, as the moon was to silver, the sun is the symbolic male partner to the female moon not only in the practice of alchemy, but also in Joseph's Biblical dreams (Gen. 37: 9). In the symbolic language of Genesis, the Gospels, and the book of Revelation, the sun is interpreted as symbolizing the archetypal father figure in a family that consists of father sun, mother moon, and offspring denoted as stars. Armenian myth also reflects this theme with an astral trinity comprising Vahagn, Anahit, and Astlik as sun, moon, and star gods-and-goddesses respectively.

**The Moon:** As mentioned above, in the mystical science of alchemy and in a natural dualism associated with night and day, the silver-blue Moon represents the feminine counterpart to a golden-male Sun. Because of its association with the monthly menstrual cycle and ocean tides the Moon has been labeled the 'queen' of the heavens in certain traditions. Paintings of goddesses such as Botticelli's famous *The Birth of Venus*[30] invariably contain moon symbolism, and as Fontana notes; "the moon goddess was almost universally perceived as the weaver of fate and the controller of destinies, in the same way that she controlled the tides, the weather, rainfall and the seasons."[31] (Please note the ongoing association with water). The Moon was a symbolic feature in the worship of the Egyptian mother-goddess Isis, the Roman goddess Diana, and the Norse moon-goddess Frigga, the wife of Odin. The moon also often factors in images or reported apparitions of the Virgin Mary, another archetypal mother-goddess figure.

**Water:** This is another primal feminine symbol. In all its many forms from snow and ice, through rivers and oceans, to clouds and mist, water remains essentially a feminine symbol. In its opposition to fire as a primary element, and in its partnership with fire as one of the pair of spiritual components of the human soul in Greek philosophy, water has a clearly defined feminine identity. In its association with the moon, the tides, the menstrual cycle, clouds and rivers as seen above, and the various ancient goddesses of the sea, we witness further connections with the feminine principle.

**Fire:** Like its original source the Sun, fire is another masculine symbol that neatly fits the chromatic profile. One of the primary symbolic elements, it represents power, heat, and energy. When connected with the Divine it is considered a positive force, such as in the life-sustaining power of the Sun or representing the presence of God in the legendary burning bush or, in the tongues of fire at Pentecost. However, when associated with the destroyer, fire is the fuel of hell and damnation; another apt association with the physical and destructive properties of the masculine color red. As previously mentioned, the ancient Greek philosophers considered fire to be one-half of the elements of the soul of mankind, the other half (interestingly enough) being water (fig.12 ♣). This in turn related to their concept of Logos, or 'Word' as the masculine attribute of the Divine, and Sophia or 'Wisdom' as the feminine aspect. Those who have any grounding in theology will surely be struck by the fundamental logic of these concepts, especially when considered in light of convoluted Christian doctrines about the nature of 'Logos' against Judaic Sophist foundations. This too, we will discuss more thoroughly in due course, but for now let us simply note the fact that this association of the dual elements of fire and water with complimentary aspects of the Divine, is also reflected in the Bible through:

- The pillar of fire, and the pillar of cloud leading the Israelites in the wilderness, (Exodus13:22)
- The burning bush and the mystical cloud over Mt Sinai, (Exodus 3:2, 24:15)
- The baptism of water, and the baptism of the Holy Spirit as tongues of fire. (Matthew 3:16, Acts 2:3)

These three listings alone challenge the traditional perception of God as a singularly-masculine figure devoid of a complimentary feminine. The symbolism here speaks out clearly beyond the literal texts themselves. Clearly, there is an emergent archetypal feminine theme despite the traditionally-patriarchal leanings of many classical scholars. (More later).

**The Rainbow:** A legendary bridge between gods and men, the awe-inspiring rainbow was naturally an object of mystical wonder and devotion before coming under the eagle-eyed scrutiny of medieval science. Worthy of note is the appearance of the rainbow in the Bible as a sign of hope after the cleansing waters of the Great Flood. Obviously, there is the connection with new creation through light, but perhaps the key points to note here are: (i) a rainbow is a commonly-accepted religious symbol of hope; (ii) each color of the rainbow has its own symbolic value; (iii) each color of the rainbow has its own scientific value; (iv) collectively, the colors of the rainbow unite to form true light (white). Thus the rainbow can be seen (symbolically) as analogous to light itself. Of historical interest perhaps is the fact that the enigmatic Joan of Arc, archetypal heroine and virgin maid, emerged out of the 'Rainbow Valley' (*Valee du Coleurs)* before rousing the French to victory in the 15th century under a blue banner.

Intriguingly, as noted in Chapter One the first American Division to land on European soil as liberators in 1917—comprising soldiers from every State in the Union—were accordingly named the 42$^{nd}$ *Rainbow* Division. Is it just happenstance one wonders, that the maximal angle of refraction for a rainbow is also 42 degrees?[32] And is there any remote connection perhaps to this number 42 being given tongue-in-cheek as the proverbial answer to the eternal 'meaning of life' question in popular books and movies?[*] The same number incidentally, that preoccupied the inscrutable Lewis Caroll in his writings; as well as being the number of months that the Bible reports 'the Beast' will hold dominion over the earth? (Rev 13:5). As a primordial number associated with the refraction of light, surely it would be no great surprise to discover the enigmatic number 42 surfacing unconsciously yet instinctively in response to these questions?

Intriguing connections aside; these are just some of the interesting parallels with the vision of hope promised by the Biblical rainbow. Regarding the 'true' colors of the rainbow the debate continues as to which, and exactly how many colors constitute its true originals. Some say six, some seven, and some even claim twelve as used in the artists' color wheel. Based upon the natural dynamics of light however, I personally incline towards the six or seven colors of the Vedic chakra system: Red, orange, yellow, green, blue, indigo, (and sometimes violet); noting the important fact that this seventh chakra is sometimes recorded by Vedic practitioners as either violet, white, or a rainbow-blend (♣ 11). Purple too is often mistakenly identified. Purple is not a natural color of the rainbow, but is a blend of red and blue; a fact that will come into play later on. The reader should thus be aware that there can be wide variances of opinion concerning color perceptions and identities even amongst the experts.

**Yin-Yang:** A relatively simple-looking symbol that is a visual metaphor for the universal principle of division and union, or harmonious dualism. Originally depicting the contrast between the shaded and sunlight slopes of a mountain, this symbol, also commonly known as the *T'ai Chi Chu*, originated in ancient Chinese cosmology and loosely defines the world of opposites that are mutually dependant upon each other for their identities and fulfillment. More simply, Yin and Yang stand for north and south, feminine and masculine, right and left, dark and light, and positive and negative principles respectively – to quote but a small listing. In respect of our earlier comments regarding black-related symbolism, the presence of

---

[*] This appears in Douglas Adam's *The Hitchhikers Guide to the Galaxy* (book and movie) as well as Monty Python's *Meaning of Life* (movie)

black in traditional Yin-Yang symbols has mistakenly led to a philosophical acceptance (amongst some) of the belief that 'good and evil' also coexist in a dynamic yin-yang-type relationship. But this understanding of 'evil' as a necessary, or balancing component of our world is now being challenged and ultimately disproved. By the conclusion of this work the reader will hopefully agree that 'evil' is not so much a harmonious partner in a cosmic philosophical Yin-Yang relationship, but rather; that 'evil' is better defined as an attack upon the Yin-Yang principle itself.

**The Cross:** Christians may be surprised to hear that the cross has been a religious symbol since ancient times, only later to become adopted by the growing Christian Church. In several ancient cultures for example, the cross represented the coming together of two dimensions, chiefly masculine and feminine. Occasionally, it also represented the intersection of heaven and earth with humanity at the central point. This corresponds to the Christological view, which places Jesus as this ultimate point of union between God and man further symbolized by the cross of the crucifixion. A thousand years before Christ however, the simple cross was an Assyrian symbol for the sky-god Anu and the ancient Chinese saw the cross as a symbol for the earth. Cross-symbols are also present in ancient Egyptian hieroglyphics. The native religions of Mexico and Central America had crosses as religious symbols long before the arrival of the Spanish Conquistadors in 1519 CE. But the Catholic Spaniards couldn't accept the (heretical) possibility that the cross was not a unique Christian symbol, so this gave rise to the legend that St. Thomas the apostle had reached this area in his travels – a rather 'doubtful' possibility.

**Stars:** Stars feature very prominently in vexillology, particularly amongst the political colors of those nations currently in the news: Israel, Iraq, and the United States for example. Once again, in reviewing 'hot' topics such as politics or religion the reader is respectfully invited to maintain a perspective of chromatic objectivity until all the facts are in.

The star is a relatively versatile symbol that often denotes abundance. In the Bible for example, stars are often symbolic of children or the chosen people, such as in the aforementioned reference made by Joseph in his dream in Genesis 37: 9. Ancient mythologies regularly reflect this theme with stars as the offspring of celestial parents. The Bible refers to 'the day star' (II Peter 1:19), and 'the morning star' (Revelation 2:28), which some scholars have concluded are symbolic references to 'the Anointed One'- the Christ. However, in Isaiah 14:12-13 Lucifer (later Satan) is called "son of the morning" which also relates to the morning star, the brightest of the heavens, but here, Lucifer is chastised for attempting to place his throne "..above the *stars* of God" which in this case refer to humanity.

In subliminal vexillology the differing shapes, forms, colors, or configurations of stars contribute to their symbolic significance. White for example, although sometimes ambiguous can generally be assumed to be a positive sign. However the five-pointed pentagram is regularly associated with magic and even Satanism and, when presented in very dark, red, or black colors on a state flag may indicate a propensity towards 'false' religion or indicate aggressive or suppressive oligarchies. This could include atheism, militant communism, fascism, oppressive fundamentalism, or even pseudo-religious despotism. When coupled with black, or red and black supporting themes, dark-colored five-pointed stars are therefore an ominous sign. The six-pointed star such as that of Judaism on the other hand could, arguably, be interpreted as two interlocking triangles, possibly male and female or yin and yang, which represent a cosmic propriety. Therefore, we may surmise that stars in different forms and colors may be symbolic of either good or evil. On the one hand; Christ, Archangels, or the traditional 'true children of God.' On the other; Satanism, Lucifer, and oppression. Alternatively, they may represent any individual or group whose character may be reflected in the colors and configuration of the star symbol.

**Birds of Prey:** Another rather less-common feature on flags are birds; usually eagles, falcons, and ravens. More prevalent in medieval times, birds of prey carry mixed symbolism in our various cultural histories. In certain cases all the admirable qualities of the majestic eagle or regal falcon are used to denote merit, such as in the Bible in Deuteronomy 32:11, where the eagle's care for her young is held up as a virtue. However, the Bible also instructs against consuming any birds of prey as meat, including the more noble eagles, ospreys, kites, nighthawks and owls. These are lumped together with other "abominable" fowls in a category that includes vultures, ravens, cuckoos, cormorants, herons, lapwings, and bats! One possible reason for this sweeping demotion is the fact that it was 'birds of prey' that claimed Abraham's failed animal sacrifice in Genesis 15:11. This in turn suggests a symbolic connection between 'birds of prey' and the forces of darkness. With a little creative interpretation it is relatively easy to thus explain the sending out of the (black) raven from Noah's Ark, preceding the (white) dove that eventually returns with an olive branch, informing Noah that it was now safe to exit the Ark. In other cultures however, birds of prey may represent lofty ideals, even deities. In Egyptian mythology for example the falcon represented the sky-god Horus, whilst the Hindu god Garuda is half man and half eagle, whose enemy is the serpent. This relates closely to the idea of God and Satan (as demonic serpent) engaged in an everlasting cosmic battle.

It would appear on the surface then, that eagle and bird-of-prey symbolism is ambiguous; that is until we include the chromo-numeric dimension. In other words, the colors of our symbolic eagles and their surrounding paraphernalia play a good part in discerning their essential meaning in any given instance. An eagle with a white head and tail such as the American bald eagle for example, which also carries the olive branch and associated blue-colored emblems has a very different symbolic value to an all-black bird, such as the Viking raven, or the double-headed black, and red-black eagles of Prussia, fascist Italy, and Nazi Germany, which traditionally represented aggressive, dictatorial institutions.

**The Circle:** The humble, but indispensable circle is mentioned here chiefly because of its connection to certain key numbers in chromonumerics, in particular the numbers three, twelve, eighteen, and thirty-six. When divided by three for example, a 360° circle produces three 120° segments. Figuratively speaking, if the start / completion point of the cosmic circle is 360 degrees, then 180 degrees is the direction of opposition, which is indicative of Satan's traditional position in relationship to God (fig.17 ♣). Interestingly, scripture records Satan's number as being 666, and 6 + 6 + 6 equals eighteen (180 degrees?). Similarly, two-thirds of a circle is 66.6%. The significance of this number lies in the unprincipled division of the cosmic circle, whereby a third of the circle is either removed or corrupted. The white (spiritual) aspect is omitted, leaving only male and female, or body and mind without the governing and balancing attributes of (Godly) spirituality. A personality or world centered solely upon physical and emotional impulses without regard to a governing morality is narcissism defined. Thus one third, the most important third of the human condition is theoretically absent, leaving only a dysfunctional 66.6% of the collective 'self' to blunder selfishly, ignorantly, and destructively through life. Worse still when black (evil) replaces the white, and the feminine (blue) aspect is denied. This leaves us with a red-black 66.6% – arguably the worst possible combination of colors.

As already mentioned, it is no secret that the number 666 is traditionally viewed as the 'mark of the beast' strongly suggesting an archetypal association with (red-black) Satan, with evil, or with similarly compromised agencies and institutions (♣ 17, 27). This is one reason given for the biblical sixty-six days of ritual cleansing of an Israelite woman after giving birth to a daughter, symbolizing the period of separation from Satan.[*]

Perhaps too it is only just coincidence that Vienna, the capital of Austria, the country that gave us Adolf Hitler and was the ancestral seat of the Germanic Holy Roman Emperors for 1,000 years, is the only city in the world that sits at a height of six hundred and sixty-six feet above sea level? The added fact that over a period of 360 years (60 x 6; or 6 x 6 x 10), eighteen Hapsburg Emperors (6 + 6 + 6?) would fly their imperial red-black eagles in the same city that hosted a young Hitler's macabre studies into the occult, surely bears more investigation?

The subject of evil and the 666 phenomenon in history will be part of a more advanced study of numeric patterns in both natural and social history which we must leave for later chapters and volumes, but I do hope this adds to the intrigue and promise of upcoming discussions. However, we must not allow ourselves to be too distracted at this early juncture.

Hoping the reader will forgive the occasional departure from the immediate topic at hand, let us now return to our study of the triadic archetype and take a closer look at some fascinating parallels in science, scripture, and society that clearly illustrate the interdependent positions of both man and the triadic archetype in today's world.

---

[*] Leviticus 12:2

# CHAPTER SIX

# SCIENCE, SEX, & SCRIPTURE

*Here we document triadic arrangements in quantum physics and natural science, later comparing them to uncannily similar patterns in both social science and Holy Scriptures. This will help to further bind the fields of science and religion together under the unified umbrella of the triadic archetype.*

The philosophical hypothesis that man is a microcosm of the universe is relatively well documented. Proponents of this idea draw attention to the fact that the same percentage of water content exists in both the earth and the human body for example. Or that trees and rivers do the same job for the earth's atmosphere as lungs and arteries do for human beings. Or the fact that just like our Earth, we are warm, moist, and messy in the center and colder and crustier on the outside. It is an interesting, but mostly speculative theory; that is until we consider the evidence of the triadic archetype that seems to confirm mankind's central position in the general 'scheme of things.'

As the evidence for a multilayered, universal, triadic archetypal system builds; the fact that humanity is very much a living microcosm will become apparent. Not so much because humanity is physically 'special' in any particular way but actually, because in fact we are not. As relative latecomers to the evolutionary stage, we are naturally comprised of many attributes of our vegetable, animal, and mineral predecessors. And even if one does not subscribe to the theory of evolution, the argument remains the same by nature of the fact that we, like most natural units, are comprised of the same fundamental 'stuff' of the universe; carbon, hydrogen, oxygen etc. Furthermore, as consumer-predators at the hierarchical apex of the natural and industrial worlds, we absorb and consume many properties of the natural world around us and as such are intimately and symbiotically linked to our natural environment. Human beings then, are a reflection of many cosmic attributes precisely because—like all other features of the universe—we are physically composed of the same fundamentals, albeit admittedly in diverse forms in varying degrees of development, and of course in varying degrees of consciousness. In other words, simple carbon-based life forms that operate along the same cosmic principles as planets and atoms and everything in-between.

As we see in Table C this theme is manifest not only in the origin-female-male, and spirit-mind-body paradigms, but can be identified in several natural progressions such as; (i) 'white' air, 'blue' water, 'red' earth (or molten core): (ii) Gas, liquid, solid, and (iii); ice-cold white, cool blue, and red hot for instance. In each case, the triad ascends or descends in parallel sequences: White through blue to red. Or, red through blue to white.

### Table C: Thematic and Practical Parallels

| White | Origin | Spirit | Air | Gas | Cold |
|-------|--------|--------|-------|--------|------|
| Blue | Female | Mind | Water | Liquid | Cool |
| Red | Male | Body | Earth | Solid | Hot |

If we can accept this logical man-as-microcosm theory then perhaps the same principles will also apply in reverse? That is to say that before we demonstrate how man is a microcosm of the universe, let us first show how he is a *macrocosm* of the elementary particles of matter. For if we can show that we are indeed constructed thematically, physically, and socially along the same biological patterns as atoms and molecules, then the rest should more easily fall into place.

We begin then with a cursory brief on quantum physics, paying particular attention to the presence of any triadic patterns that may reflect archetypal themes. Although the following might seem a little over-technical at first, the reader should find that with the triadic archetype as a reference, and in conjunction with the referenced diagrams the material should read quite easily.

## Quantum Triads

The physical universe is comprised of atoms, which in turn are the building blocks of energy, light, and life, most notably of light. Atoms join in precisely defined clusters to form molecules. Molecules (such as carbon) then come together to form 'stuff' which we can identify as separate entities such as gases, liquids, and solids. These in turn make up our natural physical environment. With one special exception that we shall look at later, atoms in turn are comprised of three basic elements; protons, neutrons, and electrons. The protons and neutrons form the central mass of the atom in what is called the nucleus, whilst a number of electrons orbit this nucleus. So we can see that atoms are generally comprised of three constant elements; (i) protons (ii) neutrons and (iii) orbiting electrons (fig.13 ♣).

However, scientists now inform us that protons and neutrons actually contain even smaller fundamental particles within their basic structures. These are (a) up quarks, and (b) down quarks, which, like atoms, also function in quantum triads. The proton for example has two 'up' quarks and one 'down' quark, whilst the neutron has one 'up' quark and two 'down' quarks (please bear with me here). The proton and neutron, comprised thus of complimentary up and down quarks, form the nucleus of the atom around which electrons are active, which, under certain conditions emit light and/or heat. Remembering that light is the prime source of color, we thus demonstrate a multilayered triadic platform at the scientific core of color theory. And although different types of atoms have different numbers of protons and neutrons in their nuclei, the triadic principles of collaborative union between (a) two pairs of three quarks, and (b) the proton, neutron, and electron remain constant. Indeed, it could be said that the proton-neutron nucleus is itself the very 'heart' of the atom. It was the splitting of this nuclear heart for example, that gave us atomic and nuclear bombs.

We can see then, that the fundamental elements of matter; quarks, protons, neutrons and electrons operate in a series of 'quantum trinities': When protons and neutrons unite, they each bring three quarks. Thus, three plus three come together to form the nucleus, making three again. Because the (blue) neutron disintegrates as an isolated particle, the (red) proton is considered the stronger element, and the life-center of the atom. The proton if you like, is the subatomic 'anchor' to which the neutron bonds for 'her' survival. The proton and the neutron can also be read to carry 'masculine' and 'feminine' properties inasmuch as they are naturally drawn together to form a productive pair. And just as human genes are composed of shared male and female sexuality in any given individual, the intrinsic identities of the proton and neutron are likewise composed of the aforementioned shared 'up' and 'down' quarks, which carry similarly-functioning properties to human sexuality. As we see in the diagram, each unit contains a ratio of 2:1, with the stronger 'up' quarks being metaphorically equivalent to human masculinity. Thus two parts 'up' quarks and one part 'down' quark equals a masculine unit; the proton. Whilst on the other hand, the feminine neutron is comprised of only one (masculine) 'up' and two (feminine) 'down' quarks. With the electron(s) then acting as the energy-glue so-to-speak keeping this nuclear unit intact, we have a veritable subatomic triad of interconnected and interdependent triadic units fusing together to produce elementary energy. And this is where we can begin to make some cross-discipline connections. For example, in an interesting metaphorical parallel with human family dynamics; before an atom can stabilize and join other atoms to eventually become a molecule (which then becomes either gas, liquid, or solid), the proton (red) and neutron (blue) must not only bond together, but must then share their (white) light, heat, and energy-emitting electrons that are in orbit around them (white, red, and blue union). Whilst these particles are obviously too small to have physically determinable colors, they not only carry the abstract masculine, feminine, and union properties of cosmic law, but the study of the energies that bond quarks together in their elementary trinities is very interestingly called "quantum chromodynamics" a phrase, which like the word 'chromosome' indicates the presence of 'color values' in the study of the most elementary particles known to man.

In summary, atomic physics employ triadic forms, patterns, and principles, which are readily matched and reflected (macrocosmically) in human genetics, social structures, and behaviors.

## Sex and Genetics

Another connecting point between these examples and the triadic archetype (fig.14 ♣) is found in the elementary components of chromosomes and DNA (deoxyribonucleic acid). Not wishing to stretch the microscopic point too far I hesitate somewhat to enter into too much detail, especially in a field in which I am not an expert. However, a few simple facts should seal this remarkable connection between the original genetic blueprint for human life and the chromonumerics of the color spectrum.

Firstly, chromosomes are sort of 'packets of information' that determine your gender and other elementary factors. The DNA found in these chromosomes determines one's unique set of hereditary characteristics and basic personality. There are two interlocking chains in DNA known as a double helix between which are nucleotides in patterns of three, as well as genetic alphabet 'bases' in units of four. Here again we see the elementary numbers of the color spectrum and ancient cosmology clearly reflected in the genetic makeup of humans. Furthermore, the different elements of DNA seek each other out in exactly the same way as masculine and feminine do, following a union, separation, and multiplication process, just like all other binary life forms. If for any reason these formulas are disrupted, then—just as there is social fallout when we defy archetypal laws in human society—genetic mutations of some sort or another will occur. When a toxic virus such as AIDS is introduced for instance, it destroys by introducing it's own genetic code into human DNA, thus reversing the normal genetic process.

Finally, as previously mentioned color-related words such as 'chromosome' are increasingly being used to define values in quantum physics. Curious, is it not, that the very elements that determine human sexuality are named 'X' and 'Y' *chromosomes*? Furthermore, red-green color blindness and night blindness can be traced to compromised X or Y-chromosomes; another connection between light, vision, and the semantics of quantum physics. And in another remarkable connection between the sexual formulas of the triadic archetype and human sexual genetics, there is a little-known condition called *Fragile-X syndrome* wherein the learning abilities of those affected is either mildly or seriously impaired. The X chromosome in question is the female element in an X-Y pair of chromosomes that join when sperm meets egg. The fact that Fragile-X Syndrome is a learning disability, with no apparent physiological effects, suggests another connection between the feminine (blue) X chromosome and the learning process, which in turn is associated with the mind, knowledge, and wisdom; all three of which are 'feminine' traits in our triadic theory. Although we could digress into related topics in support of these facts, discussing the periodic table, atomic weights, and so on, for now the clear point to establish is the physical existence of these triadic structures containing archetypal attributes even at the most elementary physical levels known to man. So, having now hopefully made a solid point of the literal-and-physical gender-specific triadic properties of elementary matter, let us divert once again into the world of symbolism to reinforce these natural connections in the socio-religious-political sphere.

**The Individual Triadic Archetype**
Already briefly covered in previous chapters, the central theme of the human triadic formula that corresponds with white, blue, and red 'values' is the spirit-mind-body progression. This illustrates the universal law that actions (red) must be preceded by thoughts or plans (blue) which in turn must be

preceded by an idea or inspiration (white). The fundamentals of this chromonumeric law are self-evident: Concept, plan, and action.

However, the astute observer will immediately note that for the very most part we live in a world governed by masculine passions, appetites, and expressions; not only in our social orders and institutions that are mostly dominated by men, but also individually in that we are primarily driven by the 'needs of the flesh' (red), and tend to allow this sphere to dominate our intellectual, emotional, and spiritual faculties. This latter condition applies equally to women as well as to men. For as Jung explains in his observations of the animus and anima, we are all comprised of a genetic unisexuality that pervades the mind as much as it does the body. In this sense, although the female has more of the nurturing and feminine (blue) traits than her male counterpart at the foundations of her psyche, she is still dominated by her female sexuality, passions, and desires, which are associated with the physical and sensual (red) values. In this manner, although men are to be primarily identified by masculine red and women by feminine blue, they both carry the intrinsic personal triadic formula of red, blue, and white *within* their masculine or feminine-based personas. Thus, as we see in fig.11 ♣, individual human beings are walking-talking expressions of their own (functional or dysfunctional) triadic formulas, whilst simultaneously being part of the general masculine or feminine elements of the triadic principle at the collective-social level.

Comparing these principles with the atomic structure in fig 13 ♣, the white electron that binds not only proton and neutron together, but also binds families of atoms into molecules, could be likened (in ideal circumstances) to the bond of love between man (red) and woman (blue) which in turn unites human families into functioning social groups (molecules?). We will see later how these themes translate into the political symbolism discussed in Chapter One.

Corroborating this atomic-familial theme is the fact that the colors of the seven-part Tantric meditation system of yoga philosophy are not only formulated along the patterns of the color spectrum, but also correlate to the chromatic values of the personal archetypal triad (fig 11 ♣). In the practice of yoga for example, we read "Tantric experts learn from a guru how to raise their psychosexual energy (Kundalini) from the base of the spine through successive focal points (chakras)." [33] These chakras are seven mystical locations on the body where it is believed that spiritual and physical energy interrelates, ascending progressively from sexual red, through the natural range of colors, through blue, to white. Hinduism and Buddhism as well as many progressive, or 'New Age' philosophies thus credit chakras with a very high level of importance in the process of human development. From the perspective of this work, it is in their representative colors that we recognize a universal verisimilitude. In his comprehensive work *The Secret Language Of Symbols* David Fontana writes;

> Each chakra has a different color associated with it, from red, the color of raw energy in the base chakra, through progressively more spiritual colors, to white in the brow chakra. The crown (head) is sometimes represented as a blaze of brilliant color." (Haloes?) [34]

Positioned at number seven, number three, and number one respectively, and associated with human development and growth, we see here the functional aspects of the various charkas confirming the thematic and progressive characteristics of color; in particular the red, blue, and white ordered triadic concept of physical, psychological, and spiritual. In other religions too, these particular colors have definitive values and meanings. We will explore this in more detail soon, but again we see a clear ascending order of spirituality associated with the red, blue, and white sequence, with full-spectrum white or a rainbow-type blaze of colors invariably rating the highest. Thus, when the rainbow appears in a religious setting such as in auras, haloes, or chakras, it is seen as indicating a very high degree of spirituality.

The relationship of the colors of the spectrum to corresponding human attributes is further confirmation that universal symbolism simultaneously reflects both religious beliefs and scientific truths despite our relative ignorance of the fact. Adding weight to this hypothesis are the mounting volumes of scientific data confirming altered states of consciousness amongst Tantric mystics. Seen as corresponding with the human endocrine system, the various color-coded chakras are physically or mentally 'massaged' by adherents to elicit altered states of consciousness to enhance their physical well-being. Without passing express judgment upon those altered states; when a tried-and-tested spiritual system parallels our findings exactly, one is obliged to concede to the proofs. This is supported in Vijaya Kumar's *Colour Therapy* booklet where he draws specific connections not only between the color red and the physical-male, but also with blue as a moral aspect of character that "reinforces your connection to Divine intelligence." Although we may differ from place to place about how we name the Divine, it is clear that Kumar too supports our findings of the ascending progression from physical reds through conscious-thinking blues, to a higher spirituality (white).

In his best-selling book *The Power of Myth* Joseph Campbell too speaks of three 'psycho-spiritual' terms in the ancient Sanskrit language that represent the jumping-off place to transcendence: "Sat" meaning 'being', "Chit" meaning 'consciousness', and "Ananda" meaning 'bliss or rapture'. Clearly there is a parallel in this ancient and revered spiritual language with our body-through-mind progression to access a higher state of existence. Furthermore, in regard to a natural cosmic order that begins with spirit, then mind, and then body; when recognizing man's disharmonious relationship with nature, in society, and within himself, we can surmise that a disproportionate preoccupation with 'the flesh' (red) effects a disruption or reversal of the cosmic order which in turn results in a dysfunctional continuum affecting all things touched by man. This of course is one explanation for our alienation from, and ongoing destruction of the natural order. We use and abuse each other and our environment chiefly for selfish reasons because our (red) base urges dominate our thinking and our decisions. The reader will recall how this relates to our previous discussion concerning the *compromised* cosmic circle, which, in the case of humanity, is generally devoid of the (white) governing spiritual aspect. This suggests a lack of principled control over the remaining 66.6% of our natures; our psychobiological desires. (Please note the surfacing of the number 666; the Biblical 'number of the beast' in this formula). Thus we tend to operate out of selfishness, or ignorance, or both. Whatever those 'spiritual' whisperings are that echo mutely in our deep subconscious, they stand little chance of being heard above the din of worldly obsessions. Hence the emphasis upon the 'wilderness' or 'vision-quest' experience and the 'control of worldly desires' in most religions: a spiritual principle emphasized but rarely clearly explained—or even understood for that matter. Evidenced in such practices as fasting, celibacy, tithing, meditation, and pilgrimages, this 'denial of the flesh' tenet, central to practically all of the world's major faith traditions is a key component in the preparation for the true religious experience, and the true spiritual quest. But it is *not* the only way (nor necessarily even the best way) to access the higher consciousness. This is a most important point to note, and will serve as the basis for later discussions on the merits, and remedial potential of triadic psychospiritual systems.

**The Biblical Triadic Archetype**
Having already alluded to the masculine and feminine symbolism present in the pages of the Christian Bible in the pillars of fire and cloud, the burning

bush, and the tongues of fire at Pentecost (12 ♣), let us move directly to probably the most intriguing and convincing evidence so far for the perennial existence of these universal archetypes in the religious realm. Because of all the psychospiritual evidence of a cosmic, universal plan, perhaps none is quite so compelling as the colors, numbers, symbols, and patterns to be found surrounding the three central, and interrelated symbols of faith in ancient Judaism; (i) the Ark of the Covenant, (ii) the Tabernacle, and (iii) the Temple of Solomon. Never before recognized in any publications,* the sheer weight of evidence is so overwhelming, and the information so pertinent today that one wonders indeed if noumenal hand(s) are not still coordinating the release of this information..?

This rather bold comment is not being made from a faith-based perspective, but rather from a purely practical viewpoint that recognizes the historical value of documents that were written thousands of years ago and as such, carry the psychic signatures of ancient societies. The added fact that many of these texts comprise the foundational scriptures for more than two-thirds of the world's religious adherents today (Judaism, Christianity, and Islam) surely requires that we afford them a little extra attention.

We might also accord extra credibility to these texts based upon the scientific accuracy of what we are about to read. Whilst a little too voluminous to engage in depth here today, the reader is cordially encouraged to visit Tony Badillo's *Solomon's Temple* website for some fascinating supporting findings related specifically to sexual, archetypal symbolism.[35] We will review some of this material in more depth in Volume Two, but for now, as we summarize the key points of ancient Hebrew symbolism the reader is invited to open their hearts and minds to the distinct probability that however the biblical patriarchs and prophets communicated with their God Jehovah, they were certainly 'tuning in' to the principles of the triadic archetype in the process. This being a methodical work, we will of course endeavor to prove our points rather than expect the reader to leap to any preemptive conclusions. To achieve this goal, we now review a short but relevant fragment from my own research, edited for brevity, which illustrates triadic chromo-dynamics in the history and structures of the Ark of the Covenant, the Tabernacle, and the Temple:

> ...the Ark of the Covenant, the Tabernacle, and later the Temple, were all structures of worship that were constructed following precise 'instructions from God' – the details of

---

* To the best of the author's knowledge

which are recorded in The Bible in the Book of Numbers. ... The Ark of the Covenant was a portable box-like article that could be carried by four men. ...The Tabernacle was a sort of temporary temple made out of tent-like materials erected in the wilderness, and the more famous Temple (of Solomon) was the later-erected permanent center of the Hebrew faith. All three were central symbolic focal points of the Hebrew faith for a period spanning 1400 years, from the time of Moses, through David, until the final destruction of The Temple by the Romans in 70 CE.

The Ark of the Covenant was covered with pure gold inside and out, with the figures of two golden cherubim on top of the lid. ...These golden cherubim formed a triangular space between them with their wings, and it was in this space that God would reportedly 'appear' to Moses, or to the High Priest. This triangular area was known as "The Mercy Seat". Inside the Ark itself rested "The Law" given by God to Moses. From Bible records, we know that the Ark was to be carried before the people of Israel in their wilderness journeys, led by the mystical column of either fire or cloud, but only to be carried by purified individuals. ...The Tent of the Tabernacle served the Israelites as the home for the Ark of The Covenant, and was the symbolic center of their faith for about four hundred years until the time of King David. This Tabernacle, (unlike the tabernacles in Catholic Churches today), was a large, semi-permanent enclosure, made to specific dimensions that housed the Ark. It was like a courtyard, partially covered by a tent. Whenever the Israelites set up camp, this Tent of the Tabernacle would be erected to house the Ark, and serve as the center of worship. The movement of the column of fire, or the pillar of cloud that rested above the Tabernacle, was the mystical-yet-substantial signal for the Israelites to break camp and move to another location. (Exodus 40:36). Interestingly enough, the Bible reports that there were forty such locations during Moses' time in the wilderness.

Solomon inherited the instructions for the building of the Temple from his father, King David. He set about building what must have been the most magnificent structure ever seen in Jerusalem, if not in the whole of the ancient world. Much of the interior was plated with Gold, Silver, and precious stones, according to the 'instructions of God' to David, and the exterior was constructed of huge, pure white blocks, mirroring the white fabric fence that previously surrounded the Tabernacle...

...and here we uncover some very interesting facts indeed, because not only were each of these constructs made to very exact, and symbolically-significant dimensions, but for some never-before-explained reason, Moses, David, and Solomon, who each served as leader of the Israelites for an interesting forty years also received specific directions about which *colors* to use in all the structural features. This ranged from the white color of the fence surrounding the Tabernacle, and the white exterior of the Temple, to the remarkable fact that only four colors were chosen for all the material coverings and priestly vestments. Would anyone like to guess? Those four colors were white, blue, red, and purple. Without offering any explanation whatsoever, the Bible records the use of these specific colors time after time following 'direct instructions from God' in all manner of sacred rites, rituals, and functions. This included their use on the coverings of the Tabernacle, the gates of the Temple, and even the colors of the sacred veil in the Holy of Holies itself. Both the abstract color-symbolism and the physical structures themselves reflect a stunning consistency. The very design of the Temple for instance is homologous with human biology, as are certain features of the Ark and the Tabernacle analogous to human growth and sexual maturity (see 18 ♣). Although being covered in greater detail in later volumes the pillars of the Temple for example, crowned by multi-seeded pomegranates, and the entrances to the Temple and the Holy of Holies are seeped in powerful sexual symbolism. Likewise, the architectural progression from Tabernacle to Temple includes the addition of priestly chambers that extend alongside the body of the Temple leading into the Holy of Holies that could arguably represent the female fallopian tubes absent from the more 'juvenile' Tabernacle design. All of which strongly suggest a 'growing-to-maturity' theme in the design of these cultural icons that matches a woman's natural development before receiving her spouse or; perhaps a nation playing the feminine archetypal role to a masculine deity? This would account for the oft-repeated term "my daughter Zion" spoken on God's behalf by the prophets:

What thing shall I liken to thee, O daughter of Jerusalem? What shall I equal to thee, that I may comfort thee, O virgin daughter of Zion? (Lamentations 2:13) [36]

Then there are the parallels with atomic structure; 'white' electrons enclosing a 'blue-and-red' nucleus, just as the white fence of the Tabernacle and the white walls of the Temple enclosed a host of red-and-blue, masculine-and-feminine themes. The numeric correlation between the 1400 years of the existence of these three central icons and the sum of the nanometer measurements of the color spectrum could of course be pure happenstance once again, but when considered along with the red, white, blue, and purple décor not only suggests an archetypal theme behind these historical icons, but also implies an archetypal author of the same. Whether this is understood in a religious or scientific sense is of course a matter for further debate. The astute reader may have noted that the additional presence of purple is on account of it being a mixture of red, white, and blue, and therefore can be observed to symbolize the unified archetypal 'royal family' of white, blue, and red.[*] Or, the restoration of the cosmic circle; the symbolic reunion of God (white, holy, spiritual) with his newly-restored children, both masculine and feminine: God, Eve, and Adam; white, blue and red; spirit, mind and body… a truly 'Holy' Trinity perhaps?

*   *   *

As we now wrap up this brief study of archetypal phenomena in science and Holy Scripture perhaps it is a good time to display a few facts and figures concerning the many appearances of colors in the Bible, which is obviously central to our efforts to link the Judeo-Christian—and to a certain extent the Islamic religious world—with our central theories. After all, for all we know there could be numerous other colors mentioned just as frequently in the Bible which would make much of what's being reported here relatively insignificant. But of course that's not the case. Of the other key colors referenced in this work, purple is mentioned in the Bible twenty-eight times in fourteen books. Black and blackness appears in twelve books a total of twenty-three times. Green appears in nineteen different books but nearly always as an adjective, and brown only appears four times in the Book of Genesis alone. The color gray gets mentioned in four books, yellow only

---

[*] With the exception of mixing red, white, and blue--resulting in purple; mixing color pigments will have a different outcome to mixing colored lights.

twice, and 'speckled' three times. Of the colors orange, pink, indigo, violet, maroon, turquoise, cyan, lavender, teal, plum, auburn, blonde, peach, khaki, tan, beige, lemon, lime, mauve, or 'mottled' there isn't a sign (did I miss any?) But gold, silver and brass on the other hand, as ornamental entities and not necessarily as colors, are frequently spoken of. The symbolism of these three metals also generally aligns with the triadic archetype; especially the masculine-feminine partnership between golden sun and silver moon, but to enter into too much research in that direction at this point would not prove practical, and so we must leave that topic for another day.

We will later review more specific examples of the colors white, blue, and red in the context of world religions. But for now we should note that when viewing the above data from a purely statistical perspective, especially when compared with the seventy-four entries of white in twenty-three different books, and the one-hundred-and-twelve entries of red, scarlet or crimson in thirty-eight books; it is plainly obvious that the two-hundred-and-forty combined entries of red, white and blue indicate the special significance of these three colors not only in Judeo-Christian scriptures, but also in any future psychospiritual-chromatic theory.

What is also very interesting from a subliminal-symbolic perspective is that there is no mention whatsoever of the (feminine) color blue in the New Testament despite the fact that blue is the third most mentioned color in the Bible as a whole. Is it just pure coincidence one wonders, that both the New Testament and early Christianity were distinctly patriarchal and authoritarian?

When we match this information with what we have learnt so far one begins to suspect the inklings of a profound and universal connection... and believe it or not, we haven't even really got going yet!

# CHAPTER SEVEN

# COLOR, MYTH, & RELIGION

*We will now explore the symbolic values of the colors white, blue, and red specific to mythology and world religions. Following this, we will consolidate our findings concerning the substantial existence of universal archetypes by readdressing our conclusions so far directly to the comparative sphere of world religions, in an effort to discern the validity of the triadic archetype in this historically-fractious field.*

Although it may appear I am belaboring the point by presenting so many examples of the triadic archetype in varied settings, we should remember that this is a recent and previously unpublished discovery, and therefore requires solid proofs for the hypothesis. Secondly, because the very credibility of the hypothesis hinges upon its universality we must also establish the comprehensiveness of the triadic archetype phenomenon. And finally and regrettably, because we each now have to deal daily with the militant excesses of religion in particular—at least in the news if not personally—I feel it is incumbent to present as wide-ranging a proof as possible in order to present a truly convincing argument of universal synchronicity. Hopefully, this may one day help to diffuse longstanding and combative, religious, and socio-political attitudes.

So let us now search within religion and mythology for any symbolic indicators that will help discern the integrity of contemporary religious traditions in relation to the triadic archetype. Any such review (provided of course it is accurate) should be of immeasurable value in identifying and evaluating the respective 'cosmic balance' of our respective faith traditions, as well as supplying useful insights into the collective psychospiritual health of society, both past and present.

## Religion and Myth

Although considered by some to be merely silly fairy-stories or legends, ancient myths are nonetheless intimately intertwined with contemporary religious thought. Indeed, the more one learns about mythology and religion the more difficult it is to differentiate between them, and so it should be. Those that argue that ancient mythologies and modern religions differ in credibility, validity, or even general orthodoxy are (I regret to say) either ill informed or selectively ignorant; since any cursory examination of cultural myths will invariably expose the central tenets, mysteries, and sacramental aspects of our modern faith traditions in some form or another. This is not an opinion, but a fact. A fact moreover, whose recognition and acceptance will contribute greatly to the ultimate diffusion of *sectarian* * neuroses.[37]

This indisputable fusion of myth and religion confirms two very important points: Firstly it challenges the validity of exclusive or sectarian doctrines (either secular or religious) and secondly, it strongly supports the Universal Truth hypothesis. Taken to the next level, this naturally leads us to the conclusion that *all* fundamental or intrinsic truths are indeed united at source. As previously implied, the only reason we haven't yet arrived at this consensus is because of the ongoing and debilitating condition of collective human ignorance that fosters the development of neurotic traditions (such as sectarian religions or ethnic-elitist political movements for instance), and encourages infantile and fear-based dependency upon society's authoritarian institutions. Nevertheless, as we learn more and more of the properties of science, anthropology, history, sociology, cosmology, mathematics, art, religion, politics, and so on…. we will it seems, be drawn to the inevitable conclusion that all our various categories and classification systems— including ancient myths and modern religions—are *at best*, simple and limited glimpses of one great Universal Truth. A Universal Truth whose principles at least in part, are reflected in the colors and numbers of the electromagnetic spectrum; which in turn—to a greater or lesser degree— comprise the documented values, themes, and symbols of our triadic archetype. Hence, the archetypal formulas presented in this work are ultimately just newly-visible manifestations of those immutable cosmic laws and processes that we violate individually or collectively to our peril. Just as the relative balance and/or completeness of the triad of white, blue, and red 'values' in science and society consistently match the character of the subject(s) under scrutiny; the same rules generally apply to religious symbolism.

---

* Sectarian: Partisan; divided; biased; narrow-minded; parochial; dogmatic

In the following brief overview that continues into Chapter Eight we will discover that in the acceptance or rejection of universal truth-formulas as defined in this work, each of the various religions tend to reflect appropriate symbolism. In other words, despite long and often convoluted traditions, the universal triadic archetype has borne subliminal witness to itself in each tradition's symbolism; either through its presence or its absence.

In particular, we note the widespread omission of blue symbolism amongst those radical or militant ideologies where feminine socio-political traits are absent (♣ 4, 7, 17, 27). This is not only reflected through matching symbolism (red, or red-black replacing blue for example), but is also typically associated with the existence or development of authoritarian and/or sectarian attitudes. These attitudes in turn are usually reinforced by an oppressive intellectual dogmatism, projected and/or protected by a militant arm or agency.

In the case of Middle Ages Christianity for instance, we see both the Dominican Inquisitors and the Teutonic Knights carrying out their often-gruesome tasks under black-colored banners (see fig.20 ♣). Later, we note the fuller inclusion of triadic symbolism amongst post-reformation Protestant sects who rejected the patriarchal and authoritarian features of the Roman Catholic tradition in favor of a more democratic, community-based model of church (fig.21 ♣). Although there are some exceptions, we also see these same symbolic leanings in those modern religions with a *truly* familial, humanistic, or natural bent, such as several tribal or New Age religions, or in those traditions rooted in ancient philosophies (fig.22 ♣). Even in the more mystical sects of patriarchal institutions such as Islamic Sufism, we see the emergence of more feminine symbolism. In Judaism's mystical Kabalistic teachings for example there are several color, symbol, and pattern line-ups in the mystical 'tree of life' that can be aligned with the triadic archetype, including the upper-central triad of *Keter*, *Choma*, and *Binah* representing God and female and male archetypes respectively (19 ♣). The three upper 'wheels' of the central column also follow appropriate chromatic propriety and align with chakras in similar positions in the Buddhist tradition. In conjunction with the two thematic gender-specific pillars labeled "the pillar of mercy" and "the pillar of severity" that undoubtedly relate to the aforementioned pillars of Solomon's Temple and the Tabernacle's pillar of fire and pillar cloud respectively (♣ 12, 18), there is sufficient material to produce a very convincing triadic Kabalistic theme that matches the characteristics of our own triadic archetype. Not least of which is the red-white-blue triangle topping the design.

In the *Zohar* too, which is amongst the leading texts of Kabalism, we read that parts of the human soul or psyche are comprised of a triad named (i) *nefesh*, (ii) *ru'ach*, and (iii) *neshamah*. Although technically dealing purely with the soul of man, they nevertheless match the triadic archetype in their intrinsic definitions as we see from the Gurunet / Wikipedia article on Kabalism, edited here for brevity:

> (i) Nefesh; the lower part, or animal part, of the soul. Is linked to instincts and bodily cravings.

> (ii) Ruach; the middle soul, the spirit. It contains the moral virtues and the ability to distinguish between good and evil.

> (iii) Neshamah; the higher soul, or super-soul. This separates man from all other lifeforms. It ..allows man to enjoy and benefit from the afterlife. It allows one ...awareness of the existence and presence of God.[38]

Clearly, there are parallels here that match our central theories, but it also needs to be said that the Kabala itself has undergone changes, additions, and adjustments through the ages arguably even since the time of Christ, and is therefore far too complex and involved for us to investigate in detail today. However, speaking both from a chromatic as well as a psychological perspective, I do believe that the Kabala as displayed in popular diagrams may respectfully, be ever so slightly out of alignment with cosmic norms.[39] The pillars of mercy and severity for example, that presumably relate to (a) the Tree of Knowledge and the Tree of Life; (b) to the Biblical pillars of cloud and fire; and (c) to the pillars of Solomon's Temple representing feminine and masculine properties respectively; do seem to have some of their symbols and characteristics inaccurately positioned – at least according to the norms of the triadic archetype. But the color symbolism on the other hand is uncannily accurate, with the pillar of mercy colored in feminine blues and greens, whilst the pillar of severity incorporates mainly masculine reds. So despite the aforementioned minor critique there are certainly enough similarities in the Kabala to align it convincingly with the triadic archetype. But that discussion must be left for another day. Enough to identify for now the consistency of gender-specific themes and symbols that generally correlate to the dynamics of the color spectrum in probably one of the most respected and fastest-growing mystical religious traditions worldwide.

Perhaps I should reiterate at this point that we are chiefly concerned with establishing the intrinsic presence of the triadic archetype in the world's most popular faith traditions and mythologies, showing that we can indeed trace certain themes and principles all the way back into antiquity. But because of the nature of religion; because it has been fashioned and shaped over the centuries by many overt and covert social forces, it is extremely unlikely that we will see an exact replica of the triadic archetype in any given tradition today. Indeed, this I believe is what lies at the heart of so much historical animosity between the differing faiths. For if we were indeed all in agreement about the fundamentals, and didn't give ourselves over so easily to superstition and conjecture, or to the need to defend our longstanding mythic traditions, perhaps we would all be arriving at the same conclusions simultaneously? But perhaps that's too idealistic a view. All the same, there are some pretty close representations to be seen, most notably in the Buddhist 'AUM' mantra; in the Vedic chakra system; in the Hindu Trimurti; and in the Christian notion of Trinity, to name but a few examples.

Because of its centrality to the main *monotheistic* [*] traditions, we will enter into additional detail concerning the appearance of specific colors in the Bible which I hope you will agree is not only very interesting (as it hasn't been done in this context before), but is also very significant when we regard the Bible both as a historical document as well as a work of scripture that is central to the beliefs of so many. So, as we review the religious and mythological realms from our new informed perspective, the reader will kindly excuse any repetition of facts previously presented as we reemphasize these important symbolic, thematic, and historical connections. Please also remain alert to appearances of our central numbers; three, four, and seven, and multiples thereof.

## White in Religion

Reinforcing our previous findings that white represents spiritual health we discover that in ancient Celtic mythology, white bulls, white clad priests, and white mistletoe were the center of a special 'cure-all' rite. This ties in with the mystical traditions of ancient Greece and Rome, whose oracles, sages and vestal virgins reportedly dressed in white. In like manner, Hindus consider white to be the color of self-illumination, whilst the closely-related Buddhist tradition deems white to be the color of self-mastery; a state that indicates a developing spirituality. For Native Americans white is symbolic of peace and happiness, and the ancient Egyptians considered white to

---

[*] Monotheism; doctrine or belief that there is only one God

represent joy. Even in traditional occultism and magic circles the color white typically represents healing, blessing, truth, peace, purity and protection.

Respected religious scholar Elaine Pagels notes that the Judaic sect of the *Essenes* who lived in first century Palestine and are rumored to have been John-the-Baptist's and possibly also Jesus' own religious community, called themselves the "sons of light" and reportedly dressed only in white.[40] Not so surprisingly this parallels Hebrew and Christian traditions where we read that the Priestly Levite tribe were arrayed in white "singing God's praises" in the Temple of Solomon (II Chronicles 5:12). The High Priest could only be clothed in white garments whenever he entered the Holy of Holies most notably on the occasion of Yom Kippur, the annual feast of atonement and repentance for the Jews. Other mentions of white in the Bible include the obvious connection with light, such as God's reported first words in the creation story "Let there be Light!" (Gen 1:3), as well as other mentions in the Psalms; where God "covers Himself with light as with a garment" (Ps 104:2), or in the description of the "likeness of the glory of Jehovah" which Ezekiel sees in a mystical vision, paraphrased here from *Insight on the Scriptures Vol 2*:

> I got to see something like the glow of electrum, like the appearance of fire... and he had a brightness all around. There was something like the appearance of the bow that occurs in a cloud mass on the day of a pouring rain. That was how the appearance was of the brightness round about.[41] (Ezekiel 1:27-28)

Here we should note the presence of the rainbow and the association with (feminine) water in the mystical language of Ezekiel. In Daniel 7:9 "The Ancient of Days" (God) is also clothed in white. Whilst in Ecclesiastes 9:8 white garments again signify goodness. All signifying religious associations between white and the Divine. White is also mentioned in association with primary sustenance through the miraculous delivery of the manna, the food God sent to his people in the desert (Ex 16:31).

In the New Testament too, we have the Holy Spirit pictured as a (white) dove descending upon Jesus, which of course has more than just metaphoric associations with the dove of Noah's Ark who similarly launched out to restart the new world four-hundred years before Abraham. Christ is also described as appearing "white as the light" during his miraculous transfiguration on the Mount. Matthew informs us that the Easter Angel too was 'clothed in white'. In John's gospel, two angels are placed at the same scene dressed in white, and in Acts 1:10 two mystical "men in white" are present at Jesus' ascension into Heaven.

In the book of Revelation, white as a color is mentioned eighteen separate times, so for the sake of brevity we will just list the central themes: There are the multitudes 'clothed in white' signifying either the faithful on earth "like righteous saints" or the "armies of heaven" who follow the "Son of Man" whose hair is white (symbolic of spiritual wisdom) suspended on white clouds; or, he who is "Faithful and True" riding on his white horse. A white stone is read to symbolize the Christ-figure, whilst 'twenty-four elders dressed in white' sit in judgment in heaven. There are another seven angels in white, and the "Wife of The Lamb" is also arrayed in white. And finally, the last entry in the Bible alluding to white is God's heavenly throne of judgment. All in all I believe, a solid ratification in the Bible of our central premise that white typically symbolizes high spirituality, true religion (an admittedly tough one to define), and the direction of union with God.

Although not officially recognizing religious icons or symbolism, in the Qur'an and other Islamic writings the word 'white' is regularly used in place of 'dawn' or 'daylight' as well as in the form of white animals, birds, or clothing that represent goodness in opposition to 'sinful' black. The red-black sacred stone of the Kabba,* Islam's holiest shrine, is traditionally believed to have originated as a white celestial stone (please note the previous paragraph) which has been turned black by the sins of man. There is also an eschatological belief that at the 'final hour' believers will be lead by the prophet Muhammad to quench their thirst forever by drinking from *al-kawthar*, a vast lake of sweet-tasting white liquid. Tradition also relates a story when the boy Muhammad was mystically cleansed of original sin in the desert by two men in white (angels) holding a "golden bowl full of snow".[42] But when legend and fact merge with strong religious convictions is, as always, an intriguing but problematic issue.

Sufism, the mystical branch of Islam operates somewhat outside of the orthodox box, using music, singing, and ecstatic spinning in its spiritual forms and rituals. Not surprisingly, its symbolism also departs from Islamic norms (fig.22 ♣). Perhaps the most famous examples are the white-robed 'whirling dervishes' of Turkish Sufism. The prophet Muhammad himself was often described as being 'dressed in white', as were angels who assisted him in battle, and there is a reported white stallion that reportedly carried him to heaven from the Temple Mount in Jerusalem. Interestingly, record is

---

* Kabba; the main temple-shrine in Mecca, Saudi Arabia. Not to be confused with the Cabala (sometimes spelt 'Kabala' or 'Kabbala'); the book and philosophy of Jewish mysticism

also made in Islamic texts of the time when God allocated a white standard (flag) to Adam, and a black one to Iblis (Satan), representing the earthly battle between good and evil – which in turn was handed down to Abel and Cain and their descendants respectively.[43] This is of particular interest to us not only because it confirms the Cain-and-Abel dynamic in pre-*and*-post Abrahamic history (this will be covered in Volume Two), but also because the armies of 7th century Islam were subsequently recorded as flying black or green flags in battle. Interestingly, Muhammad's own personal standard was an all-black flag that sometimes exhibited a falcon in its center. In a *providential* [*] context, this *could* of course be symbolic confirmation of the Muslim-Arab world's traditional 'Cain' position in relation to Judeo-Christianity. But caution must be exercised here. We should remember that the 'Cain' position is the position of direct providential struggle—the 'older son' position with the authority to either comply or destroy—and thus may respond in either direction; either good or evil. Of course, we would still expect the symbolism to follow suit. Caution before judgment however should remain the rule of thumb.

In contrast to the disciplined orthodoxies of the monotheistic Abrahamic traditions, Hinduism, with its abundant proliferation of colorful deities is religious amorphism defined. Yet in spite of its apparent lack of theological constraint, in certain key areas Hindu symbolism still adheres to archetypal chromatic principles. Vedic texts for example associate white with 'nirvana' (ultimate peace), as well as with the crown chakra. It is also generally understood to represent goodness, purity, and spiritual wisdom, just as in Buddhism, Sikhism, and Zoroastrianism.

In contemporary religious understandings of the color white, spiritual healer Edgar Cayce says that white is the perfect aura. "If our souls were in perfect balance, then all our color vibrations would blend and we would have an aura of pure white."[44] Using religious terminology, chromatist Betty Wood describes white as associated with "wholeness, purity, and innocence and is a most sacred color, (representing) ..spiritual authority."[45]

Therefore we may conclude that when the color white appears in religion or mythology, it has traditionally represented God, spirituality, goodness, wholeness, and purity. Not so surprisingly, these are the same general themes found in our study of color in science and history, only with a slightly differing reading and vocabulary.

---

[*] Providential; pertaining to a Divine plan for human history

## Blue in Religion

In mythology and ancient religions, blue has always held a special place as the color of the heavens, and of the sea, and through association, the Moon and the archetypal mother figure. The Greek goddess Demeter was clothed in a blue cloak for example; a tradition carried on in Catholic images of the Virgin Mary. Whilst in Celtic mythology blue was the color of the bard or poet-minstrel, which also has feminine-emotional overtones. Supporting this feminine / maternal / emotional / contemplative theme; in the Kabalistic tradition (Jewish mysticism) blue is the color of mercy, whilst in Buddhist thought blue is the color of wisdom (again). The Cherokee Indians have a saying; "He is entirely blue" which is the equivalent of the emotional 'feeling blue' concept in modern English.

In the Bible the feminine theme is also closely affiliated with the color blue especially in rituals associated with Israel's preparation as a bride for the Messiah. From Exodus 25:4 through 39:31 blue is mentioned thirty-four times in association with fine finishing work associated with the priestly vestments, and with the Tent of the Tabernacle. We will see later how the Tabernacle itself carries a profound sexual theme that can be read to symbolize the development of the pubescent female – seen as a mature female in the symbolism of Solomon's Temple (Fig.18 ♣).

In Numbers 4: 6-12 "cloths of blue" are mentioned several times in reference to wrapping sacred items and covering the altar with the food for offering to God. There are also two possible references to an association of blue with "whoredom" in Numbers 15:38, and Ezekiel 23:6, where we find blue affiliated with both the memory of whoredom and with the act of adultery. But whether there is a direct connection to the acts of adultery and prostitution as opposed to a general connection with 'feminine sexuality' is an arguable point. Regardless, this does not necessarily challenge but instead can be read to support the overall feminine theme of the color blue in scripture. As we have already shown, blue also featured in the Tabernacle and in the building of Solomon's Temple along with red, white, and purple (II Chronicles 2). The only other references to blue in the Bible are descriptive of clothing and sails, yet the color blue is not mentioned at all in the New Testament – an omission that bears subliminal witness amongst other things to the distinct patriarchy of early Christianity.

In Islamic writings, the Sufi disciples of Sheikh Hassan Asrakpush dressed only in blue garments considering this to be a reflection of the color of heaven. Blue turbans too, were the mark of the philosopher. But apart from this particular sect's use of the color, blue is noticeably absent in the Qur'an and in Rumi's *Mathnavi* is even regarded a sign of hypocrisy, although this is possibly for its association with the abovementioned sect who were frowned upon by the orthodox Muslim establishment of the day.[46] A tradition amongst Arabs to this day is to paint the doors of their houses blue to ward of the 'evil eye'. Considered a heavenly color, blue is believed to carry spiritual powers, but legend also associates this 'evil eye' with the blue-eyed Crusaders who wrought such devastation amongst Middle Ages Muslims and Jews. Observing the distinct lack of blue in traditional Islamic iconography and political colors, we should of course note that strict Islamic rule is generally considered an oppressive system, particularly of the (blue) feminine elements of the psyche, and of the (blue) female population.

In our observations in Chapter Seven we concluded that blue moves us towards the more spiritual aspects of life and away from the physical level. Also "spiritually stimulating," blue is "the color of the soul, and of purity." Cayce reiterates these concepts stating that "blue has always been the color of the spirit, the symbol of contemplation, prayer and heaven". Referring to diagram 24 ♣, we see that the emotional-spiritual realm occupied by the mind, psyche, and soul moves progressively from blue towards spiritual white as we move away from selfish individuality towards a collective spirituality. This not only matches Cayce's understanding of the soul's blue value, but underscores the chromatic connection between the color red and selfishness, passion and desires, and flesh-centered masculine properties; whilst the more contemplative and spiritual values are associated with the colors blue and white. Furthermore, it reinforces the theoretical connection between the natural (ideal) development of the human being—spirit, mind, and body—vs. the obvious imbalances we see in society today.

Betty Wood describes the values connected to blue as "truth, revelation, wisdom, loyalty, fertility, constancy, and chastity"; concepts also reflected in traditional heraldry that likewise attributes the values of truth and loyalty to blue. Not surprisingly, Wood also connects this color with "the raising of consciousness to a spiritual level" and "the feminine principle, the Great Mother,.. comfort, peace, compassion, and healing" – further confirmation of the archetypal association linking the color blue and the feminine. In an interesting note concerning healing Wood adds that blue "is only superceded by its higher counterpart.. indigo, the ray of spirituality" (sometimes read as violet or purple).[47] This supports our understanding that purple, as a mixture of white, blue, and red, ranks high in symbolic importance, approaching equal status with white; in that it can represent the harmonious conjunction of spirit, mind, and body as seen in the symbolism of Solomon's Temple and in the notion of a unified cosmic 'royal family' comprising God (white), cosmic man (red), and cosmic woman (blue).

**Red in Religion**

Of the three colors covered here red is both the most dramatic and, in certain ways, the most ambiguous to define. This is because in a chiefly male-dominated history red is representative of a much broader range of behaviors and themes. In addition, as the color of the basest urges and emotions, and as representative of the physical over the psycho-spiritual, red has a far more prevalent and well-developed symbolism in society than its less-dominant psychological (blue) and spiritual (white) counterparts. This will be explained fully in a moment, but for now, in reading the following definitions of red in religion the reader should not be too perturbed at the apparent breadth of diversity amongst the associated themes. For, from heroes to demons, and from military might to martyrdom, the overall theme of masculinity and physicality remains throughout.

In mythology red regularly surfaces as the traditional color of the hero such as in the color of Hercules' cloak (Greek and Roman), or Cuchulain's cloak (Celtic), both of whom suffer remarkably similar adventures to the archetypal Greek hero Prometheus and another counterpart; Odin of Norse legend. The pattern of being tied to a rock or tree and being wounded or attacked by ravens or eagles (representing evil or Satan), is common throughout. Journeying to the underworld and shedding blood in a sacrificial act is also familiar to these and other religious figures such as the ancient Persian god Mithras who strongly influenced Roman Christology. Of course, the same themes are intriguingly present in the passion of Christ, who incidentally also wears a scarlet cloak in the gospel of Matthew before being marched to his crucifixion and later descent to the underworld (hell). In the Old Testament, the prophet Elijah too—arguably *the* most important of the Hebrew prophets—leaves his red mantle behind for his successor Elisha after ascending miraculously to heaven. Obviously, the red mantle in this case is a metaphor for Elijah's messianic-type masculine mission. Red was also the color of Set, the typhoon god of the ancient Egyptians, underlining a connection with masculine force, or power.

Supporting these themes, oriental philosophy places the red chakra at the base of the spine where it is considered 'the root' and source of physical energy – especially sexual energy. Red is also associated with (red) earth, which in turn translates into the word 'Adam' in Hebrew. In Native American tradition, *Lone Man* (or Adam) set up a totem pole and painted it red at the beginning of time, whilst in Cherokee symbolism red is symbolic of success in war, in play, and in love, and was the color of both the war-club and the shield. According to legend the messianic 'Red Robe' will return one day to liberate the Native Americans and restore them to their rightful heritage. Edgar Cayce tells us that in ancient symbolism 'red represented the body' (as opposed to the mind-spirit), whilst in his closing color chart Cayce gives us the three words; 'force', 'vigor' and 'energy' to define red. In occultism too, red is again associated with lust, strength, courage, power, health, energy and vitality.

In the monotheistic Sikh tradition, just as in our earlier findings red is symbolic of egotism and selfish sensuality. Whereas in the Muslim Qur'an, Muhammad is regularly described in conjunction with red tents or clothing, appropriate for a man of high position in a patriarchy. In the increasingly popular Baha'i faith, which emerged out of Islam in 1844, the prophet-patriarch Baha'u'llah is understood by adherents to be the manifestation of the aforementioned 'Red Robe'. This title originated in the legend of an Adamic robe made by God in the Garden of Eden which was subsequently passed through a chain of biblical hero-figures that included Enoch, Noah, Shem, Abraham and Moses; as well as prophet-messengers from other faiths such as Krishna, Buddha, Zoroaster, Jesus, Muhammad, and the Baha'i's own founding prophet, the Bab. In Baha'i texts, mention is also made of the fact that Baha'u'llah actually wore a red robe all his life.[48]

In the Bible the words red, crimson and scarlet appear over a hundred times, beginning with the aforementioned reference to Adam meaning "red earth" in Hebrew. As with white, there are two main uses of these words—either descriptive or symbolic—or a combination of both. In relation to future discussions about the archetypal hero-type roles of key personalities in history, legend and myth, it is especially important here to maintain focus as we explore the significance of the following:

In Genesis 25:25 Esau, one of Isaac's twin sons, is described as "red all over" at birth, and red is intriguingly mentioned once again as the color of the food given by Jacob in exchange for Esau's birthright. Because Jacob and Esau are amongst the founding ancestors of the Arabs and the Jews their stories bear special import, especially when we consider how the associated colors align exactly with archetypal themes. This will be discussed in more detail in Volume Two. Later, when Tamar gives birth to Judah's twin sons Pharez and Zarah (descendants of Jacob), Zarah sticks his hand out of the womb first and a red thread is tied to it (Gen 28:39). Why red one might ask? This too has significant symbolic meaning connected to Semitic lineage. In Isaiah 1:18 sins are described as "scarlet" and "red like crimson" and in Isaiah 63:1-2, red garments denote might, power, and greatness. "Mighty and valiant men" (soldiers) dress in scarlet in Nahum 2:3, whilst a red rope is used to save Joshua's spies in Joshua 2. In II Samuel 1: 24, and Proverbs 31 scarlet clothing is a sign of material prosperity, which is further reflected in the book of Daniel where the dream interpreter is "rewarded with scarlet". The one notable mention of red in the gospels and the only time Jesus is associated with red, is the aforementioned occasion when Jesus is mocked as a king in the scarlet robe during his torture, but interestingly, in the other gospels Jesus' robe is purple. The division of this garment amongst the soldiers at his crucifixion is of course representational of the physical defeat of the cosmic hero-figure of the day.

In spite of its obscure mystical language the Book of Revelation remains an official part of the Christian Bible, and some religious scholars continue to believe that the symbolic language contained therein does indeed have contemporary value. It should be noted however, that the six symbolic mentions of red and scarlet in the Book of Revelation are open to a wide variety of subjective interpretations, and as such have been the source of considerable acrimonious debate as differing groups interpret the allegorical language according to their own sectarian leanings. However, with the proofs of this work to guide us, connections with historical or contemporary figures or institutions can hopefully be more accurately discerned – depending of course on whether or not one believes literally in Bible prophecy in the first place. Many have argued quite convincingly that prophecy in effect countermands human responsibility, and therefore is literally impossible if man indeed has such a thing as 'free will'. "If the Bible already predicts world events" they ask, "then what's the point or purpose of having choices?" Or if primordial cosmic 'patterns' such as the triadic archetype actually dictate the course of history, then where does personal responsibility come into play? Interesting questions indeed. But a debate we must, for the sake of clarity and expediency, save for later.

What is clear however, is that when it comes to apocalyptic literature there are many differing interpretations on the table. With a little imagination for instance, any of the upcoming figurative descriptions from the Book of Revelation could well be applied to political or religious institutions both past and current that appear in this book. Among possible candidates for these allegorical entities are certain features of; (i) the Imperial Roman Empire, (ii) the Holy Roman Empire, (iii) Roman Catholicism, (iv) Christianity, (v) Communism, (vi) Fascism, (vii) Protestant Fundamentalism, (viii) Islam, (ix) authoritarianism, or (x) secular materialism. Depending upon one's cultural, political, or religious position, there is quite a selection of potential 'bad guys' to choose from here.

For instance; there is the 'red horse' with the great sword that will "take peace from the earth" in Rev 6:4; or the 'red dragon' in Rev 12:3 that fights with Michael the Archangel and wants to "devour the child" (savior). Or, the 'woman dressed in scarlet', sitting on a scarlet beast who is "the mother of all harlots" and a great threat to God's people. If one is a Christian democrat for instance, then the abovementioned 'red horse' could very well be Soviet Communism – splitting the world with its 'sword' (militant ideology). If one is a regular Christian, then the 'red dragon' is obviously Satan, or agents thereof. If one is a reform Protestant, then the 'woman in scarlet' is clearly the Roman Catholic Church, ..and so on. We must remember amongst all this striking symbolism that the greatest danger is in making ill-informed subjective interpretations. The real enemy is ignorance and enmity, and pious justifications for hateful attitudes. We must resist the temptation to use this knowledge to further divide society. In every case, we should first apply these archetypal findings in a frank critique of our own cultures and faith traditions before ever daring to apply such to others. In doing so we may very well be surprised as to who in fact are really the 'good guys' and who are the bad. Again, caution and humility should be the rule of thumb.

In any event, we now know that whenever we see symbols of oppression mixed with red, such as appearances of black birds-of-prey; an absence of blue; and/or a predominance of red in any given institution's symbolism; we may be reasonably sure that we are looking at agencies of oppression, suppression, or destruction – of archetypal formulas and values – in some form or other. Recalling Chapter Four; "Mixing red with black is considered the worst possible combination, but red (alone) can be either positive or negative" ..which brings us to a most important point of clarification.

## Thematic Subdivisions of the Color Red

The reader will no doubt have noticed the aforementioned broad array of sometimes-contradictory symbolic definitions within the range of the color red. From 'sin' to 'savior', 'priest' to 'prostitute' ('harlot') and 'Church' to 'Communism' for instance. Coming up with just one central theme for the color red is therefore inappropriate, and rightly so. Because especially in a religious context, red is different to the other colors we are studying having the confusing properties of representing three different archetypal categories which we will provisionally term here: (i) the original male, (ii) the perverse male, and (iii) the hero figure. Notwithstanding these three different classifications however, the common unifying elements of masculinity and physicality remains across the board (♣ 16).

This three-stage classification of archetypal red values fits particularly well with the traditional monotheistic understanding that mankind fell from a state of primordial grace, and has since been engaged in the struggle against evil (black) in order to regain that state of original purity (white); for which role of course we need religious heroes, messiahs, or saviors. Hence we have an original 'perfect' male (in this viewpoint) who is connected to God (i); namely Adam *before* the fall (white and red). Then, we have the perverse male figure that has come under the influence of evil (ii). Remembering our discussion of the cosmic circle (♣ 17), this is where the white 'holy' spiritual area has been replaced by black, as well as the feminine-compassionate blue being excluded; thus creating a perverse red-black entity comprising 66.6% of the original cosmic circle. This red-black category includes Adam *after* the fall, his older son Cain the murderer, and of course Satan, as the (male) fallen angel of light and orchestrator of evil. In the fall-from-grace theory, implicated in this second category of course are all human males who have not yet reached a state of 'perfection' or reunion with God. Such agencies as (red-black) Nazism typify the worst of this category in a social-historical setting, but any excessive or violent use of masculine energies is symptomatic of this condition. Finally, the third category (iii) is the hero figure (red), sometimes known as "Red Robe" embodied (or mythologized) in the various legends and myths of folklore, as well as in popular religion. Here we have salvific-oriented male figures such as Moses, Elijah, or Jesus, but it should also be noted that whether they subscribe to the fall-from-grace theory or not, nearly all religious traditions have central figures that fit this hero-mold.

In the context of red-white symbolism, all male figures that have attained a high degree of spiritual awareness and have lived their lives accordingly may thus be viewed as 'cosmic hero' types, inasmuch as they have striven to reflect the ideal male archetype, or have contributed substantially to advancing that model. Based upon chromonumeric parallels this category could include Zoroaster, Abraham, Buddha, John-the-Baptist, Muhammad, Baha'u'llah, Gandhi, and many, many more who have in some way or other hosted the providential spirit – even if only partially, and for limited periods of time. Whether done at the local-personal, or international-historical level, it is the role, not the person that defines the symbolism.[*] As we shall see in Part Two, this rule applies equally to many mythological figures as well as to several secular heroes in history, for we must not forget that religion per se is but one of many features of everyday life that we should (ideally) be employing to better ourselves. The fields of science, politics, and academic pursuits also have their deep vocational properties as

---

[*] An upcoming work entitled *Monsters, Maidens, and Messiahs* will explore the phenomenon of providential figures in history. See http://color-of-truth.com for more details.

well as their own homegrown heroes. Indeed, the properties of true moral integrity are often to be found in equal, if not greater abundance and consistency amongst the ranks of inspired academics, scientists, and common men than in the relatively narrow world of career religionists. 'Holiness' after all, is surely descriptive of the Divine reflection as made manifest in all individuals and society; and are we not constantly being told that we are *all* God's children? In any event, any God-Creator must logically have been a creative scientist before ever He was a religionist (if ever indeed He was one). Therefore if we are to attribute any intrinsic partisan or political bias to God, then surely it must be a humanistic-and-scientific one?

But back to the topic: As we saw in our studies of political insignia, the perverse male archetype is usually represented with the color red in conjunction with the color black, or, at least without the presence of the color blue. We need only look to popular culture to confirm this; a red-eyed, black-cloaked Darth Vader in the Star Trek movies, or other stereotypical villains, typecast in their black pajamas and red bandanas. And although the colors of the hero are definitely red *and* white—as were the colors of the original male (the Adam archetype)—the presence of white in certain red-black situations (such as the Nazi flag) may simply be due to the *absence* of color. Similarly, when red is present in isolation it may only be representative of the male, or other masculine traits such as patriarchy, physical strength, or aggression. For as we all well know, many male hero figures in history from popes to priests, and from kings to emperors have all too often succumbed to their baser traits. But who can identify any hero in history or mythology who did not have to put up a fight of some sort?

Thus, when assessing the potential values of red symbolism in specific situations it is especially important to seek out additional evidence to confirm one's chromatically-based assumptions. When it comes to the religious realm in particular it is probably wiser at first to presume the possible presence of 'good' red symbolism in each case, given the conviction that it is indeed through the subliminal avenues of True spirituality or True religion (with a capital 'T') that any benign noumenal force has the best chance of getting through to us. In the same vein however, the presence of dark or historically-destructive symbolism amongst the semiotics of any particular religious or political tradition should never be overlooked, for evil's best disguise is to masquerade as truth: "What better disguise for the master of lies than to pose as a preacher on Sundays." Nevertheless, caution and humility should still remain the rule of thumb.

## The Absent Feminine

Noting the very important fact that we do not have the same multiplication of archetypal themes at the blue end of the spectrum raises the interesting question of why we only have one blue symbolic interpretation, and not three, as with the color red? This is almost certainly because the feminine dimension has for the greater part of history been suppressed and oppressed (by the male), and besides, she does not intrinsically carry the same type of physical energies as her masculine counterpart – destructive or otherwise. Hence she has not emerged as a well-developed or dominant political force; at least not yet. But it could equally have something to do with the fact that according to one interpretation of archetypal propriety, the feminine (blue) aspect of society cannot be developed, reformed, or redeemed, until *after* the red aspects have first been dealt with. The question is; can the collective 'he' or 'we' do it without 'her' help?

Well, in context of a cosmos that is comprised of multiple masculine *and* feminine properties, the answer to this question is rather obvious. 'She' is of course indispensable. But this interesting development takes us into the theoretical realm of providential mechanics, and the role of gender in human history; a discussion that we must for the moment put to one side. But even as we put aside this discussion, we should keep in mind the fact that any social construct that is deficient in its cosmic feminine properties is ultimately doomed to failure or destruction through the excesses of the male. This reality is becoming more and more apparent as we struggle for social, historical, and political balance in a world ever more divided between generally-democratic red-white-and blues, and the reds and red-blacks of more radical societies.

So, having taken a rather broad overview of the perceived values of the colors white, blue, and red in religion and mythology, let us now review in a little more detail some specific appearances of the triadic archetype in the world's major faith traditions.

# CHAPTER EIGHT

# RELIGIOUS TRIADIC ARCHETYPES

*A brief but specific review of examples of the triadic archetype in the histories and current expressions of the world's most popular faith traditions.*

Despite religions' assumed mystical origins, or should we say precisely *because* of its mystical origins, religion is awash with powerful symbolism in many shapes and forms. Rituals, traditions, and priestly vestments for instance: or icons, statues and stained-glass windows. Some groups express symbolism in their sacred texts in metaphor, poetry, and myth, or through sacraments and singing, or in symbolic treks and pilgrimages. Others symbolize their faith internally, or accord special importance to their scriptures; the Torah, the Upanishads, the Holy Bible, or the Sacred Qur'an for example; or see their tradition's central figures as sacred icons and symbols in-and-of themselves. In short, there are a multitude of ways that any particular religious group symbolizes their faith and practices. But today, we are chiefly concerned with visual, color-specific symbolism. In particular; archetypal, triadic-based symbolism. Therefore whilst acknowledging the profound importance of other symbol forms to various religious groups, we will of necessity only focus upon what appear to be expressions of—or part expressions of—the triadic archetype.

Naturally, we cannot but briefly allude to the specific theologies or philosophies underlying these symbol-forms. Nor would we want to get embroiled in the tortuous complexities of religious dogmas and doctrines and their associated manifestations in religious practice; this work being in part a specific attempt to help resolve some of those convolutions. So whilst recognizing that the information we are about to review is being delivered from an objective, archetypal perspective, and as such may not be seen as

101

fully 'orthodox' by any particular tradition's adherents; we will nevertheless endeavor to illustrate how the world's religions are in fact already subliminally united along triadic archetypal themes—at least partially—and show how it is mainly due to the excesses and deficiencies of ignorance and sectarianism that an underlying consensus is not already in place. As we shall see, the proofs of the triadic archetype strongly suggest that rigid orthodoxies and other modern interpretations of the Divine originally sprouted from the same archetypal origins, but over time have suffered many unqualified interpretations. This, brought about chiefly by ignorance and through liberal or conservative excesses respectively. In the following accounts for example, one area of potential misunderstanding is where we list examples of the triadic archetype as either 'trinitarian' or 'triadic'. Sacrosanct to many, religious fervor runs high when we inadvertently promote a mere triad to the status of a Trinity, or relegate one tradition's 'Ultimate Being' to a relatively junior position in a divine hierarchy, or to the status of a mere partner in a divine duality. But the plain fact is that mythological and religious triads through the ages have reflected very similar properties. Indeed, grasping this fact is key to fully appreciating this research. Homer's triad of *Zeus, Poseidon, and Hades* in Ancient Greece for example, although all technically male, did in fact represent the sky, the sea, and the underworld respectively – white sky, blue ocean, red-black underworld. There is also the ancient Babylonian triad of *Anu, Enil, and Ea;* or Egypt's *Osiris, Isis, and Horus;* or Japan's *Sun, Moon, and Storm gods;* all ancient triads with divine status and corresponding archetypal properties. Or we can resurrect the Norse gods of *Odin, Thor, and Frey,* or their Roman counterparts of *Jupiter, Juno, and Minerva..* or for that matter the Inca gods of South America; *Viracocha, Inti, and Illapa.* Each in turn *could* be interpreted as having loose, if not specific associations with the triadic archetype as described herein, as well as with contemporary religious triads. But these mythologies, like many others before and since underwent changes in form and content even whilst functioning as the well-established religions of their day. The blending of cultures and ideologies, wars and military conquests, the needs and requirements of commerce and politics, the effects of religious indoctrination over the years, and the evolution of societies steeped in myth and superstition; all of these helped shape our religious heritage today. But untangling all of these overt influences from each tradition's archetypal origins is a massive and extremely complex undertaking, not to mention very time consuming. Consequently, traveling down those particular misty corridors for more proofs of the triadic archetype at this early stage may prove more confusing than fruitful. So I must leave it to the reader to probe further in that direction if they are so inclined, or, wait for that particular volume to come out in print. Meanwhile, we must busy ourselves with more contemporary examples of archetypal origins that are either self-evident or relatively easy to verify.

The reader may at this point enquire why it is we are spending so much time on religious iconography – to which I offer the following brief reply: Firstly, because the majority of readers will identify one way or another with some of the religious beliefs presented in this work. Secondly, because the inappropriate application of religious beliefs in history accounts for the bulk of human suffering. Thirdly, because the very definition of 'archetype' is that it permeates all of society, past, present, and future. And finally, because one of the greatest promises offered by the discovery of the triadic archetype is that it may help nullify elitist religious sectarianism whilst simultaneously binding us together in a more wholesome and productive, collective spirituality.

Nevertheless, and perhaps not surprisingly, making pointed comparisons between the various religious models is likely to upset denominational purists. However, not wanting to lose even the most entrenched religionist at this point, let me politely reiterate that we have an important and specific task to accomplish here, and therefore must not allow ourselves to be restrained or distracted by any particular set of religious beliefs or orthodox terminologies. Our task is to simply prove the case for the triadic archetype by identifying collaborative themes in modern religions associated primarily with groupings of various gods, goddesses, and other theological constructs. This being said however, I do sincerely hope that this search for archetypal parallels amongst the world's major religions will not provoke any unwarranted offense or indignation. Those who may incline towards defensive reactions are respectfully invited once again to consider the factual and systematic nature of the content so far, and to graciously allow for the generalizations and oversimplifications that must of necessity accompany this research.

## Hinduism

Hinduism itself almost defies specific academic definition, for not only is there no listed founder of Hinduism, but there are no formal doctrines such as we find in monotheistic traditions. This reflects the overall understanding amongst Hindus that 'God' or 'Ultimate Reality' is beyond full comprehension, but is nevertheless expressed in diverse forms and situations according to environmental circumstances and the faith-position of the individual believer. Hence Hinduism displays an apparent multitude of discrete deities. It would be more accurate however, to recognize these deities as manifestations of the One Absolute Reality – only in different roles. More or less equivalent to you or I holding different job titles according to whether we are parenting, cooking, laboring, teaching or whatever.. at any given moment. As a result, we find many rich and colorful allegories in Hindu philosophy, equally reflected in its symbolism (figs.15 & 22 ♣). Texts such as the Upanishads and the Vedas for instance which were written several centuries before Christ, carry all of the central themes of other *cosmogonic*[*] myths; Divine creation, magical symbolism, and cosmic hero figures to name but a few. Occasionally the authors used colors in their attempts to define both corporeal and mystical concepts, as we see in this extract from Volume 2 of the Upanishads referring to the path to Ultimate Reality (Brahman):

> "On that path they say that there is white, or blue, or yellow, or green, or red; that path was found by Brahman, and on it goes whoever knows Brahman, and who has done good, and obtained splendor."[†]

The very expansiveness of Hinduism, and the fact that it doggedly refuses to be trimmed and bracketed into logical creeds and dogmas makes it both a worthy model of universalism in principle, as well as an extremely difficult religious model to quantify systematically. Nevertheless, from the perspective of this work it is very intriguing to discover a core triad known collectively as the Trimurti (trinity), that comprises the three central deities accompanied by their respective consorts, who carry an assortment of characteristics that match the archetypal (religious) values of the colors white, blue, and red. With a little conceptual flexibility, and whilst allowing for the inevitable thematic convolutions when dealing with a million junior deities, the central premises of the triadic archetype can still be identified in the following symbolism: (♣ 15; color frames added by the author).

Firstly there is 'white' Brahma (God the Creator), from "Brahman" the Ultimate Cosmic Principle, who is interestingly partnered by Saraswati, the goddess of knowledge and wisdom (blue?). Secondly we have Shiva, another primary deity colored blue and associated with both procreation and destruction, and matched with his consort Kali, the (often red-black) goddess of power, destruction, and transformation. Thirdly there is Vishnu,

---

[*] Cosmogonic; the study of the origins of the Universe
[†] Brahman is the Hindu name for Ultimate Reality

preserver of the Universe, also usually colored dark blue and associated with primordial waters, or, sometimes colored black and reclining on a great serpent. Vishnu can manifest himself in avatars (human embodiments) also in various colors. His consort Lakshmi, is the goddess of love, beauty, and delight.

Although the symbolism, like Hinduism in general is somewhat difficult to pin down, we do see certain parallels between the triadic principle and the respective attributes of archetypal white, blues, and reds as discussed in this work. Equally, in the practice of yoga as a path to enlightenment Hindus recognize the validity of various disciplines that correlate to our progressive theories as we shall see in a moment. Not forgetting of course the aforementioned Sanskrit triad of *Sat* (being), *Chit* (consciousness), and *Ananda* (spiritual bliss), rooted deep in the same Hindu culture. When allowing for the lack of constraint upon individual Hindus in matters of faith and religious expression it is actually quite remarkable that the triadic archetype has apparently still managed to hold its subliminal ground. Most important of all perhaps is the recognition that the Trimurti, as a core belief amongst Hindus offers a common base with Christian theology (the Holy Trinity); with human theory (spirit, mind, body); and within quantum science (proton, neutron, electron) in our search for universal truths.

Remarkably, this triadic core also presents itself in the sacred "AUM" chant. AUM is the Hindu syllable of 'Supreme Reality'; sometimes pronounced "OOM" or "OM" and revered in both audible and visible forms by Hindus, Buddhists and Sikhs alike. When chanted, the three sounds of A, U, and M represent the aforementioned Hindu Trimurti of Brahma, Vishnu, and Shiva. In addition, AUM symbolizes totality, completeness, and the whole universe. There is also an interesting literal connection between the sound of "AUM" and God-related terms in the English language such as: "Amen, Omnipotent, Omnipresent," and "Alpha-and-Omega."

In scientific language there is another possible connection too; 'AU' is the periodic table's sign for gold, the metal most often associated with religious ceremonies and the male deity, and it may also factor in the word "Aura", the spiritual radiation phenomenon associated with the concept of haloes. In Islam too, the word "amin" (amen), and the Islamic letter for "Allah" look remarkably similar to the literal AUM symbol, and the Muslim Tuaregs of North Africa use a similar pseudo-religious term to describe the precious 'water of life' as "ammam imman". Finally and most conclusively; during ritualized chants in the Buddhist tradition, each of the three audible sounds represents three aspects of the mystical process of communication, which not surprisingly are:

- The Three Chakras; the inner eye, the throat, and the heart
- The Three Practices; the secret, the inner, and the outer
- The Three Colors; white, blue, and red

This brief exposition of the AUM mantra—I hope you'll agree—is a powerful ratification of our central theory, binding the core principles and beliefs specifically of Hinduism, Buddhism, and Sikhism with the central themes and colors of the triadic archetype.

## Buddhist Taras

Buddhism grew out of ancient Hinduism, refining its beliefs and practices along the foundations set by its founder Guatama Buddha in the 6th century BCE. Although officially rejecting monotheistic doctrines 'The Way' (of the Buddha) has many features in common with monotheistic traditions and, not unlike Hindus, Buddhists identify with a broad collection of manifestations of the Buddha's characteristics. Some, known as *Taras* are manifestations of the feminine (divine) or expressions of the female *Buddha of Enlightened Activity*. Please note here the association between 'enlightenment' and the feminine-wisdom traits of the triadic archetype. Once again a remarkable consistency is displayed when the color-symbolism relates to the characteristics, rather than just the stated gender of these deities. What must be taken into account of course is the fact that these applied mystical color-characteristics originated long before science had discovered and charted the chromonumeric properties of the electromagnetic spectrum.

In his book *In Praise of Tara: Songs to the Savioress,* Martin Wilson translates Buddhist scripture regarding the origins of the primordial Tara as follows: "In the past, many eons ago... in the Universe called Manifold Light, there lived a princess by the name of Moon of Wisdom-knowledge."[49] This moon-wisdom-knowledge theme exactly correlates to the feminine goddess-principle who, once fully enlightened, adopts the role of "Liberator" (of the feminine traits) in a masculine-dominated world. Once again, this corresponds to the idea of an intermediary blue wisdom-entity ('Sophia?') seeking to redress the red, masculine, physical imbalances of patriarchal, and materialistic societies. And although there are twenty-one different manifestations of Tara, she is nevertheless often referred to collectively as 'The Mother of all Buddhas:'

> Tara is known as the "Mother of all Buddhas." This is
> because she is the wisdom of reality, and all Buddhas and
> bodhisattvas are born from this wisdom. This wisdom is also
> the fundamental cause of happiness, and our own spiritual
> growth comes from this wisdom. That is why Tara is called
> the Mother. And Mother Tara has much wisdom to manifest
> many aspects, sometimes peaceful, sometimes wrathful, in
> different colours – all to help sentient beings.[50]

The above quote seems almost tailor-made to fit with our triadic archetype.
It speaks of the connection between the divine feminine and Wisdom, as
well as the fact that "our own spiritual growth *comes from* this wisdom".
This reinforces the progression from mind to spirit as well as reminding us
that Wisdom (or the fruitful functioning of the mind) is essential to spiritual
growth (figs. 24 ♣). Switch off the mind – switch off the spirit. This theme
challenges the validity of those faith traditions that are built upon stringent
dogmatics and blind faith, which by implication suppress the activities of
the mind.

In addition to these core parallels with other religious mother-figures,
the colors of each of the respective Taras are uncannily close to the
chromatic values discovered in this work, with white representing high
spirituality, enlightenment and peace; blue often being associated with
wisdom; red being an indicator of heroism and physical power; and
whenever black appears it is invariably associated with wrath, vengeance,
and aggression, most notably when partnered by red as we can see in the
following examples taken from the website of the *Amitabha Buddhist
Center*: First of all there is the Tara who fulfills all active functions, her
body colored white and radiating varicolored lights, holding the green flask
from whence come all magical attainments. This is a clear association with
light itself, the colors of the spectrum, and the position of the color green at
the center of creation. Then there is the Tara 'white as the autumn moon'
who defeats diseases and evil spirits, holding the white flask that pacifies.
This same white flask is also capable of defeating all terrors whilst
bestowing good fortune, cleansing sins and obscurations, pacifying the
poison of the 'lu' serpents, and dispelling poison and disease. Remembering
that red is associated with things physical, active, and dynamic, and in its
pure form is also associated with the messiah or hero figure, we discover the
Tara swift and heroic who destroys hindering demons and heals injuries.
This Tara's body is colored red and blazing like fire, holding the red flask
that protects from obstacles, and subjugates, tames, and defeats all 'du'

demons and obstructions. And lastly, there is the aforesaid Blue Buddha associated with the properties of wisdom, and the mystical blue "flask of knowledge" which subdues evil spirits.[51]

There are two features of the color black identified in this work that are also common to Buddhism. These are (a) the connection with Satan, darkness, and the underworld, and (b), as an ominous masculine portent when mixed with the color red. The reader will recall that red-and-black in combination represent the most destructive aspects of male energy. Although sometimes benign we see these two themes reflected in some of the following Tara figures: There is "Tara the Terrifier" victorious of the triple world with frowning brows who tames hindering demons, her body colored red-black, holding the aforementioned blue flask that confounds ghosts and awakened corpses. There is also Mother Tara whose body is colored black, and holds the black flask that averts magic mantras, whilst a third red-black Tara holding a red flask defeats 'chi' demons and enemies. Yet another red-black Tara is known as 'Tara the Pulverizer', collectively conjuring up a broad range of rather masculine images of the goddess. Here we see a good example of the principle of role-over-gender, where symbolically speaking the most important factor for determining the imagery is the activity, rather than just the gender of the subject.

## Taoism and 'The Way'

Another ancient tradition that originated in China, Taoism has brought to the Western sphere a spiritual awareness that promotes reverence and understanding of the natural order. Definitely more a mystical-wisdom-philosophical tradition than a conservative orthodoxy, Taoism too has three 'Pure Ones' or deities, as pseudo-personifications of its central themes: The Jade Pure, the Upper Pure, and the Great Pure. Originally developed from the *Tao Te Ching* (or *Dao De Jing*) Taoism's central manuscript is believed to have been written by the Chinese philosopher Lao Tse (604-520 B.C.), although scholars generally agree that a school of philosophy probably worked in collaboration to produce the work. Perhaps the most-translated of all Chinese texts, the *Tao Te Ching* is described in Wikipedia as a book whose "content focuses mainly on mystical, political, and practical wisdom". But we are also told that the language is so obscure at times, that it has produced completely different translations; so much so that the debate continues as to its exact meanings. For the purposes of this work however, it is reasonably safe to say that Taoism in its own words, is based upon a triad of mind (the cognitive), heart (the affective), and body (the behavioral). Replacing the somewhat imprecise 'heart' with 'soul' in this triad would of course align this philosophy very neatly with the triadic archetype. In his anthology of world religions Huston Smith writes:

> The object of philosophical Taoism is to align one's daily life with the Tao, to ride its boundless tide and delight in its flow... a force that is infinitely subtle and intricate, ...it lives by a vitality that has no need of abruptness, much less violence. The Tao flows in and flows out again, turning life into a dance that is neither feverish nor unbalanced.[52]

The technical meaning of the word *Tao* is generally interpreted as 'The Way,' with the word *Te* meaning 'integrity and power,' and *Ching* referring to the sacred text itself. Supported by the aforementioned 'Jade, Upper, and Great Pure Ones'; this conceptual triad again correlates to a three-system spirituality comprising an inspirational aspect (Tao), a theoretical aspect (Ching), and an active aspect (Te), which in turn nicely coincides with the Wikipedia description of Taoism's central text as focusing upon "mystical, political, and practical" aspects. Again, this directly albeit loosely translates into; (i) concept, plan, and action; (ii) spirit, mind, and body; (iii) white, blue, and red.

## Judaism, Christianity and Islam

The wealth and breadth of symbolism within each of these three traditions deserve to be presented as topics in their own right – as will be done in later volumes. But we group these mainstream traditions together today for good reasons. Because in a very telling and historically-accurate display; by studying them in concert we uncover a far more balanced and condensed archetypal picture than if we study them as distinct institutions individually. There are strong symbolic links connecting all three in other words, which shouldn't be too surprising if one is familiar with their respective histories. If one believes in a divine providence this could, possibly, indicate either a combined social-historical mission or, more pessimistically, a succession of historical failures or lapses in key areas by each tradition in turn. For as we shall soon see, when viewed as interrelated historical institutions a very interesting picture emerges.

First a little history: As Judaism predates Christianity and Islam by 2,000 and 2,700 years respectively and was arguably the direct progenitor of both traditions; it is not surprising that these three religions have certain features in common. Monotheism, or the belief in One God is probably the chief unifying factor, as well as a traditional respect for Abraham as their original 'father of faith'. Acceptance of the story of Adam and Eve as generally representative of the origins of man is another unifying creed. But after this, the three faiths diverge dramatically in several directions including different positions on the role and importance of their various central figures; Abraham's sons Ishmael and Isaac, Jesus of Nazareth, Mary his mother, and Mohammad for example. Whose holy scriptures are in fact the most holy is another area of dissention. Is it the Torah, the Bible or the Qur'an? Sadly, as we all well know, religious divisions between these three traditions as well as amongst their internal sects and denominations probably accounts for the greater part of the horrors of human history. All the more exciting then to discover some new thematic parallels between them when we view their respective histories via the themes and principles of the triadic archetype.

Remembering that Christianity and Islam were not merely religious movements, but were also political empires in their own right for centuries; Christianity arguably for a thousand years in Europe from 800 to 1800 CE, and Islam in the Middle East, North Africa, and Spain from 632 until around 1492 and beyond. But Judaism on the other hand existed without political sovereignty for 1800 years until the recent creation of the State of Israel in 1948. As far as their historical origins and development are concerned, the political symbolism of these combined religions comprises an interestingly mixed bag of colors and symbols. These include the colors blue, white, red, green, and black; variously supported by stars, crosses, and sun and moon symbols at various points in time. Although there will be some exceptions to these rules, generally speaking we can say that the political symbolism of Judaism comprises a blue star on a white background. Early Christianity on the other hand tended to sport sun-symbolism and white crosses on red backgrounds; whilst Islam expanded its territories in the 7th century under crescent-moon symbolism—usually backed by the colors green, white, or black—still evident in many political flags today. Red also surfaced as a dominant color as Islam became a militant religion. So as we can see; quite a mixture of colors, symbols, and themes to digest. The question is; what's the connection between them (if any) – and with the triadic archetype?

**Celestial Symbolism**
We begin by informing the reader that both Christianity and Islam are infused with a considerable amount of what orthodoxy terms 'pagan' symbolism; in particular the sun and the moon respectively. In regard to the use of the terms 'orthodox' and 'pagan' in a historical setting; in most cases the term 'orthodoxy' refers to the accepted beliefs of the prevailing religion

at any given time – in any given place. Even today, more dogmatic religions still tend to declare themselves 'orthodox' whilst those perceived as outsiders are denounced as unbelievers, infidels, heretics, atheists, gentiles, heathens or pagans. The term 'pagan' however, goes back much further and is a relative expression originally meaning 'country-folk' or 'simple folk' and by implication, the 'silly religions' of those *pagani*. Interestingly, but not too flatteringly, before Christianity adopted the term as a pejorative the Romans applied the same to the Christians and the Jews. But from our now more enlightened perspective, we can reasonably assume that the pagan celestial symbolism that predates these religions is in fact connected to the same aforesaid universal (archetypal) principles as modern orthodoxies. Be that as it may, Christianity and Islam in particular still contain more than a peppering of 'dark and disturbing' signs and colors. The observant reader will already have noted certain unhealthy themes and trends both in the histories and symbolism of our most populous religions. Suffice for now to note that the aggressive and destructive aspects of Christianity and Islam— by far the two most militant religions in history—can quickly be matched to corresponding 'excessive male' and authoritarian red or red-black symbolism in their internal, historical structures. The primary colors of Christendom until the Reformation for instance were red and white (see fig.20 ♣), and those of early Islam were green and white, although black also featured very prominently both in the bloody Inquisition years as well as in Muhammad's own tribal colors (22 ♣). Black is also prominent in other Islamic symbols such as the black Kabba of Mecca—the central icon of Islam—and as discussed earlier, along with red, remains evident in many modern Arab-Islamic political colors (♣ 7). The lack of blue in both these traditions is a reflection of the belief that Allah (or God) is a singular, masculine entity (although in Christianity's case He is also mysteriously personified in the Trinity). Blue-and-white Judaism on the other hand, lacking any political standing since before the rise of Christianity has been notably devoid of the reds and red-blacks of her progenies. Interestingly though, when Judaism was a strong political entity with a successful army during the time of King David around 1000 BCE; its national symbol was a (masculine) red star on a white background. One has to reasonably assume that this *Red Star of David* was archetypically linked to the role of David as a hero-redeemer-warrior king. In Christianity's case however the pervasive reds were not—as one might expect—directly and purely linked to Christ in a similar messianic role; but were for the most part inherited from the traditional colors of the (authoritarian and 'pagan') Roman Empire, which in turn were directly linked with Mithraic sun-worship; the preexistent exclusively-male belief system at the time Christianity merged with Roman paganism in the 4th century; during the reign of Constantine the Great.

Here perhaps we should briefly digress to explain that the Emperor Constantine mentioned here (288-337 CE) has long been regarded the secular 'father' of Christianity inasmuch as he legalized Christianity in 313 CE, and then set about establishing what is now recognized as the Christian Roman Empire. What is not so commonly known however, is that Constantine saw Christ to all intents and purposes as the embodiment of the sun-god Mithras. Not only was the cult of Mithras exclusively male and the traditional religion of the Roman Legions (red), but Mithraic mythology contains several key themes long held as original to Christianity: Mithras was reportedly born on December 25th for example, surrounded by shepherds, and called "the light of the world". A dualistic tradition that originated in Persia, Mithraism included rituals such as baptism, a sacred meal (communion) and the belief in Mithras' miraculous resurrection, to give but a few examples. Furthermore, Constantine himself maintained his Imperial 'pagan' identity as a Roman god throughout his whole supposed conversion to Christianity, only being baptized a Christian on his deathbed. These facts not only help account for the strongly patriarchal direction of post 4th century Christianity, and for its political structures, but also for the solar symbolism and other Roman emblems forming as part of Roman Christian iconography that existed at the time of the rise of Islam in the 7th century.

Islam on the other hand most likely picked up the crescent-moon symbolism that we see in political colors today from its equally 'pagan' associations with the moon god Hubal, who was considered the greatest of the 360-or so gods of pre-Islamic Mecca (fig.22 ♣). Scholars inform us that the common name for Hubal as the highest deity, was 'Allah' or 'Allat'. In his book *In Defense of the Faith* David Hunt states;

> Allah is not a generic Arabic word for God but a name of a particular god among many deities traditionally honored in ancient times by nomadic tribes in Arabia. Allah was the chief god among the approximately 360 idols in the Kaaba in Mecca...Allah is a contraction of AL-ilah, the name of the Moon God [Hubal] of the local Quraysh, Mohammed's tribe...Allah's symbol was a crescent moon, which Muhammad carried over into Islam. This symbol is seen on Mosques, minarets, shrines, and Arab flags. [53]

Here we see a direct connection between Islam and feminine moon symbolism, which, in Islam's early development was actually quite appropriate. For although it later gathered a reputation as a religion of barbarians (due in large part to Christian propaganda), Islam actually began as a compassionate and unifying monotheism that did much to elevate and protect the social position of women whilst advancing learning and education in occupied lands. We should perhaps explain that despite the religious wars of the time, Muslim scholars effectively brought the Judeo-Christian world out of the Dark Ages, and unlike contemporary attitudes amongst Muslim fringe fanatics, expressed remarkable tolerance for those adherents of Christianity and Judaism who lived amongst them. Hence the feminine and unifying traits of wisdom and scientific knowledge respectively were very evident in the growth of early Islam whilst being alarmingly deficient in the Christian Kingdoms of the day. But although being a relatively 'progressive' religion as far as women's social roles were concerned, the philosophical progressiveness of Islam soon succumbed to the more militant demands of spreading a new 'holy' empire after Muhammad's death. The masculine elements soon overshadowed the feminine ones in other words. Hence the social policies of modern Arab states which by and large maintain an 'orthodox' (as in unchanged) 7th century Islamic approach towards their womenfolk, and generally speaking—in terms of global norms—continue to suppress the feminine elements of their cultures and societies.

As far as the color green in Islam is concerned, as the obvious color of nature it is not surprising that this harks back to the days when Islamic culture emerged out of the deserts of Arabia, subsequently dominating the natural sciences; philosophy, art, architecture, and music. Remembering the central position of the color green in the visible spectrum, and whilst allowing for this 'green as oasis-in-the-desert' theme, the *unifying* and *scientific* features of early Islam further qualify the subliminal choice of greens in its traditional symbolism. The traditional blacks and red-blacks on the other hand (fig.22 ♣) will require a closer look in later volumes where we will explore the historical development and political role of Islamic states today in light of the potential development of society along the idealistic lines of the triadic archetype.

Returning to the 7th century CE, if we now recall our exploration of symbols associated with the archetypal masculine and feminine, we begin to see an interesting dualistic model emerging between the respective sun and moon symbols of Christianity and Islam, further reflected in their choice of calendars: Solar for Christendom and lunar for Islam. Christianity was overtly patriarchal (masculine) whilst Islam was covertly educational (feminine), at least inasmuch as the latter carried the wisdom of the ancients into newly-occupied lands. This is very interesting, for does it not seem appropriate (from an archetypal-providential perspective) for feminine moon symbolism to be present in a socio-political religious movement (Islam) that drew from Hellenistic (Greek) wisdom traditions and aimed to correct rampant polytheism, and a strongly patriarchal Dark Ages Christianity: A militant and generally suppressive Christianity governed from Rome and Constantinople, whose origins and character were not only distinctly masculine and authoritarian, but were also fused with Constantinian sun-worship?

But this of course leads us back to the question of the potentially-matching sun-moon symbolism, and of the role of a distinctly unpolitical and displaced Judaism in the equation; because obviously there was no enduring 'holy marriage' between these conflicting religions. Nevertheless the symbolic potential between Christianity and Islam remains tantalizingly there. Could it be possible perhaps, that despite the ignorance of such themes at the time; that the noumenal, or subliminal influences behind this sun and moon symbolism were somehow reaching out through (archetypal) 'pagan' connections (Mithras and Hubal) to somehow achieve the balanced union of two great, but archetypically-incomplete religious movements, and two great but socially-imbalanced cultures? For although the colors don't seem quite right on the Islamic side (no blue), the feminine moon symbolism is definitely there, and the rapid advance of Islam in those first hundred years between 632 and 732 CE was remarkable to say the least. Still, our archetypal male-and-female-union theory appears to stumble on the acknowledgement that there were no complimentary feminine blue representations in early Islam, nor in the ancient or modern colors of traditional Muslim or Arab cultures (figs.7, 22 ♣). We are therefore left with the inescapable conclusion that 'archetypal wisdom' (blue) must, at the time of the expansion of Islam have been busy elsewhere. Or was She? Maybe there's another explanation.

Let's take another look at the symbolism here. More specifically, let's look at what's *not* here. Based upon what we have discovered so far, specifically the human spirit-mind-body triad; the white-blue-red, and red-blue-green color triads (fig.10 ♣); and the family triad of father, mother, and children; and whilst remembering that in the Bible the sun and the moon in Joseph's dream are recognized as representing his father and mother respectively (Genesis 37: 9-10). With all this in mind, when we look at the historical symbolic set up of 7th century Christianity and Islam with (a) the sun and the moon, and (b) the combination of reds, whites, and greens; we can see that we have two parts of three possible archetypal triads:

1. The color spectrum trinity of red at one end, blue at the other end, and green in the center. *Blue is missing.*
2. The triad of red, white, and blue. Once again*, blue is missing.*
3. The symbolic 'family' trinity of sun, moon, and stars. *The stars are missing.*

Maybe what's missing from the formula… is a blue star? (Fig. 23 ♣)

Exciting, paradoxical, yet strangely probable. With a modest grasp of archetypal constructs it now seems quite reasonable to assume that noumenal forces (in whatever shape or form we choose to identify them) were attempting to orchestrate a benevolent union between three competing religious traditions, who each had so much to learn from each other, and who each would make their mark on history. In a curious and admittedly rather convoluted orchestration, the symbolism can now be read to identify God (or Allah) as the Origin (white). Then sequentially the (blue) 'virgin daughter Zion' as ancient Judaism, who then matures to give birth to a male hero-figure (Christ) whose followers erect a patriarchal and authoritarian (red) religion sadly devoid of the feminine. Seven centuries later, a potential union (green) is somehow orchestrated through the agency of early Islam, centered geographically in the Middle East, which not only lifts a struggling Christendom out of the Dark Ages, but also provides a possible socio-political link between the Western and Eastern worlds and their respective religions. The chromatic sequence is correct: First white, then blue, then red, and finally; the potential of union between blue and red at the central green point. Add to all this the fact that each tradition in turn used a different calendar: Christianity the Julian solar calendar; Islam the lunar calendar; and Judaism a combination lunar-solar calendar; a thematic blend that places the Jewish star at the mid point between the Christian sun, and Muslim moon respectively; and we are thus presented with the visible symbolism of yet another possible cosmic 'family'.

But as we now know, unity was not ultimately achieved, although to give credit where it is due; the early Muslims did in fact have a pretty good crack at it. Because when they originally converged on 8th century Spain, the Muslim Moors were placed in the unique situation of entering a divided Christian country with a large (albeit oft-persecuted) Jewish minority. Holding power intermittently for several centuries, it is notable that by the time of the last Christian reconquest in 1492, certain areas under Muslim rule had enjoyed a 'Golden Age' of unparalleled unity and cooperation between Jews, Christians, and Muslims, as well as achieving truly great advances in philosophy, science, architecture and the arts. Indeed, it was in this enlightened environment that Jewish mysticism in the form of the Kabala began to take shape and form. Increasingly popular today, this Spanish Kabalism was a well-thought-out attempt to unify the realm of the Divine with the created world. Echoing many of the themes in this book, mention is made of archetypes, mystical numbers, and planes of existence that not only relate to the cosmos, but very interestingly, also expound upon the workings of human history. Intriguing too that although Kabalistic thought is believed to have existed since before the time of Christ, it didn't really become popular until this time, emerging from post-Islamic Spain as an alternative theosophy to the prevailing strict orthodoxies of Judaism, Christianity, and Islam. Here we need only note that Kabalism is definitely a mystical-wisdom tradition, which would also confer upon it the colors blue and white in the face of the reds and red-blacks of the patriarchal and often militant religions of the day.

But back to the story: The Christian reconquest of Spain prompted the expulsion of the Jews and the arrival of the infamous Spanish Inquisition in 1478 CE. Complete with appropriate red-black symbolism, the Inquisitors enforced mass expulsions and 'conversions' to Christianity at the point of the sword and thus drove a fatal and far-reaching wedge between Muslims, Jews, and Christians alike. Sadly once again, man used religion as a justification for the most horrific abuses.

So it appears that this (if any) providential attempt at unity (via the agency of Islam in Spain) was not to endure. At least that's what the current enmities between Jews, Muslims, and Christians would suggest. The discrepancies of each of these three faith movements appears to have exacerbated since the 15th century, with pious elitism, paranoia, dogmatism, pride, arrogance, and the scourges of sectarianism and nationalism reinforcing the negatives in each tradition (please excuse the generalizations). As a result we are left with; (i) a Judaism that is for the most part still locked into Old Testament thinking *without* her (red) messiah and who, like the archetypal female (blue and white), has struggled both ideologically and politically throughout history to survive in a hostile society surrounded by masculine reds and red-blacks; the Roman Empire, middle-ages Christianity, the Spanish Inquisition, Nazism, Communism, the Arab League, the P.L.O., Hamas, Hezbollah, etc. (ii) A Christianity that continues to be plagued with patriarchal attitudes (red), often suffering the excesses and deficiencies of the masculine; most evident in its more authoritarian forms such as strict Roman Catholicism or Protestant Fundamentalism (21 ♣). (iii) A modern Islam that appears to have lost the compassionate flavor of its origins, and has for the most part exchanged its thrust for scientific knowledge and social justice (green) with a narrow minded and often-radical fundamentalism (red and black). Sadly, the symbols and the colors all confirm these facts with modern Judaism still carrying no red, and Roman Catholicism and Islam still displaying no blue in their vexillologies* (figs. 7, 20, 21 ♣) – although it should be reiterated that certain Protestant sects have indeed chosen red, white, and blue as their official standards since the turn of the 20th century. Interesting is it not, that this should mirror the inclusion of women into their executives, as well as a more democratic approach to their respective ministries?

Meanwhile in the oldest established branch of Christianity, namely Roman Catholicism; whilst age-old patriarchal attitudes, structures, and doctrines do remain generally in force, we have nevertheless witnessed the gradual promotion of the enigmatic Virgin Mary (blue and white) to a position of co-redemptrix with Jesus (red and white). Although the theology and the Mariology surrounding this development is convoluted and confusing even to the trained religious scholar,[54] the solid fact remains that the original, subliminal triadic archetype as defined in this work has once again presented itself to the collective consciousness in symbolic-and-sensory, albeit mystical forms: Christ as hero-redeemer and King, the 'Second Adam' and son of God; the original male archetype almost always depicted in red and white. And Mary, Queen of Heaven; also regularly known as 'Queen of the Universe' or the 'Second Eve' fulfilling all the mystical requirements of the archetypal mother figure, habitually dressed in blues and whites both in popular paintings and whenever 'She' makes a mystical appearance (figs.25, 27 ♣). And although the historical reality of Mary's maternal role to Jesus is not in question; what does beg an answer is how indeed Jesus and Mary have come to be recognized in Catholic doctrine as archetypal son and daughter under God; brother and sister; and redeemer and co-redemptrix? Not to mention mystical spouses in union with the Holy Ghost in their roles as the cosmic 'Second Adam' and 'Second Eve' respectively; adorned jointly in white, red, and blue.

Could the answer lie in subliminal archetypes one wonders?

---

* Due to his personal devotion to Our Lady, the late Pope John Paul II carried blue in his personal standard

# The Color of Truth - Volume I:  Diagrams and Illustrations

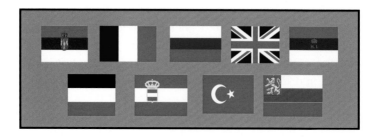

### FIG. 1 THE ALLIES (TOP) AND THE CENTRAL POWERS DURING WWI

(Top L-R) Serbia: France: Russia: Britain: Montenegro: Germany: A-Hungary: Turkey: Bulgaria

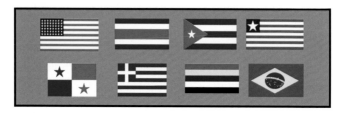

### FIG. 2 THE UNITED STATES AND EIGHT ALLIES JOIN THE WAR IN 1917

(Top L-R) United States: Costa Rica: Cuba: Liberia: Siam: Panama: Greece: China: Brazil:

### FIG. 3 TARGETS OF JAPANESE AGGRESSION DURING THE WAR YEARS

(L to R) China: Korea: Russia: Japan

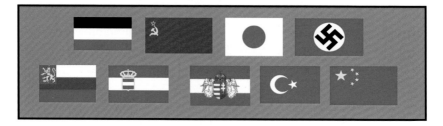

### FIG. 4 VARIOUS 'OPPOSITION' FORCES IN THE TWENTIETH CENTURY

Germany: USSR: Japan: Nazis: Bulgaria: Austria-Hungary: Romania: Turkey: Red China

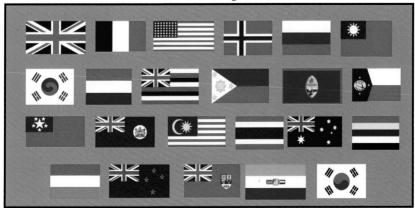

## FIG. 5 THE REMARKABLE DISPLAY OF RED, WHITE, AND BLUE SYMBOLISM

(From Top L) Britain: France: USA: Norway: Russia: Allied China (now Taiwan): (old) Korea: Netherlands: Hawaii: Philippines: Guam: Wake Is: Midway Is: Hong Kong: British Malaya: Thailand: Australia: (old) China: Luxembourg: New Zealand: Canada: S. Korea: South Africa

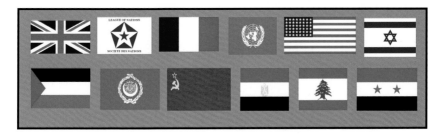

## FIG. 6 POLITICAL SYMBOLISM OF THE MIDDLE EAST

(Top) Great Britain: League of Nations: France: United Nations: USA: Israel: (Bottom) PLO: Arab League: USSR: Egypt: Lebanon: Syria

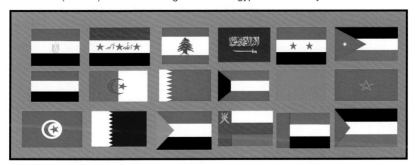

## FIG. 7 NATIONS OF THE ARAB LEAGUE C. 1960

(From Top, L to R) Egypt (H.Q. of Arab League): Iraq: Lebanon: Saudi Arabia: Syria: Transjordan (now Jordan): Yemen: Algeria: Bahrain: Kuwait: Libya: Morocco: Tunisia: Qatar: Sudan: Oman: the UAE: the PLO

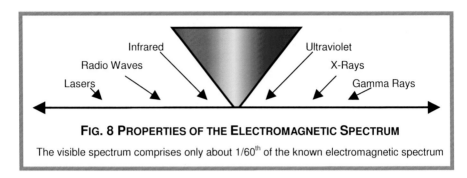

**FIG. 8 PROPERTIES OF THE ELECTROMAGNETIC SPECTRUM**

The visible spectrum comprises only about 1/60th of the known electromagnetic spectrum

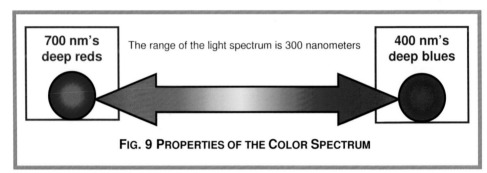

**FIG. 9 PROPERTIES OF THE COLOR SPECTRUM**

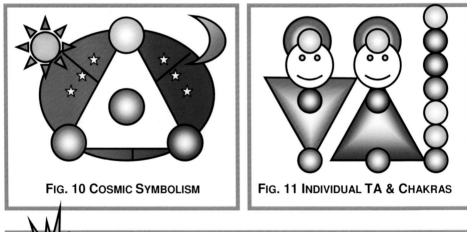

**FIG. 10 COSMIC SYMBOLISM**

**FIG. 11 INDIVIDUAL TA & CHAKRAS**

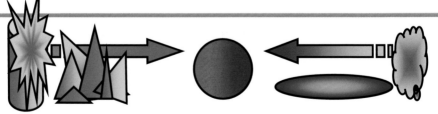

**FIG. 12 SYMBOLIC ELEMENTS OF THE GREEK SOUL & BIBLICAL SYMBOLISM**

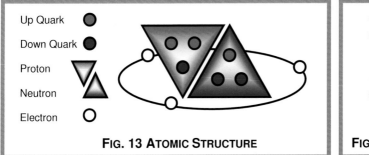

Up Quark ●

Down Quark ●

Proton ▽

Neutron △

Electron ○

**FIG. 13 ATOMIC STRUCTURE**

**FIG. 14 DNA**

**FIG. 15 THE HINDU TRIMURTI AND A.U.M.**

| First male archetype, health, energy, vitality, male, power, greatness, pioneering, leadership, sexual energy, all things physical, strength, heroism, positive, the body, vigor, stimulating, passion, material prosperity | Lust, sins, dragon, fights-with- angel, devours-the-Savior, takes away peace, threat to God's people, mother of harlots, Communism, war, opposition to white, absence of feminine, Fascism, Nazism, rage, force, anger | The hero, male, central figure, first-out-of-womb, birthright, red cloak, sacrifice, ritual, conqueror of evil, strong, valiant, true, savior, life, will, power, leadership, battles, martyrs, pioneers, victorious |

**Fig. 16 Thematic Subdivisions of the Color Red**

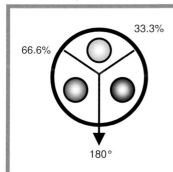

33.3%

66.6%

180°

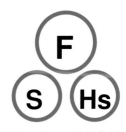

Father, Son, & Holy Spirit

**FIG. 17 COSMIC CIRCLE; NAZI & FASCIST SYMBOLISM; THE HOLY TRINITY**

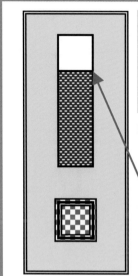
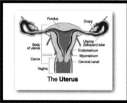
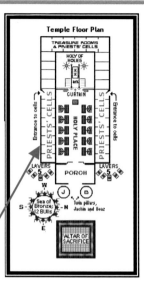

Both the Tabernacle and the Temple physically resemble a uterus. The red-white-blue veil separating the Holy of Holies (white) from the Priests' area (blue) is symbolic of the hymen. The younger Tabernacle (L) lacks the symbolic fallopian tubes of the later Temple (R). The entrance passes between two pillars (legs?)

**FIG. 18 SEXUAL SYMBOLISM OF THE TABERNACLE AND THE TEMPLE**

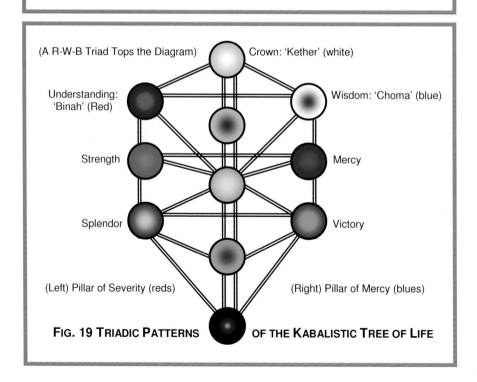

(A R-W-B Triad Tops the Diagram)        Crown: 'Kether' (white)

Understanding: 'Binah' (Red)        Wisdom: 'Choma' (blue)

Strength        Mercy

Splendor        Victory

(Left) Pillar of Severity (reds)        (Right) Pillar of Mercy (blues)

**FIG. 19 TRIADIC PATTERNS OF THE KABALISTIC TREE OF LIFE**

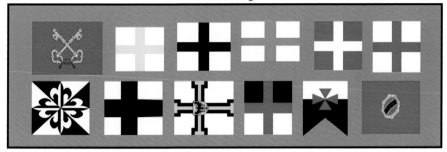

**FIG. 20 PRE-REFORMATION FLAGS OF CHRISTIANITY**

From Top L to R: French Papal Enclave c. 1300, 5 Crusader Cross Flags (12 Century),
Dominican Order, 2 Teutonic Knights Flags, 2 Knights Templar Flags, Pontificate Territories

**FIG. 21 SOME POST-REFORMATION CHRISTIAN FLAGS**

Christian Flag, Anglican, Episcopalian, Anglican Australian, Ch. of England, Ch. of Wales,
Scottish Presbyterian, Salvation Army, 4-Square Gospel, Churches of Christ, Mormons,
Baptists, Assemblies of God, Methodists USA, Papacy in 1669, Vatican State (Roman Catholic)

**FIG. 22 FLAGS ASSOCIATED WITH OTHER RELIGIONS**

Buddhism, Flag of Shiva (Hinduism), Baha'i's, Indian Sufi Brotherhood, Sikhism
Islam: Flag of Quraish, Era of the Prophet, Umayyad, Ottoman Muslims, OIC, Nation of Islam

**FIG. 23 COSMIC SYMBOLISM AND MONOTHEISTIC TRADITIONS**

Christianity and Sun (left), Judaism and Star (center), Islam and Moon (right)

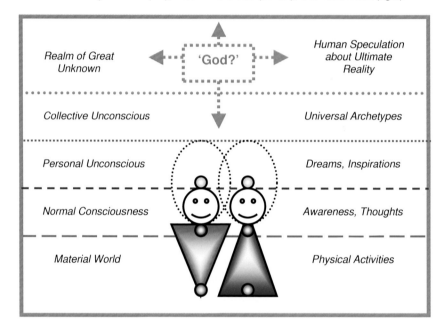

**FIG. 24 STAGES OF HUMAN CONSCIOUSNESS AND THE TRIADIC ARCHETYPE**

**FIG. 25 ANIMUS & ANIMA / JESUS & MARY AS ARCHETYPES / YIN YANG**

Profound similarities exist between the concepts, themes, and functions of dualistic archetypes

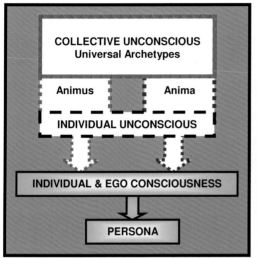
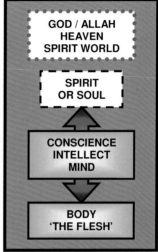

## FIG. 26 JUNGIAN THEORY OF PERSONALITY & RELIGIOUS THEORY

## Fig. 27 Some Traditional Hero, Heroine, & Anti-Hero Figures

Dali Lama, Santa Claus, Jesus Christ, Prometheus, Gameboy 'Hero'
Mother Theresa, Lady Liberty, 'Our Lady', Joan of Arc, Gameboy 'Heroine'
Count Dracula, Darth Vader, the Devil (or Satan), cartoon 'Villain'

## SELECTED FEATURES OF THE TRIADIC ARCHETYPE: EXAMPLES 1-8

*Remembering that each individual human hosts their own specific triadic sequence despite their primary designation as either male or female respectively (fig.11 ♣), so do many of the charted aspects, themes, attributes, or agencies listed here carry their own intrinsic triadic formulae despite being part of a greater or larger triadic theme.*

*Therefore whilst the propriety of many of the listed triads are clearly self-evident, we should also allow for the fact that (a) this is not yet a fully developed science;(b) that all human taxonomies are ultimately somewhat limited and artificial; (c) that a certain amount of intersection and overlapping amongst listed themes is unavoidable; and (d) that some of the triads listed have yet to be discussed in the text. (See extra notes\*).*

*We also need to note that the following tables display the information in a horizontal linear mode, but many of the triads listed might be better represented in vertical, triangular, or even circular mode, such as the spirit-mind-body triad (vertical descending), the white-blue-red triad (triangular), and the proton-neutron-electron (circular).*

*I also humbly acknowledge that alterations or adjustments may be necessary in the future in order to 'tighten-up', add, or even eliminate some of the more abstract triads, and I eagerly await suggestions from those who may be more experienced in any given field.*

*In short, please be patient with a very inadequate taxonomy, and simply observe the striking consistency of the triadic archetype phenomenon in so many shapes, forms, and disciplines.*

## Example 1: Science / Quantum Physics / Numeric

|   | Red | White | Blue |
|---|---|---|---|
| A | Deep Reds | Light | Deep Blues |
| B | Infrared | Color Spectrum | Ultraviolet |
| C | Proton | Electron | Neutron |
| D | Up Quarks | Gluons | Down Quarks |
| E | Electricity | Electromagnetic Spectrum | Magnetism |
| F | 700 nanometers | One, 300nms, or Infinity | 400 nanometers |
| G | Positive | Fusion / Union | Negative |
| H | Experimentation | Observation | Reflection |

## Example 2: Ontological / Thematic / General

|   | Red | White | Blue |
|---|---|---|---|
| A | Masculine Elements | Original Principle | Feminine Elements |
| B | Creation | Cosmic Truth | Knowledge |
| C | The Word | The Way | Wisdom |
| D | External | Eternal | Internal |
| E | Action | Concept | Plan |
| F | Energy | Inspiration | Reason |
| G | Body | Spirit | Mind |
| H | Justice | Life | Liberty |
| J | Blood | Oxygen | Water |
| K | Fire | Air | Water |
| L | When? | Why? | How? |
| M | Solution | Problem | Analysis |
| N | Achievement | Desire | Purpose |
| P | Achieve | Concieve | Believe |
| Q | Logos | Ethos | Pathos |
| R | Yang | Union | Yin |
| S* | Left | Center | Right |

## Example 3: Psychological / Psychospiritual

|   | Red | White | Blue |
|---|---|---|---|
| A* | Material | Spiritual | Social |
| B | Actual | Noumenal | Ideal |
| C | Reality | Inspirations / Dreams | Thoughts |
| D | Creativity | Unconsciousness | Consciousness |
| E | Extrinsic | Questers | Intrinsic |
| F | Personal Choice | Genetics | Environment |
| G* | Animus | Psyche / Persona | Anima |
| H | Masculinity | Integrated Psyche | Femininity |

## Example 4: Human / Relational / Social

|   | Red | White | Blue |
|---|---|---|---|
| A | Body | Soul | Mind |
| B | Physical | Spiritual | Emotional |
| C | Masculine | Creation | Feminine |
| D | Man | Love | Woman |
| E | Father / Husband | Parental / Conjugal Love | Mother / Wife |
| F | Brother / Son | Sibling / Filial Love | Sister / Daughter |
| G | Individual | Community | Family |
| H | Productive | Inspirational / Creative | Intellectual |
| J | Man | Union and Creation | Woman |
| K | Sperm | Conception | Egg |

## Example 5: Biblical / Judeo-Christian / Theological

|   | Red | White | Blue |
|---|---|---|---|
| A | Adam | God | Eve |
| B | Tree of Life | Paradise | Tree of Knowledge |
| C | Logos | God / Yahweh | Sophia |
| D | The Word | God | Wisdom |
| E | Messiah, Redeemer | Jehovah | Bride, Co-Redeemer |
| F | Burning Bush | Presence of God | Enveloping Cloud |
| G | Pillar of Fire | Mercy Seat | Pillar of Cloud |
| H | Temple | Ark of Covenant | Tabernacle |
| J* | Pillar; "Joachim" | The Temple | Pillar; "Boaz" |
| K | Outer Courtyard | Holy of Holies | Inner Sanctuary |
| L | Baptism of Fire | Baptism of Spirit | Baptism of Water |
| M | Charity | Faith | Hope |
| N | Flesh | Soul | Conscience |
| P* | The Son | The Father | Holy Spirit |

## Example 6: Other Religious / Mystical / Mythological

|   | Red | White | Blue |
|---|---|---|---|
| A | Body | Spirit | Mind |
| B | Healthy | Holy | Happy |
| C | M | A | U |
| D | Red Chakra | Crown Chakra | Blue Chakra |
| E* | Heart | Inner Eye | Throat |
| F* | Outer | Secret | Inner |
| G* | Sat | Ananda | Chit |
| H | Vishnu | Brahma | Shiva |
| J | Te | Tao | Ching |
| K | Jade Pure | Great Pure | Upper Pure |

| | | | |
|---|---|---|---|
| L | Yang | Nirvana | Yin |
| M* | Binah | Keter | Choma |
| N* | Ru'ach | Neshemah | Nefesh |
| P* | Lingam | Conception | Yoni |
| Q | Actual Truth | True Religious Experience | Conceptual Truth |
| R | Ritual | Meditation | Prayer |
| S | Charity | Love | Compassion |
| T* | Astlik | Vahagn | Anahit |
| U* | Hades | Zeus | Poseidon |
| V* | Horus | Osiris | Isis |
| W* | Inti | Viracocha | Illapa |
| X | Sun | The Heavens | Moon |

## Example 7: Historical / Political / Sociological

| | Red | White | Blue |
|---|---|---|---|
| A | Industrial Revolution | Renaissance | Enlightenment |
| B | Products | Ideas | Plans |
| C | Mechanical | Artistic | Philosophical |
| D | Technical Skills | Morality | Academics |
| E | Industry | Government / Law | Education |
| F | Military | Executive | Legislative |
| G | Society | Religion | Science |
| H | Individualism | Universalism | Collectivism |
| J | Capitalism | Democracy | Socialism |
| K | Practice | Ideology | Theory |
| L* | Holy Roman Empire | Papacy | Kingdom of France |

## Example 8: Other Possible Representations

| | Red | White | Blue |
|---|---|---|---|
| A | Sun | Stars | Moon |
| B | Earth | Sky | Oceans |
| C | Fire | Air | Water |
| D | Solid | Gas | Liquid |
| E | Core | Atmosphere | Surface |
| F | Hot | Cold | Cool |
| G* | Experiential | Attitudinal | Creative |
| H | Act | Feel | Think |
| J | Pragmatism | Morality | Ethics |
| K | Get | Want | Plan |
| L | Comprehend | Observe | Interpret |
| M | End | Beginning | Middle |

## * Examples 1-8: Explanatory Notes

2S: Left and right positions may be reversible

3A: Sociologist William James' social theory

3F: Religious personality types as viewed in the study of the Psychology of Religion

3G: Concepts from Jungian psychology

5J: Pillars of Solomon's temple were named 'Smiter' and 'Sustainer' respectively

5P: Although listed here in idealized format, the Christian Trinity has traditionally been conceptually devoid of the feminine (♣ 17)

6E & F: Aspects of the Hindu and Buddhist Chakra systems

6G: From Joseph Campbell's *The Power of Myth*, ancient Sanskrit language: "Sat" meaning 'being', "Chit" meaning 'consciousness', and "Ananda" meaning 'bliss or rapture'

6M: The crowning triad of the Kabala in Jewish mysticism (♣ 19)

6N: From Jewish mysticism's Zohar; the three aspects of the psyche or soul

6P: Hindu genitalia worship; 'Lingam' being the male organ; Yoni the female

6T, U, V, W: From the mythologies of Armenia, Greece, Egyptian, and Incan civilizations

7L: This topic is discussed fully in Volume II

8G: From Stephen Covey's *Seven Habits of Highly Effective People*

# PART TWO
# REFLECTIONS

*Where we delve deeper into the fields of philosophy, religion, psychology, and numerology, as we endeavor to place the phenomenon of the triadic archetype in context to our world today*

# CHAPTER NINE

# TALKING ABOUT TRUTH

*We open Part Two with a detailed discussion about the meaning and significance of the much-abused term 'truth' before moving on to consider additional examples of the triadic archetype in philosophy, mythology, religion, geometrics, and psychology, and their possible relevance to us today.*

Until now, we have looked chiefly at facts and figures and closely related hypotheses, basing our provisional conclusions upon the evidence put before us. In other words, for the main part we have simply reported the facts and allowed truth to be its own witness. But here in Part Two we will be encroaching upon more speculative territory, including the realms of social science, philosophy, psychology, and mysticism as we search for more evidence and better understandings of the triadic archetype and what it means to us today. But we still want to remain as methodical and systematic as possible. So before we engage the triadic archetype in more depth we first need to clarify a few important points about contemporary understandings of the nature of truth. In engaging prevailing religious beliefs on this topic we need to be frank and uncompromising in confronting any and all perspectives that may obstruct a full and reasonable acceptance of our research. Therefore the reader is respectfully advised (and encouraged) to absorb the following central points thoughtfully and patiently; not merely as a defense against any contrary opinions, but also as a preamble for the dramatic evidence to come.

**Defining Truth**

Truth is a much-disputed term. In certain circles, even the title of this book might give rise to charges of presumptuousness inasmuch as 'Truth' is understood with a capital 'T'. But truth can also be understood simply as 'that which corresponds with facts or reality' and it is chiefly this latter concept that lies behind the title *The Color of Truth*. By 'facts and reality' I am of course referring to tangible truths that can be verified through simple observation or commonsense logic. This is in contrast to those more personal truths or experiences that may be colored by one's own cultural or religious perspectives. In short, the difference between 'objective' and 'subjective' reality. 'Subjective'; indicating a personal viewpoint that may or may not be 'true' to others; and 'objective' meaning 'seen from the broader collective viewpoint'. But of course, inasmuch as there are smaller and larger groupings within nations, cultures, and religions for example, and therefore lesser and greater 'collective viewpoints' within any given society, then we might expect varying levels of subjectivity and objectivity in any given argument. Some would argue that it is impossible *not* to have a subjective viewpoint, but I strongly disagree. This, based upon the fact that any lasting solution to the world's problems must arise from a global (objective) perspective that places the fate of the world and of society above the (subjective) interests of any given nation, religion, political party, agency, or individual thereof: The quest for a universal reality in other words. Certainly we still have a long way to go before human institutions align along a common collective objectivity, but undoubtedly this is our destiny. Seen in the formation of institutions like the League of Nations, the Interfaith Councils, the United Nations and so on; as well as in the move away from authoritarianism towards democracy; and in those occasional sparks of enlightened objectivity that have emerged in the lives and teachings of some of history's greats. The alternative; a world ideologically divided and constantly at war is simply unacceptable: Especially when the latter is ultimately a product of human ignorance.

In writing this book I have endeavored as much as possible — and as well as I am able — to adhere to the (objective) universal-collective viewpoint. Whilst acknowledging that I too am a product of certain cultural influences and limitations, I have nevertheless avoided presenting my own subjective opinions or beliefs insofar as I can identify and separate them from the objective facts. This is not to say that I do not *personally* sense some profound association between universal Truth (with a capital T) and the discoveries in this book, but there is an unwritten rule in the hierarchy of academics that states that one must always temper one's opinions with an objective humility, and never *ever* presume to have a handle on absolute truths. Even when a scholar or scientist may believe that their argument is inviolable, the academic establishment requires that they present their hypothesis giving due respect and acknowledgement to established positions on the subject – even contrary ones – or should I say *most especially* the contrary ones. In this manner, scientific debate manages to avoid over-personalizing any particular issue and thus typically escapes becoming embroiled in redundant emotional disputes. With the added security of systematic testing and the stringent proofs of the scientific method to depend upon, we can see how this rule of objectivity, humility, and mutual respect is indeed a good one that clearly serves the process of discovery and edification. All the same, there are times when tactful diplomacy must give way to candor and frankness.

The scientific method for establishing facts is typically based upon the formula: (1) observation, (2) hypothesis, (3) experiment, (4) report results, (5) others repeat the experiment and achieve the same results, (6) interpretation of results, and (7) formal documentation of facts. But whenever scientists dare to approach the subject of 'truth-in-religion' they quickly find that the rules are very different. Indeed one might even argue that there are in fact no rules when compared to the scientific method.

For instance, most religious beliefs are based upon personal revelation, doctrines, faith, and tradition, and not necessarily upon knowledge or even reasonable hypotheses. Secondly, matters of religion are highly subjective and emotive to the faithful adherent, who frequently interprets any critique of his or her chosen belief system as a direct personal attack – or worse still, as a direct attack upon their God. This presents the evangelizing scientist with a considerable problem: Either to try to overcome the prevailing unawareness, suspicion, and/or emotional hostility of the non-scientific mindset or simply (and more safely), to confine one's activities to the scientific arena. Regrettably (but perhaps wisely) most have chosen the latter course. But this only serves to widen the science-religion divide, and polarize these two different approaches to 'truth'. The problem is greatly exacerbated when, in discussing matters of religion, well-intentioned scholars mistakenly apply the scientific rules of objectivity and respect to religious hypotheses. This gives the untrained observer the impression that such beliefs and doctrines are in fact credible in the first place. And whilst we should never withdraw the requirements for objectivity and respect in any type of debate, we need also acknowledge the vast differences between promoting truths that are based upon the scientific method, and the often-sectarian speculations of the religious world. According professional respect to fractious belief systems that continue to cause friction, confusion, and division whilst simultaneously flying in the face of scientific facts does little more than provide a pseudo-scientific platform for the promotion of untenable ideologies. There are times and places when calling a spade a spade – without apologetics or deferments – is the right and only course to take. But this requires an uncommon amount of courage, conviction, and vocational resolve, especially amongst scholars or scientists who may find themselves bound by their material or social dependence upon their host communities.

In the science-religion debate the principle of respect and freedom for other perspectives certainly needs to be honored, but more importantly, it needs to be applied with discernment and wisdom. Otherwise, as history testifies all too vividly, we find ourselves pandering to ideologies that are rooted in direct opposition to these very same principles of freedom and mutual respect. Oppressive authoritarian institutions for example – whether political or religious – can only survive and repopulate in a vacuum of relative ignorance. In totalitarian regimes at least there is no pretense, and the vacuum of ignorance is enforced by overtly brutal means. On the other hand, in so-called 'educated' countries more subtle exploitations are required: Ideological indoctrination of the young; political and religious propaganda; fostering emotional and/or material dependency; or other subtle forms of suppression have become the norm. Whether social, political or religious, this hardly translates into freedom or respect; let alone true education. For there is a crucial difference between indoctrinations that instruct the student in any particular belief or ideology with the expectation of unconditional acceptance; vs. a genuine education, which enlightens and informs a student using logic and reason in the process of rational self-discovery. Each has its place in the learning process but there are certain forms of instruction, most notably in philosophical or religious discussions that should *never* involve indoctrination. For indoctrination is not really concerned with the enlightenment of the mind, but primarily with the conformation and obedience of the student. You are told; and you are expected to believe. Hence its popularity with authoritarian institutions who by and large fear the advances of true enlightenment and genuine personal freedoms. On the other hand, self-evident truths such as the findings of science are far better disposed to the educational process. There is no fear there, only the firm but gentle admonition to disciplined and persistent research. Truth after all will reveal herself (says science) when enough questioning layers are peeled away. But indoctrinations on the other hand— when not rooted in empirical facts and data—can all too easily become deeply obstructive mental strata to the uncovering of universal Truths (with a capital T). Given that our discoveries concerning the triadic archetype are, in my opinion, part of that larger body of collective Truths (with a capital T), then the greatest obstacle to their understanding will probably come from unsubstantiated, conflicting religious beliefs and traditions. The reason for such misunderstandings is chiefly due to the inappropriate use of indoctrination under the guise of 'religious education'. Indeed, in context of any given religion's attempts to suppress any other forms of learning, the term 'religious education' is both a misnomer and an *oxymoron*[*].

For example, vehicle mechanics is one subject well-suited to the indoctrination process – provided of course that it is followed up with an educational experience. This is simply because there is only *one* right way to assemble an engine, or replace a spare wheel. The facts are plain to see and if you get it wrong, well, the engine might just explode or your wheel will fall off. With the facts so clear, and with such risks at stake, a primary indoctrination is both appropriate and necessary. But with subjects that are not based upon clear, tangible, logical facts and data, (such as religion or spirituality for instance) indoctrination is plainly inappropriate. More seriously, inasmuch as education aims for truth and enlightenment, in such cases attempts at indoctrination are fundamentally dishonest, and most certainly infringe upon the true education process and the genuine (spiritual) enlightenment of the individual. For as we all well know, even in the face of undeniable realities, traditional religious beliefs in particular die hard. Rooted in the deepest and most credulous reaches of the mind, many questionable beliefs have been meticulously cultivated over the years through repetition, tradition and ritual, and dutifully sunk in mental concrete so-to-speak as a bastion against the challenges and disappointments of reality. Getting through to those concrete boxes, let alone trying to move or uproot them is probably the greatest challenge facing educators of integrity today. But we must try. Before we can hope for any success however, we must first understand how and why we think and believe as we do, and why we often choose to elevate our personal, cultural, or religious beliefs over the scientific facts of life.

So with this somewhat provocative opening statement behind us, let us now continue our journey into Part Two of *The Color of Truth Volume I* by exploring some of the taxonomies employed in the information-gathering processes common to the human mind; the classification systems used everywhere in research, academics, and religious pursuits at both the

---

[*] Oxymoron; when contradictory terms are combined, such as; 'a deafening silence'

individual and the institutionalized level. With apologies for some of the more unfamiliar terms being used, this discussion is nevertheless crucially important in understanding both the necessity for, yet the profound limitations of human classification systems in the face of a universal, or truly objective reality.

## Subjectivity, Objectivity, and Taxonomies

As evidenced by the resolute albeit often contradictory convictions of various philosophical schools, the cognitive education process—most especially in partisan or religious circles—remains plagued by problems that continue to obstruct the objectives of true erudition. In short, I propose that any sectarian-based 'education' is not in fact real education.

Having already briefly discussed the issue of indoctrination, let us now review the closely-related problem of elitist thinking; that rather proud tendency of humans to think subjectively-and-exclusively, vs. objectively-and-inclusively, the latter being the truer definition of the authentic educational mindset. Although deliberately advanced by many false teachings, the exclusive-elitist mindset (in opposition to the inclusive-collective mindset) is inadvertently fostered by two other factors common to all spheres of learning and instruction. Those factors are (i) subjectivity, and (ii) inadequate taxonomies. Subjectivity we have already discussed; taxonomies on the other hand are simply our traditional ways of cataloging and sorting out different 'stuff'. Insofar as these are present in the learning process they often obstruct the accumulation of consensual or universal knowledge. To put it another way; we differ and argue about various 'truths' chiefly because of the existence of personal perspectives, and 'artificial' classification systems.

Firstly let's revisit the matter of subjectivity: Since all human beings are both unique and subjective, information is understandably processed in a unique and generally subjective way. Thus, different opinions are not only unavoidable, but are arguably the very essence of collective truth (but only when viewed objectively of course). As Oscar Wilde astutely put it; "A truth ceases to be true when more than one person believes in it."[55] By this we may assume he was referring to the deeply personal and uniquely subjective aspect of each human mind as it accepts or rejects 'truths' in life. He may also of course have been alluding to the vast difference between a personally-*experienced* truth and a second-hand *belief* – the profound difference between knowledge and faith that very few dogmatists have ever given serious thought to. Perhaps Wilde should have said that any truth ceases to be true precisely *because* a person *believes in it* – rather than actually *knowing* it to be true – in which case even one person simply *believing* in any given truth is reason enough to question its validity. The act of believing is itself the main issue of concern; not just the object or idea that it refers to. The greater danger then arises when we allow our personal subjective beliefs to coagulate into elitist social structures (usually in the form of religious institutions), thus giving a false sense of reality and substance to unverified opinions that rightly still belong on the philosophers desk. And although faith is arguably a great human virtue under certain circumstances; solidifying our religious or philosophical hypotheses with traditions and rituals serves chiefly to justify, fuel, and even sanctify our ignorance and our arrogance. Again, please excuse the clumsy generalizations. In other words, in the absence of a greater personal knowledge or experience, we tend to use religious rituals and creeds to substantiate our beliefs, and then somehow try to force the universe to defer to our viewpoint. And if the universe stubbornly resists, well, we still have 'our faith' to comfort us. But as we mentioned before, although we are each at liberty to believe anything we wish, such beliefs may, and often are, very, very far removed from the truth. Sadly and inevitably, someone somewhere will pay the price for our ignorance and our intransigence.

Secondly, and compounding this first subjective factor are those myriad complications arising out of the inexact nature of the *etymological**  classification systems common to the sciences and religions, as well as our individual usage and understanding of them. In other words, the incompleteness and artificiality of academic categories. This not only includes standard scientific taxonomies such as the labels 'mathematics, biology, chemistry, geography' etc., but also the verbal gymnastics associated with various hypotheses, theories, doctrines, dogmas, opinions, and beliefs, as well as other semantic complications.

For instance; what I may perceive as 'true' or 'real' or 'scientific' or 'religious' or this-or-that, may very well be different to your perceptions and understandings. This is simply due to the unavoidable inconsistencies that arise out of our differing interpretations of particular words or ideas, from time to time and from culture to culture. Words are only metaphors after all. You say "God" and I say "Ultimate Reality". You say "truth" and I think "sincerity". You see a beautiful fish swimming in an aquarium – and I see lunch. As unique individuals we each have a right to a unique perspective but there is always a greater reality. This is not a matter of 'right' and 'wrong' per se, but more a matter of seeing the bigger truth above-and-

---

* Etymology; the branch of linguistics that deals with the origin and development of words

beyond individual perspectives. That fish may indeed become my lunch later on but right now, it is also your beautiful fish. In either case it is still a fish. It would be pointless to fight about who had the 'truest' perspective. But we usually do, don't we?

Culture, social environment, education, and the accurate use of language – all have their bearing upon our ability to communicate effectively. Naturally, the further apart the perspectives or the less familiar the person, the topic, or the situation, the higher the likelihood of misinterpretations. Even when scholars of the same genre debate, misconceptions and misunderstandings are common, although perhaps nominally masked by the requisite diplomacy of civilized discussions. Thankfully however, the rules of the scientific method minimize these misunderstandings. Obviously, at lesser-educated or more superstitious levels of society we may expect more acrimony. The more abstract or complex the topic (such as religion and spirituality for instance), the greater the risk of subjective interpretations, and there is always the danger of irrational beliefs and opinions further clouding the issue. When such differences of opinion arise they may or may not result in enmity and discord but they do invariably distract from the matter at hand, which *should* be the accurate discovery and efficient accumulation of knowledge and truth. In short, our inherent subjectivity (i), coupled with inadequate taxonomies (ii), and poor individual comprehension skills (iii), are the greatest impediments to objective learning. The 'normal' human interpretation process in other words, is fundamentally flawed. But if this is actually the case, then what then is the solution?

Well, what is apparently needed is a comprehensive, universal language that can neither be misquoted nor misunderstood. 'Perfect' communication in other words that only reflects fundamental truths. Instead of using human language to try to convey to others piecemeal what we merely *believe* to be true, perhaps we would have been better advised to first find out what is in fact universally true, and *then* build our language systems around it? Such as with the 'languages' of science and mathematics for example, where errors of understanding are relatively rare even across international boundaries. Instead of limited languages trying to define truth, truth in these cases defines the language. It is a simple case of *not* putting the cart before the horse. Ethical scientists have always followed this rule but many career religionists and pseudo-scientists on the other hand have made a life's work of ignoring it. Indeed, most of religion's historical difficulties can be traced to the proud tendency of religious scholars to presume to put into words that which privately, they knew was beyond their grasp. But as we mentioned in Chapter Three; whether based in faith or not, longstanding religious institutions are not built upon vague concepts. Just like political ideologies they too must have authority for their existence and justifications for that authority. Rock-solid concrete creeds and doctrines conveniently supply that authority; constructs that in turn give rise to a new type of social parasite; those who (well-intentioned or not) prostitute their intellects building careers out of constructing clever, but ultimately misleading apologetics for speculative dogmas and doctrines. The mountains of such materials gathering dust in the religious archives serves mostly to intimidate would-be searchers-of-truth who, in their admirable but misguided humility and believing in the intellectual greatness of esteemed church scholars, dare not presume to challenge long established creeds; let alone engage the daunting task of unraveling complex and intricate dogmatics. Their understandable mistake of course is in not recognizing the ultimate smallness of such intellectuals, who have in many cases done no less than sell their sycophantic souls. And we, trusting, all too often follow them unwittingly into the abyss.

The reader should at this point understand that these rather challenging and confrontational statements are not being made to arbitrarily attack religion per se, but more to challenge our own personal credulity; our historical gullibility; our disturbing willingness to allow others to do our thinking for us. Surely, after so much bloodshed in history—still ongoing today, and mostly carried out by well-intentioned but naive religionists—nobody will argue this point. Furthermore, because much of the data that surrounds the triadic archetype challenges many long-established beliefs, we also need to bolster our objectivity and courage as we make determined and purposeful inroads into the traditional territory of dogmatists and absolutists. Shedding light into dark and secretive places can be particularly disquieting, especially for those who have made themselves comfortable there. But truth and light are one-and-the-same, and it has been my experience that True revelation (with a capital 'T') ultimately and eventually bears witness to itself. However it rarely, if ever, translates manifestly into absolute dogma.

So, if we are agreed that this particular education vs. indoctrination, and subjectivity vs. objectivity problem arises in the first place out of presumptuous and/or preemptive dogmatics, based upon (at best) partly-comprehended truths; we may justly surmise that if we can somehow acquire a universal language-form that parallels universal principles and laws, and *then* apply that language to our existing limited taxonomies and religious-truth claims, then hopefully the final outcome will be the elimination of conceptual errors and the fusing of previously discrete taxonomies into one universal *etymology:*[*] In short, the materialization of a comprehensive language-of-truth that would simply bear witness to itself.

The natural consequences of the emergence of any such comprehensive language would finally mark the end of non-collaborative, or non-interdependent thinking such as exists in sectarian ideologies. Sectarianism in all its destructive forms would then be exposed as the ignorant foolishness it really is and we could all then begin the collective journey of true, whole, and objective education.

Of course, this all sounds wonderful until we realize that in order to get to that place of discernment where we can accurately judge what is and is not 'universally true', and before we can translate such into any new *lexicon,*[†] we first have to process all manner of information through our faulty, and very subjective human minds, and through equally-limited artificial taxonomies. Understanding this process is obviously crucial to the accurate discernment of truth as and when it emerges, and by consequence, also vital to the clear identification of existing errors.

**Universal Truth Theory**

All human systems of learning that incorporate a subject-and-object, student-and-teacher model require some form of classification system for data. Whether the teacher in the model is a person such as a schoolteacher, parent, cleric, or college professor, or whether the object of instruction is in inanimate form such as an article, book, or media outlet the rule is the same: Information is imparted to the student, reader, or observer through the process of organizing and classifying information into digestible bytes.

For example; at the most preliminary level we have the literary classification of language both written and spoken, beginning with our ABC's and advancing through words, to sentences, to paragraphs. Then we have further classifications such as literature, academics, politics, religion, science, economics, and so forth, all of which use common language as a tool wherein we tailor the information to be imparted into further sub-categories; again, for ease of understanding and assimilation. This is the traditional way human beings have educated each other since the rise of consciousness. We start with little bytes, to snacks, to huge great mouthfuls of information, but only (if we are wise) moving onto the next greater category once we have digested the previous one(s). If we change the

---

[*] Etymology; the branch of linguistics that deals with the origin and development of words
[†] Lexicon; dictionary or stock of terms used for a particular language

sequence by proffering too large a mouthful before the smaller ones have been fully digested, we will only achieve mental indigestion so-to-speak, resulting in confusion and half-truths. After all, one cannot expect to understand Shakespeare without first learning one's ABC's. Nor can we expect to run before we have crawled. In this manner human education processes follow the dictates of that cosmic law that states that things *must* occur in sequence one after the other, in the correct order: The concept precedes the plan, which in turn precedes the action. Formation precedes development and growth, which in turn precedes maturity. The seed precedes the sapling that becomes the tree, and so on. We crawl, then we walk, and then we run. In almost any area of life, we can identify such three-stage developments that generally correspond to these principles, and whilst human intelligence obviously introduces a whole new range of complexities the principles do remain the same. We observe, we interpret, we comprehend. We feel, we think, we act. We want, we plan, we get, and so on. All corresponding neatly to the principles of the triadic archetype (see midsection Tables 1-8). We may, by force of will try to interfere with these principles, but always ultimately to our cost. When we take action for example without thinking through the project beforehand, we usually (unless we are very fortunate) come to grief. At very least, we cause unnecessary stress or difficulties either for ourselves or for others through mistakes, delays, inefficiencies etc. Likewise, responding blindly to our passions (or our beliefs) without rational consideration also has its cost.

For now we need but acknowledge the simple and obvious fact that we human beings—both as individuals and in collective groups—are at very best in a constant process of observing, absorbing, and assimilating fragments of information in categorical bytes. What's more, and contrary to the often-asinine intimations of far too many religionists, we undoubtedly still have a great deal to learn before we even dare to approach anything resembling 'absoluteness'. Truly absolute statements should ideally only reflect total, complete, and comprehensive knowledge. Hence, absolutism as a religious tenet is fundamentally contradictory. It is inappropriate, ill conceived, and ultimately born of ignorance and pride. It is no coincidence that both absolutism and sectarianism share these vices, for indeed they are very closely related. Both presuppose the superiority of one's own opinions, or of one's peer group over heathen or enemy 'others' without being in full possession of all the facts. Absolute judgments—just like sectarian judgments—arise from a base of relative ignorance or, from a condescending subjective bias.

As seen in the rise of religious terrorism worldwide; ignorance and absolutist thinking—combined with elitism—constitute a very dangerous mix. Humility and dogmatic arrogance cannot coexist; hence the profession of humility as a core spiritual virtue in the founding principles of the major faith traditions as well as in the aforementioned scientific method. Sadly, it is not practiced with nearly as much vigor as it is advertised. In an ideal world we would make a lifelong habit of rethinking our partisan and absolutist tendencies from this 'humility first' perspective. For as long as we realize and humbly accept that we are 'just learning', most of the attitudes and beliefs that fuel the destructive excesses of sectarianism simply could not develop. One day in the distant future perhaps we might indeed be qualified to claim a comprehensive understanding of cosmic truth. But based upon the improbability of any of us alive today reaching that goal, we may safely surmise that the notion of universal or absolute truth will for the time being remain an objective *concept* as opposed to the partial and subjective *theories* that most of us carry around with us: Theories, (especially when in the form of religious beliefs) that although having no substantial reality we nonetheless confidently declare as "Truth."

That which is both subjective and partial however, cannot by any definition be 'complete' in the universal sense – and therefore cannot be defined as 'universally true'. The same rule applies to all areas of human endeavor; whether science, academics, religion or whatever, no isolated agency has the right to declare anything 'absolute' unless it can be unequivocally recognized as such by all other human agencies at face value. Even in the event of such a consensus the wiser ones amongst us would still no doubt caution against presumptuous declarations.

So, whilst rightfully congratulating ourselves upon the great leaps and bounds of learning achieved during recent decades, we must at the same time acknowledge the limitations of the traditional approach to learning that is represented by our piecemeal categories-and-classifications systems and ask the very important question: "What if none of these academic, scientific, and religious categories actually exist in universal reality?"

To understand the correlation between human knowledge and universal reality let us now explore this process of systems-based learning through a simple illustration that clarifies three main points, beginning with point number one; the observation that human beings evaluate and think *phenomenologically*:[*]

---

[*] Phenomenological; (in context of this work) – of the senses; tastes, likes-and-dislikes

## Phenomenological Evaluations

In context of this work 'phenomenology' is both a philosophy and a psychology that suggests that our perceptions of any given 'thing' at any given time are uniquely flavored by our current tastes, values, and attitudes. For example; to identify any substantial object at the most elementary level we usually employ one or more of the five senses. That is to say that through the primary agents of sight, hearing, taste, smell, or touch, we embark upon the often unconscious process of recognizing, classifying, and categorizing any given thing – thus giving it both a value and an identity that our mind can grasp. Indeed, without such discerning activity we couldn't function as intelligent beings. However, such value judgments and identity-recognition procedures are highly subjective observations, depending almost completely upon our current phenomenological perspectives. Or to put it another way; what makes current sense to us. These value judgments (or classifications) fluctuate wildly according to our present tastes, knowledge, accuracy of perception, or prevailing circumstances. For example; when we see ripe golden bananas we recognize them as 'food', 'fruit', and 'bananas' (three classifications) and evaluate them according to our preexistent tastes; 'like' or 'dislike' (two more classifications). However, if we happen to be very hungry then the bananas' perceived value (another classification) becomes amplified in direct proportion to our hunger level. All being equal, if a fruit vendor is auctioning rather than selling the bananas at a set price, the hungrier customers will pay more for their bananas simply because their desire is greater and thus they value the bananas more highly. On the other hand, if we have just departed a banana banquet we may not even wish to acknowledge any additional bananas' existence. So, in this simple example we see that 'value' as a classification system represents a very personal and subjective approach to truth judgments that is limited to, and governed by, one's current needs, wants, desires, and level of universal knowledge. To summarize; we evaluate phenomenologically. This is the first point.

## Reductive Classifications

The second point is that we have been trained to classify reductively. In other words, partly because we can digest only so much information at a time (usually the less the better) and partly because we have definitive rather than abstractive thinking, we have learnt to classify everything into single, discrete, identifiable units wherever possible. For example; upon being told to collect "some food" from the banquet table we immediately enquire about what *sort* of food to collect. In reply, we are told "some fruit." To which we naturally respond "what *type* of fruit?"… and so on. Obviously, the more specific the definition at the outset, the less potential for confusion. If we are specifically directed to collect "five large golden bananas.." at the outset, then our mind is satisfied, we can embark on our task and life can go on. Such specificity not only minimizes unnecessary confusions, but also saves precious time that can then be used for more important things – such as eating bananas of course. Very rarely is our mind satisfied with blanket categorizations such as 'food' when there is a more specific definition at hand. When it comes to matters of personal importance in any sphere we simply don't handle generalizations very well. We invariably tend to seek more specific descriptions, definitions, and classifications. We just want that added detail. Hence we may conclude that we classify reductively, and specifically. This is the second point.

**Universality**
The third point is both immeasurably complex in its ontology, yet absolutely simple in its *teleology* * and is plainly this: That everything in the known and unknown universe both tangible and intangible, noumenal and phenomenal, is inescapably interconnected at some, several, or possibly all levels of existence – past, present, and future. In simpler language; everything and every non-thing is connected. This all-inclusive monistic principle includes such abstracts as thoughts, concepts, and beliefs—even erroneous ones—as well as the whole physical realm of existence, and thus establishes a theoretical connection between all aspects and features of life.

In other words, no matter how advanced we become at identifying apparently discrete specifics, whether it be atoms, ideas, planets, beliefs, or bananas; from a universal perspective all we are managing to do (at best) is identify a fragmentary piece of 'life' in one form or another in temporary, and artificial separation from the cosmically-unified macro-organism we call the Universe. Or, in metaphysical terms perhaps we might say 'Ultimate Reality' 'God' or 'Truth' with a capital 'T'. Under such circumstances Truth would appear as a unified whole rather than as an overlapping confederation of discrete groupings of knowledge that invariably contain gaps, omissions, and errors. And of course it is due to these very gaps, omissions, and errors, and our associated beliefs and presumptions that we have so much acrimony and confusion in the first place.

The solution obviously lies in somehow 'filling-in' the blank spots, but as we said before most importantly; filling-in the blank spots with self-

---

* Teleology; the study of design or purpose in natural phenomena – towards some objective

evident truths and *not* the traditional nebulous beliefs or hypotheses of either pseudo-religion or pseudoscience.

But as we have just demonstrated humans tend to process information reductively (i), specifically (ii), and phenomenologically (iii). Yet paradoxically, we are also predisposed to holistic, or comprehensive thinking. In other words, we just don't like empty spaces in our theories. When such 'gaps in understanding' present themselves we invariably plug the hole with the nearest available hypothesis or belief. There is barely enough time to think, let alone consider the possibility that the Cosmic Divine might yet try to squeeze through that particular gap. So few have yet to understand that genuine faith means living with uncertainty, not certainty. And although religious fundamentalists might argue that their lives are indeed based in faith, it might be more accurate to define this type of faith-position as credulous or naïve. Certainly most such beliefs cannot be described as either sophisticated or scientifically credible. Complicated perhaps, even clever and complex, but ultimately incredible from a scientific perspective.

As previously explained faith is only supposed to be a transitory state where we dwell in temporary uncertainty whilst pursuing knowledge or direct experience, and was never supposed to be an objective in-and-of itself. But regrettably this hasn't stopped the evangelists, the proselytizers, or the indoctrinators from pressing their case. The resulting dogmatic 'faith' that is rooted in absolute convictions leaves little room for uncertainty or doubt, and therefore little or no room for questions or further learning. Arguably, this isn't really faith at all, but a psychological escape from it – into an imagined world of self-created absolutes.

Thus the true objective of faith (further learning and knowledge) is inadvertently forestalled. Accordingly, instead of being innately aware of our ignorance and of all the gaps, omissions, and errors in our knowledge, we tend to be blissfully unaware of them. For obviously; we cannot be both "absolutely sure" and consciously aware of our ignorance at the same time can we? Whether scholar or fool, genius or gullible, critical or credulous; under normal circumstances the only time that we experience a (usually very temporary) sense of our own ignorance is when we have a fleeting moment of enlightenment, unexpectedly declaring to ourselves "Mmm, I didn't realize I didn't know that!" For a brief second, the ego is made aware of the fact that it still has more to learn, but that moment soon passes and before long we return to our normal presumptuous condition of believing that we already know just about everything we really need to know, and that whatever other knowledge is still 'out there' is just proverbial icing on the cake. This is the troubling human condition that gave rise to the maxim "ignorance is bliss" but with the recent upsurge of so many appalling crimes of 'selective ignorance' on the international front—especially those based on improvable religious beliefs—we are only now beginning to realize the awful price for such historic bliss.

The reality of an *anastomotic*[*] universe of united and indivisible truth will remain difficult for many to accept because it first of all involves contemplating our own relative insignificance as 'just another cosmic fraction of existence' (although that need not necessarily be the case) and because such a belief also presupposes an existing state of profound human ignorance.

Despite colorful and loquacious declarations of belief in a transcendent realm and the imperfection of man; for those religious absolutists who "already have all the answers" or for those—secular or religious—whose neuroses are camouflaged by sectarian affiliations, these humbling hypotheses are fundamentally untenable. For to concur with the concept of universalness is to automatically discredit exclusivist paradigms. This in turn exposes the relative ignorance, inadequacies, and insignificance of separatist thinking and the irrelevance of sectarian agencies. This includes all forms of partisan thought, both secular and religious.

Whether in the form of radical nationalism or religious extremism; perhaps best exemplified in the totalitarian regimes of the 20th century, and in the fundamentalist religious States of today, the presumption of ascendancy over others, and the willingness to enforce that presumed authority by any means necessary remains the same. Hence those whose identities, careers, neuroses or psychoses are intertwined with sectarian philosophies face the unsettling reality that they are living in a *myopia*;[†] a myopia what's more that is ultimately a contradiction, an oxymoron in-and-of itself. Those with staunch denominational religious beliefs will sooner or later find themselves living the ultimate paradox; tacitly denying the existence of Universal Truth through the strident practice of prejudicial religion. Or, denying hard-core realities in favor of dearly-held beliefs.

This obvious, yet mostly unobserved fact is affirmed in the many fixed doctrinal statements of the major orthodoxies that effectively prohibited discovery or revelation; whether scientific or religious. Meanwhile, the silent miracle of creation bears daily testament to the cosmic values of change, growth, and discovery:

---

[*] Anastomotic; an integrated network of systems such as blood vessels
[†] Myopia; nearsighted; the state or condition of metaphorically 'living in a bubble'

For the invisible things of Him from the creation of the world are clearly seen, being understood by the things that are made, even his eternal power and Godhead; so that they are without excuse. (Romans 1:20).

In colloquial terms 'God' continuously reveals Himself through the agency of natural law, yet dogmatic religionists often stubbornly refuse to hear Him. How tragically ironic. In the face of so much evidence to the contrary it is painful to listen to increasingly absurd theories as fundamentalists refute cold hard facts in favor of fantastic and ultimately incredible declarations of faith. Not surprisingly, this continued state of denial also accounts for the marked absence of true spirituality amongst staunch denominationalists. For as long as they remain immersed in delusion and fantasy—especially dogmatic delusions—they can never encounter the living truth.

In conclusion, and serving as the preamble to the following chapters let us respectfully remind ourselves that there is indeed a vast difference between mere beliefs and actual knowledge. Although religious convictions have undoubtedly served many of us meaningfully in times of hope, faith, doubt, uncertainty, or despair; and religious institutions themselves have carried out much admirable humanitarian work over the centuries; in these times of great scientific advances in knowledge and understanding and with so much information at our fingertips, perhaps we might be better employed investing our energies into the activities of discovery rather than continuing to defend or reinforce traditional and often questionable beliefs.

For surely it is in this personal leap of courageous faith, away from the security and safety of doctrine and dogma, and into a place of genuine humility and open-mindedness that we each stand the best chance of truly engaging the truth?

# CHAPTER TEN

# SCIENCE, RELIGION, & ARCHETYPES

*Placing the triadic archetype in context of prevailing psycho-spiritual theories; and in the process, unveiling yet more evidence to support our central theory.*

A central theme of our findings so far is that certain indeterminable forces, or subliminal energies, or perhaps even a cosmic super-intelligence is somehow systematically at work beyond the realm of normal human consciousness. Of course, this idea is not new having been presented by philosophers, scientists, prophets, and theologians in one form or another since the dawn of consciousness. But our particular findings here are somewhat different inasmuch as they concern a triadic archetype that produces *substantial* and *observable* symbolism whilst simultaneously being rooted in the fundamental principles of light and energy. This takes the ontological discussion to a new level of synchronicity. Instead of arguing purely abstract theories we can now check our abstractions against the combined weight of historical facts, empirical data, psychoanalytical theory, religious traditions, theological speculations, and the newly-discovered visible proofs of the triadic archetype as presented in this book. In combination, these sources provide a newer and more substantial base for our investigations into the noumenal-transcendental realms than that traditionally provided by religious or purely philosophical hypotheses. In applying the corroborative evidence of these sources discerningly it becomes increasingly clear that there is indeed some sort of subliminal influence playing out its fateful role behind the oft-impenetrable veil of human consciousness.

This provocative assertion is fortified by contemporary research derived from psychoanalyst Sigmund Freud's detection of the realm of the unconscious in the late 1800s and Carl Gustav Jung's subsequent discovery of universal archetypes and symbols; both of which opened the way for scientific bridging discoveries into the traditionally mysterious realms of religion and spirituality. Coining new scientific terms for age-old religious concepts, Freud and Jung brought the religious journey slowly into focus discussing the concepts of God, spirituality, the soul, the mind, and religion in such terms as "the numinous realm, the unconscious, the superego, ego, and id, the individual subconscious, archetypes, the animus and anima, complexes and neuroses" and so forth, thus introducing a new scientific lexicon for what was traditionally considered 'spiritual' subject matter. However, having been reasonably settled in their respective fields for over a century this invasion by psychologists into sacrosanct religious territory caused ripples of disturbance on both sides of the divide. The uneasy truce that had been in effect since Enlightenment times had been violated, and predictably, Freud and his findings were censured and demonized. Consequently both science and religion took up the call to either explore further or defend existing beliefs respectively. The resulting sharp polarizations produced a rash of new definitions, interpretations, terminologies and classifications that have since been handed down to us from both sides of the divide, regrettably causing much confusion. As a result the fields of theology and psychology have increasingly become the domain of specialists, often veiled in obscure language and frequently unintelligible to the layman. For this reason, and in order to avoid exacerbating existing misunderstandings I have put together a simplified, generalized table of comparative views that jointly outline the central characteristics of the theories that we will be discussing. Table D is in turn supported by diagrams ♣ 24, 25, & 26).

The tabular form of the chart should not be read to suggest that there are *exact* delineations between the contents of these columns and rows in any direction either within theories, or cross-theoretically. For indeed as previously explained, categories and classifications are at best limited forms of information-gathering, and in this psycho-spiritual sphere of operations it is precisely because we have not yet reached a consensus of appropriate concepts and terminologies that we need to consider any new perspective in the first place. As we better comprehend the Freudian, Jungian, and religious theories through the following definitions and discussions and gain a general understanding of prevailing beliefs in the respective fields, we should be better placed to evaluate the potential for any new theory based upon the principles of the triadic archetype. This theory we will tentatively name 'The Psychospiritual Theory'. But before we examine this new theory in depth, let us first take a brief look at arguably the three most prominent theories dealing with this subject matter in the fields of science and religion respectively, beginning with the 'Father of psychoanalysis' himself.

### Table D: Psycho-Spiritual Theories – Thematic Comparatives

| Freudian | Jungian | Religious | Psychospiritual |
|---|---|---|---|
| (un-named realm) | Noumenal Realm | God / Heaven? | Realm of Great Unknown |
| (Deep) Unconscious | Collective Unconscious Archetypes | Spirit World or Spirit Realm | Realm of Collective Unconscious |
| Psyche: (Id) & Subconscious | Personal Unconscious Dreams | Soul or Spirit | Personal Unconscious |
| Psyche: Id, Ego, Consciousness | Consciousness | Spirit or Mind | Inspirational Self |
| Psyche: Ego, Libido, Superego | Ego, Consciousness | Mind, Free Will | Thinking Self |
| Ego & Personality | Persona | Body, The Flesh | Active Self |

## Freudian Theory

As the father of psychoanalysis, Sigmund Freud (1856 – 1939) introduced the world to such concepts as the subconscious, the ego, the id, the libido, psychosexuality, the superego and the interpretation of dreams; as he pioneered the study of the mind, its ailments and its healing. Amongst some of his most outstanding students were the psychologist Otto Rank who wrote *Myth of the Birth of the Hero* (1909); psychiatrist Alfred Adler *(inferiority complexes);* and Carl Gustav Jung (1875–1961) who, amongst other notable achievements first documented the existence of archetypes in the collective unconscious.

It is not necessary to enter into great depth into Freud's understandings of various terms in order to make our point today, but the brief (and admittedly inexact) summary represented in Table D along with the following concise definitions of Freudian theory should assist the reader in understanding and evaluating the general similarities and differences between Freudian and Jungian theory, conventional religious theory, and our own psychospiritual theory based upon the triadic archetype. The hope and intention is that with at least a generalized understanding of these theories, the laypersons amongst us will see the pertinence and value of the triadic archetype as a guide to contemporary studies of the mind and the spirit. Naturally, we should assume a progression from the top from whites, through blues, to reds. The color-notes following each Freudian definition below are merely generalized indicators of alignment with the psychospiritual theory (see fig.24 ♣).

*The Ego:* The ego is that conscious part of the psyche or mind that deals with realities, thoughts, and behaviors, and is influenced by social forces. The ego is one of three components of the human personality, mind, or psyche, and is sometimes defined as one's concept of 'self', usually comprising mind and body elements (blue and red).

*The Superego:* Roughly corresponding to a social conscience, the superego controls and regulates instinctual impulses, urges, and thoughts. The superego develops as the individual is exposed to value systems through the normal process of social growth (white-blues).

*The Id:* The id is comprised of mainly unconscious pleasure-oriented impulses, which exert influences upon the individual driving them towards immediate gratification (blue, deep reds).

*The Libido:* Often described as the manifestation of the creative energies of the Id frequently in sexual expression (more physical-sexual reds).

*The Unconscious:* Also sometimes referred to as the subconscious; is that part of the mind that contains fears, feelings, wishes, memories, ideas, dreams and the like, that are not directly expressed consciously, but nevertheless influence many conscious processes in subtle or covert ways, including being expressed as neuroses (blue-white).

*Psychosexual Theory:* Hypothesis that suggested that all mental disturbances originate in sexually-related experiences or behaviors. Two of Freud's better-known theories in this area were the Oedipus complex and infantile sexuality.

Not everyone of course agrees with Freud's psychosexual theories. As we can see by the added color-notes, Freud's theories do appear to be less structured and systematic, and less in exact alignment with the triadic archetype than either Jungian or religious theory. But there are some intriguing parallels all the same. One interesting example that may be familiar to the reader was the theme in a 90's Hollywood thriller entitled *Final Analysis* and starring Richard Gere in the role of a therapist delving into patient's dreams. From the perspective of this work, worthy of note were the associations between the colors of certain flowers and archetypal themes, drawn directly from Freud's research. For example, Freud associates (white) lilies with purity and chastity, pink (or red) carnations with carnal, sexual phallic themes, and (blue-purple) violets as representing feminine sexuality.[56] Although he goes into considerable detail discussing word associations as well as other more complex themes, the fundamental link between reds and masculine, blues and feminine, and white and purity is evident. The main point to note is not so much the diminishing applications of some of the afore-listed terms and theories in modern psychoanalysis, for certainly there have been many recent advances in the field; but more so to observe the fundamental tenets that gave birth to the discipline of psychoanalysis in the first place. These fundamentals still persist today and correspond at least generally with the principles of the triadic archetype. By taking a brief look at the Psychospiritual Theory outlined in Table D and figs.24 & 26 ♣ for instance, we can see how Freud's *superego* and *id* concepts correspond fairly well with the 'inspirational and emotional self' whilst his notions of *ego* and *personality* likewise parallel the 'thinking self' and the 'active person' respectively. If colored, the chart would progress from whites, through blues, to reds, from top-to-bottom of course and although matching the various themes exactly is not possible, I hope the reader can acknowledge the general parallels. One of the beauties of diagrams of course, is that a picture is supposed to paint a thousand words, at which cue I will resist the temptation to over-explain everything and move on to the man who first coined the term 'archetypes'.

**Jungian Archetypes**

Born in 1875, Carl Gustav Jung was directly responsible for a great many innovations in psychology, and although viewed as the natural successor to Freud for many years Jung eventually branched out along different lines founding the analytical school of psychology and focusing upon groundbreaking work with universal archetypes. In particular he focused on the analysis of dreams where he showed how the accurate interpretation of primordial manifestations in dreams could lead to dramatic resolutions of psychological disturbances. He later developed such techniques as *word association*, and defined the *introvert* and *extrovert* personality types.

A truly religious man, Jung also became famous for applying psychological understandings to the religious field and for suggesting the possible universal synchronicity of all things. However, Jung's insistence upon empirical and academic integrity, instead of being viewed as an admirable trait by his religionist detractors, led to a reactionary rejection of many of his precise scientific definitions of religious subject material, and it was really only after his passing in 1961 that Jung began to receive some of the respect he deserved from the religious world. Scientists too had difficulty accepting Jung's definition of what was in fact 'empirical' (meaning "verifiable by observation or experiment") which Jung saw as applying to any personal experience whether mystical or otherwise. In my opinion this rejection of Jung's theories was a great tragedy. For if both the religious and scientific world had been more receptive to his explanations of religious phenomena, we would undoubtedly be living in a better-educated and therefore less dogmatic, and less divided world today. Having made this respectful comment however, our concern with Jungian theory today centers chiefly on his findings concerning archetypes and the collective unconscious for as we shall soon see there are some remarkable connections between (a) worldwide reports of mystical religious experiences; (b) Jung's discoveries concerning the collective unconscious, and; (c) our own reported findings in this book.

Jung's professional journey into mythology, religion, and psychotic fantasies stemmed from his doubts about the comprehensiveness of his mentor's psychosexual theories in explaining mental and emotional disturbances, and led to the eventual discovery that there were apparently 'universal' and unconscious forces at work that were integral to the resolution of imbalances in humanity's search for personal fulfillment. Jung believed that prototypical, conceptual 'inhabitants' of the subliminal realms communicated to us through our dreams, our neuroses, our myths, and our religions and, being beyond the *conscious* influence of man, remained theoretically 'uncorrupted.' Here we should underline the bridging potential of these themes between the traditionally-competing fields of psychology and religion.

Arguably Jung's most influential work was *The Psychology of the Unconscious* (1917) wherein he promoted the existence of these universal energies first naming them "archetypes", describing them as a form of unconscious primordial symbolism common to all humanity. Ancient Greek philosophers Plato and Aristotle first discussed this concept believing that reality consisted of such archetypes, or fundamental truth-forms, beyond the reach of normal sensory perceptions.[*] Unfortunately for us, that is largely where these phenomena have remained; hidden in the silent shadows of the collective unconscious unnoticed, unavailable, and unable to compete with the frantic distractions of everyday life in a very material world. I say 'unfortunately' because I do not subscribe to the belief that 'hidden truths' have been cosmically engineered to escape our understandings, but rather

---

[*] The word 'archetype' is taken from the Greek word 'archetypos' meaning 'first of its kind'.

that any such 'hidden truths' can only serve their cosmic purpose through human discovery and understanding. The fact that they remain 'hidden' is simply a testament to our collective unenlightenment; to the fact that human consciousness has not yet fully matured. Indeed, we will know when human consciousness is approaching maturity when there are no more hidden scientific truths or arcane religious mysteries to solve.

So, taking into account the fact that we are still very much upon the collective journey to enlightenment, of particular interest to us today is the fact that Dr. Jung eventually concluded that the archetypal projections he found through his research were nothing less than manifestations of some ultimate cosmic truth-language. In his own words, Jung defines archetypes as follows:

> The concept of the archetype... is derived from the repeated observation that, for instance, the myths and fairytales of world literature contain definite motifs which crop up everywhere. We meet these same motifs in the fantasies, dreams, deliria, and delusions of individuals living today. These typical images and associations are what I call archetypal ideas. ... They impress, influence, and fascinate us. They have their origin in the archetype, which in itself is an irrepresentable, unconscious, pre-existent form that seems to be part of the inherited structure of the psyche and can therefore manifest itself spontaneously anywhere, at any time.[57]

Jung goes on to explain; "The archetype in itself is empty and purely formal, nothing but a *facultas praeformandi,* a possibility of representation that is given a priori." Here he is referring indirectly to the inability of the subjective mindset to truly grasp and articulate objective realities – as discussed in the previous chapter. In more common language Jung is explaining that although archetypes definitely exist in the unconscious realm, their 'true' original form is inaccessible and rather meaningless to us without being packed out with images and associations that the (subjective) conscious mind can relate to. He adds; "...it seems to me probable that the real nature of the archetype is not capable of being made conscious, that it is transcendent, on which account I will call it *psychoid.*" *

---

* Psychoid; term used by Jung to define noumenal-type archetypes

## Delving Deeper

Basically, and with allowances for the ambiguity of the term; there are three levels of Jungian 'awareness' to consider here: Firstly (a) the personal consciousness. Secondly (b) the personal unconscious (or subconscious); and thirdly (c) Jung's realm of collective unconsciousness (see fig.24 ♣). Loosely speaking these three levels of human awareness correspond to our psychospiritual theory as: (a) our personal experiences and emotions in daily life; (b) our hidden dreams and suppressed fears; and (c) the common gateway to collective archetypes, human spirituality, and the Great Unknown. Each of us without exception has a unique perspective on life that generally aligns along these three levels (whether we are conscious of them or not). But most of us remain only partly aware even of the first level (a); hence the term 'consciousness' – although perhaps the term 'partial-consciousness' might be more appropriate? Not surprisingly, to access the deeper personal subconscious (b) usually requires medication or psychotherapy; whilst access beyond this realm is rarely reported or documented scientifically.

One way to explain the mysterious realm of collective unconsciousness (c); (where Jung surmises archetypes emanate from) is to use the illustration of individual swimming pools in the back gardens of our various homes: Each swimming pool has been uniquely designed to reflect the likes and character of the owner; its shape, length and depth, the surrounding foliage, and the decorations all represent the individual consciousness (a). This is the place where we 'swim' daily. We like to keep the water a certain temperature, and, when we want to play a little, we bring out our beloved rubber ducks and floating armchairs. This is my own personal pool, where I feel safe and comfortable. It is what I know—what I am used to—what I am familiar with. It represents my culture and my personal history, and the 'stuff' of my everyday life. It could therefore be decorated with all manner of political or religious symbolism, family photos, or even sexy pinups for that matter. If I am a true-blooded American, then I may have a Stars-and-Stripes theme predominating. If I am a fun-loving youngster, then there might be a Caribbean bar with beer and dance music. If I am a little unsure of myself then the pool may be a bit secluded, and so on. The water of course represents my personal flow of consciousness, and the pool's environment my cultural location, surroundings, and beliefs. It can be a fun exercise imagining what one's own psychological 'pool' of consciousness would look like – and how we would decorate it using our own specific social and personal paraphernalia.

The unconscious or subconscious realm (b); or more specifically the *personal* unconscious, is represented by the deeper water of the pool. Still part of our personal pool of course, but somewhat removed from the surface it is not such a comfortable place to be. Usually colder and darker, we don't hear or see so well there – let alone breathe or run around. Neither does it contain the familiar stimulations of the surface. Because try as we might it is very difficult bringing our personal 'stuff' underwater; especially material stuff of course, and/or the thoughts and images of daily reality. The more of that personal 'stuff' that we attempt to hang on to (our ego-consciousness and persona) the less chance we have of being able to descend below the surface. Rather like trying to dive underwater dragging our rubber ducks and floating beds with us. Or, in more realistic terms; trying to sleep whilst playing sport.. or dreaming whilst engrossed in a stimulating conversation for example. One activity is conscious – the other is unconscious, so they can't be done simultaneously. Accordingly, if we do wish to access the subconscious (or super-conscious) realms, we need to somehow temporarily 'let go' of our attachments to sensory and material things, and of our overriding need to 'be in control'. But this is harder than it sounds. That's why the subconscious remains such an unvisited realm. Here we may recall parallels between the traditional mystical quest and the denial of the flesh; the 'letting-go' of the ego and materialistic preoccupations. As a result, the only time we visit this deep water of the subconscious under normal circumstances is in our sleep. But hypnotism, psychotherapy, and certain religious practices can also take us there. But having little or no sensory stimulation, it is for most an unfamiliar, unappealing, and therefore often-uncomfortable place to stay for very long.

Then we have the realm of the collective unconsciousness (c); the place identified by Jung as holding those key motifs and patterns inherited at birth; 'psychoid' themes as he called them that are common to all humanity. This then is the realm of archetypes that is somehow connected both to our unconscious mind (b) as well as to what I term the Realm of Great Unknown. If not the origin thereof, then this surely is an early source of the energies of the triadic archetype. In the analogy, this collective unconsciousness is like an even larger lake of water; pure and clean, that unbeknownst to us supplies all our personal swimming pools from a common source. Like a huge subterranean sea of consciousness if you like; where all our individual 'pools' (personas) are ultimately rooted. This accounts for the regular surfacing of particular social patterns common to all cultures throughout history, as well as for the existence of subliminal archetypes. But the access points to this universal flow of Truth are so deep and well-hidden in the depths of the psyche that hardly anyone consciously *knows* about them, let alone has visited there. Those few who have made that profound journey have had such difficulty explaining the experience or translating the wisdom glanced there when they return to 'the surface' that we either deify or crucify them – sometimes both. Not wanting to let go of our own ideas, beliefs, or possessions; or scared of being swept away from our own personally-designed pools-of-consciousness, we stubbornly resist the call to explore so deeply. Indeed we may even deny the existence of such a place. Rather than change the shapes of our own pools of consciousness to accommodate a greater truth; we would rather suppress, ignore, or deny that greater truth. But the call remains all the same. If we do choose to believe in the source's existence, it is often in a prosthetic sense, and we simply latch onto one religion or another 'in faith' as a newly-converted member. Only to find—if we are truly awake—that all we have done is join another larger swimming club that has its own, self-constructed and relatively shallow 'collective pool' where we all share the same superficial consciousness, and where we still don't have to dive too deeply.

The great difficulty that Jung identified, and the reason that he considered archetypes as being incapable of being made manifest consciously, was because any Great Truths being drawn from this uncorrupted source must be viewed through the murky perspectives of our personal, subjective pools of awareness. A personal consciousness all cluttered up with our own particularized junk, our individual perspectives, our subjective and biased opinions, our emotional baggage, and our personal beliefs. This applies to both the individual psyche as well as to the collective, or group dynamic. This is one reason why true objectivity is so vitally important, and why ignorance—especially selective or sectarian ignorance—simply cannot be allowed to prevail.

### The Animus and Anima

In his voluminous works on dreams, mythology, alchemy, religious symbolism, mystical phenomena, and the science of psychology, Jung continued to present proof after proof of this yet-to-be-consciously-deciphered archetypal realm that was 'speaking' to us from that place he termed "the collective unconscious." A place populated with mythological figures; heroes and heroines, mother-figures, crones, virgins, and tricksters, to name but a few. From our perspective, amongst his most poignant discoveries was the uncovering of the presence of the *Animus* and *Anima;* the feminine and masculine subconscious archetypes of the male and female psyche, whose functions he described as follows: (♣ 25, 26)

> The natural function of the animus (as well as the anima) is to remain in (their) place between individual consciousness and the collective unconscious (q.v.); exactly as the persona (q.v.) is a sort of stratum between the ego-consciousness and the objects of the external world. The animus and the anima should function as a bridge, or a door, leading to the images of the collective unconscious, as the persona should be a sort of bridge unto the world.[58]

In our diagrams of the individual triadic archetypes (♣ 11), the animus and the anima may be represented by the smaller, or subliminal presence of opposing sexuality in everyone's personal makeup. Subconscious most of the time, but nevertheless crucial to an integrated worldview, it is here that we find the 'spiritual balance' so-to-speak, that keep us (psychologically) in tune with the cosmos. Thus, Jung paints a picture of gender-sensitive conscious and unconscious 'doors' of the psyche opening and closing under certain circumstances, revealing or suppressing 'truths' as the case may be, depending upon our state of consciousness. As previously mentioned the strong inference is that this collective unconscious (c)—precisely *because* it has escaped conscious human influences—contains universal truths that have not yet suffered corruption by human agency. However, the related implication is that under normal circumstances we are cognitively alienated from this archetypal source and, whenever messages from this collective unconscious are somehow channeled through human agents or agencies there is invariably a corresponding subjective 'corruption' of the original content or theme. Although this subjective interpretation process *seems* unavoidable the theoretical implication is that the human mind should be as 'pure' and free from any false, limited, or artificial interpretative bias in order to guarantee the most accurate interpretations from this uncorrupted source; a truly objective, or 'open' mind in other words – as previously discussed. But such a state of pure objectivity can only be achieved where there is a total absence of subjective thinking; where the preoccupations of the ego are replaced by a higher state of awareness. Interestingly enough, most spiritual exercises such as fasting, praying, meditation, and chanting are specifically designed for this purpose; to quiet the ego and worldly desires, and to open up the mind (or spirit) to a higher state of consciousness. A regular occurrence amongst genuine mystics; some even call the process "connecting with God." This helps explain the prevalence of spiritual exercises that strongly emphasize corporal suffering, especially amongst those faith traditions that subscribe to the dualistic body-and-soul paradigm; mortification of the flesh in Catholicism for instance, or ritualized flagellation in Shiite Muslim sects. Because as previously explained, the traditional belief is that in order to access higher consciousness one must first deny the comforts and desires of the flesh. In this case through self-inflicted pain. However, the associated covert subjugation of the mind during such practices should not go unnoted. In light of recent research, it is my sincere opinion that this approach to 'spiritual enlightenment' is not only ill advised, but it is also potentially counter-productive; simply because the mind too obviously needs to be included in any truly integrated state of 'holiness' or wholeness. We will discuss this shortly.

By contrast psychology, as a science of the mind generally *employs* the psyche during therapy as an aid to accessing the higher (or deeper) consciousness – and from there to effect a result. Counseling psychology, psychoanalysis and hypnosis for example each engage the mind in dynamic processes. In simple terms, and accepting that both religion and science are ultimately aiming for the same goal of human enlightenment, is it not intriguing that the two models are so very different? One appears to negate the mind as a potential hindrance in the battle between the good (spirit) and the evil (flesh), whilst the other integrates body *and* mind in the quest for a healthier whole (♣ 26). The religious model tends to deny the truly questing mind, whilst the transcendent 'spirit' on the other hand, is typically neglected in the scientific model. By comparison, the triadic archetype-model would align more closely with the integrated scientific arrangement, only with a stronger emphasis first on developing, and then including a sacred, or spiritual aspect. In color-terms, and speaking rather generally once again; the religious model is based upon a white-versus-red dualism (spirit *vs.* body), whilst science employs a red-and-blue approach (body *and* mind). The triadic archetype model of course incorporates all three colors in a unified symbiosis (spirit, mind, and body). This observation now leads us to a brief overview of the religious theory and the place of the (feminine-blue) mind in respect to human development and in respect to a genuine spirituality.

**The Religious Theory**
In Table D and fig.26 ♣ 'religious theory' refers loosely and generally to the monotheistic / Christian belief system that is admittedly not representative of all religions, nor even of all Christian denominations in their different interpretations of the psychological / spiritual / noumenal realm(s). However, because the main purpose of this comparative collaboration of theories is to validate the triadic archetype as well as authenticate and more

accurately define such phenomena as the 'true religious experience' (a phenomenon that is not denomination-specific except by interpretation), the general-Christian theory is chosen here because it claims the largest amount of followers worldwide, and more importantly, because the author believes it is *generally* representative of many other religious theories, especially Judaism and Islam, and will therefore have points familiar to most readers. Hopefully, once the findings of this book are independently confirmed the resultant psychospiritual hypothesis based upon the triadic archetype should be equally applicable to other theories of the mind or spirit, whether scientific, secular, or religious. Other volumes will discuss the religious perspective in greater depth. We do not want to cloud the central arguments too much at this stage, and so must be satisfied with an admittedly sketchy overview of three central themes in these popular religions that relate directly to the triadic archetype: (i) The absence of a strong and active 'feminine' element; inasmuch as the theological focus is on a male deity, and the institution is governed and staffed predominantly by men. (ii) The suppression of the enquiring mind; inasmuch as the techniques of indoctrination, faith, and obedience prevail as the main instruction techniques: And (iii) the presumed antagonism between spirit and flesh; inasmuch as the central teachings of the major monotheistic traditions presume upon a polarized humanity living in a polarized universe.

Let us begin with a rather oversimplified summary of the religious theory before considering it in context of the triadic archetype. Please take particular note of the place (or the absence) of the (feminine-blue) mind in the following outline:

## A Simplified Overview of the Religious Theory

- God (Yahweh, Jehovah, Allah) created everything, including mankind.
- Man is comprised of a material body (red), and a transcendent soul (white).
- Mankind has fallen from grace due to sinful 'weaknesses of the flesh' (red-blacks).
- The purpose of the religious life is to reconnect with God (white).
- 'The flesh' and associated sinful *thinking* must be subdued in this redemption process (subjugate the reds, and any problematic blues).
- The place and function of 'the mind' in these processes is unclear (feminine-blues).
- Good-and-evil are generally synonymous with (i) God-and-Satan, (ii) spirit-and-flesh, (iii) sacred religion vs. secular society.

The main point to note is the absence of recognition of an empowered feminine aspect in monotheistic traditions, and a parallel disassociation or subjugation of the mind amongst their memberships. We should also note the aforementioned dualistic paradigm based on a good-versus-evil model that is (in religious settings) believed to be intrinsic to human nature. Again, I must emphasize that these are very broad generalizations and should not distract the reader from the central fact that any form of indoctrination can only subsist upon a foundation of suppression of the mind – at least at some level. Well-intentioned or not, religious indoctrination is a form of instruction that requires tacit acceptance from the student *without* the presentation of tangible proofs. Given the nature of the material being taught this may indeed be necessary. But the question we should really be asking is whether or not this is the best or most wholesome way to prepare for the journey of life?

In attempting to present a clearer alternative to traditional theories, the strong implication is that we need more (blue) feminine-mind energy and activity to compensate for some of the (red-black) authoritarian excesses in certain well-established areas. For if (blue) science cannot yet explain certain 'religious' concepts, then perhaps this is simply because our brightest and best-educated minds cannot logically come to terms with them. In which case, we might then ask how and why religionists claim to be able to do so... even going as far as inventing a specialized lexicon for the purpose? As we have shown, this specialized lexicon serves the primary purpose not actually of true erudition, but more to add sophisticated 'meat' so-to-speak to the bones of religious conjecture; thus creating another form of 'reality' that many of us believe we are experiencing in the mysteries, sacraments, and traditions of our chosen faiths. But those special 'somethings' we experience during times of prayer or meditation may actually have little or no relation to the religious doctrines we have been taught to accept. And before any of us feel obliged to leap to an emotive defense of these personal objects of faith, we should first recall the simple beliefs and convictions of our childhood years; of Santa Claus and Halloween perhaps, of the tooth fairy, of hobgoblins and leprechauns, and compare the emotive power and sense of reality of those legends and fables with the beliefs, themes, and sensations we often encounter in the practice of our religions. The *feelings* are indeed very real to us on an individual level... but the *beliefs* they are attached to are not. When so-called 'mysteries of faith' are not even supposed to be understood by the clergy, it encourages a broad collective superstition, and a generally dependent and disempowered population. Any such population is easily manipulated for objectives that sadly, have often been far from holy. Any cursory glance in the history books will surely confirm this. Such beliefs in most cases have been tacitly 'accepted on faith' purely on the word of trusted mentors and clerics without any real regard for the believer's understanding of the origins of those beliefs. Indeed, there are numerous examples in history of religious censorship and suppression whenever awkward questions arose. This is not to disparage religion per se, nor to belittle genuine spirituality, but more to keep us on a logical and pragmatic track as we evaluate the contextual place not only of the triadic archetype, but also of our own personal beliefs in context of universal truths and realities.

**Religious Terminology**

As previously noted there are a great many ongoing debates within the various faith traditions as well as within the discipline of psychology about the true nature and meaning of overlapping terms such as 'mind, spirit, heart, soul,' and 'spirituality' and of their place and meaning in the journey of life. For although these terms attempt to encompass metaphysical concepts, feelings, or experiences and are therefore often technically imprecise and nebulous in nature, scientists and theologians alike accept the existence of an experiential realm beyond—but somehow related to—the realm of consciousness. In religion this is the place where the soul connects with God. In science, it is the realm of collective consciousness, or, of the psychoid realm and beyond.

Of course, as shown in Table D the debate about specific meanings and understandings continues to prevent close collaboration between scientists and religionists chiefly because of the aforesaid differences in defining the parameters of what constitutes objective reality and truth. For scientists for instance, truth is evaluated against a backdrop of reason, whilst theologians on the other hand often base their arguments upon revelation, that is; matters of faith, not reason. So despite the fact that the aforementioned metaphysical terms are more-at-home-in and specific to the religious life, this clarity-of-definition issue is usually (and somewhat ironically) far more convoluted in the religious field. Wishing to avoid a long and unnecessary exposé of complex and confusing religious terminology, the reader is invited to accept this writer's personal testament based upon several years of interreligious interactions; that there is hardly a theologian or cleric let alone a religious layperson who has a clear and unequivocal understanding of the meanings of such terms (spirit, mind, soul etc.,) and for very good reason. In a simple experiment conducted on a variety of denominational groups noted for their dogmatic views including Roman Catholics, Southern Baptists, Seventh Day

Adventists, Mormons, Unificationists, and Jehovah's Witnesses, between eight and a dozen persons attending a topical seminar were unexpectedly invited to list three words or a short phrase to define each of the following: (i) God, (ii) heaven, (iii) hell, (iv) spirit or soul, (v) prayer, (vi) religion, and (vii) spirituality. Rather surprisingly, there was hardly an instance where two people in any particular denominational group listed the very same properties or definitions *even for any one item* on the list. On several occasions none of the answers matched at all, thus accumulating so many abstract nouns, adjectives, ideas, and concepts, so as to render the subject under discussion practically meaningless; if not as a philosophical topic then certainly as a collective doctrine. The tendency on the part of the surveyed subjects to *sciolistic*[*] definitions was very high, and the subsequent discussions invariably revealed considerable confusion, unacknowledged questions, and/or unquestioning acceptance of *imperspicuous*[†] doctrines. This confirms not only the relativity and subjectivity of beliefs concerning these seven particular topics even amongst denominationally orthodox thinkers, but in combination with science's traditional reluctance to engage such religious terminology, also demonstrates the urgent need for an intelligible taxonomy that can be generally recognized.[59]

## Some Common Ground

Referring back to Table D both the subconscious and spiritual realms as respectively defined by science and religion do have one central thing in common; neither is fully understood. This point is surely beyond argument. This fact alone unites them at least in the possibility that the subconscious and spiritual realms do indeed have much in common if not in fact, actually being one and the same thing? In any event, given our lack of knowledge on these subjects it simply cannot be argued that they are *not* interconnected in some way.

Similarly, the characteristics of the soul, spirit, or conscience as defined in religious thought relate closely to psychology's definitions of the psyche, superego, id, or subconscious, as do the mechanisms of prayer, meditation, and mystical trances correlate to the measurable effects of hypnosis, hypnoanalysis, or other mental states induced in psychiatric experiments. On top of this, research has been conducted comparing religious phenomena with known neuropsychological factors in an effort to isolate the biological and the psychical features from the potentially 'spiritual', and evidence

---

[*] Sciolistic: having a superficial and/or pretentious attitude of scholarship
[†] Imperspicuous: Unclear, vague, fuzzy, poorly-defined

continues to mount that now explains 'mysterious' religious phenomena in purely empirical terms. Indeed, during now-famous experiments conducted under laboratory conditions in the 1960s by psychologists Schachter and Singer, it was found that persons tended to interpret the sensations and sentiments experienced under controlled conditions as either 'religious' or 'non-religious' (for example) depending purely and specifically upon their environmental surrounds.[60] In simple terms, it was shown that people could quite easily be conditioned to interpret plain old normal events as spiritual / religious / supernatural or whatever, through the application of related stimuli. Such experiments obviously go a long way to explaining how and why natural phenomena are often considered 'mysterious' in religious circles. But at the same time the experiments also raised new questions about universal parallels that link certain types of religious experiences that *cannot* presently be dismissed as purely biological or psychological phenomena. The incidences of the aforementioned mystical or 'peak' experiences for instance, also sometimes referred to as 'an epiphany' and usually depicted as an enlightening flow of wisdom, peace, and universal cognition; or described as ecstatic, mystical, spiritual or transcendental. Reported in various faith traditions worldwide this profound, personal spiritual experience is experienced as an uplifting numinous event whereupon subjectivity and objectivity fuse as a unified whole. The individual mind, psyche, or spirit merges with that of the universe, and we "become perfect like (our) Heavenly Father is perfect" (Matt.5:48) at least in theory, if only for a moment or two. In short; a moment of holiness, or wholeness, as Jung might say. This is thematically consistent to an individual experiencing a 'moment of light' when the red, blue, and white aspects of their being unite in temporary fusion with the higher reaches of the collective unconscious or even—one might say—of the 'mind' of the Universe. Most often reported by the trained mystics of the major faith traditions; Buddhist monks, Christian contemplatives, Jewish Kabalists, or Sufi mystics for instance, it is no mere coincidence that along with reports of 'incredibly beautiful lights' during these encounters the respective underlying theologies are populated with color-coded deities or principles. From the Christian Trinity to the Hindu Trimurti, or from Buddhist chakras to the iconic designs of the Old Testament Jews, or the signs and symbols of the Kabala. Mystical light it seems is the one aspect of religious experiences that remains consistent across the board.

Equally intriguing are the reported color-choices of religious figures seen in visions and apparitions; the red-and-white Christ figure, or a blue-and-white Holy Virgin for instance. And although the findings of psychological research often challenge religious interpretations of both natural and 'supernatural' phenomena, we can see in the data mutual consistencies that add indirect weight to the theory of universality. That is, the theory that there is indeed a universal source of 'outside' stimulus common to us all that suffers being interpreted individually, subjectively, emotionally, psychologically, and sometimes… even religiously.

## Becoming Whole

So, having uncovered convincing symbolism that correlates to Jung's archetypal findings which, whilst being tied to the substantial world evidently originate somewhere *beyond* consciousness; we may reasonably conclude that these multidimensional yet consistent patterns are no less than sensory expressions of Jung's "archetype of wholeness" which he further defines as "producing a symbolism which has always characterized and expressed the Deity.." Remembering that he was not personally aware of the *substantial* symbolism presented in this work, we can nevertheless draw upon Jung's observations of the subconscious and his theories regarding psychology and religion when he declared:

> It is only through the psyche that we can establish that God acts upon us, but we are unable to distinguish whether these actions emanate from God or from the unconscious..[61]

Referring back to our swimming-pool analogy, this is akin to saying that although we know the water comes from 'somewhere', we cannot accurately discern where or what that 'somewhere' is. Unless of course we can somehow travel to that mystical depth or, alternatively, identify evidence of that mystical source at the level of daily consciousness: Such as through symbols and colors perhaps?

Using data to explain that the access point for the true (mystical) religious experience is indeed via the unconscious, Jung goes on to state with conviction; "..empirically it can be established, with a sufficient degree of probability, that there is in the unconscious an archetype of wholeness.." One might even be tempted to interpret this as an archetype of holiness? Speaking religiously, and not forgetting the multiple appearances of the white, red, and blue phenomenon in scripture as well as in natural science, we are thus left to contemplate the distinct and very real possibility that any all-permeating symbolism such as that partially reflected in the triadic archetype is no less than a historical 'message from God' – or perhaps even a 'reflection of God' as experienced directly by some in mystical religious experiences. In more scientific language, we may refer to the same in Jung's words concerning his interpretation of the 'God-image' or *imago Dei* as; [*]

> ...an archetype of wholeness which manifests itself spontaneously in dreams, ...from the psychological point of view, a symbol of the self *(q.v.)*, of psychic wholeness..

...which in turn he clarifies:

> One can, then, explain the God-image.....as a reflection of the self, or, conversely, explain the self as an *imago Dei* in man.

These definitions of Jung's 'archetype-of-wholeness' or 'God-image' can of course be directly transferred to our discoveries concerning the triadic archetype. What Jung identified in the realm of the unconscious we have today identified in nature, science, religion, history, mythology, art, and politics. His "invisible, psychoid, and transcendent noumena" that whispered secretly to him from folklore and dreams have apparently been here with us all along, marching side by side, leaving their archetypal footprints and signatures in the signs, symbols, and colors of human history.

Perhaps it should be clarified that the 'self' Jung is referring to is the unconscious or true inner self of an individual as opposed to the persona, or outer aspect of the personality. Very interestingly, in its sub-reference to 'self' in Jungian psychology the *Encarta Encyclopedia* refers to the anima as; "The feminine inner personality, as present in the unconscious of the male. It is in contrast to the animus, which represents masculine characteristics." Please note the secondary and 'inner' position as said of the feminine unconscious in relation to the masculine-themed persona.

This not only corresponds to our subatomic findings concerning the structure of matter; where proton and neutron share up and down quarks in respect of their quantum 'gender' whilst bonded by the electron, but we also have yet another direct reference to the human progression from masculinity through femininity to spirituality: External, to internal, to eternal: Body to mind to spirit: Red to blue to white. (♣ 24, 25, 26).

---

[*] Latin term constructed by Church Fathers for what may be equated with the 'true religious experience'

Inasmuch as we now have a sort of symbolic litmus test against which to assess the cosmic balance of any particular institution, agency, or organization, this is where the proofs of the triadic archetype promise to be of greatest service. Where religious beliefs display a cosmic propriety formulated along the triadic principles discussed in this work, they may now safely be elevated at least to semi-scientific status as opposed to being dismissed out-of-hand by empiricists as mere superstitious conjecture. In particular, by using the categories of the psychospiritual theory in Table D to loosely incorporate matching religious terminology, we can reduce the hugely complicated and confusing religious debate to at least five scientifically-debatable areas namely; (i) the active self, (ii) the thinking self, (iii) the inspirational self, (iv) the personal unconscious, and (v) the collective unconscious respectively; all relatively stable concepts in science and psychology as we have seen. This leaves only the *Noumenal Realm*, or the *Realm of Great Unknown* as a refuge for supra-sensory or mysterious concepts, thus reducing the area of religious and theological conflict from an area that previously encompassed all aspects of life and learning, to only that which is still beyond the reach of science.

Establishing definitive patterns in symbolism that correspond to the triadic archetype moves us ever closer to the understanding that collectively, human development and history appears to be advancing along a general red, blue, white sequence corresponding to physiological, through psychological, to spiritual. At the same time however, and rather confusingly; we each have our own personal progressions to contend with in achieving physical health, psychological well-being, and spiritual balance in an environment that is far, far from being ideal. Because most of us are still inching our way up the scale it is natural to surmise that as we reach each level of awareness, we will of necessity need to reevaluate our understandings of life and adapt accordingly. Just like painting a picture first with one color, and then two, three, and four colors, we realize at each step the great improvements that can be made to our painting as new tools and shades and hues are made available to us. One day, in that ideal world, we prospective artists-of-life will have all the colors at our disposal, and it will be then, and only then, that we can approach our craft as true masters in the natural sequence: First concept or inspiration, then the plan or sketch, and finally a full-color masterpiece. For the time being however, we junior apprentices have our hands and minds full just coming to terms with the few colors and concepts available to us – not to mention the difficulty of keeping those colors pure and unsullied. But as long as we keep trying, there is always hope of a better tomorrow. In the meantime, as we approach the next level of collective education, we need to focus on understanding the full meaning of the triadic archetype, and its implications for us today.

With the discovery of the triadic archetype, the theory of universal truth suggested by Jung's subliminal archetypes can now be substantiated at least partially, in the conscious, sensory, and substantial realm, and once accepted, the laborious process of untying the metaphorical blindfolds of sectarian belief systems can begin in earnest. By demonstrating the existence of this archetypal realm through observable examples of its manifestation in daily life we may just have the tentative and admittedly humble beginnings of a comprehensive 'universal theory of life' that incorporates both scientific and sacred aspects.

But no 'universal theory of life' should subsist on 'mere' theories and coincidences, no matter how colorful or exciting. What we need right now I believe, are some more concrete facts and figures to back up our hypotheses so far. So before we discuss any more examples of the triadic archetype at work in history, let us first return to that most basic of languages respected and acknowledged all over the planet; the language of numbers.

# CHAPTER ELEVEN

# ARCHETYPAL MECHANICS

*Here we look at numeric formulas and associated theories that correspond to the triadic archetype in some form or another. This brief study will form the basis for a tentative 'meaning of life' hypothesis that accommodates previous and upcoming examples of substantial archetypes in the lives of certain key figures, agencies, and events in history.*

The political and religious color phenomena outlined in earlier chapters is for the most part clearly self-evident, as are the psychological theories of Jung. But when we start dealing with mystical numbers, alleged 'providential' time periods, and supposedly 'divinely-ordained' historical persons or events we open up a particularly perplexing 'can of worms' not least of all because of the numerous competing theories and hypotheses centering upon these themes already in existence. But this focus upon what I term 'archetypal mechanics' should not be mistaken as a tentative adventure in occult numerology, nor some foray into mystical gematria (the study of corresponding themes between the letters and numbers of the Hebrew alphabet). Nor are we going to leap from the self-evident facts and figures of previous chapters into pure speculation. Indeed, the reader should be made aware that I have harbored concerns about diluting the existing evidence with an overemphasis upon any numerical aspect, especially if it might result in exposing our central theory to too much critical speculation. But after considering the matter at length, and after research unearthed volumes of supporting material, I decided this information was too important to ignore. Indeed, the discovery of this added dimension to the triadic archetype added such quantities of material to my research, that I realized that a second, third, and even fourth volume may be needed to accommodate it all. Adding to my conviction that I should include this numerical aspect in the book was the unearthing of striking symbolism that surrounded many of those key figures and important historical events.

In discovering symbolic parallels in the recorded lives of Noah, Abraham, Moses, David, and Jesus for example in the Biblical sphere; or Zoroaster, Buddha, Mohammad, and Baha'u'llah, in the interreligious sphere; or Constantine, Charlemagne, Napoleon, Mussolini, and Hitler in the political sphere; or even Cleopatra, Joan of Arc, Marie Antoinette, Eva Braun, and Indira Gandhi.. to give just a few examples—and then to note many other themes linking their lives and missions respectively—naturally I felt obliged to attempt to make some sense of it all. The results of my admittedly limited research and studies so far indicate very strongly that key individuals, groups, nations, and historical events align numerically along subliminal archetypal lines in a process that may best be described as providential mechanics, which in turn align with the color-related findings of this book. For practical reasons, the detailed study of this intriguing topic will have to be continued in upcoming volumes, but to summarize; these providential mechanics appear to operate in numerical sequences as if necessary for the advancement or correction of human society, for as we shall see, the players involved at the center of these patterns have invariably affected the course of history either for good or for ill, or, in a combination of both. In other words what I hope to demonstrate is evidence of a systematic pattern—or series of interconnected social patterns—that center upon major historical figures and events; which in turn indicates human adherence to proactive, yet subliminal 'providential' activity – that also corresponds to the triadic archetype. However, in proffering the term 'providential' to define this activity the reader should not anticipate any improvable claims of divine orchestration, but should understand the term in the broadest sense of the word, and in light of the fact that the dictionary is still short on words to describe this particular phenomenon. In collating this data certain reasonable deductions can of course be drawn. But before we leap to any unfounded conclusions concerning the possible origins and meanings of these activities, let us be patient and wait until the evidence is in. So, with the fundamental understanding that human history has always been bound by numbers in one form or another let's begin our review with some basic observations.

**Numbers are Important**
Numbers are obviously very important. Numerical formulas make sense where abstract concepts are often difficult to grasp. They are essential in the language of science and mathematics and are key to practically all of our social endeavors. All the known laws of the universe first had to be numerically identified and quantified before they could be translated into common language. By studying the paths of the stars, tracking their courses,

timing the days, months and seasons, measuring speeds and distances, forms, shapes and volumes, such icons as Pythagoras, Plato, Aristotle, Michelangelo, Leonardo Da Vinci, Copernicus, Galileo, Newton, Hamilton and Einstein, were able to bring to our limited intellects an understandable and logical universe. They used numbers. The reason they used numbers was not simply because the laws of the universe could be translated into numerical context, but rather (I propose) because the language of cosmic law is already numerical to begin with. In other words, our scientific geniuses have collectively been engaged in the process of discovering, understanding, and translating the preexisting numerical language of cosmic law. Proponents of the chaos theory might debate this point, but as science learns more and more about the fundamentals of matter, a growing consensus is leaning in the direction of a systematic and organized universe. As the *GuruNet Wikipedia 2005* states under the heading of numerology:

> Pythagoras, the Greek mathematician and philosopher, was so enamored with the concept of numbers that he almost succeeded in developing a complete religion centered around the premise that the universe is based on a mathematical algorithm. Although his ideas may have seemed far fetched in his day, as we approach the 21st century scientists are only just now beginning to realize that there is truth to his thinking processes..
>
> As modern scientists are able to break the atomic structure into protons, electrons and neutrons, and those primary building blocks down into smaller subatomic particles, they are beginning to realize that these structures are so minute that their building blocks must be based (upon) some higher force. [62]

The bearing of this introductory statement to our discussion of providential mechanics is to simply acknowledge and accept that whatever numerical formulas lie at the heart of creation must by definition be archetypal formulas. Cosmic numeric blueprints in other words. Just as we have discovered subliminal attachments to certain symbolic themes or collections of colors in culture, politics, and religion, so might we reasonably expect to find matching numeric patterns in natural history that correspond in some way to the dynamics of the electromagnetic spectrum. Already hinted at in events listed in Chapter One, in the geometrics of atomic composition, and in conjunction with the color and symbol proofs of previous chapters; this study of key numbers linked with the triadic archetype in both natural and human history should help construct yet another anchor for our speculative development of a comprehensive 'unified theory of life'. Dealing with a broad range of data, the reader will of course understand that we can only cover some of the better-known facts, people, and events of history in this condensed study. But first, lets consider a few basics.

## Some Common Sense

To begin with an almost absurd observation; let us simply inquire whether or not a square remains a square if it has five sides? Or what does it become with only three sides? Or can a circle have more or less than 360 degrees and still remain a true circle? Of course not. So we recognize these laws in our mathematics. If we didn't grasp these fundamental principles then hardly a house would stand, or a school be established. If our ancestors had not recognized the existence and validity of the systems, rules, and formulas that comprise natural law, then we could never have 'evolved' out of a primal state of elementary ignorance. And although we are arguably still very ignorant of many of the secrets of the universe there is no doubting the rapid advances in civilization whenever we make scientific, mathematical breakthroughs such as Newton's documenting of the laws of gravity, or Einstein's general theory of relativity.

As previously stated the fabric of life itself, light and energy, is system-based, as are all the other systems that support life in all its myriad forms in the natural world; all the plants and animals, and even our methods of communication, education, learning and life experience are numerically encompassed, shaped or bound in some form or another. Even light and sound can be numerically recorded as we have seen. This means that everything that gives our lives meaning; from our concepts of time and space to the functioning dynamics of our social institutions, is shaped by, and subject to, inviolable numeric laws.

The simplicity of these statements seems that I am overstating the case, but at the risk of insulting the reader's intelligence I must also ensure that everybody who reads this work fully grasps and acknowledges these simple yet cardinal truths: We live in a mathematical universe, governed by numeric laws that affect every part of our daily lives, which we ignore or circumvent to our cost.

In relating this rule back to the symbolism covered so far, we recall the proposal that the coalescence of red, white, and blue somehow thematically represents either the original blueprint for creation or, when present in politics, psychology, or religion in particular, represents the remedial pattern for restoration of that blueprint. Inasmuch as we can find numeric parallels that align with these concepts whilst simultaneously matching the respective color-dynamics of universal symbolism, then we may be reasonably assured that we have uncovered some additional numeric aspect(s) of the triadic archetype either in its original or remedial forms.

Referring back to our diagram of the visible spectrum (♣ 9) we see that the main numbers we are looking at are three, four, seven, and ten, and multiples thereof. The particular cosmic, remedial, or symbolic values of each of these numbers will become apparent as we progress, but I must reiterate very strongly, that the data presented in the various numerical tables in this book are comprised only of that which I have had time to personally research, and so I remain open to seeing many, many additions to these tables from different cultural perspectives, academic disciplines, and time periods that will hopefully further confirm our findings. But I'm sure you'll agree that the existing evidence is still very compelling. Please now take a moment to review Tables B, H, J, K, & L  (see page viii).

There is always the chance of course that some of these figures are merely coincidental, and therefore have no place in a systematic theory of archetypal numerics, but to discern that clearly at this early stage would require a comprehensive knowledge of the history of the world – something regrettably I do not possess. Besides, in later volumes I intend to qualify most if not all of the data reported here, as well as introducing many additional facts to support our central theories so far. But at the same time I wish to restate the fact that just because we have apparent evidence of subliminal and systematic orchestrations in history, does not automatically allow us to make unwarranted conclusions about the possible involvement of the hand of the Divine. But on the other hand, we may reasonably conclude that there are definite archetypal associations between the surfacing of these cosmic patterns and the strivings of religion to theologize their meanings in history. But discerning whether it is 'the hand of God' or 'universal archetypes' or just 'natural cosmic mechanics' at work behind these phenomena is not in my opinion as important as simply recognizing the striking unifying features. Because if this theory of the triadic archetype is to hold any weight in bringing people closer together, it will be chiefly in its ability to bear witness to itself in scientific terms, and not as a pseudo-religious appendage to existing religious beliefs. Therefore we must always and only consider the facts as they are presented, and resist the temptation to seek out justifications and partial verifications for our own subjective beliefs.

**Cosmic Numbers**

In reconsidering the dynamics of the electromagnetic spectrum as representative of the energies of the universe, we can logically interpret the colors of the spectrum as a visible model of universal balance or perfection. Considering these two features in symbolic form; (i) *universal energy*, and (ii) *universal balance*, we find ourselves presented with a rainbow of symbolic color-options in natural and human history that *could* represent all the varying stages of origin, growth, development, and/or disease and dysfunction, both in the ecosystem and in society. This is a rather mind-boggling concept if we think about it for too long. But thanks to the colors and themes of the triadic archetype, it need no longer be quite so indecipherable.

*Universal energy* (i) for instance is obviously represented by the full range of the color spectrum or by the color white alone, whilst *universal balance* (ii) seems to be best represented in social circumstances by the colors of the triadic archetype; either a combination of white, blue, and red (fig.11 ♣) or, in natural circumstances by *green*, blue, and red (♣ 10). But, any *dualistic* model of cosmic balance would I propose, ideally consist of the colors blue and red in harmonious synchrony, both in natural and social situations, as discussed throughout the book (♣ 11, 12, 13, 25). In contrast, cosmic imbalance or inappropriate destruction is usually represented by deep reds in isolation, or red-blacks (♣ 16, 17, 27 etc). But blue, being the feminine nurturing color will rarely if ever be seen accompanying destructive symbolism (♣ 27). These facts need to be kept in mind as we progress through the following review. All the while remembering of course that we are generally concerned with symbolism that is related to natural science or to 'core' individuals, agencies and events in history.

So far, we have focused chiefly on this color-related symbolism and its meanings, showing how the color red for example, both in nature and in history has traditionally represented the strong, masculine, physical, and aggressive elements, whilst the more feminine traits of contemplation, wisdom, and compassion are characterized by blue. We noted experiments where the playing of red or blue lights on plants and captive animals had remarkable effects relating to the masculine and feminine properties respectively. We also noted the same themes repeated throughout mythology and in certain contemporary religions, although sometimes only by their absence. In short, and although there is yet more color-related evidence to come, I believe we have clearly demonstrated the centrality and importance of these particular colors both as subliminal and substantial influences in human and natural history. But now we are talking about numbers that correspond both with the visible spectrum as well as with intriguing synchronistic phenomena in human history. We will show for example how the key numbers of three, four, seven, and ten are not only predominant amongst the world's major faith traditions, but are equally evident in the mechanics of the visible spectrum, in quantum physics, the periodic table, and now, as we shall see in Tables H-through-L, are also to be seen surrounding certain key time periods, agencies, and individuals in history. The big question of course is what's the connection?

To answer this question logically we first need to return briefly to Greek philosophy.

## Quantum Philosophy

For a long time, the atom was considered the smallest identifiable element of matter. The word 'atom' in ancient Greek means 'indivisible' and was first coined by the Greek philosophers to identify what they believed was the smallest component of matter which in turn, related directly to their concept of an 'Original Cosmic Principle' or 'Universal Reality' or 'God'. Later, the stoic philosopher Heraclitus would translate this concept of 'God-in-action' as the aforementioned 'Logos' when he used the term to define the Cosmic Principle in mediation between God and man. This all-pervading divine life force (God), or Original Cosmic Principle of the ancient Greeks was thought to be reflected in the immortal souls of humans, which in turn were believed to be a mystical mixture of fire and water (see fig.12 ♣). Consequently, fire and water were symbolically understood to be mystical manifestations of the Logos. [Here the reader is invited to reflect upon the strong parallels with Jungian archetypes – in particular the role of the Animus and the Anima as mediators between mankind and the truths of the collective unconscious (♣ 24, 25, 26)].

Thus we see that the original Logos concept included both feminine and masculine properties as blue-and-red, water-and-fire elements respectively, and it was only when the feminine blue aspect of Logos was dropped (or ignored) by the early Christians that we see the emergence of an all-male, Christ-as-Logos figure complete with red-and-white symbolism heading an imperialistic ecclesiastic patriarchy (♣ 25). Accordingly, in light of the respective numbers of the extremes of the visible spectrum (700 for red, and 400 for blue), one could say that the feminine blue was substantially absent not only from the mission of Christ, but also from early Judaism, Christianity, and Islam, thus resulting in the aforementioned patriarchal imbalances, and the need for the theoretical restoration of the (blue) number 400, or 40. This, in the same way perhaps as a (red) proton would seek out

177

its blue counterpart the neutron, in order to achieve cosmic balance? Could this 'seeking-the-feminine' theme perchance have anything at all to do with the profusion of appearances of the number four and its multiples? Not only throughout Christ's lifetime and the Pentecost period, but also in the preparatory history of the Jews as recorded in the Bible, most notably in the activities of Moses, Saul, David, and Solomon, and later reportedly in the lifetime of the prophet Muhammad and pervading later Islamic empires? Keeping these intriguing suggestions in mind, let's now continue with our investigation.

Since the time of the indivisible atom of the Greeks it has of course been proven that the atom is indeed divisible, releasing huge amounts of energy in the form of the atomic bomb. We also have nuclear power from the same source, although it could be argued that the splitting of the atom was a breach of cosmic law that has brought more harm than good. This based upon the fact that the natural nuclear reactions occurring in the sun are a *fusion* of atoms rather than a splitting of them. Hence the differing terms 'fusion' and 'fission'; the latter meaning to divide, or split. The sun generates life-giving solar energy using a unifying process (fusion), whilst we appear to be manufacturing a potentially destructive energy-source using a divisive process (fission). Anyway, whatever one's opinion the fact remains that we can and do split the atom, and by doing so have learnt a great deal about the makeup of our world. Whether or not we should have done so in the first place is another debate. However, this brings us to a point of clarification about cosmic law and how it operates. For we need to make a clear distinction between (i) natural cosmic laws that follow their own predetermined intrinsic processes, and (ii) those creative or destructive forces engineered or manipulated by man, that in turn can interfere with those laws. Having already identified certain colors and symbols that can generally be aligned with creative, destructive, or remedial processes in human history, this investigation of numerical sequences or patterns matching the same should help us appreciate some additional mathematical aspects of the triadic archetype.

## Creative Formulas

Having already acknowledged the fact that there are fundamental, inviolable cosmic laws, we need also recognize that there is a creative dimension to natural law which, for ease of reference today we will name here 'the realm of creative formulas'. Whereas cosmic law determines the elementary numeric information of the elements, forces, and energies of nature; 'creative formulas' serve to unite these elements, forces, and energies during the creative process. For example, if we use the analogy of a seedling, some water, and some sunlight, we can see that each of these three entities can be identified as an independent element in itself in numeric terms; by weight, shape, size, volume, chemical composition, electromagnetic waves, etc. In this example, these three (admittedly more complex than fundamental) elements represent by analogy any three elementary principles of cosmic law. Bringing them together to produce a fruit laden apple tree requires a creative formula: In this case, the simple formula would be $(S + W + L = T)$; seed (S), plus water (W), plus light (L), equals a tree. In this case, and if all goes according to plan, there will be a dynamic harmonious union of these three elements resulting in a new creation; the apple tree. But if any of these individual contributing components are removed from the formula or altered or interfered with substantially, then obviously the development and fruition of the tree is in jeopardy.

Another simple analogy is that of the artist (A), his paints (P), his brushes (B), and his canvas (C). Each is a discrete entity in its own right which when combined can result in a wonderful masterpiece. But remove just one of them from the formula $(A + P + B + C)$ and you will not have much of a painting. In such a manner, we can understand that although the cosmic law of the Universe is itself inviolable under all circumstances, the dynamic *creative formulas* that engender life here on Earth are not. This means that under certain circumstances creative formulas are subject to 'outside' (human) interference or manipulation, and the results of any such intervention could possibly be detrimental (but not necessarily so). The aforementioned 'unnatural' splitting of the atom is a case in point, as is the manufacture of highly toxic substances for short-term commercial or military uses. Thus we may define cosmic law and creative formulas respectively as follows:

- **'Cosmic Law'** is the term that defines the inviolable, elementary governing principles of the universe – also known as 'Universal Law'.

- **'Creative Formulas'** refers to the processes of uniting and/or combining elements of cosmic law to generate energies, entities, life-supporting systems, or produce inanimate and animate creations. These processes are *not* inviolable, but can be manipulated by us to produce 'other than natural' outcomes.

Man it seems, is the only known psycho-biological agent capable of consciously manipulating creative formulas for either good or ill. This places us in a rather special relationship between cosmic law and Mother Nature. Using the triadic archetype as a model, it could even be suggested that mankind holds the middle (blue) position of 'conscious reason' between a (white) cosmic Origin of the Universe and the (red-green) energies of substantial creation—both natural and man-made—which would of course fit nicely with the Biblical admonition to Adam and Eve to become stewards of the earth?[63] In any event, the main point to be taken from these observations is the recognition that nature, when left to her own designs has always managed to function in harmonious synchrony. There is a consistent if sometimes terrible beauty to natural mechanics. Even allowing for the inherent violence of nature in the predator-prey dynamic, or in the devastation wreaked by storms, droughts, ice-ages or volcanoes, Mother Nature always manages to recover and go on. But at the point of human intervention we witness regular and chronic disruptions of the cosmic order that produce sinister outcomes. At the natural level such occurrences as pollution, deforestation and global warming are cases in point. Or at the social level; broken families, community crime, and international warfare; not to mention preventable famine and disease, or the long-term aftereffects of nuclear radiation from spent fuel rods or, of nuclear fallout if global nuclear war ever becomes a reality. These 'unnatural' phenomena can be traced to a point where humanity has failed to harmonize with cosmic law in one form or another—whether through ignorance or design—and the results are ominous to say the least. In the same way that we would be deeply concerned if our apple trees started producing poisonous fungi instead of healthy fruit, so should we be equally concerned about troubling phenomena in our societies and in the natural world. Which part of the fundamental formula for producing healthy apples is being compromised or interfered with we might ask? Or, who messed up the painting? Which aspects of creative formulas are we unconsciously or consciously violating in order to be engineering such a disturbing natural and social environment? What indeed is missing from the formula for cosmic balance in each specific case?

Personally, I believe the answer lies not in social or scientific theory alone, but in our ability to clearly define the mathematical principles behind the construction and development of human society, and from there, to critically compare those facts and figures with the fundamentals of cosmic law to see where we might be going amiss. And whilst I will readily admit that the information in this book will fall well short of answering these crucial questions in depth, I also feel that the discovery of a symbolic, chromatic, *and* geometric triadic archetype might well lead us one step closer to an understanding thereof. For if we are agreed that even we super-intelligent and super-civilized humans are essentially composed of the same cosmic stuff as planets, pigs, and potatoes, then perhaps the formulas for light and energy that govern and define all cosmic behaviors might also have something to teach us? But before we go on to identify and explore some examples of those specific numbers, let us also acknowledge the fundamental principle of restoration or repair: In other words, if we do somehow violate these cosmic formulas, and damage or injury or dysfunction occurs, then a system of repair and restoration must obviously be initiated if we are ever to regain our previously healthy state.

## Repair and Restoration

When injury or damage occurs, cosmic formulae also govern the subsequent repair process. Therefore, any such processes must first (theoretically) recognize and identify the problem before presenting a plan of restoration and then executing repair: Concept, plan, and action – white, then blue, then red. In other words, one cannot provide the solution (except by an accidental fluke) without first knowing and understanding what the problem is. Neither can one ignore the damage already caused when seeking to bring about repair. Simply put; 'broke stuff' whether material or ethereal, actual or conceptual, individual or global… stays broke, until it's fixed. There are no short cuts to this process. We can't just 'wish' the problem fixed. Regardless of our personal beliefs and convictions, if we don't recognize that a problem has occurred in the first place and then take the appropriate restorative action, the problem can't and won't get fixed. Even in the case of 'passive healing' in its various forms, there are always active forces at work.

To press home this important point let's use a simplified imaginary formula for human flight. Let's pretend that the following numbers represent the appropriate values for gravity, speed, weight, volume, lift and thrust, and when applied correctly will result in actual human flight. So here we have the 'cosmic' numbers of; 1, 2, 36, 40, and 100, combined as the 'creative formula' for human flight; because we need *one* person, who weighs *one hundred* pounds, with *two* wings measuring *forty* feet across, traveling at *thirty-six* miles per hour off the roof… to achieve human flight. (Please do not try this at home!) If any of the numbers in the 'creative formula' are violated; for example if the wingspan is only thirty feet instead of forty, then the objective (human flight) cannot be achieved.

Now, I respectfully ask the reader to please pay attention to what is perhaps the most important point of all: No matter how much we *wish;* no matter how much we *hope;* no matter how much we *believe;* and no matter how hard we *pray;* the plain and simple truth is if that wingspan is not constructed to the right dimensions, or if any of the other factors are not 'on spec' then we will not fly. This is plainly and simply how the universe works and, on the rare occasions when these laws appear to be getting suspended or broken such as in the cases of reported miracles or supernatural events, I see more a confirmation of our collective lack of knowledge and understanding rather than a literal suspension of these laws. I do sincerely believe by the way, that it is our collective destiny to continually advance in understanding until knowledge and wisdom eventually replaces (blind) faith and adherence to tradition, as the preferred religio-spiritual virtues of choice.

**Cosmic Themes**
Rationally speaking it is logical to deduce that where there are numeric cosmic laws there must be some origin of those laws. Whether one believes a cosmic explosion such as the 'Big Bang' theory is that source, or an almighty benevolent life force (God), or even little green men from Mars is not so important at this point. We only need acknowledge that the origin or source of these laws operates by or through, or at least in conjunction with these same numeric principles. Whether this is merely the unconscious machinations of cosmic propriety in natural action, or is devolving from some Supreme Intelligence is a secondary point to accepting the logic of a geometric origin of geometric laws. For as we have already shown, the fundamental principles that govern elementary matter are present both at the microcosmic and macrocosmic levels as well as being reflected in human physiology, psychology, and society, and all are therefore bound by similar archetypal principles. To recap;

- Light is visible energy, which travels at 300,000km per second. Light can thus circumnavigate the globe seven times in one second.

- In subatomic science; protons, neutrons, and electrons operate as a quantum trinity to form an atom.[*]

- 'Up' and 'Down' quarks within protons and neutrons also function as three fundamental units in union with each other, using the formula; 2 + 1.

---

[*] Hydrogen atoms do not have a neutron, and are therefore an exception to this rule.

- When protons and neutrons unite, they each bring three quarks. Thus 3 plus 3 come together to form the nucleus (adding 1), thus creating the number seven.

- The (female) neutron disintegrates as an isolated particle, thus the (male) proton is considered the stronger element, and the life-center of the atom.

- When protons and neutrons are compared to the red and blue extremities of the visible spectrum, we see strong and weak correlations respectively between the red and blue (masculine and feminine) colors.

- Using the temperature scale and social symbolism as a guide; red equals heat, activity, and masculinity, whilst blue represents cooler temperatures, passivity, and femininity.

- The red extremity of the visible spectrum is numbered at 700 nanometers whilst the blue end is recorded as 400. Hence a 300 nanometer span between them.

- When functioning maturely and productively the human psyche operates upon the principle; first concept, then plan, and then action, although the usual developmental progression from youth to maturity is the reverse; red, then blue, then white; physical, then emotional, then spiritual.

- Human DNA is comprised of nucleotides in patterns of three, as well as genetic alphabet 'bases' in units of four.

- Human society, when functioning ecologically, reflects the same basic numeric and thematic principles as the dynamics of fundamental energy.

Focusing primarily upon these facts, we note some intriguingly consistent physiological parallels between atomic principles and human relations centering on the numbers three, four, and seven. These include the many synchronistic patterns where electrons pursue regular cycles around the nuclei (center) of atoms in sequences of threes, fours, and especially sevens (13 ♣). Apparently, there are many variables as atoms become more complex, but the patterns of the lowest energy states are clearly following some predetermined mathematical principles.

If we now briefly look at the next stage of the structure of matter we will see that atoms, through the electrons in orbit about them, connect with each other to form molecules, which then assume various forms of matter. Once again, there are inviolable laws to this process. For example, when different atoms unite they 'share' each other's electrons, which is how they bond together as a molecule. Not unlike individuals in healthy human families share in (blue) communication, (white) love-energy, and (red) material support, we also see a parallel between human emotions and the activity of gluons; so named because they make quarks stick together so-to-speak; and the further gluons are spatially apart, the more intense the glue-like effect. The *Gurunet Questia Encyclopedia* describes the functions of gluons eminently more scientifically as follows: (Please keep in mind the aforementioned parallels between human relations and quantum physics *noted here in italics*, as we patiently try to digest all this technical stuff).

> **gluon,** an elementary particle that mediates, or carries, the strong, or nuclear, force. In quantum *chromodynamics* (QCD), ...the interaction of quarks to form protons, neutrons, and other elementary particles is described in terms of gluons – so called because *they "glue" the quarks together*. Gluons are massless, travel at the speed of light, and *possess a property called color....analogous to positive and negative charges...* Quarks change their color as they emit and absorb gluons, and *the exchange of gluons maintains proper quark color balance.*

> Unlike other forces, the force between quarks increases as the distance between the quarks increases. Up to distances about the diameter of a proton, *quarks behave as if they were free of one another*, a condition called asymptotic freedom. As the quarks move farther apart, the gluons that move between them utilize the energy that they draw from the quark's motion to create more gluons.. *The gluons thus appear to lock the quarks inside the elementary particles, a condition called confinement.* Gluons can also bind with one another to form composite particles called glueballs.[*]

---

[*] Gurunet quote edited for brevity, and italics added – STM

Not wanting to bog the reader down in concepts and quantum mechanics that I too must admit to having difficulty following at times, may I simply suggest that in equating (a) raw human emotion to gluons, (b) personality and gender traits to quarks, and (c) individual personalities to either proton or neutron as male and female respectively; we have the basic dynamics that contribute to forming a human family. The concept obviously needs refining, but the principles are indeed there. Even the curiously-named 'glueballs' above have their counterpart in the strong feelings of familial attachment when we operate as independent individuals within the family circle. When we then suggest that the electron (white) represents the good love-energy in a healthy family, we can see the parallel atomic value in the electron's binding of the atom as a harmoniously functioning unit. And as we recall from Chapter Six there is a further analogous comparison between atoms becoming molecules, and human families becoming communities. This process is achieved by sharing the love-energy (white) of healthy family units or, in microscopic parallel, sharing electrons around clusters of atoms to form a molecule. To try to put these microcosmic concepts into some sort of perspective, we should understand that one single drop of water contains millions of millions of billions of hydrogen and oxygen atoms. The following table should help summarize our main points so far:

### Table E: Subatomic Elements and Social Parallels

| Element | Character | Social Parallel |
|---------|-----------|-----------------|
| Gluons | Force that binds quarks together | Emotions |
| Quarks | Operate in 2:1 triadic patterns | M/F Personality |
| Neutron | 'Feminine' character because dependant.. | Woman |
| Proton | 'Masculine' character because dominant.. | Man |
| Electron | Bonding part of atom, required for molecules | Love |
| Nucleus | Proton and neutron combined | Sexual Union |
| Atom | 'Complete' unit; electron, proton and neutron | Family |
| Molecule | Conjoined atoms surrounded by electrons | Community |

Furthermore, and adding a little more speculative fuel to our 'coincidental' fire; science informs us of five elements that exist in all living organisms on Earth; carbon, hydrogen, oxygen, nitrogen, and phosphorus. These five elements are amongst at least 150 others listed in the updated periodic table that have each been given different numeric values. [64] This, according to their atomic 'weight' and respective quantum properties, such as the number of protons in their respective nuclei. What is interesting from the perspective of this book is that the atomic weight numbers assigned to each of these cardinal elements (with the exception of hydrogen which is a special case), are either multiples of, or are divisible by the numbers three, four, seven, and ten, and whilst arguably this may be mere coincidence once again, there might equally be more than happenstance to observe here:

**Table F: Primary Elements and Archetypal Numbers**

| Element | A # | Atomic Weight | T/A Number |
|---------|-----|---------------|------------|
| Hydrogen | 1 | 1 | (Special Case) |
| Carbon | 6 | 12 | 3 x 4 |
| Nitrogen | 7 | 14 | 7 + 7 |
| Oxygen | 8 | 16 | 4 x 4 |
| Phosphorus | 15 | 30 | 3 x 10 |

In fact, according to the NASA-affiliated PSRDA (*Planetary Science Research Discoveries Agency*), only hydrogen, carbon, nitrogen, and oxygen are actually essential for life. This brings us neatly back to our 'feminine' and life-sustaining number four once again. On the other hand and continuing with our thematic parallels; what makes hydrogen a special case is the fact that in its most usual form it is comprised only of a proton and an electron (red-white) – without the usual balancing neutron (blue). It is also the lightest and most abundant element in the universe, key to the formation of stars, and features critically in the Big Bang theory. However, hydrogen atoms can still only function 'creatively' when bonded to other atoms in the form of molecules, and thus are bound by the same general principles.

There may yet be some corresponding values between the abundance of hydrogen in our universe (red-white) and the fact that human history has for the most part been a 'red-white' story so far? As a red-white 'masculine' element hydrogen could (at a stretch) be symbolically aligned with the traditional 'creative male' figures; God-the-Creator, cosmic heroes, redeemers and messiahs for instance, chiefly through associations with (a) the cosmic number one, (b) through its primal presence in the universe, (c) because of its 'explosive' star-making creativeness, and (d) because of the absence of a feminine neutron. Combined with oxygen it could also be numerically aligned with the mystical "water of life". Water, being made up of one hydrogen and two oxygen atoms ($H_2O$) combine to give us the number thirty-three, which is not only the possible missing 33% of the compromised cosmic circle, but also represents the feminine, symbolic aspect of the triadic archetype. But I must confess to indulging in a little dubious speculation here. But who knows, perhaps some eminent physicist will spot some correlation in these abstractions that can help draw the fields of science and religion closer together?

But, speculation about the symbolic potential of hydrogen atoms aside; there are still the remarkable bonding properties of carbon 12 to consider, another essential life-producing element. Carbon is understood to be produced at the heart of a collapsing star at temperatures exceeding a hundred million degrees when three *alpha particles* of helium (atomic weight # 4) fuse together in a dynamic procedure called the *triple-alpha process*. Interestingly, these alpha particles are also comprised of two pairs of protons and neutrons each, giving us not only another masculine-feminine and red-and-blue parallel, but also an interesting total of twelve units that also match our earlier 3 x 4 discoveries of Chapter Five (Table B). When we add to this the 100,000,000° figure mentioned above, and the scientific conclusion that "The energy released by the reaction is approximately proportional to the temperature to the *40$^{th}$ power*, and the density *squared*" [65] we are inescapably brought back to our creative feminine-blue fours, with our other key numbers of ten and three as steady partners in these cosmic creative formulas.

Now I'm not claiming to be able to fully understand or grasp all the implications of the data we have unearthed concerning quantum physics, nor exactly how such may be applied by more capable others; but in considering the 150-or-so different-numbered elements of the periodic table that could (theoretically) have been involved in the abovementioned formulas; the parallels and numeric connections here with the central numbers of one, three, four, seven, and ten are undeniable.

In emphasizing the importance of these parallels between our key numbers, human society, subatomic physics and cosmic energies, I hope to be able to demonstrate that the central reason behind the continuous repetition of these numbers in nature and human history is because they represent both creative, and restorative (or repair) process that are intrinsic to life itself. Recognizing the numeric values of cosmic laws, it makes perfectly good sense to conclude that one possible explanation for the uncanny coincidences and repetitions of numbers and colors in human history (shown in Tables A through L) is that they are indicators of some cosmic attempt to either create something, or, put something right. Given the fact that our world is riddled with ignorance, fear, superstition, sickness, pollution, prejudice, bigotry, corruption and cruelty, perhaps we should be more disposed to the conclusion that if anything at all is being orchestrated at the cosmic level, then it is most likely some sort of repair or restorative process rather than something purely creative. However, this does not necessarily discount the third option; the possibility that we are all collectively and currently involved in an apparently-chaotic and untidy progression from our early animal origins towards our future 'divine' human potential. We will develop these theories as we progress, but meanwhile the real trick in making any sense of all this will be in discerning between the purely creative formulas of nature, and the aforementioned remedial formulas within human history. For therein lies the potential both for the greatest truth, and for the greatest confusion.

If then as suggested in this chapter, the numbers three, four, seven, and ten are central to the restorative-creative process, then naturally we can conclude that they also relate to the original problem and/or the original plan or formula in some way, at a time *before* the damage occurred. For example, if we see our aviator friend trying to add a 10ft section of wing to a 30ft section we can conclude that a wingspan of 40ft is probably part of the original formula for flight. Similarly, if it can be proven that the numbers three, four, seven and ten, are truly connected to a restorative process on a cosmic scale, then any original model or formula for creation must also relate to those numbers in some way. In other words, if mankind can in fact manipulate certain aspects of cosmic law through either ignorance or selfishness (which we all know we can), then we may assume that there are many ongoing problems associated with mankind's misuse (or abuse) of creative formulas that need to be addressed not only today, but also continuously throughout history. Hence the concept of a socio-spiritual messiah, or a divine providence of restoration designed somehow to address 'sinful' social dysfunctions: Our personal sins and vices; global pollution and disease; economic imbalances between nations; religious dissention; crime and warfare; corporate greed and deception; political oppression; and human rights violations for instance. These issues are not compatible with a wholesome and fruitful world that is functioning harmoniously, and therefore must be addressed if we are to restore cosmic balance.

The multiple and synchronistic repetitions of colors, numbers, themes, signs, and symbols associated with human history strongly suggests the possibility that *somehow* the universe is trying to make corrective (or at least progressive) adjustments to address gross imbalances instigated by us in natural and social history. Whether 'the Universe' and the activities thereof are to be read in a scientific or religious sense will be fully debated in Volumes II and III, but before we enter into specific historical detail, we first need to undertake a general overview of this phenomenon of archetypal numbers in science, nature, and history associated with the color spectrum.

By the conclusion of Chapter Twelve, I hope to have presented enough numerical and synchronistic evidence to the reader to place this theory of a substantial, geometric, and color-based triadic archetype firmly on the historical map.

# CHAPTER TWELVE

# PROVIDENTIAL PATTERNS

*Having shown the centrality of certain key numbers in science and nature, we will now revisit specific examples of those numbers from a perspective that considers their possible providential influence on human history.*

In this chapter and in subsequent volumes we will present specific examples in human history where for some yet-unexplained reason, certain key numbers associated with the triadic archetype appear to overshadow if not actually orchestrate the evolvement of history. Scientifically speaking this is a radical claim to put in writing, and religiously speaking, in a world regrettably possessed more of ignorance than enlightenment this might even prove to be a dangerous one as well. Because in the following pages we will attempt to answer that heavily-pregnant question posed in Chapter One; "is it really feasible that collectively we are somehow being unwittingly influenced? That we are unconsciously involved in fulfilling a greater historical plan ...a providential plan that can apparently affect nations, ideologies, and individual destinies like so many pieces on a cosmic chessboard at least to *some* extent?" In attempting to answer in the positive it is unavoidable that we will step upon some sensitive toes – so sensitive in fact, that unless we were to neutralize the upcoming facts with endless sycophantic platitudes, there could be no guarantee that offense will not be taken. Scientists I am not too concerned about, as I welcome the opportunity to be educated, enlightened, or challenged as the case may be so as to improve the quality and credibility of my research. But certain religious fundamentalists on the other hand are probably going to see either a ratification of their own beliefs in the following facts and hypothesis, or, are going to perceive the following as an attack upon them. In either case I would be deeply concerned, for one of the main purposes of this book is to attempt to draw us all together around a logical and systematic premise that may serve as a unifying base for further discussions. This is why I try my best to report the facts as objectively as possible, and from there, with as little bias as I can muster, to offer reasonable hypotheses. But having had some experience in this field, I can state with some confidence that certain ultra-denominationalists will react strongly to the conclusions indicated. I can but reiterate that the original concept and proofs of the triadic archetype are not my personal invention, but simply the documented results of many years of sincere research and study where my personal quest has been to uncover universal Truths (with a capital 'T') over and above any single philosophy or doctrine – most especially the exclusivist ones. Therefore, whilst endeavoring to offer reasonable respect to existing philosophies or doctrines, the reader will I hope understand that an accurate reporting of the subject material requires that I be as forthright in my findings as I can. This having been said, let's now take a look at the hypothesis of an orchestrated providence.

## Providential Mechanics

Let's imagine for a moment it was possible to somehow erase the blue end of the spectrum with all of its symbolic and literal associations, without of course destroying the universe in the process. Then, in response to the terrible imbalances poured out on the cosmos because of this, the remaining (red) units of creation would chase around frantically searching for the retrieval of the blue in order to survive. As 400 is the number assigned to blue by science (400 nanometers), we might reasonably expect those remedial endeavors to be centered upon that very number right? Especially if we tabulate our efforts in keeping with the laws of quantum mathematics. All this of course presumes upon the inviolability of natural law inasmuch as it will always seek to repair itself or restore equilibrium; especially whenever creative formulas go awry in some form or other. For despite our enthusiastic attempts to destroy the population and poison the planet, Mother Nature continues in her attempts to redress the balance. In those cosmic attempts we may expect to see the mechanics of natural law following their prescribed corrective courses; this type of imbalance requires that type of response, and this omission requires that insertion.. and so on, but always following natural law.

For instance, a seedling that sprouts in a shadow will naturally seek out the sunlight, just as different varieties of flowers in the same region bloom alternately in order to maximize their chances of pollination. Wildlife migrates with the seasons, and will go to extraordinary lengths to fulfill their instinctual obligations to mate and reproduce. Likewise in quantum physics, an atom simply cannot materialize without the inclusion of both (male) proton and (female) neutron.[*] They must, by force of cosmic law seek each other out in order to continue to exist and develop to the next molecular level (♣ 13). But as previously mentioned, when it comes to human interactions things can and do go amiss outside the boundaries of natural law. This is where we might expect to find the remedial principles of the triadic archetype at work in human society and history; as opposed to the normal, natural, and balanced mechanics of Mother Nature. This in great part accounts (provisionally) for the otherwise inexplicable series of colors, signs, numbers, themes and symbols identified in this book that appear to be following predetermined designs. For as we shall continue to see, these archetypal patterns—either constructive or remedial—align uncannily with key events or individuals in history in an apparent attempt to either (a) promote development, or (b) redress imbalances or omissions caused by harmful human activity. The real trick of course, is in discerning which is which.

In explaining the basic idea behind this notion of providential mechanics, perhaps the analogy of a human family might be a good place to start: For the family to develop and procreate naturally, the (red) masculine figure must of course find a receptive (blue) female partner before he can expect to become a parent. In numerical terms, and taking the red physical entity as the starting point, this would be a quest centering on the number four, or multiples thereof, because this is the number of the feminine blue. Maybe the number 300 (nanometers) would also be involved in some way as the distance between red and blue? But whatever the case, in literal terms we would state that he is "seeking a mate". In symbolic terms we could say "he is searching for blue", and in numerical terms we would say "he seeks 400". Each statement means the same thing in context of this discussion, which ultimately leads to birth, rebirth, or a new creation by, through, or in conjunction with the female. Having thus acquired the female and achieved natural union, we might then anticipate a merging or summation of the numbers 700 and 400 – and/or 300 – as an indicator of harmonious success.

In 'normal' human *developmental* sequence therefore, where we homo sapiens start our lives in the (red) physical before moving towards the (blue-white) emotional-intellectual and spiritual, we might expect the sequence to begin with 700 (the number of red), through 300 (as the distance between

---

[*] One exception to this law is a hydrogen atom, which only has a proton and an electron

red and blue), and then onto 400 (the number of blue). But as regards the *original* blueprint for creation; the 'Great Plan' behind the cosmic scheme of things as-it-were that applies uniformly to all other aspects of creation, the sequence is opposite: First concept, then plan, and then action. White, then blue, then red. The fact that this sequence applies to natural law but not necessarily to human social development indicates that mankind, as previously explained, has not yet (collectively at least) reached that place in our development as a species where we are in harmony with the universe. This is chiefly because we are still seeking that missing body of collective knowledge or awareness, or state of enlightenment that could unanimously be identified as 'spiritual' or 'superconsciousness'. Either that, or we somehow 'fell from grace' as suggested in several religious texts. But either way the end result is the same; a prevailing state of disharmony and ignorance as we collectively seek out enlightenment.

Once this spiritual knowledge is identified and understood by the collective consciousness of course, we should have a much better idea of our place—both collectively and as individuals—in the grand old cosmic scheme of things. This would then serve to lift us out of our current state of chaos, confusion, and destruction, and into our rightful positions as benevolent stewards of the earth. But seeing as we do not yet have that collective level of 'spiritual' awareness, then we cannot know for sure what the symbolic number of Ultimate Origin is – the source of the original (white) concept previously discussed, and therefore we cannot construct a *complete* numeric formula for whatever providential activity *might* be occurring under our very noses. Tempting though it is to find some arbitrary number or theory to fill this irksome gap, we must nevertheless be patient, deal with the facts at hand, and see how it all comes together. So in order to maintain credibility and scientific objectivity, we will try to steer clear of anything that might compromise the authority of the facts being presented. But we still have to make a few tentative speculations here and there. For instance, perhaps the number three would fit the missing slot of 'Ultimate Origin' not only as the number of cosmic balance, but also as derived from the aforesaid number of the speed of light at 300,000km per second?[*] Although purely speculative at this point, this would give us a neat and tidy sequence of three, then four, and then seven (or their multiples) as the numeric equivalents of the natural cosmic process of creation. This would reflect the primary archetypal color sequence of white, then blue, and then red: Concept, plan, and action. (Please bear with me here). But as regards

---

[*] For scientific purists, the speed is actually 299,792,458 meters per second.

*remedial* activities centering upon either of these themes, that is, (i) *natural* corrective formulas associated with the original blueprint for creation, or (ii) *providential* corrective formulas associated with human history and development; we might expect to see any mixed combination, or amalgamations of apparently-jumbled combinations of these themes-and-numbers, in response to whatever specific problem is being addressed at any particular point in time. I know this sounds tremendously complicated, and indeed it has taken a great deal of time and research to untangle – even to this limited point. But using the chromonumeric parameters of the triadic archetype as a guide, we can I believe, now begin to make some logical, sequential inroads into the convoluted mechanics of some of the key areas of human history.

For example; going back to Chapter Eight and our discussion of the combined symbolism of Judaism, Christianity, and Islam, is it not curious that the Old Testament (blue-Jewish) era from Adam to the birth of Christ spans a legendary 4,000 years, and the subsequent period of Roman-Christian emergence (red) until the time of Islam (green) was also a chromatically-appropriate seven centuries? Surely one wonders if this might be an example of archetypal mechanics? Or to give a more contemporary example; the fact that (red) Soviet Communism lasted seventy years, and the Berlin Wall came down at the birth of the new unified Germany after exactly forty years? Or conversely on an individual level; the forty weeks of pregnancy followed by the traditional seven years to the so-called 'age of reason'? In short, wherever we find a convergence of the numbers, colors, and themes of the triadic archetype within a particular historical context in tight formation, or in repeated patterns, then we may be reasonably assured that we are on to something that is; (i) probably beyond mere coincidence; (ii) is (at least in parts) beyond the direct conscious influence of man; and (iii) may in fact be evidence of something much more exciting indeed.

More specifically, any such convergence of affiliated themes, numbers, and symbols is probably evidence of either (a) natural cosmic formulas, or (b) remedial providential activity at work. But although the following evidence is, in my opinion very convincing, I must reemphasize the tentative and exploratory nature of these conclusions. All the evidence in other words, is not yet in. So in order to minimize unnecessary confusion; in our quest for any such historical convergences we will be looking chiefly at the better-known events of history, not so much because they are more or less important, but rather because they will be more familiar to the general reader, and therefore less likely to give rise to dissention.

## Complex Patterns; Simple Themes

Before actually discussing specific examples of the aforementioned numbers I would first like to offer a simplified assessment of the thematic meanings of the numbers three, four, seven, and ten in context of a theory of an orchestrated providence. This, in a manner that respects their appearances in science, history, and religious scriptures and their respective positions of alignment within the visible spectrum: In other words a general, but credible summary of their scientific, religious, and historical characteristics. As with our previous study of the meaning of colours; conclusions about the value-meanings of these numbers (or tentative conclusions to be more exact) are deduced from a broad range of sources. The taking of so many examples from the Bible is a reflection of my own personal schooling in that area, as well as the aforementioned recognition of the centrality of the Judeo-Christian Bible both as a historical document, and as the central scripture for most of the word's faithful.

Dealing first with the number three we note its fundamental connection with the triadic archetype as the cosmic number of equilibrium. As the first linear geometric shape that can 'contain' material, the triangle also has a primal substantial character that is further reflected in the term 'three-dimensional'. (Please see 'Triangle' in Ch. 5). Coupled with its copious appearances in religion and mythology along with sacred or providential themes, the number three is apparently both fundamental and indispensable. In addition to the many triadic themes in nature and sociology (as listed in Examples 1–8 in the midsection), we also note numerous instances of the number three affiliated with the mission preparation for various hero-figures in the Bible, such as the size of Noah's Ark at 300 cubits; the three miracles Moses used to move a *recalcitrant*[*] Pharaoh; or the gifts of the three Wise men at Bethlehem. Thus I propose that appearances of the number three or its multiples at important times in history, especially when in association with archetypal symbolism or themes, represents a time or occasion of *preparation,* or is a literal or symbolic *foundation* for subsequent activity.

Secondly, the number four and its multiples: As previously noted there is a theme of seeking-the-feminine, or waiting for birth as in the forty weeks of pregnancy. A time of preparation for a new and different future, or union with the feminine to bring forth new life. The number four has traditionally represented the four corners of ('Mother') Earth, the four seasons, and the four aspects of creation in Greek philosophy (fire, water, air, and earth) that combine in the cycles of life (♣ 10). Once again, it appears repeatedly in the

---

[*] Recalcitrant; stubborn, willful, obstinate; resistant to guidance or authority

lives of many of history's greats as they themselves were 'reborn' to a new mission or achieved some outstanding social accomplishment (Tables H, J, K). Of considerable significance is the four-thousand-year Axial Age period wherein we witness the uncannily-parallel rise of several world religions, including Hinduism, Buddhism, Taoism, Confucianism, Zoroastrianism, and the Hebrew faith – the latter which in turn gave birth directly or indirectly to Christianity and Islam. In *A History of God* by professor Karen Armstrong we read:

> The period 800-200 BCE has been termed the Axial Age. In all the main regions of the civilized world, people created new ideologies that have continued to be crucial and formative. The new religious systems reflected the changed economic and social conditions. For reasons that we do not entirely understand, all the cheif civilizations developed along parallel lines, even when there was no commercial contact [as between China and the European area].[66]

As we saw in Chapter One, the number four-hundred also holds special significance, most particularly around 1917 marking the four-hundredth anniversary of the Protestant Reformation; the victories of leading democracies over autocratic societies; and representing the emergence of the feminine in the suffragette movement – amongst several other 'blue-flavored' happenings and events at that specific time. Hence we will summarize appearances of the number four and its multiples as representative of that time of *new beginning*; a time of *birth or rebirth* through, by, or with the feminine.

Thirdly we have the number seven, another mystical number associated with the masculine color red (700 nm) which, as in the seven Biblical days of creation can be interpreted as a period of *creative activity,* or a providential *mission of restoration*, usually carried out by the male hero figure; in this particular case God the Father (red and white). This emphasis upon the male hero vs. the female heroine should not be misinterpreted here as a subjective masculine bias. This male-dominance theme simply reflects the grave and extremely disturbing absence of the feminine archetype both in history and in contemporary society, especially in the major orthodoxies. But in regards to humans achieving any particular mission in their lifetimes, it is interesting to note that according to the official *human scale* [*] the lifespan of a human is approximately seventy years.

Finally there is the number ten, which is a little difficult to summarize because there are so many possible interpretations. But for our discussion today, and in relation to some of the examples to be shown, the number ten and its multiples appear to symbolize either (i) *periods of necessary deferment*, or, (ii) *periods of completion* of any given event, episode, epoch, or era.

As a quick reference I have tabulated these summaries in Table G but wish to remind the reader that we do not want to stray too far into the world of numerology in order to make our case of a possibly-orchestrated providence. Undoubtedly there is a great deal more to be explored in this fascinating field, but from the perspective of this work these numeric themes, theories, and data are presented chiefly in support of an exposition of the triadic archetype. Any brief search of the Internet will show that many scholars and historians have already noted the existence of apparently-synchronistic time periods in history. But in the absence of a more comprehensive explanation, may I suggest that the surfacing of these key numbers in history is at least as likely to be associated with the dynamics of the electromagnetic spectrum as it is to any less scientific theory. All the same, I humbly acknowledge the many credibility issues that accompany new research. Therefore, as we peruse the examples of the following pages we should of course bear in mind the limitations of this study – namely my own unintentional cultural or personal biases, and the practical limits of my research – and be satisfied at this point with only a partial demonstration of this numeric phenomenon. Hopefully, the upcoming facts and figures will both justify and support their inclusion in this overview of a numeric dimension to the triadic archetype.

**Table G: Possible Meanings of Providential Numbers**

| Number | Possible Providential Meaning |
|---|---|
| Three, 30, 300, etc. | Foundation. Beginning. Preparation. Stable Primary Group. |
| Four, 40, 400, etc. | Preparation for Birth, Rebirth, Union, Renewal, or Growth. |
| Seven, 70, 700, etc. | Period of 'Creative' Activity.[†] Masculine Mission. |
| Ten, 100, 1,000 etc. | Period of Deferment, Change, or Completion. |

---

[*] Generally-accepted numbers that relate to the human being.
[†] This 'creative activity' may be destructive if negative red-black symbolism is present.

Even so, and after all of this explanatory preamble, we are, appropriately, still presented with a disturbing scenario of relative chaos; where apparently neither (i) the original blueprint for creation, nor (ii) the natural developmental processes for human society, nor (iii) any providential remedies are fully in alignment, nor yet fully complete. This should be expected of course seeing as we do not yet live in a 'perfect' world. But placing this frustrating detail aside for the moment, the accumulated data still shows plenty of evidence to suggest the existence of an orchestrated providence being painstakingly engineered either somewhere in the subliminal depths of the collective human psyche, or in supra-conscious cosmic mechanics: If not indeed in the mind of some Supreme Divine.

## Key Numbers

We now begin our exposé of key numbers (and their multiples) based first of all upon their appearances in the Bible. This is chiefly in recognition of the importance of the Bible to the majority of religious adherents today, and in respect of its historical influence and effect upon modern cultures. It also keeps open the debate of how indeed such numbers, themes, colors, and formulas are as evident in the pages of ancient scriptures and mythology as they are in the events of modern history. We must remember however that when reading the Bible, although comprised of psalms, poetry, parables, legends, and social laws it is also comprised of much historical fact, particularly in the Old Testament, but of course not all of it is to be taken literally. There is a certain point where history, myth, and legend merge. This requires a flexible and well-informed interpretation. For example; according to modern scientific theory regarding evolution and the existence of dinosaurs, the generational numbers given in the Bible for Adam and his descendants are simply untenable. Neither a 6,000 year-old Earth, nor 900 year-old patriarchs make much sense to the geologist or the anthropologist. All the more interesting then, to see the same numeric patterns and themes even in these admittedly legendary accounts of the origins of mankind – taking us intriguingly across that line between prehistoric cosmogony and documented history.

Because the greater part of this book documents triadic phenomena, and seeing as many of the examples to be studied are already multiples of ten, we will confine our discussion chiefly to the numbers four and seven, with intermittent references to the numbers three and ten as they arise. In subsequent volumes it will become increasingly evident that all four of these numbers are very significant in context of this study of a possibly-orchestrated providence. Yet still, although it is generally accepted amongst religious scholars that the numbers three, four, seven, and ten (and their multiples) are somehow 'very important to God's providence', as far as I am aware no one has yet given a credible scientific explanation of why we see so many repetitions of these colors and numbers throughout both Biblical and modern history, or, what the connection between them (if any) might be. Apart from a few rather obscure pseudo-religious treatise that attempt to explain the phenomena and one or two numerological theories that appear overtly biased in their construction and therefore technically questionable, I have yet to find a solid and rational explanation that does not take us into purely speculative territory. [67] Personally, as I think I've made clear by now, I think the answer lies in the numeric dynamics of the visible spectrum in conjunction with a progressive understanding of the triadic archetype at work in history; not so much in respect of a singularly-specific messianic mission per se, but more as an ongoing and all-pervading cosmic rehabilitation process that will continue through history from generation unto generation until the objective is finally achieved; namely, the full and wholesome enlightenment of mankind.

## The Number Four

First of all, let me state with conviction that I believe the number four to be representative of rebirth, especially in the form of the number forty. There are many reasons for this including the aforementioned forty weeks of human pregnancy, and the several periods of preparation for special missions that many of the saints and prophets undertook, as well as other historically-important secular figures. Each had to go through a period of personal, if not providential preparation and rebirth. This includes the three forty-year periods whilst Noah built the Ark, and the forty-days of rain before the great flood and the rebirth of a new generation of humanity through Noah's family. Then there are the three matching forty-year courses of Moses, each of which initiated a new providential mission; first as a prince of Egypt, then as a nomadic shepherd, and finally leading the oppressed Israelites out of bondage. The fact that Moses was three months old when discovered floating down the Nile in his own mini-ark may also have significance, as does the symbolism of the water. Very interestingly, in Hebrew Gematria the term for 'water' also holds the numeric value of forty: "M = mem = water = 40". [68] Then there were the successive forty-year reigns of Kings Saul, David, and Solomon, each of whom carried great historical responsibilities. Jesus too was tempted for forty days before his baptism with water, and the start of his new mission, reflected in the modern Christian tradition of Lent where believers repent for past transgressions and prepare for spiritual renewal. The forty hours when Christ was in the tomb before his supernatural resurrection (or rebirth) is another little-known fact, most people believing he was in the tomb for three 'days'. Not to mention the subsequent forty-day pre-Ascension period before Christ reportedly ascended to heaven. Whether the supernatural resurrection and ascension literally happened as reported in the gospels is, in context of this discussion, secondary to the fact that the number forty mysteriously appears again within two of the central beliefs of the world's most populous religion. But what exactly is the implication here?

Well, in looking back at the visible spectrum we recall that science assigned the number 400 to the color blue. Blue of course is the color of the feminine; the vessel of rebirth. Considering the undeniable fact that the feminine has been repressed, suppressed, and generally ignored for the most part of known history, it would be most appropriate for male providential agents in history (in particular) to go through this forty hours, days, weeks, months, or years period of symbolic 'rebirth' as they sought to restore, or find, or promote, or unite with the (lost) feminine. Or for that matter, before they were reborn themselves into a new providential paradigm or mission. This could be either literal or symbolic of course, either as an internal, personal, spiritual-educational quest, or in actually seeking a bride or complimentary-blue partner in some form or another. This includes not only religious individuals such as those mentioned above, but as we can see in Table H also includes many so-called 'secular' individuals, groups, organizations, and even nations and empires, in potentially-providential roles – or anti-providential roles as the case may be. Please allow for the lack of specificity of details, the non-sequential record, and for the author's interpretation of 'Feminine Themes', as most entries will be duly discussed.

**Table H: Some Instances of the Number Forty in History and Scripture**

| Duration | Central Figure / Agency | Feminine Theme |
| --- | --- | --- |
| 4,000 yrs | Fundamentalist belief; from Adam to Jesus | Prep. for messiah |
| 400 years | Period from Moses to David | Birth of Israel |
| 400 years | Tabernacle serves as centre-point of faith | Feminine symbolism |
| 400 miles | Abraham's journey to Canaan | Birth of Judaism |
| 400 men | Esau's army waiting for Jacob's family | Sibling unity |
| 40 camps | During Israelites' wilderness journey | Seeking new home |
| 40 | Generations; Abraham to Jesus (Matt.) | Birth of messiah |
| 40 | Authors of the Bible (approx) | Inspiration |
| 40 | Caliphs over 700 year period | Formation of Islam |

| | | |
|---|---|---|
| 40 years | Age of Esau at marriage | Female partner |
| 40 years | Moses' age when leaving Egypt (40 & 80) | To promised land |
| 40 years | Age of Joshua; spying Canaan for 40 days | Seeking new home |
| 40 years | Reign of Saul; first Israelite King | Israeli sovereignty |
| 40 years | David's reign, 7 yrs plus 33 yrs | Expands Israel |
| 40 years | Reign of Solomon, man of wisdom | Builds Temple |
| 40 years | When Confucius "has no more doubts" | Advent of wisdom |
| 40 years | St Patrick's age upon returning to Ireland | Celtic Christianity |
| 40 years | Clovis when he became 1st Christian King | New political era |
| 40 years | Charlemagne is "Protector of the Church" | Protection / Nurture |
| 40 years | Galileo's age at major discoveries | Scientific knowledge |
| 40 years | Copernicus' age at major discoveries | Scientific knowledge |
| 40 years | Muhammad's age at time of visions | Spiritual birth |
| 40 years | Age of Muhammad's wife at marriage | Marriage |
| 40 years | From 1st Hegira (Islam) to death of Ali | End of early Islam |
| 40 years | Age of Columbus on journey of discovery | New World |
| 40 years | Age of Queen Isabella & King Ferdinand of Spain when supporting Columbus | New World discoveries |
| 40 years | Duration of Great Schism 1378-1417 | Unity of Church |
| 40 years | Reign of Maria Theresa of Austria | 1st Female 'Emperor' |
| 40 years | Luther's Bible copied 100,000 times | Education |
| 40 years | Age when Ulrich Zwingli (reformer) marries | Female partner |
| 40 years | Baha'i prophet Baha'u'llah exiled | New religion |
| 40 years | Jung; "Psychology of the Unconscious" | Feminine psychology |
| 40 years | Age when Einstein marries | Female partner |
| 40 years | Mussolini's age when seizing power; 1922 | Birth of Fascism |
| 40 years | Age when Hitler's father changes his name | New dynasty |
| 40 years | Age when Hitler first meets Eva Braun, 1929 | Female partner |
| 40 years | East Germany to fall of Berlin Wall, 1949-89 | German reunification |
| 40 years | Helen Keller writes; Light in my Darkness | Education |
| 40 years | Age of Yassir Arafat when chairman of PLO | Change in life |
| 40 days | Of rain; before 40 days of Great Flood | Rebirth of Humanity |
| 40 days | Moses up mountain (10 commandments) | New religion |
| 40 days | Temptation of Christ | Baptism / Mission |
| 40 days | Resurrection to Ascension | Spiritual rebirth |
| 40 days | Battle of Bulge; last German offensive | End of war |
| 40 days | Duration of Desert Storm invasion of Iraq | End of dictatorship |
| 40 days | Time of mourning in Islamic culture | Spiritual rebirth |
| 40 hours | Jesus in tomb | Resurrection |

It is also probably no mere coincidence that in Hindu philosophy blue, the color of emotional growth and self-expression is positioned at the third position in the Vedic sequence, mid-way between spiritual white and base red; which in turn, appropriately, is situated at the seventh location.

Sticking with the Bible for the present though, it is possible that the origins of each of the key providential numbers discussed here began with Adam and his family: Adam had three sons for example, the third being Seth, the direct ancestor of Noah, who in turn also had three sons, a theme to be repeated in many historical families of import both in religious and secular history – as we shall see in Volume II. Considering our premise that the hero operates on a foundation of sevens, perhaps it is just coincidence that there are seven generations between Adam and Enoch, who was reportedly so holy that he "walked with God" rather than dying a mortal death after siring Methuselah at the interesting age of 300 years? Then a further three generations to Noah gives us a tidy three-seven-three sequence closing with a neat ten generations between Adam and Noah. It may also be just happenstance that Adam's first two sons Cain and Abel were born in the opening verses of Chapter Four of the Book of Genesis? ..but maybe we're reaching just a little bit here. Unfortunately, we are not given Cain and Abel's ages, but their respective roles have great providential and archetypal import, a subject yet to be discussed. Adam meanwhile lived a further 800 years after Seth's birth, giving us a two possible 400-year sequences where 'something' of substance could or should have happened perhaps? Similarly, Adam's age of 130 at Seth's birth could symbolize a hundred-year period of deferment for the Cain-and-Abel failure followed by a preparatory period of thirty before restarting with Seth? I don't want to stretch the numeric connections too thin at this early stage, but it is probably not mere chance that the number thirteen recurs time and again in history and scriptures in classic Cain-and-Abel type situations which we will be looking at in Volume Two. But I am digressing here, and need to take us back to our number forty:

The directions for building Solomon's Temple are riddled with the number forty, and as we shall see later, the Temple itself is architecturally symbolic of the developing female form – complete with conception and birth-giving symbolism which in turn would account for God's prophets addressing Israel as his chosen nation, his daughter Zion; the proverbial cosmic groom awaiting his bride (♣ 18). Other examples of providential rebirth might include the aforementioned forty days of rain during the Great Flood; the Ark's forty days on Mt. Ararat, and the 400 years between Noah and Abraham where otherwise there is very little in the way of 'religious' history going on. Abraham's 400-mile journey to Canaan, and his son Isaac's age at marriage are further examples, as is the reported 4,000 years between Adam and Jesus. Furthermore, Matthew's gospel lists forty generations between Abraham and Jesus, the latter being a reported thirty years old at the start of his public mission. Esau too, as a great-ancestor of the Arabs was also married at forty, suggesting that this is the appropriate period of time for preparation to receive one's bride. The Israelites' desperate wanderings in the desert with the Tabernacle consisted of forty campsites over forty years, and later, the spying out of the promised land of Canaan also lasted forty days, overseen by a forty-year old Joshua—the land of Canaan being that which "flowed with milk and honey"—feminine symbolism again. Moses too spent forty days on Mt. Sinai where he received the Ten Commandments whilst the mountain was shrouded by a great (feminine) cloud, and there were a further forty generations between Moses and King David, arguably the greatest leaders the Jews ever had, corresponding with great historical and sociological changes. Later we have Christ's parallel forty days of temptation in the desert where he survived three trials before being anointed and joined with the Holy Spirit at his baptism in the river Jordan (note the feminine water symbolism again). His reported forty days of preaching after the crucifixion was followed by the Pentecost period ten days later, where 120 disciples (3 x 40) hid in fear before exploding into the community 'reborn' and 'afire with the Holy Spirit' – again after an intriguing forty days of preparation.

In Islam too, the fact that Muhammad, the founder of Islam began experiencing his mystical visions in 610 CE at the age of forty is worthy of note, as is the fact that his wife was forty years old when he married her. Interesting too that Islam would spread after the Prophet's death for exactly 100 years before being stopped by Charlemagne's grandfather in 732 CE. Depending upon which particular scholars you research, you will also find forty Sultans and Caliphs listed as rulers of the Ottoman Empire covering a period spanning nearly seven centuries. The most notable amongst them was probably Selim I who arose to power after a three-year campaign of "amazing victories" against the Mamelukes, dressed (according to the image accompanying the Encyclopedia article)[69] in red, white, and blue. By assuming the Caliphate of Islam in 1517 Selim made himself and his successors spiritual as well as temporal heads of a theocratic empire that would last exactly 400 years until 1917.

With all these numbers aligning so neatly, this could be interpreted as Islam's historical opportunity to achieve certain objectives during those years wherein it was most politically and economically influential.

Interesting is it not that 1917 would witness so many such political events associated with the change-over from masculine reds to feminine blues – and vice versa?

**Table J: 400 and the Cosmic Feminine in 1917**

| Event | Feminine Theme |
|---|---|
| End 400-year Ottoman (Muslim) Empire 1517-1917 | Breakthrough of Democracy |
| 400th anniversary; rise of Protestantism 1517-1917 | Change from Catholicism |
| Rise of Suffragette Movement 1917 | Female Empowerment |
| First women politicians in US and Europe 1917-18 | Female Empowerment |
| US enters WWI in 1917 & RWB flags phenomenon | Expansion of Democracy |
| Balfour Declaration: Jews end 1800 yrs *Diaspora*[*] | Biblical daughter returns home |
| Emergence of Anti-Israeli Arab League | None |
| Bolshevik Revolution: Rise of Communism | Arguably; socialism[†] |
| Appearances of Our Lady of Fatima 1917 | Feminine Archetype Visions? |

The strong suggestion of course, is that these events were 'somehow' either orchestrated providentially; or are the historical results of subliminal, archetypal feminine activity. The full implications of this sequence of events will be covered in Volume II, but the reader should be aware that it is my considered opinion—based both upon the facts and the symbolism—that 1917 was a major breakthrough point in modern history for the dynamic emergence of the feminine; in religion, politics and in society in general.

But back to the number four: In 507 CE a forty-year old King Clovis I[‡] was not only the first Catholic King of the Franks, but by defeating the Visigoths of Spain he lay the foundations for modern France before leaving his Christian Kingdom to his four sons, a short four years later. Popular tradition regards Clovis as the first true King of France, a fact reflected in the litany of successors who took his name (translated "Louis") in later years.

Charlemagne too, the first official Holy Roman Emperor was anointed by the pope on Christmas day in the year 800, (2 x 400 after Christ) and held the official title "protector of the church" also for a full forty years before the collapse of his kingdom under his three warring sons. Not to be confused

---

[*] The Jews, evicted by Romans in 135 CE; returned in 1936 under terms of the Balfour Decl.

[†] In pure form, socialism *could* be considered a move beyond Imperialism. Soviet Communism was a social failure due chiefly to masculine excesses (red): See Vol II.

[‡] Sources are unsure about Clovis' birth date; generally assumed to have been c. 465-466

with the earlier Roman Empire that arguably lasted 400 years from the time of Christ to the sacking of Rome in 410 CE, and the subsequent launch of 400 years of relative political and religious chaos around the Mediterranean and beyond until the rise of Charlemagne. Interestingly, Rome was sacked only once previously in the year 390 BCE by the Celts; exactly 800 years earlier and about 120-130 years *after* the Romans forced out the Etruscans, who in turn were dominant in the area for about four centuries. This gives us a direct historical parallel to Adam's 130 years before the birth of his third son Seth, and his subsequent 800 years lifespan, matching the abovementioned 800 years of Roman influence in the Mediterranean region. Perhaps the Romans too were being accorded a certain period of time to accomplish certain goals?

**Table K: Selected examples of 400-year political periods**

| Dates | Agency | Period |
|---|---|---|
| 1600-1200 BCE | Mycenaean Greece | 400 yrs |
| 1200-800 BCE | Greek Dark Ages | 400 yrs |
| 2070-1600 BCE | Xia Dynasty (1st Chinese) | 470 yrs |
| 1200-400 BCE | Olmec (South America) | 800 (2 x 400 yrs) |
| c.2300-1900 BCE | Ancient Semites; Noah-Abram | 400 yrs |
| 776-323 BCE | Ancient Greece | 453 yrs |
| 1400-1000 BCE | Israel: Moses to David | 400 yrs |
| c. 400 to 6-0 BCE | Israel: Malachi to Christ | 400 yrs |
| 202 BCE to 220 CE | Han Dynasty; China | 402 yrs |
| 146 BCE to 1453 CE | Roman and Byzantine Greece | 1,599 (4 x 400 yrs) |
| 190 BCE to 224 CE | Parthians in Mesopotamia | 414 yrs |
| 794-1185 CE | Heian Samurai period (Japan) | 391 yrs |
| 1323-1720 | Iberian Kingdom of Sardinia | 397 yrs |
| 1386-1797 | Venetian Period ; Corfu / Italy | 411 yrs |
| 1517-1917 CE | Ottoman Empire (Turkey) | 400 yrs |
| 1517-1917 CE | Reformation to Canon Law | 400 yrs |

Even in glancing briefly at the historical duration of other ancient empires we see uncanny repetitions of the number 400 or very closely thereof. The *Wikipedia Encyclopedia* lists the following dates for successive Greek Empires for example: Mycenaean Greece ca.1600-1200 BC, and the Greek Dark Ages ca..1200-800 BC; both terms of 400 years. Ancient Greece is listed as spanning 453 years, and Roman and Byzantine Greece as spanning

1600 yrs (146 BC-1453 AD). And finally, Middle Ages Ottoman Greece is listed as a period of 379 years. All-in-all, not a bad ratio, with six out of eight periods being exact multiples of 400, and the remaining two being close thereof. The only remaining quote was that of the untidy and rather ambiguous 177 years of Hellenism, which eventually blended with Roman culture by the 1st century CE.

The Parthians too "intermittently controlled Mesopotamia between ca 190 BCE and 224 CE" – another period of just over 400 years, whilst in the Far East, Japan's highest cultural era was arguably the Heian period (meaning 'peaceful') that gave rise to the Samurai class of warriors in 794-1185 CE, another four century period, and I am quite sure that a more thorough search will unearth many more empires and dynasties of significance that appear bound by these 400-year term limits for some curious reason.

Going back to individual examples though, we continue with the famous forty Catholic Martyrs of England and Wales, who died between 1535 and 1679 CE during a 144-year persecution period in post-Reformation England. These comprised some of the more famous Catholics who refused to acknowledge the Queen as the head of the newly-reformed Church of England, and were imprisoned, tortured, and put to death for their faith. Arguably, this particular group of forty does not exactly fit with our subliminal formulas inasmuch as it was the Catholic hierarchy who later decided on the mystical number to be canonized, and therefore may have done so on existing numeric tradition. The 144-year duration of their collective persecution is however worthy of note as a possible symbolic match to the Biblical 'people of God'; the 144,000 of Revelation (14:1).

In the medieval scientific world, both Copernicus and Galileo were at their creative peaks at age forty,[*] as was English physicist Charles Barkla when he received his Nobel Prize in physics for his work on x-rays in the providentially-pregnant year of 1917, the same year incidentally that Jung wrote his groundbreaking work *Psychology of the Unconscious*. Two years later in 1919 Albert Einstein married in his fortieth year, the same year that a solar eclipse confirmed his General Theory of Relativity. The famous deaf and blind American activist Helen Keller helped found the American Civil Liberties Union in 1920 at age forty, as well as writing the acclaimed *Light in my Darkness*, published forty years later. Meanwhile, back in the medieval religious world it took the fledgling presses of Protestantism a full

---

[*] 1514 Copernicus writes on his heliocentric hypothesis. 1602-04 Galileo investigates the laws of gravitation and oscillation.

forty years to publish 100,000 copies of Martin Luther's translation of the Bible into common German, around the same time that the leader of the Swiss Reformation, Ulrich Zwingli broke his priestly vows at age forty to marry Anna Meyer. His German counterpart Luther also married an ex-nun but apparently a little belatedly at age 41. But perhaps we can excuse the delay based upon Luther's lack of experience in the dating game. Even St. Patrick (385-461CE), the originally Welsh-English patron saint of Ireland did not commence his mission until age forty, after many years of slavery, hardship, and scholarly training. The Baha'i prophet Bahaullah (1817 – 1892) likewise suffered a forty-year period of persecution at the hands of Islamic authorities before his teachings exploded onto the world scene – now the second widest represented religion in the world today. Interestingly, his followers knew Baha'u'llah as "Red Robe" (♣ 27).

In the lead-up to the birth of the French Republic in 1789, Empress Maria-Theresa of Austria, the Germanic mother of Marie Antoinette, and the first major female political figure in Europe for centuries also reigned for a history-changing forty years. The formal union of the Germanic Austro-Hungarian 'Holy Roman Empire' (red) with the Kingdom of France (blue) through marriage is but one of the direct results of her activities, and in great part accounts for the emergence of the French tricolour of red, white, and blue after 1,000 years of conflict between (blue) France and (red) Germany (800-1801 CE).

There are intriguing parallels in modern history too. There is the fact that the E.E.C Treaty of Rome in 1957 marked forty years from the Bolshevik Revolution mentioned in Chapter One, and the fact that the Berlin Wall, the visible symbol of Communist domination of Eastern Europe fell after exactly forty years of Soviet occupation of East Germany (1949-1989), opening the political gates to a new albeit rather untidy state of developing democracy. It is also perhaps no mere coincidence that Russia changed her national colors back to red, white, and blue shortly afterwards.

The Battle of the Bulge in WW II, described by Winston Churchill as "the most important American battle of the war," and arguably the battle that finally marked the end of Germany's ambitions in Europe lasted for a bloody forty days. Desert Storm too, the opening battle for Iraq in 2003 also lasted for exactly forty days, where three red, white, blue nations aligned to remove Saddam Hussein from power (captured at age 66 incidentally), and as of this writing, moves are reportedly afoot to introduce a new blue-based national Iraqi flag. Our dearly-departed Yassir Arafat was also aged forty when he became chairman of the PLO in 1969, thus introducing the possibility that certain so-called 'hero figures' can indeed be engaged more in destructive than constructive enterprises. In the case of Arafat though, the red and black symbolism of the PLO is admittedly a bit of a giveaway, as is the fascist symbolism of Mussolini who became dictator of Italy in 1922, his $40^{th}$ year. Hitler too was forty when the Nazis rose to political power, the same year he met Eva Braun – later to become his clandestine mistress.[*] And whilst we are on the topic of historical bad guys, we might as well mention that it was a forty-year old Joseph Stalin who advocated the purge of Bolshevik enemies through the 'Red Terror' campaign that claimed several thousand Russian lives in 1918.[†] In each of these latter cases the red, or red-black symbolism tells its own story.

As can be seen from the extended list in Tables H, J and K, and by reviewing the examples in Chapter One, there are many more examples of the appearance of the number forty or four hundred that could be interpreted as providential attempts to either renew or give birth to the feminine principle in some form or another. In some cases is it benign and productive, whilst in others as we can see, these forty-year sequences can give birth to monsters – both literally and figuratively. Usually, the associated symbolism is the giveaway, either indicating an approach to, or an attack upon feminine principles. Or, an attack upon 'feminine' agents, agencies or nations. Most notable in modern history perhaps is the fall of the 400-year autocratic Ottoman Empire whose ruler held the title 'Caliph of Islam' since 1517, and the 400-year anniversary of the Protestant Reformation also in the year of 1917 along with that long list of possibly providential happenings that converged on that date. Both of these events were marked by the appropriate symbolism, with the British and her allies taking Baghdad under the red, white, and blue Union Jack, and the fledgling Protestants (who would later chose red, white, and blue symbolism) rejecting the oppressive patriarchal authority of the medieval Catholic Church (♣ 20, 21). Although Britain was still emerging from a long period of imperialism, and the Reformers of the $16^{th}$ century were far from being shrinking violets, both events were significant moments in history where the more democratic powers of the feminine first challenged and then (arguably) subjugated prevailing authoritarian institutions and societies.

As regards the rise of the feminine in history, and paraphrasing from Chapter One it is interesting is it not that 1917 also; "...witnessed the rise of the Women's Suffragette Movement... the appointment of the first woman, Jeanette Rankin to the U.S. House of Representatives... the birth of

---

[*] Hitler's Nazi (or socialist) Party won the Bavarian elections in 1929

[†] According to the birth register of Uspensky, Georgia, Stalin was born on Dec 6th 1878.

India's first female prime minister, Mrs. Indira Gandhi, ...and the first mystical appearances of Our Lady of Fatima... explicitly warning the world of 'imminent danger' from Russia." And although numerically out of sequence, perhaps we should also mention the fact that 1917 marked the beginning of a covert 66-year period of U.S. Government-sponsored forced sterilization of women (and 'other undesirables') – an intriguing fact that corresponds uncannily with the instructions for ritual cleansing in the Bible upon the birth of a female child; (Leviticus 12:5). In conjunction with the numerous instances of the numbers forty and four-hundred as reported in Chapter One and Tables H, J and K, surely we may conclude that perhaps indeed some great cosmic-feminine emergence occurred on that date?

**The Number Seven**
Seven has traditionally been regarded as a sacred or mystical number in many faith traditions as well as in the magic arts, chiefly in its association with the days of the week and the Ancient Greek gods. But from a chromo-numeric perspective the number seven is primarily representative of the masculine end of the spectrum. Therefore we may expect to see sevens or multiples thereof in association with red-centered activity, particularly concerning hero or messiah figures. But instead of rebirth-type activities as with the number four and its multiples, in this case activities associated with the number seven will include creative or construction type-themes such as the seven days of creation; the seven days for Noah to load the Ark; or the seven years it took to build Solomon's Temple. Remembering of course that we have three subdivisions of the color red when it comes to religious symbolism; (i) the original male, (ii) the perverse male, and (iii) the hero figure (♣ 16, 27) we should expect a broader array of associated themes, including connections with the 'darker' unwholesome reds as seen in the previous category; therefore some considerable discernment is required.

The seventy years of Babylonian captivity of the Jews (586-516 BCE), or the parallel-named exile of the Papacy (1309-78 CE) and the seventy years of modern Soviet Communism (1917-87) might be cases in point. But because a comprehensive understanding of the above themes would require a vast amount of detail and historical research, and because at this point this is still a developing albeit hopefully convincing theory, (and because we will be expounding on this subject anyway in later volumes); I will simply present my case today giving indications here and there of what I believe each to represent, either (i), (ii), or (iii) above. But first perhaps we need remind ourselves that the greater part of history so far has been engaged in the struggle by red archetypal themes seeking to reclaim or rediscover the

209

providential feminine – unwittingly or not. So naturally it will only be later in history (perhaps in 1917?) that we may expect to see the substantial emergence of feminine blue activities as proposed in this theory.

But back to the topic at hand: Beginning with the original male archetype (i) looking first to the Bible we see that Adam (meaning 'red earth' in Hebrew) is naturally associated with the seven Biblical days of creation, although he was admittedly created on the sixth day. But after Adam's fall from grace, no-one else can actually claim this 'original male' title, except of course the masculine aspect of any non-compromised Divine being; the Original Male archetype in other words. Adam's fall necessitated the creation of a hero-figure or redeemer (iii) who appears first as Enoch, seven generations later, a man who "walked with God". Enoch was the great-grandfather of Noah, who would restart the providence ten generations after Adam, after the Great Flood. The next notable example might be the seven days allowed for Noah to get all the creatures into the Ark, which he is instructed; "bring the clean beasts" and the "fowls of the air" not in twos as is commonly believed, but "in sevens"(Genesis 7:2).

Then there are three seven-day periods where Noah dispatches a dove to find land, and on the third attempt, she doesn't return, telling Noah it is safe to evacuate the Ark. All these events are symbolic gestures surrounding the providential hero figure as he prepares the way for a new beginning. The added fact that Noah's father Lamech lived to be 777 years old, or that Kenan (4th descendant from Adam) begat Noah's ancestor at age seventy may of course be nothing more than coincidence. But the numbers in Kenan's case match uncannily the patterns of Adam's life; except that in Kenan's case they fit the theme of a *successful* providential hypothesis, whereas the 130 years before Adam sired Seth have a different symbolic meaning. God did tell Cain however, that he would be protected 'sevenfold' from those who might do him harm.

Abraham's father too was seventy years old at the birth of his three sons, and then there are Jacob's three seven-year courses of service to his uncle Laban before reuniting with his brother Esau and journeying with seventy members of his family to Egypt. Interestingly, an embittered Esau was waiting for his brother with 400 soldiers until Jacob won his heart with three gifts sent in advance – another example of a new beginning. During the Exodus, as the (feminine) cloud rested on Mt. Sinai for seven days, seventy priestly elders prayed for Moses, who, upon returning to find his people engaged in idolatry, slew 3,000 of them before returning a second time up the mountain for forty more days. Here again we see all the central numbers and themes of the triadic archetype aligning in a mythology that has never been fully explained before.

Adding to the intrigue are the Seven Wise Men of Greece; a group of 7th and 6th century BCE philosophers who arguably founded the institutions of modern science and democracy. Known collectively as *the Pleiades*, the same group name was later respectfully given to seven outstanding poets of 3rd century BCE Alexandria, as well as to another seven-man assembly of 16th century French poets. Then there are the seventy (undoubtedly male) scholars who first translated the Hebrew Bible into Greek—the language of the early Christian church—some three hundred years before Christ. Now known as the Septuagint, in conjunction with other writings this translation forms the basis of the Christian Bible today. Could there be any possible association one wonders, between the creative enterprises of those seventy ancient scholars and the fact that the Bible as a whole is overtly masculine? Also interesting to note that the historian Manetho writing in that same 3rd century BCE lists a group of seventy Egyptian Kings ruling for seventy days in the Seventh Dynasty, launching a time of anarchy in Egypt that lasted for three further dynasties. Once again, masculine themes linking the number seven with important historical events.

In later Israelite history too the Babylonian Captivity lasted for seventy years before a reported forty thousand Jews were allowed by King Nebuchadnessar to return to rebuild their Temple. Here, the number four-hundred features in another time of historical rebirth and new beginnings. The City of Tyre would also "be forgotten for seventy years" for her sins (Isaiah 23:15). The numbers and themes repeat time and time again, and all are creative or corrective enterprises of some description leading to new foundations. Later, Jesus too would for some reason send precisely seventy disciples out to preach to the chosen people; and recent research places Halley's Comet "in the sky for more than seventy days" in the year 6 BCE, a fact that would match several scholars' suggestions that this was in fact the mystical Star of Bethlehem.[70] Staying with Jesus, it was also a reported seven years after the start of Christ's public mission that Stephen, one of the seven original 'Christian' deacons was martyred on charges of blasphemy by the Jewish religious authorities, watched by a recalcitrant Saul. Saul would later be converted on the road to Damascus taking the new Christian name of Paul, and becoming the major directing force of subsequent Christianity thirteen years later. In this case, it could be argued that the martyrdom of Stephen marked either the end, or the beginning of 'true' or at least early Christianity. In any event, not only did the Romans put down a Jewish rebellion in 70 CE and destroy the all-important Temple, but according to *Wikipedia* they then spent "a span of seventy years" expelling the Jews from Jerusalem and its surrounds. The area of Judea was renamed Palestina, and the Jews would not return there as a nation for 1800 years. Incidentally, in Jewish Rabbinical Law, any court that administers capital punishment more than once in seventy years is known as a "destroyer". Once again, a red, masculine theme connected to the number seven.

In later history, and remaining with the aforementioned historical figures, Charlemagne's empire would be divided in 870 CE, seventy years after his coronation, and the subsequent reign of German Carolingian Kings would also last an interesting seventy years. For practical reasons we must explore the significance of this and other related parallels in post-biblical history in later volumes, but any quick check of the history books will reinforce the importance of these events in world history.

In the early 7th century too it took Muhammad a reported seven years to dictate the Qur'an, whilst the Third French Republic—a republican parliamentary democracy that succeeded the French Revolution—flew under the red, white, blue tricolor for seventy years, from 1870 until the invasion of Hitler in 1940 under a red-and-black swastika. It would also be an interesting seven months after the U.S. declaration of war in 1917 before American troops from the 42nd Rainbow Division would land on European soil three years after the advent of WWI. The same seventy year period repeats between the founding of the Zionist movement in 1897 to the Jewish occupation of Jerusalem in 1967 during the Six-Day War between Israel (blue) and the combined nations of the Arab League (no blues)… and the list goes on and on…

Although there are many, many more examples of the number seven and its multiples that could be quoted in the context of providential, creative or repair formulas, I believe we have made our point for the time being: The recognition of important parallel themes in history, scripture, and mythology that center on the number seven and it's multiples. Themes that also align with the red, creative (or destructive) activities, which in turn correspond to the masculine end of the color spectrum, and the measurement of 700 nanometers.

Anticipating the argument that these numbers have merely been 'fished' out of the history books, I respectfully counter by reiterating that those listed here are but a sampling of those parallels that I have uncovered, and besides, at this early juncture are only presented in support of our central theory of a natural-historical triadic archetype.

## Table L: Examples of Seven and its Multiples in History and Scripture

| Period | Event |
|---|---|
| 7 days | Creation Story |
| 7 days | Animals into the Ark (by sevens) & Flight of Dove |
| 7 gods | Greek and Roman, and days of the week |
| 70 people | Jacob's family come to Egypt |
| 70 years | Age of Terah when Abraham was born |
| 70 years | Age of Confucius' father at his birth |
| 70 years | Age of Socrates at death |
| 7 years | Jacob 'earns' his wives and flocks (3 x 7 years) |
| 70 elders | Pray with Moses at Sinai (plus 7-day cloud) |
| 7 years | Building Solomon's Temple c. 1,000 BCE |
| 7 days | Duration of Temple Festival on $7^{th}$ day of $7^{th}$ month |
| 70 years | Babylonian Captivity 586-516 BCE |
| 70 scholars | Of the Septuagint; (early Bible translation) |
| 70 days | Halley's Comet (Star of Bethlehem?) over Palestine |
| 70 disciples | Sent out by Jesus to preach to the Jews |
| 7 weeks | Crucifixion to Pentecost |
| 7 years | Jesus to Stephen ($1^{st}$ Christian Martyr) |
| 70 CE | Temple destroyed, and Jews expelled; duration 70 yrs |
| 7 years | Muhammad dictates the Qur'an |
| 70 years | Charlemagne Crowned to Empire Divided 800-870 |
| 70 years | Reign of Carolingian Kings |
| 70 years | Duration of Third French Republic 1870-1940 |
| 70 years | Papacy in Exile – Great Schism 1309-78 |
| 70 years | Zionism to Jewish occupation of Jerusalem 1897-1967 |
| 70 years | Communism / Soviet Union 1917-87 |

So hopefully, as we now approach the conclusions of this first volume of *The Color of Truth*, we have established not only the credibility of a chromo-numeric triadic archetype, but also of its dramatic and continuing effects in history. Hopefully too, the facts and data presented so far in this condensed introduction will be stimulation enough for the reader to pursue a fuller understanding of the range and effects of the triadic archetype in successive volumes.

But regrettably, there still remains amongst us that disturbing tendency to polarize and demonize any insights or interpretations that originate outside of our own faith tradition. This will of course include any new philosophy, no matter how colorful and exciting the evidence. Sadly, this too is a reflection of the ongoing cosmic battle with mankind at the center; not between good and evil so much, but rather between wisdom and ignorance; between truth and superstition; and between knowledge and blind credulity.

Indeed in many parts of the world there remains a belief that many if not all of the evils in human society are there either by divine design, or as the direct result of external demonic interference. Although already briefly touched upon in Chapter Ten, and whilst not wanting to bog the reader down in theological complexities, we must nevertheless take a closer look at the longstanding issue of dualism—this tendency to polarize and divide— both as a secular ideology as well as a religious belief. This is very important inasmuch as any such belief may conflict—at least in parts—with any integrated model of spirit, mind, and body, or with any other fundamental expression of the triadic archetype.

# CHAPTER THIRTEEN

# A DIABOLIC DUALISM

*Continuing our discussion of the psycho-spiritual implications of our discoveries, we now readdress the topic of dualism as a prevailing belief that has the potential to obstruct a full understanding of an integrated triadic archetype. Dealing with important issues in the religion-science divide as well as in secular society, the reader is once again respectfully invited to maintain an objective perspective and allow for certain necessary generalizations, as we bring Volume I, Part Two to a close.*

Contemporary wisdom suggests that when presenting any new thesis or theory, it is best to present your findings in a purely positive light and avoid any areas of conflict incase it distracts from the central discussion – or lest it offends the reader. Offended readers do not make particularly good listeners. But when writing on matters of 'truth' and 'reality' it is necessary to engage the so-called 'darker side' of human beliefs—the arena of dark forces; of devils, demons, and fallen angels— especially when ideas centered therein may obstruct or even run contrary to our central premise. For as we have seen, the blueprint suggested by the triadic archetype does not contain an inherently 'evil' aspect. Nor does any such infection contaminate the natural world. But humanity on the other hand does arguably, play host to 'evil' in various forms. The very fact that so many worldviews contain a philosophy of evil is surely sufficient cause to study its origins. Certainly, there are enough perversions of the natural order in so-called 'civilization' to have earned a study of the phenomenon of social evil and to prompt an understanding thereof.

There is also the tricky issue of the color black in context of its aforementioned symbolic association with evil, darkness, and demonic forces, and the question of how and why such symbolism has surfaced so regularly in some of our most prestigious social institutions. What, if anything could this mean? What exactly does this represent, and what historical lessons are to be learnt here? In particular, in viewing the appearances of destructive-masculine symbolism (red-black) amongst some of our more revered religious institutions, along with the notable absence of feminine blues, we first need to qualify the religious understanding of the mind and its workings, for as we have seen, a theology of the mind is not at all a well-developed area. Indeed, contrary to the equilibrium of the triadic archetype, the mind (feminine, blue) is not viewed in conservative theologies as a particularly important player amongst its more dominant body and soul partners (red and white). The big question is, why not?

**An Unnatural Dualism**

Basically, Christian *ontology*[*] revolves around a discordant dualistic paradigm wherein the body and the soul are set against each other in a state of unnatural friction: The flesh versus the spirit, and the secular versus the sacred for example. This is the general understanding amongst monotheistic religions today, particularly amongst orthodox Muslims and Jews and most Christian sects, and is espoused by a great many liberal believers as well. Born out of the emotive and politically charged early years of Christianity that saw 'outsiders' such as the Romans, Jews, and various supposed heretics as 'demonic' adversaries; I do not believe we can overestimate the difficulties this mindset has caused. Sadly, after two thousand years of reinforcement this combative dualistic mindset is now intrinsic in society. Rooted deep in the collective psyche and clearly evident in the denigration of all political, cultural, or religious 'outsiders', this ingrained dualism accounts in great part for the litany of hostility that has stained human history. We will discuss the personification of 'the devil' in a moment, but first we need to address this issue of body-spirit dualism as a potentially serious obstacle to the acceptance of a universal and integrated body-mind-spirit paradigm.

Within the dualistic paradigm, apparent opposites are set at variance. In particular, there is a distinct and seditious separation between the supposedly 'secular' (worldly) and 'sacred' (spiritual) realms; duly personified in the figures of Satan and God respectively. The purpose of the religious life (it is understood) is to subdue and conquer the sinful flesh by appropriate soul-work or, through the reception of salvific graces (♣ 26). As indicated in our brief summary of the religious theory in Chapter Ten; the

---

[*] Ontology; in metaphysics, the study of 'the nature of being'.

human condition is perceived as variously 'lost, separated, ignorant, sinful, disconnected-from-God,' and generally 'living in spiritual and moral darkness.' Thus estranged, religion promises to provide the sinner with the methods and the means for reconnection. The salvific processes of resurrection, restoration, redemption, and/or renewal each depend upon accessing this estranged realm through prayer, meditation, and/or good works via the agency of the soul, mind, heart, or spirit. But regardless of the semantics, the general understanding is that there is an everlasting battle between the body and the soul, with the 'educated mind' playing a minimal role, if indeed any role at all in the equation. Where the intellect is in fact accorded an active role in the life of faith, it is usually that of a pernicious and untrustworthy collaborator in human sinfulness: An agent of secular corruption at variance with true spirituality; as evidenced in the suspicion with which certain religious fundamentalists view the profession of psychology for example. This contrasts substantially with our notion of a harmonious triad of spirit, mind, and body at the heart of the human psyche.

Although the unified spirit-mind-body paradigm as outlined in this book has become noticeably more popular in New Age and progressive faith traditions of late, it remains a sadly disturbing fact that the more authoritarian religious institutions rely upon a relatively disempowered membership for their existence. This is usually achieved by the systematic suppression of enquiring minds either through religious indoctrinations or more subtle forms of coercion; guilt complexes, longstanding emotive traditions and rituals, social pressures etc. The inclination to personal self-enlightenment through outside study (using the mind) is usually discouraged in favor of partisan creeds; and the activities of the intellect are reduced to simply listening obediently to the (by now) well-indoctrinated personal conscience under the watchful guidance of authoritarian clerics. Again, please excuse the necessary generalizations. The independent use of the mind is seen at best as unnecessary, and at worst as a threat. It is the clerics' job to do the thinking, theologizing, and mediating-with-God for you. Your job is simply to maintain faith and obedience; 'virtues' that require little if any deployment of one's rational or intellectual faculties. On the other hand, the scientific approach to personal education or development is almost exclusively based on the exercise of one's reason and intellect.

Nevertheless, although the methods of authoritarian religious traditions are in effect counterintuitive to the process of genuine enlightenment, the principal *declared* directive remains the same: That of endeavoring to access a higher realm or state of being—(or state of holiness or enlightenment in religions' case)—through the subjugation of worldly desires. The objective (it is claimed) is to develop one's 'spirituality' by controlling carnal desires or, in the case of psychology; to achieve a 'higher state of mental equilibrium' through the control of dysfunctional behaviors. Eradicate 'sin' or 'dysfunction' respectively by controlling our unprincipled errors or excesses in other words. In this pursuit at least both psychology and religion are united, although the fact that it is impossible to reach a state of higher consciousness whilst possessed of psychoneurotic fantasies seems to have somehow escaped the attention of the indoctrinators.

My own opinion (which is born of personal experience in both fields) is that instead of subjugating anything we should be empowering. Empowering the mind and the spirit through education and experience to the point where the flesh and any of its unwholesome demands are *naturally* relegated to the third tier in the soul-mind-body paradigm. I reemphasize the term 'naturally' as indicative of redressing an imbalance in the spirit-mind-body paradigm as opposed to isolating and/or suppressing one of these vital aspects of the full human experience. Building a natural unified triad vs. reinforcing an unnatural contentious dualism in other words. This approach produces stronger, not weaker souls, as well as stronger minds and bodies. For a body disciplined, under mindful control and with a deep sense of purpose is indeed a force to be reckoned with. But perhaps this is precisely the reason why authoritarian institutions—both secular and religious— hesitate to employ such liberating and empowering tactics with their members?

Just as the body is key to the survival of the mind and spirit on this earthly plane, so is the mind vital to the development of the human psyche (or spirit) and is therefore not too well served by membership in suppressive authoritarian institutions. True salvation surely implies true and wholesome empowerment? If so, then the mind simply *must* be engaged in the process. And fully engaged to whit. Whether they realize it or not, ideologies that advocate blind faith or dogmatics over healthy and provocative questions are in fact denying their members the true journey of enlightenment; the true 'food' of the soul. Subjugation of the mind is NOT the way to educate it, and never will be, and any so-called 'education' process that is centered on censorship and fear is going to be intrinsically flawed. Rather than deny the flesh or the mind its essentials, we would be better employed in realigning the spirit-mind-body paradigm to reflect a natural balance. Temporarily subjugate where necessary yes! But only temporarily, and only whilst we are devoting at least as much energy into building up the deficiencies in other areas. Stop the bad habits whilst simultaneously developing better ones in other words. According to the principles of the triadic archetype, we should first seek a strong moral education based upon cosmic laws and values, and then interpret and regulate our worldly desires through that paradigm. But more often than not, authoritarian agencies dismiss the need for that cosmic education, and instead besiege the mind and the body with fear-based indoctrinations that can do little else but suffocate the psyche, and fuel a debilitating dichotomy between the embattled flesh and the spirit. The flesh is not to be trusted they say, and the spirit, being a mystery, is not supposed to be understood. So we live in a limbo-like state of dependence upon self-appointed spiritual guides, in alienation from the very vessels scripture tells us were designed as the "temples of the Holy Spirit" – our bodies (1 Cor 6:19). Living thus in enmity within our own selves it is inevitable that an unnatural state of division will split the individual psyche. The sinful (red) flesh and its passions are internally demonized and strictly constrained, whilst the (white) spiritual realm is elevated to that of supernatural importance; yet remains a utopian mystery set at a distance to which we can only vainly aspire. Self-loathing and an uncompromising religious faith combined thus become the neurotic and psychotic forces that intimidate healthy young minds into silence, acceptance, and obedience. Meanwhile, somewhere in the middle, the edifying and unifying graces of feminine wisdom are discarded lovelessly from their rightful place between body and spirit, and replaced instead with a macabre red-black concoction; a demonic adversary, clever and super-intelligent, whose central role in this perverse drama is to maintain, justify, and fuel the body-spirit dichotomy.

**Satan and the Psyche**

It may surprise many to discover that the modern concept of a personalized Satan, the traditional diabolical enemy of the One True God is a relatively recent invention. Born out of the political and religious debates of early Christianity in conjunction with prevailing Middle-eastern mythologies and later transmuted into selected texts of the Bible as Lucifer or Satan, and then in the Qur'an as Iblis; the notion of a single demonic entity in direct opposition to Almighty God did not exist as such in ancient Judaic texts. Which if we recall, were in many ways the founding origins of Christian and Islamic scriptures. In fact, the word "devil" is itself a corruption of the Greek *diabolos*, meaning "adversary, prosecutor", which in turn is a translation of the Hebrew "ha-satan" (the satan). Hence 'Satan' was not originally a proper name, but rather an occupational title for one of the agents of the divine court. That agent had the job of watching humanity and reporting any shenanigans back to God. Something akin to a modern U.S. State Prosecutor perhaps? Our modern concept of Satan as archenemy of

God only began to materialize when early Christian evangelists interpreted their contemporary adversaries as 'demonic' in order to coalesce the fledgling Christian communities against their common enemies; first the orthodox Jews, then the pagan Romans, and then the supposed 'heretics' within their own ranks.

In her book *The Origins of Satan* Professor Elaine Pagels makes the striking point that in polarizing God vs. Satan, and then using this paradigm to separate Christians from the rest of the world, the early Church fathers set an antagonistic and elitist religious precedent that has lasted for millennia and permeated practically all of our social structures. A precedent what's more that is nowhere present in the natural world – or should I say, in *God's* natural world. Even in the Biblical story of Noah's Ark, it was only the *unclean* beasts that were loaded proverbially "two-by-two".

Here we should perhaps remember that even at the atomic level, the dualistic processes of nature are almost exclusively of creative unions. Even when we do witness examples of healthy cells dividing themselves, they are invariably doing so in *creative* processes. Interesting that the exceptions to this rule are to be found in either cancer cells or in the aids virus: Both diseases that operate on a 'divide-and-conquer' theme. In a disturbing social parallel, this matches those theologies that advocate a divided body-and-spirit theme. Each of these examples thrives by consuming and destroying the host. I mention this here because of the powerful imagery invoked when we consider the cosmic battle between good and evil; with God on the one side, Satan on the other, and humanity torn between the two in the middle. God (it is said) is master of the heavenly realm, whilst Satan, "the Prince of this world" possesses the flesh and the material world. Thus the spirit is 'good', and the flesh and the material world is bad or evil, and is therefore not to be trusted. Equally our mind, the source of so many temptations and desires needs to be kept in serious check, lest it lead us into the domain of Satan. The picture this conjures up in our young minds when first receiving religious instruction is one of an everlasting struggle for our souls to which we hold the ultimate key. As beings of consciousness vs. mere animal instinct, in our choices, thoughts, and actions we can (we are told), influence the direction of that cosmic battle one way or the other, so we must always be on our guard against the devil and his agents. Those agents, more often than not are possessed of the same crafty intelligence that marks their master; the Archangel of Light, Lucifer, the most intelligent being of God's creation. (The reader will of course note here the clear association between evil and the enquiring mind). Shakespeare's quote "The devil can cite scripture to his purpose" was eagerly, if somewhat ironically, adopted by the clergy of the day to emphasize the dangers of listening to false prophets. Circulated most vigorously during the Inquisition and Reformation years, this hubristic doctrine has today been deftly reassigned to those scholars and academics, most notably psychologists and questing theologians who advocate theories that challenge fundamentalist doctrines. The solution? Absolute trust and obedience to the agents of the Church, (or the Temple, Mosque, or Synagogue) of course. Don't trust those who would offer clever answers to age-old religious mysteries we are told. And don't forget that Lucifer too thought he had all the answers. Difficult to argue with I must confess. Hence education itself is held suspect (blue), a theme that harkens back to the darkest ages of European history, where suppression and censorship of all non-Christian beliefs or ideas was at its peak.

Most people today may believe that the forces of good will eventually prevail, but living in a dualistic (religious) culture still promotes the fear that any one of us could all-too-easily fall prey to 'demonically-contrived' outside teachings or activities, and thus end up in the eternal fires of hell – either literally or metaphorically. As far as religious institutions are concerned I'm sure we can all picture vivid examples of this doctrine as displayed in the radical activities of religious extremists. In political institutions, perhaps the contemporary example of communist North Korea with its closed borders and cult-based paranoia of the West, or the wholesale denunciation of the USA by Islamic States as 'the Great Satan' best embodies these views. Not forgetting of course the marked historical tendency of Christianity and the West to attach the very same labels to their enemies when politically expedient to do so.

So is Satan 'real'? Or is he, as suggested above, merely an aberration of ancient scriptures conveniently and passionately given shape and form by oppressed and persecuted Christians in their darkest hours, and later elevated by the authoritarian Church to the position of 'Prince of this (evil) world'? Should we, based upon the historical evidence, reject the notion of a supernatural individual who is intrinsically evil? Or, should we more realistically perhaps acknowledge the tendency of humans to group together in elitist and fear-based unions; who then seek moral justification for their prejudices by evoking the persona of Satan as being embedded within the ranks of outside others?

Well, in context of this work it is important to acknowledge the existence of evil at least as one aspect of human character. To name that aspect 'Satan' and give it outside shape and form is perhaps, as Professor Pagels intimates, an act of psychological denial that allows us not only to imagine that we can separate ourselves from 'him' through rigid religious activity, but more disturbingly, it allows us to believe that Satan has possessed our enemies so fully that we are justified in destroying them. Projected onto heathen others, it becomes the right and duty of enlightened believers no less, to destroy Satan's agents through denunciations, persecutions, holy wars, inquisitions, jihads, excommunications, beheadings, or suicide bombings as the case may be. Crazy though we may judge them to be; there is no doubting the sincerity and conviction of those who give their lives in acts of religious terrorism (or martyrdom – depending upon one's viewpoint). They most assuredly believe in Satan, and see him clearly personified in their enemies.

In this sense, inasmuch as there is a cause-and-effect: the cause being a belief that Satan is amongst the ranks of 'the enemy', and the effect being the outpouring of sectarian bitterness, Satan is indeed very 'real'. In the aftermath of so much bloodshed under this very pretext we certainly have a philosophical argument that Satan does exist. But let's not get our 'realities' too mixed up here. Let's differentiate between subjective beliefs and objective reality. Certainly evil exists in our world as a result of human choices and decisions. But does Satan really exist as a discrete personal agent bent on devouring our immortal souls?

## Satan as Archetype

I think we now need to see the traditional figure of Satan more as a perverse archetype that cannot actively possess us, but *can* be *possessed by* any individual, agency, or society in history depending upon their particular circumstances and choices. Arising out of our contraventions of cosmic law, it is in the damage done to nature and human society that we identify the results of evil choices. Ever-present, such a concept of evil can be as much a product of human consciousness as any of the noble virtues. I propose therefore that evil cannot direct our consciousness, but rather is subject to it. Even by orthodox definitions Satan *only* operates through human agency. 'He' needs our conscious co-operation in other words. The superstitious notion of a demonic entity visiting plague, pestilence, and death on the population has long been laid to rest in favor of scientific understandings and human accountability – at least amongst the enlightened. The signature of evil in society is distinctly human in other words – not superhuman. For there are clearly-identifiable stages of social evil; from personal, to group, to national, and even historical evils. This should prompt us to consider from whence any such devil gains his power and authority if not exclusively from the depths of the human psyche. There is no 'Satan' per se waiting in the wings to pounce upon and devour us, but evil, as a product of human choice is always an option. There is no Satan—other than our ancestors and very own selves—to whom we can point the finger and accuse of the horrors and evils of history. There is no demonic scapegoat whereupon we may cast the blame for our sins and avoid cosmic accountability; other than the force of human evil as personified in myself first and foremost, and then collectively amongst us all.

Such thinking removes the awful 'us-versus-them' elitism from the equation, and replaces it instead with an understanding that we are all continuously, constantly, and collectively in danger of succumbing to evil. Instead of artificially splitting our personal, psychological, and social resources into two combative and judgmental camps, we should instead follow the model of the triadic archetype and seek to unify all human goodness in spirit, mind, and body; thereby tackling the collective problems of human ignorance and evil as a unified whole. In replacing the contentious duality of body-versus-spirit with a unified triad of spirit, mind, and body, we serve to unite humanity in its struggle *against* evil; rather than give tacit respectability to evil by implying that it naturally somehow 'belongs' in the machinery of cosmic law. By promoting the belief that Satan can infiltrate human agencies and possess certain individuals at a personal level, we only aid in polarizing the problem and thus facilitate the fabrication of false and artificial sects who can each then claim to be singularly "on the side of good," and can then project evil onto others. Sadly, there are plenty of contemporary examples to be seen of this type of radical judgmental religiosity. The battle between good and evil in each and every human heart is one that needs to be understood as a collective and ongoing problem that should be tackled with all of our faculties; bodies, minds, and spirits, and not, as so many religious groups suggest, by demonizing the body and alienating the mind. Such an approach only takes us further into the realms of confusion and superstition as we wander aimlessly in the psychedelic world of spiritual mythologies, simultaneously surrendering our intellects to dogmatic persuasions, and our bodies to unnatural stresses and denials. Surely, a more wholesome spirituality would engage the minds and hearts of humanity in the collective struggle against that which threatens us all, and encourage the full use of *all* our faculties in the quest for enlightenment, salvation, redemption, restoration, development, improvement or perfection, as the case may be? In each of these noble pursuits there is ample room for developing a healthy body with advanced artistic or technical skills; a well-educated, wise and discerning mind; and a deep and profound sense of the sacred. But the higher reaches of the mind simply *must* be involved in these processes. Suppressing the mind and denying the body all the wonderful joys and flavors of life only takes us out of the true richness of the human experience wherein we may hope to uncover the personal keys to fulfillment. Not in decadent licentiousness of course, but in the aforesaid wholesome integration of spirit, mind, and body in the fullest experience of being human. Many New Age religions and progressive practitioners in psychotherapy and alternative healing techniques already adhere to this view, but the great difficulty when approaching the conservative traditionalist is in overcoming this deeply-ingrained unnatural dualism, and finding some common ground from where to initiate the debate. It is a terribly difficult thing to be able to let go of an idea that one has become accustomed to over a lifetime – even when that idea is clearly proven to be wrong. It is a sad fact that as we age we tend more towards conservatism than change, and prefer not to be drawn out of our old familiar haunts for fear of what we might discover 'out there', and in fear of what those discoveries might demand of us.

## Taking Responsibility

In context of this work however, one relatively painless place to begin 'letting-go' of our ingrained ideas is in recognizing the dynamics of the triadic archetype as they relate to our personal environments, cultures, and histories. Understanding that each person is the accumulated product of (i) his or her genetics, (ii) one's social environment, and (iii) one's own personal choices, helps us to accept the reality of who we are as historical agents with the personal responsibility, literally, to change the world – even if only in some small way. A full discussion on these three themes must be held for later volumes, but in realizing that we are the direct products of the societies and lineages of the past—complete with the subliminal, psychological, and physical attributes of our ancestors—who amongst us can still deny accountability for the errors of the past, or defer our responsibility to future generations?

If as I hope I have shown, this tradition of aggressive dualism based upon a mistaken good-versus-evil, and God-versus-Satan model is largely the cause of past human sufferings, then surely we should seek to eliminate it from our lives whenever we come across it? Using the colors of the triadic archetype as a guide we can now identify the truer meaning behind the symbolism traditionally attached to the figure of Satan in classical paintings and in popular culture. Invariably dressed in the reds and red-blacks of the perverse male as discussed in Chapter Seven, and associated with the macabre fires of hell and the sins of the flesh (red-black) the absence of the feminine compassionate blues in Satanic iconography is very telling. How disturbing then to see the very same color symbolism adorning not only Fascism and Communism, but also pre-reformation Christianity, radical Islam, and other authoritarian social institutions today (figs.7, 17, 20, 22 ♣).

The question obviously needs to be asked: Could 'he' (as perverse archetype or in the form of human agency) have somehow infiltrated these prominent social institutions under the red-black banner of authoritarianism? Could this demonic 'he' have taken form and substance in the polarized and unenlightened minds of the indoctrinated? Could 'he' still be there today, spouting divisive political ideologies, or, cloaked in dogma and orthodoxy, still stubbornly resisting the emergence of the cosmic feminine and the enlightenment of the masses? Sober thoughts to consider indeed.

Undoubtedly, some will contest the validity of these assertions, especially those who have become attached to a personalized Satan – even if only as their spiritual archenemy. (Please recall our personal 'pools' of consciousness, and the challenges of 'delving deeper'). Others will no doubt suffer the aforementioned pious outrage at any negative implications directed at their faith – as should be expected of course. Meanwhile more pragmatic others may persist in their rejection of any cosmology that includes a 'spiritual' or sacred aspect – even in such negative forms. But even so, and despite such passionate resistance and denials; the facts, the historical record, and the symbolism are there for all to see. We must therefore bravely continue to encourage the debate. Like all self-evident truths, it is only a matter of time before the proverbial penny drops.

In the meantime though, let us simply acknowledge the fact that this historical tendency to polarize good and evil, and God and Satan, and ourselves against heathen others has forged a collective mindset throughout the past two thousand years in particular, that has given us the mistaken notion that 'redemption' or 'salvation' (in the religious sense) can only be acquired through a blinkered, if not blind faith at the expense of the temporal aspects of the body and the mind. Or in more serious cases, at the direct expense of personal, emotional, and psychological development; and at the expense of the safety and well-being of our neighbors-now-turned-enemies. When our faith directs us to destroy our neighbors, surely we can concede that there is a disturbing absence not only of the compassionate feminine aspects, but equally of the discerning mind (blue), which is instructed by all of the major faith traditions to "do unto others as you would have them do unto you". But as one might imagine, pondering sentimental aphorisms such as "love thy neighbor" does tend to encumber the demonizing process – both of others, and of one's own sins.

Religions are of course a crucial aspect of social development that serve very important functions in our world, and there are undoubtedly many insights yet to be gleaned from the combined realms of religion, mythology, folklore, and the world's wisdom traditions. Indeed, much such research is contained in upcoming volumes. But the answer lies not in promoting one unsubstantiated theory or doctrine over another, but in seeking out comparative beliefs that serve to unite, rather than divide humanity further. In turn, these comparative beliefs need to be double-checked against current scientific knowledge and common sense in order to weed out those ideologies that spring either from elitism or ignorance or both. Then, we have to have the courage and fortitude to stop teaching questionable ideas to our youth, regardless of how emotionally attached to those beliefs we may be. Captivating they may be; longstanding and well established too. But are they really True (with a capital 'T')?

Tough though these comments may be to listen to, I ask the reader most sincerely to consider the facts objectively so that we may make some space in our personal archives not only for the discoveries presented in this book, but more importantly, for the ongoing education poured out onto us daily through the wonders of nature; through the mysteries of the cosmos, via the miracle of the human mind.

**In Closing..**

In viewing the natural patterns of the universe so clearly evident in the mechanisms of nature, and the lack or absence thereof in the annals of human history; we are drawn to the inescapable conclusion that if humanity is ever to function fully in harmony with the cosmos, we must learn to emulate those patterns in society. In recognising that humanity is the *only* aspect of creation that operates either in part-fulfilment, or in direct contradiction to these laws, we must, if we are to claim any sort of True collective integrity (with a capital 'T' of course), endeavor to understand and adopt these laws into our fundamental understandings of the meaning of life.

In their repeated appearances in our mythologies and religions, especially when manifested as remedial or corrective symbolism, the recurrent patterns of the triadic archetype need to be seriously heeded. We need to urgently accept the fact that the Universe is trying to tell us something very, very important indeed. Whether we interpret the surfacing of remedial archetypal patterns in human history as 'Divinely inspired' or not, the inescapable conclusion is that the Original Energies of the Universe are somehow coordinating these happenings in an attempt to achieve equilibrium not only between man and the natural environment, but more importantly perhaps, within the spiritual core of each and every human being.

We humans have a great and terrible responsibility. Great because of the incredible potential that awaits us; and terrible because of the horrors and destruction we have visited upon Earth and its inhabitants because of our ignorance and greed. Instead of managing our earthly inheritance with the grace and responsibility that comes with an elevated universal consciousness, we have, chiefly through our ignorance and our arrogance, slowly transformed this jewel of the universe into what can only be described as the proverbial kingdom of hell on Earth.

By studying the profound messages of the triadic archetype, we may yet have the beginnings of a global consensus that could—one day—lead us into a more unified understanding of the True meaning of life.

If the reader will excuse my frankness; in my considered opinion, it is the duty and responsibility of all capable members of society no less, to encourage and promote the quest for a better and more integrated understanding of life. In particular, an informed understanding of humanity's role as one great, unified, and super-conscious organism that gives purpose and meaning to creation itself. For if we continue to be found lacking in this department – why indeed should the universe continue to tolerate us?

Just as wayward children are warned and chastised, so it would seem is the watchful universe—here in the guise of the triadic archetype—admonishing us to urgently change our ways.

The real question is; who amongst us has the courage to heed that call?

# PREAMBLE TO VOLUMES II AND III OF THE COLOR OF TRUTH

Thank you for reading through *The Color of Truth Volume I*. I hope the material so far has stimulated, excited, and provoked you (in the nicest possible way of course) ..at least enough for you to be intrigued about the contents of future volumes. For although this book may be considered a work in its own right, it is of course only the opening third of the larger manuscript which would, in ideal circumstances have been entitled *The Color of Truth; Patterns in Light, Parallels in Life, and Principles to Live By*. Naturally, I would have preferred to produce one single 1,000-page book detailing all the research and discoveries so far, but the logistics of publishing just wouldn't support the production of such a large book – hence this series of successive works. The decision to produce three relatively-detailed volumes was to facilitate a more thorough understanding of the material, which I hope you'll agree would not be too well served by tight abbreviations or mere synopses. In other words, whilst wishing I had the skill, expertise, and resources to deliver the full contents to the reader in briefer form, I have so far found it impractical to do so.

So now at the end of Volume I—but also, only at the beginning of Volumes II and III—I feel obliged to encourage the reader respectfully but resolutely, to continue the quest. Hopefully you will not now need too much convincing. For if the contents of this first Volume were of any interest to you at all, then I can assure you with confidence that Volumes II and III will certainly not disappoint. In order to give the reader some insight as to what to expect, I now offer the following provisional summaries of the contents of Volumes II and III.

## PREVIEW OF VOLUME II; PARALLELS IN LIFE

Opening with a one-chapter condensed synopsis of the findings of this book, *Volume II: Parallels in Life* will take a closer look at the symbolism surrounding those core agencies and individuals who have shaped human history. This will include investigations of some of the major themes in history and how each in turn (possibly) fits with our theory of an archetypally-orchestrated providence. Empires, kingdoms, and dynasties will be reviewed; as will their battles, wars, and conflicts. From Alexander the Great to Nero and Constantine. From Clovis to Charlemagne and beyond, and on through the Holy Roman Empire; from the rise of Prussia to the emergence of the Nazis. From the kings and queens and princes of Europe; to the priests, popes, and radical reformers. From the Hapsburgs to

228

the House of Windsor, and from Leo the Great to Martin Luther; each investigation in turn reveals a stunning consistency in vital symbols, colors, themes, patterns, and family structures that at very least challenge us to explain why indeed this has never been explained before?

The symbolism of the world's major religions will also be revisited from a socio-political perspective, where we will reveal many more archetypal patterns and themes that illustrate and identify their real roles in history so far. More challenging perhaps will be the acknowledgement of where and what they are today – not from their own internal standpoints of course, but rather from the universal perspective as viewed through the proofs of the triadic archetype. Their achievements too will be noted, as will the emergence and growth of other major social movements; from the Renaissance, through the Reformation and Enlightenment periods, to the American, Industrial, and Bolshevik Revolutions. Then there are the legendary personalities at the center of these events: George Washington, Napoleon Bonaparte, Lenin, and Hitler for example; or the great prophets and sages of both East and West. We will find out how and why each has helped shape our common heritage, once again uncovering dramatic, even startling details that link their respective historical roles. There is also the feminine dimension of history to consider. In this vein we will explore the impact of such notables as Joan of Arc, Catherine De Medici, Maria Theresa of Austria, Queen Victoria, and Indira Gandhi; not forgetting of course the enigmatic Lady of the mystical visions at Guadalupe, Lourdes, and Fatima, whose true identity has been lost and misinterpreted for centuries. This too will be revealed for the very first time in print.

We will also examine other intriguing patterns in history, such as the ever-present Cain-and-Abel dynamic – so named because of its 'older brother kills younger brother' theme, so sadly reflected in many dualistic cultures. In the process, we will clarify and put into perspective some of the more pressing issues of today; the conflict in the Middle East between Arabs and Jews for example, the emergence of religious terrorism, and the role of America and her allies both from a secular as well as a religious perspective. In short, we will continue our quest for clues as to 'the meaning of life' as expressed in the parallels to be found linking the triadic archetype with so many individuals, agencies, and events in history. In doing so, we will come another step closer to answering the profound questions posed at the beginning of this book.

## PREVIEW OF VOLUME III; PRINCIPLES TO LIVE BY

In *Volume III; Principles to Live By* we will put forward two possible explanations for the existence of the triadic archetype that accounts for most, if not all of the supporting evidence of Volumes I and II. Already briefly alluded to; both these theories carry the potential to explain the phenomenon of the triadic archetype in-and-of-themselves. More exciting perhaps is the possibility that some combination of the two theories may in fact produce the proverbial 'big answer' to so many of our even bigger questions.

First of all we will explore the traditional *Fall From Grace Theory*—promoted by so many traditional religions in one form or another— as one explanation for the remedial activities of the triadic archetype. In the stimulating process of comparing longstanding religious themes and beliefs against the proofs of the triadic archetype, we will uncover certain previously unpublished realities that challenge the prevailing dualism in Western ideologies and theologies, and replace it instead with a wholesome and integrated model of 'grace and salvation' that is rooted in logic and reality rather than mystery, fear and superstition.

Following this we will outline a *Theory of Progressive Development* for humanity, wherein the triadic archetype is seen as a reflection of the Universe's natural attempts to nurse mankind into a fully-integrated position in the earth's ecosystem, as well as in the cosmos at large. Based upon the presumption that there is in fact nothing intrinsically 'wrong' or 'evil' with human nature in-and-of itself, we will nevertheless explore the phenomena of personal and social evils as a direct by-product of ignorance and other social and developmental handicaps. Arguing that these problems are chiefly due to our collective lack of cosmic maturity (vs. the 'fall from grace' scenario), an alternative model of life will be presented that not only absorbs and accommodates the bulk of existing religious theories; but also presents a healthier alternative to dualistic, divisive, or elitist understandings of the proverbial 'meaning of life'.

We will close Volume III with a provisional outline of an idealized 'universal theory of everything' which—it can only be hoped—can at some better time, be integrated and applied in each of our lives for the greater benefit of creation, and for the futures of all our children.

# CONDENSED GLOSSARY

Anastomotic: An integrated network of systems such as blood vessels
Archetype: An original model, or prototype (see definition at front of book)
Axiomatic: Certain, self-evident, beyond doubt
Chromatic: Relating to colors
Chromodynamic: Activity associated with colours (specific to this work)
Chromonumeric: Relating to colors and numbers
Chromomeres: Smaller particles in a chromosome
Chromosomes: Threadlike strands within DNA
Cosmogonic: Study of the origins of the Universe
Dichotomy: Division into two usually-contradictory parts
Empirical: Derived from observation or experiment; provable; testable
Etymology: Branch of linguistics; the origin and development of words
Hypostatic: Intrinsic essence; the substance; the underlying reality
Iconography: The study of images or symbols
Lexicon: Dictionary, or stock of terms used for a particular language
Monotheism: Doctrine or belief that there is only one God
Myopia: Nearsightedness; condition of metaphorically 'living in a bubble'
Noumenal: Not of the physical senses; psychological term for spiritual realm
Objective: Lack of personal bias; detached observation; impartial;
Ontology: The study of the nature of being; of existence itself
Orthodox: Adhering to the accepted viewpoint; conservative; mainstream
Oxymoron: A combination of contradictory terms, e.g. 'a deafening silence'
Phenomenon: A thing, event, or occurrence perceivable by the mind; or/and
something unusual or remarkable
Phenomenological: To do with one's senses, tastes, likes-and-dislikes
Providential: Pertaining to a Divine plan for human history
Psyche: The spirit, soul, and/or mind – usually a psychological term
Psychoid: Term used by Jung to define noumenal-type archetypes
Psychospiritual: Relating to the mind and the spirit, and specifically to the
'Psychospiritual Theory' as dealt with in Chapter Ten
Recalcitrant: Stubborn, wilful, obstinate; resistant to guidance or authority
Sectarian: Partisan; divided; biased; narrow-minded; parochial; dogmatic
Subjective: Particular to a given individual; personal; limited; introspective
Subliminal: Subconscious; below the threshold of conscious perception
Synesthetic: When one sensation evokes the stimulation of another
Taxonomy: Classifications; ordered groups and classes; a systematic listing;
Teleology: Study of purposeful design or functions in natural phenomena
Vexillology: The study of flags and their origins

# BIBLIOGRAPHY by BOOK TITLE, AUTHOR, and PUBLISHER

*A Handbook of Greek Mythology* H.J.Rose © 1964 University Paperbacks

*A History of Pagan Europe* Jones and Pennick © 1995 Barnes & Noble

*A Mind Awake; an Anthology of C.S.Lewis* edited Clyde S.Kilby © 1968 Harvest / HBJ Books, New York & London

*An Introduction To Color Energy* Inger Naess c 1998 Color Energy Corp.

*Antichrist- Two Thousand Years of the Human Fascination with Evil* Bernard McGinn © 1994 Harper Collins Publishers, New York

*Aristotle on God* Joseph Owens, C.Ss. R. 1977 Learned Publications Inc.

*Auras* Edgar Cayce © 1973 Assn. for Research and Enlightenment, Inc.

*Behind The Sex of God* Carol Ochs c 1977 Beacon Press.

*Bernadette and Lourdes* Michel de Saint-Pierre © 1954 Farrar, Straus & Young, Inc

*Bible Almanac* Anna Trimiew © 1988 Publications International Ltd, USA

*Care of the Soul* Thomas Moore © 1992. Harper Collins, New York

*Christ, A Symbol of the Self* Carl G. Jung

*Collaborative Ministry* Loughlan Sofield & Caroll Juliano © 1987 Ave Maria Press

*Collected Works of C.G.Jung (abstracts of)* edited Carrie Lee Rothgeb 1978. USA DHEW Publication No. (ADM)78-743

*Color and Culture* John Gage © 1999. University of California Press

*Color and Meaning* John Gage © 1999. University of California Press

*Color Codes* Charles A. Riley II © 1995 University Press of New England

*Color Therapy* Vijaya Kumar © 2004 New Dawn Press

*Counseling Psychology* Charles J. Gelso and Bruce R. Fretz © 1992 Holt, Rhinehart and Wilson. Harcourt Brace College Publishers, Orlando, FL USA

*Coming to Terms With Death* David Bakan. Article appearing in *Personality and Religion* edited William A. Sadler, Jr. © 1970 SCM Press Ltd, London.

*Crises in Personality Development* Anton Boisen. Article appearing in *Personality and Religion* edited William A. Sadler, Jr. © 1970 SCM Press Ltd, London.

*Death-of-God Theology* Eric C. Meyer, C.P. 1977 Learned Publications Inc. N.Y

*Eerdmans' Handbook to the History of Christianity* © 1977 Lion Publishing

*Encyclopedia of Psychological Problems* Clyde M. Narramore © 1966 Zondervan Publishing, Michigan, USA

*Essays in Radical Empiricism* William James, Ch 2 "A World of Pure Experience". Longman Green and Co (1912) New York.

*Ethics – a brief introduction* Robert C. Solomon © 1984 McGraw-Hill

*Explaining Unification Thought* Sang Hun Lee © 1981 Unification Thought Inst.

*Exposition of The Divine Principle* Sun Myung Moon © 1996 HSAUWC

*Faith, Religion, and Theology* Brennan R. Hill, Paul Knitter & William Madges © 1997 Twenty-Third Publications, Mystic, CT

*Fascinating Bible Facts* David M. Howard and Gary M. Burge © 1988 Pub's. Int.

*Father and Son in Christianity and Confucianism* Robert N. Bellah. Article in *Personality and Religion* ed. William A. Sadler, Jr. © 1970 SCM Press Ltd. UK.

232

*Formation of the Need to Achieve* David C. McCelland. Article appearing in *Personality and Religion* edited William A. Sadler, Jr. © 1970 SCM Press Ltd. UK

*Gandhi* Louis Fischer © 1954, 1982 Penguin Books

*Gleanings From the Writings of Baha'u'llah* translated Shogi Effendi © 1976 National Spiritual Assembly of the Baha'is of the United States

*God in African Thought and Life* Charles E. Fuller 1977 Learned Pub's Inc. NY

*God in Analytic Philosophy* David Stagaman, S.J. 1977 Learned Publications Inc.

*God in the Biblical-Rabbinic Tradition* Simon Greenberg 1977 Learned Pub's. Inc.

*Healing and The Mind* Bill Moyers © 1993 Bantam Doubleday Dell Publishing

*Hellenistic Religions* Luther H. Martin © 1987 Oxford University Press Inc.

*History of Doctrines Vol II* K. R. Hagenbach © MDCCCLIX

*Holy Bible, King James Version* © 1989 – 1994 Franklin Electronic Publisher

*In Defense of the Faith* David Hunt (Publisher Unknown)

*Insight on the Scriptures* © 1988 Watchtower Bible and Tract Society of Pennsylvania, published Brooklyn, New York

*Individual and Social Narcissism* Erich Fromm. Article appearing in *Personality and Religion* edited William A. Sadler, Jr. © 1970 SCM Press Ltd, London.

*Inneractions* Stephen C. Paul © 1992 Harper Collins, New York

*Illuminations* Stephen C. Paul © 1991 Harper Collins, New York

*Is the Virgin Mary Dead or Alive?* Danny Vierra © 1997 Modern Manna Ministries

*Knowledge of God in Islam* Robert E. Carter 1977 Learned Publications Inc. NY

*Legio Mariae (official handbook of the Legion of Mary)* © 1993 C. Legionis Mariae

*Life Colors* Pamela Oslie © 1991 New World Library

*Light, Color, & the Environment* Faber Birren. © 1969 Van Nostrand Rheinhold Co

*Man and His Symbols* Carl Gustav Jung © 1964 Aldus Books, London, UK

*Maria Legionis Vol. 43, No.3, 2000*

*Mary and Modern Man* Thomas Burke S.J. © 1954 The America Press

*Memories, Dreams, Reflections* C.G.Jung © 1965 Random House Inc.

*Models of Religious Education* Harold W. Burgess © 1996 Victor Books

*Muhammad: His Life Based on the Earliest Sources.* © 1983 Martin Lings. George Allen & Unwin. London.

*Mysticism: St. John of the Cross* Robert A. Herrera 1977. Learned Publications Inc.

*Mythology* Edith Hamilton © 1940, 1969 Penguin Books

*New American Bible* © 1991 Confraternity of Christian Doctrine, Washington D.C.

*New World Translation of Holy Scriptures* © 1984 Watchtower Bible & Tract Soc.

*Obsessive Actions and Religious Practices* Sigmund Freud. Article appearing in *Personality and Religion* edited William A. Sadler, Jr. © 1970 SCM Press Ltd. UK

*On Becoming a Counselor* Eugene Kennedy and Sara C. Charles © 1990 The Continuum Publishing Company, New York

*Paradoxes of Religious Belief* Milton Rokeach. Article appearing in *Personality and Religion* edited William A. Sadler, Jr. © 1970 SCM Press Ltd, London.

*Paul J. Tillich on Natural Theology* Joseph Fitzer 1977 Learned Publications Inc.

*People of the Lie* M. Scott Peck © 1983 Touchstone Books, New York

233

*Personality and Religion* ed; William A, Sadler, Jr. © 1970. SCM Press Ltd. UK
*Platonic and Christian Theism* John P. Rowan 1977 Learned Publications Inc. NY
*Practical Ethics for You* Eiji Uehiro, Japan (publisher unknown)
*Psychoanalysis and Religion* Erich Fromm © 1950 Yale University Press
*Psychology and Religion* Carl Gustav Jung© 1938 Yale University Press
*Psychology, Symbolism, & the Sacred* S. T. Manning © 2006 CheckPoint Press
*Psychometric Testing* Philip Carter and Ken Russell © 2001 John Wiley & Sons UK
*Quantum Healing* Deepak Chopra © 1990 Bantam books
*Religion in Times of Social Distress* Thomas F. O'Dea. Article appearing in
*Personality and Religion* edited William A. Sadler, Jr. © 1970 SCM Press Ltd. UK
*Religious Aspects of Peak Experiences* Abraham H. Maslow. Article appearing in
*Personality and Religion* edited William A. Sadler, Jr. © 1970 SCM Press Ltd. UK
*Religious Education As A Second Language* Gabriel Moran © 1989 Rel. Ed. Press
*Reshaping Religious Education* Harris and Moran © 1998. Westminister John Knox
Press, Kentucky USA
*Science and Health* Mary Baker Eddy © 1934 Christian Science Board of Directors
*Sects, 'Cults' and Alternative Religions* David V. Barrett © 1996 Blandford
Publishing UK, & Sterling Publishing, New York
*Shrines to Our Lady* Zsolt Aradi © 1954 Murray Printing Company
*Symbols of Freemasonry* Daniel Beresniak © 2000 Assouline Publishing, New York
*Symbols of Islam* Malek Chebel © 2000 Assouline Publishing, New York
*Tales of a Magic Monastery* Theophane the Monk © 1981 Cistercian Abbey of
Spencer Inc. Crossroads Publishing Company, New York
*The Battle for God* Karen Armstrong © 2002. Ballantines Publishing Group
*The Book of Mormon* translated by Joseph Smith Jr. © 1981 Intellectual Reserve Inc
*The Bulletproof George Washington* David Barton
*The Christian Science Way of Life* Dewitt John © 1990 Christian Science Pub. Soc.
*The Color Code – A Revolutionary Eating Plan for Optimum Health* by James A.
Joseph, Daniel A. Nadeau, and Anne Underwood © 2002 The Philip Lief Group
*The Color Code – A new way to see yourself, your relationships, and your life*
Taylor Hartman © 1998 Fireside – Simon and Schuster
*The Common Enemy* Karl Menninger. Article appearing in *Personality and Religion*
edited William A. Sadler, Jr. © 1970 SCM Press Ltd, London.
*The Complete Idiot's Guide to Philosophy* Jay Stevenson © 1998 Alpha Books
*The Complete Idiot's Guide to Psychology* Joni E. Johnston, © 2000 Alpha Books
*The Complete Idiot's Guide to The World's Religions* Brandon Toropov and Fr.
Luke Buckles © 1997 Alpha Books
*The Complete Book of Bible Lists* H.L.Willmington © 1987 Tyndale House Pub's
*The Concept of God in Confucian Thought* Te-Sheng Meng and P.K. Sih 1977
Learned Publications Inc. New York
*The Concept of God in the Reformation Tradition* Geddes MacGregor 1977 (Ibid)
*The Creed* Bernard Marthaler© 1993. Twenty-Third Publications, Mystic, CT
*The Demon-Haunted World* Carl Sagan ©1996. Ballantine Publishing USA
*The Duality of Human Existence* David Bakan© 1966 Rand McNally & Company

*The Existence of God* edited John Hick © 1964 Macmillan Publishing co., Inc.

*The Feminine Dimension of the Divine* Joan Chamberlain Engelsman © 1979 Westminster Press

*The Growth of Medieval Theology* Jaroslav Pelikan © 1978 University of Chicago

*The Healing Power of Color* Betty Wood © 1998 Destiny Books

*The Hindu Concept of God* Francis W. Vineeth 1977 Learned Publications Inc.

*The Holy Qu'ran* Published Amana Corporation © 1989 Maryland USA

*The Illustrated Book of Myths* Neil Philip © 1995 Dorling Kindersly

*The Illuminated Rumi* © 1997 Barks and Green. Broadway Books, Doubleday, NY

*The Jesuits: The Society of Jesus and the Betrayal of the Roman Catholic Church* by Malachi Martin © 1987 Touchstone Books, Simon and Schuster

*The Left Hand of God* Adolf Holl © 1997 Bantam Books

*The Luscher Color Test* Translated and Edited Ian A. Scott © 1969 Max Luscher. Washington Square Press. New York.

*The Millionaire Course* Marc Allen © 2003 New World Library

*The Myth Behind The Sex of God* Carol Ochs © 1977 Beacon Press

*The Origin of Satan* Elaine Pagels © 1995 Random House Inc. New York

*The Oxford Study Bible* © 1992 Oxford University Press

*The Portable Thoreau* edited Carl Bode © 1947, 1975 Viking Penguin Inc.

*The Possible Human* Jean Houston © 1982 J.P. Tarcher, Inc, CA

*The Power of Myth* Joseph Campbell © 1988 Apostrophe S Productions

*The Power of Now* Eckhart Tolle © 1999. New World Library, CA, USA

*The Prophet* Kahlil Gibran © 1923 & 1951 Random House, New York

*The Prophet* Max Weber. Article appearing in *Personality and Religion* edited William A. Sadler, Jr. © 1970 SCM Press Ltd, London.

*The Psychologist's Book of Self-Tests* Louis Janda © 1996 Berkley Publishing NY

*The Psychology of Religion – An Empirical Approach* Hood, Spilka, Hunsberger, & Gorsuch 2nd ed.© 1996 The Guildford Press, New York *(see sub-quotes at end)*

*The Religious Context of Prejudice* Gordon W. Allport. Article appearing in *Personality and Religion* edited William A. Sadler, Jr. © 1970 SCM Press Ltd. UK

*The Religious Dimension of Human Experience* Dorothy Lee. Article appearing in *Personality and Religion* edited William A. Sadler, Jr. © 1970 SCM Press Ltd,. UK

*The Scientific Study of Religion and Personality* Article appearing in *Personality and Religion* edited by William A. Sadler, Jr. © 1970 SCM Press Ltd, London.

*The Scientist in the Crib* Gopnik, Meltzoff, & Kuhl © 1999 William Morrow & Co.

*The Secret Language of Dreams* David Fontana © 1994 Duncan Baird Publishers

*The Secret Language of Symbols* David Fontana © 1993 Duncan Baird Publishers

*The Selected Writings of Ralph Waldo Emerson* Ed; Brooks Atkinson © 1992 Random House.

*The Shining Wilderness* Thomas Merton © 1988 Darton, Longman & Todd Ltd. UK

*The Story of Christianity Vol. 1 & 2* Justo L.Gonzalez © 1985 HarperCollins

*The Symbolism of Color* Faber Birren © 1988 Citadel Press, N.J. USA

*The Timetables of History* Bernard Grun © 1991 Simon & Schuster Inc.

*The Varieties of Religious Experience* William James. New American Library

*The Wanderer* Kahlil Gibran © 1932 & 1960 Mary Gibran. Random House
*The World's First Love* Bishop Fulton Sheen © 1952 McGraw-Hill Book Co
*Thought Organization in Religion* Paul Pruyser. Article appearing in *Personality and Religion* edited William A. Sadler, Jr. © 1970 SCM Press Ltd, London.
*Unconditional Life* Deepak Chopra © 1991 Bantam books
*Unification Thought* © 1973 Unification Thought Institute, New York
*What Is Islam?* Dr. Muhammad Ansart, Islamic Federation of New Jersey, Inc. USA
*What is Scientology?* (L.Ron Hubbard) © 1998 Church of Scientology
*When Religion becomes Evil* Charles Kimball© 2002. HarperCollins New York
*When Science Meets Religion* Ian G. Barbour © 2000. HarperCollins, New York
*Who's Who in the Bible* © 1988 Publications International Ltd, USA
*Who's Who in the Bible* © 1994 Reader's Digest Association
*Who's Who of Religions* edited John R. Hinnells © Macmillan Press 1991
*Wisdom's Book, The Sophia Anthology* Arthur Versluis © 2000 Paragon House US
*Woman and the History of Philosophy* Nancy Tuana © 1992 Paragon House USA
*World History* edited Jeremy Black © 1999 Parragon Publishing, Bath, UK
*World Religions Vol. 1; Living Religions of the Middle East* Young Oon Kim ©
*World Religions Vol. 2; India's Religious Quest* Young Oon Kim © 1976 (Ibid)
*World Religions Vol. 3; Faiths of the Far East* Young Oon Kim © 1976 HSAUWC
*World's Religions* Huston Smith © 1994 Harper Collins Publishers
*World Scripture, A Comparative Anthology of Sacred Texts* Andrew Wilson © 1995 Paragon House Publishing, USA.

Psychology of Religion sub-quotes:
- Carroll, M.P. (1986). *The cult of the Virgin Mary: Psychological Origins,* Princeton, N.J: Princeton University Press.
- Perry, N., & Echeverria, L. (1988). *Under the heal of Mary.* London: Routlefge and Kegan Paul.
- Warner, M. (1976). *Alone of all her sex: The myth and cult of the Virgin Mary.* New York: Knopf.
- Carroll, M.P. (1983). Vision of the Virgin Mary: The effects of family structures on Marian apparitions. *Journal for the Scientific Study of Religion. 22, 205-221*

Websites:
Color of Truth - http://color-of-truth.com
Colour Energy - www.colourenergy.com
Allen Wood - http://www.allentwood.com/
Paul Volk - http://www.newstartplus.org/
Luscher Color Testing - www.luscher-color.com
Baha'I Faith - http://www.bahaifaith.net/kabbalah.htm
Flags of the World - http://www.crwflags.com/fotw/flags/
Paul Goldin Clinics - http://www.paulgoldin.com/colorgenics.htm
Tony Badillo; Solomon's Temple - http://home.earthlink.net/~tonybadillo/

# REFERENCES and ENDNOTES

CHAPTER ONE:
[1] *The Timetables of History* by Bernard Grun © 1991 Simon & Schuster Inc. – p167

CHAPTER TWO:
[2] See "Color" Microsoft Encarta Reference Suite 99.
[3] Paul Volk: *New Start Plus* Seminars; http://www.newstartplus.org/
[4] *The Color Code – A Revolutionary Eating Plan for Optimum Health* by James A. Joseph, Daniel A. Nadeau, and Anne Underwood © 2002 The Philip Lief Group, Inc.
[5] www.colourenergy.com see music section
[6] (1) Luscher Color Systems @ www.luscher-color.com (2) Paul Golden Clinic: See *"Colorgenics"* website. Dublin, Ireland (3) *The Color Code – A new way to see yourself, your relationships, and your life* by Taylor Hartman © 1998 Fireside – Simon and Schuster
[7] *Color and Meaning* by John Gage © 1999 University of California Press. P 13
[8] *Color Codes* by Charles A. Riley II © 1995 University Press of New England p1.
[9] See *Psychology, Symbolism, and the Sacred* 2nd Ed.© 2007 by this author for a fuller discussion on the religious question.

CHAPTER THREE:
[10] *The Varieties of Religious Experience,* by William James, (1902) New Amer. Lib – Lec 20.
[11] Herman Melville (1819–91), U.S. author. *Moby-Dick,* ch. 114 (1851).
[12] *Holy Bible KJV* Genesis 26-27
[13] *The Healing Power of Color* by Betty Wood © 1998 Destiny Books p31
[14] *Auras* by Edgar Cayce © 1973 Association for Research and Enlightenment, Inc.

CHAPTER FOUR:
[15] *Light, Color, and the Environment* by Faber Birren. © 1969 NY: Van Nostrand Rheinhold
[16] *The Secret Language of Symbols* by David Fontana © 1993 Duncan Baird – p67
[17] Ibid – p66
[18] http://www.colour-affects.co.uk/psyprop.html
[19] *Color Therapy* by Vijaya Kumar © 2004 New Dawn Press pp.35, 36.
[20] Reported in; *Color and Human Response* by Faber Birren. © 1978 New York: Van Nostrand Rheinhold Co Inc.
[21] *The Healing Power of Color* by Betty Wood © 1998 Destiny Books pp50, 51, & 105
[22] *Auras* by Edgar Cayce © 1973 Association for Research and Enlightenment, Inc.
[23] Ibid – p66
[24] *The Luscher Color Test* Translated and Edited by Ian A. Scott © 1969 by Max Luscher. Washington Square Press. New York p18, 19.
[25] *Color Coding* Journal Article by Olivia Guide; Art Journal, Vol 58, 1999
[26] http://www.pha.jhu.edu/~kgb/cosspec/

CHAPTER FIVE:
[27] *Old Testament*; Genesis & Exodus (Moses); Samuel I; Samuel II; Chronicles I; Psalms;
[28] See Jung's many discussions on the Anima and Animus eg; *The Syzygy: Animus and Anima.* In Collected Works of C.G.Jung Vol. 9, Part 2. 2nd ed., Princeton Uni. Press, 1968
[29] Ibid – p54
[30] Painting by Botticelli (1445-1510)
[31] *The Secret Language of Symbols* by David Fontana © 1993 Duncan Baird Pub. – p120

CHAPTER SIX:
[32] See GuruNet Wikipedia "Rainbow".
[33] *The Encarta® 99 Desk Encyclopedia* Copyright © & ☐ 1998 Microsoft Corporation.
[34] *The Secret Language of Symbols* by David Fontana © 1993 Duncan Baird Pub. – p183
[35] http://home.earthlink.net/~tonybadillo/
[36] See the *Books of Lamentations* and *Micah* for repeated examples of the term "daughter Zion" in the Bible.

CHAPTER SEVEN:
[37] See website: "POCM"--(The Pagan Origins of the Christ Myth)
[38] Gurunet / Wikipedia article on Kabalism
[39] See http://www.crystalinks.com/kabala.html for images and further information.
[40] *The Origin of Satan* by Elaine Pagels © 1995, Random House. p58
[41] Translation: *Insight on the Scriptures* Vol 2 © 1988 by Watchtower Books p253 "Light"
[42] *Muhammad: His Life Based on the Earliest Sources.* © 1983 by Martin Lings. p27
[43] *The Mathnavi of Rumi*, Vol 6. (E.H.Whinfeld translation)
[44] *Auras* by Edgar Cayce © 1973 Association for Research and Enlightenment, Inc.
[45] *The Healing Power of Color* by Betty Wood © 1998 Destiny Books
[46] The Mathnavi of Rumi, Vol 1. (E.H.Whinfeld translation)
[47] *The Healing Power of Color* by Betty Wood © 1998 Destiny Books. p94
[48] See http://www.bahaifaith.net/kabbalah.htm

CHAPTER EIGHT:
[49] *In Praise of Tara: Songs to the Saviouress* by Martin Willson, Wisdom Publications. (see website of Amitabha Buddhist Centre)
[50] From the teachings of Ven Lama Thubten Yeshe (see website of *Amitabha Buddhist Centre*) http://www.meditationinbristol.org/
[51] For a full listing of Buddhist Tara's color values, a visit to the website of *Amitabha Buddhist Centre* is recommended.
[52] *Upanishads vol. 2, Brihadaranyaka-Upanishad Part 3*, verse 9.
[52] *World's Religions* by Huston Smith © 1994 Harper Collins Publishers – p135
[53] *In Defense of the Faith* by David Hunt (Publisher Unknown) – p37 & 38
[54] Please see *Mariology; Resolving the Confusion* by this author at http://color-of-truth.com

CHAPTER NINE:
[55] Oscar Wilde (1854–1900), Anglo-Irish playwright, author. *Phrases and Philosophies for the Use of the Young*, in *Chameleon* (London, Dec. 1894)

CHAPTER TEN:
[56] *The Interpretation of Dreams* Sigmund Freud (1900) Chapter 6 (part 2) *The Dream-Work*
[57] *Memories, Dreams, Reflections* by C.G.Jung © 1965 Random House Inc. – p392
[58] Ibid. – p392
[59] The growing problem of religious fundamentalism is discussed in more depth in *Psychology, Symbolism, and the Sacred; Confronting Religious Dysfunction in a Changing World* © 2004-2007 2nd Edition, by this author.

CHAPTER ELEVEN:
[60] *The Psychology of Religion – An Empirical Approach* by Hood, Spilka, Hunsberger, & Gorsuch 2nd ed.© 1996 The Guildford Press, New York. – p192
[61] *Memories, Dreams, Reflections* by C.G.Jung © 1965 Random House Inc. – p395

CHAPTER TWELVE:
[62] See *GuruNet Wikipedia 2005* under the title "Numerology".
[63] *Holy Bible* Genesis 1:26 – 28 KJV
[64] See *GuruNet Encyclopedia* under the title "Periodic Table"
[65] See *Triple-Alpha Process*; Wikipedia
[66] *A History of God* by Karen Armstrong p27
[67] See *Wikipedia* under "70 days"


CHAPTER THIRTEEN:
[67] Korean evangelist Rev. Sun Myung Moon's *Divine Principle* contains a numeric theory of a historical, numeric providence that places the subject as the locus of history. Under scrutiny however, certain critical claims and themes appear to have been modified to fit the theme. For a critical evaluation of the *Divine Principle* please see http://www.allentwood.com/. For the official Unificationist view see http://www.unification.net/dp96/
[68] Understanding Hebrew: A search for the pure language. By Randall Shortridge 1999
[69] See *Chronicle Encyclopedia of History* under "1517" in CD format 1997


List of Websites Referenced:

www.colourenergy.com
www.luscher-color.com
http://color-of-truth.com/
http://checkpointpress.com
http://www.allentwood.com/
http://www.newstartplus.org/
http://www.unification.net/dp96/
http://www.meditationinbristol.org/
http://home.earthlink.net/~tonybadillo/
http://www.bahaifaith.net/kabbalah.htm
http://www.paulgoldin.com/colorgenics.htm
http://www.colour-affects.co.uk/psyprop.html
Flags of the World: http://www.crwflags.com/fotw/flags/